The European Union: How does it work?

Develop your understanding of European Union politics with the New European Union Series, created to give you clear and comprehensive coverage of essential topics in the area.

THE NEW EUROPEAN UNION SERIES

Series editors: John Peterson and Helen Wallace

The European Union presents an ever more daunting analytical challenge to students of politics, economics, history, law, and the social sciences. It is the most successful experiment in modern international cooperation but also a target of fierce criticism.

The European Union of the twenty-first century faces multiple crises, not least Brexit - the United Kingdom's departure from the EU – as well as core policy challenges, particularly in transnational arenas such as migration, management of the eurozone, and climate change. As a result, the evolving European Union requires continuous reassessment by both scholars and practitioners.

THE NEW EUROPEAN UNION SERIES brings together the expertise of leading scholars and practitioners to analyse EU politics and policies for an interntional readership. Build your knowledge with regularly updated editions on:

ORIGINS AND EVOLUTION OF THE EUROPEAN UNION

POLICY-MAKING AND THE EUROPEAN UNION

THE EUROPEAN UNION: HOW DOES IT WORK?

THE INSTITUTIONS OF THE EUROPEAN UNION

THE MEMBER STATES OF THE EUROPEAN UNION

INTERNATIONAL RELATIONS AND THE EUROPEAN UNION

For more information on the titles available in the New European Union Series, visit the OUP website at:

www.oup.com/academic/content/series/n/new-european-union-series-neu

Make your voice heard: join the OUP Politics Student Panel.

To help us make sure we develop the best possible textbooks for you, the student, we have set up a student panel to hear your opinions and feedback.

To find out more, visit www.oxfordtextbooks.co.uk/politics/studentpanel

THE EUROPEAN UNION
HOW DOES IT WORK?

Fifth Edition

Daniel Kenealy, John Peterson,
and Richard Corbett

OXFORD
UNIVERSITY PRESS

OXFORD

UNIVERSITY PRESS

Great Clarendon Street, Oxford, OX2 6DP,
United Kingdom

Oxford University Press is a department of the University of Oxford.
It furthers the University's objective of excellence in research, scholarship,
and education by publishing worldwide. Oxford is a registered trade mark of
Oxford University Press in the UK and in certain other countries

Published in the United States of America by Oxford University Press
198 Madison Avenue, New York, NY 10016, United States of America

British Library Cataloguing in Publication Data
Data available

Library of Congress Control Number: 2018950863

ISBN 978–0–19–880749–0

Printed in Great Britain by
Bell & Bain Ltd., Glasgow

Links to third party websites are provided by Oxford in good faith and
for information only. Oxford disclaims any responsibility for the materials
contained in any third party website referenced in this work.

OUTLINE CONTENTS

DETAILED CONTENTS

PREFACE AND ACKNOWLEDGEMENTS

Previous editions of this book have emphasized change as a constant in the world of European Union (EU) politics and public policy. That certainly applies to the EU since the fourth edition was published in 2015. As we concluded writing the fourth edition the EU had seemingly emerged from the depths of the global financial crisis that had rocked the Eurozone between 2010 and 2012. As we finalized that edition, the global refugee crisis was emerging as the EU's latest crisis, a reality that has crystallized since 2015. Meanwhile Europe's leaders struggled with a revanchist Russia, under President Vladimir Putin, which intervened in the Donbass region of Ukraine in 2014, creating a frozen conflict that persisted despite efforts by the French and German governments to alleviate the situation.

As we approach the present fifth edition of the book our task remains a daunting one. The most challenging days of the financial crisis do seem to be behind the EU. However, significant and complicated public policy challenges persist as the EU—and particularly the 19 member states who use the euro as their currency—tries to complete the project of a banking union and looks for new institutional mechanisms to strengthen the governance of the Eurozone and its ability to absorb the effects of, and counter, any future economic crisis. Similarly, although the refugee crisis is less intense in 2018 than it was in 2015, significant challenges remain as EU member states struggle to absorb those who have arrived over recent years. There remains a pressing need for the EU to speak with a strong and coherent voice on the global stage as Russia extends its influence in the EU's neighbourhood, as multiple crises and conflicts continue to unfold in North Africa and the Middle East, and as China seeks to extend its economic influence and leverage globally via its Belt and Road Initiative. The policy agenda in Brussels remains a full one.

These significant policy challenges—and there are more not mentioned here—are made even more difficult by a rising tide of populist political sentiment across the EU and beyond. The election of Donald Trump as US president in November 2016 added yet another volatile and unpredictable element to the mix given the importance of the transatlantic relationship both economically and in terms of security. In several member states—notably Poland and Hungary—a form of illiberal democracy is taking root, which poses a challenge to some of the EU's founding principles. Euroscepticism, a phenomenon linked politically to populism, remains an issue for the EU. Anti-EU parties made significant gains in the 2014 European Parliament election. As we completed the fourth edition, we remarked on the prospect of an existing member state—the United Kingdom (UK)—voting to leave the EU. On 23 June 2016, citizens of the UK did vote to leave the EU. This event was a seismic one that shook the Union to its core: the first time in the EU's 60-year history that its membership will shrink, from 28 to 27. Brexit—as it has come to be called—poses a major challenge for the EU as it attempts to minimize the disruption and turbulence caused by the departure of a member state, and to maintain the integrity of the Union for its remaining 27 members.

As in previous editions, we the editors—and our authors—can offer little more than educated guesses about what the effects of these institutional, political, and economic changes will be. The status quo looked fragile as we went to press, suggesting that more changes were likely to be in the offing. We (or most of us) are, by now, battle-hardened as to how much and fast the ground can shift in European integration. What the Union does, how it does it, and with what consequences, have all altered or intensified in some (usually significant) ways since the fourth edition of this volume was published.

We have tried to reflect the most important of these changes in this new edition. Each individual chapter has been significantly updated (three years is a long time in EU affairs), especially, but not only, to take account of the UK's vote to leave the EU. We have added several new authors to be sure that, even as we offer a basic introduction to the Union, our book reflects findings from the very latest and most perceptive research on European integration. The editorial team remains the same as it was for the fourth edition.

Our core mission remains the same: to produce a clear, concise, truly introductory text for students and the curious general reader. No experience required. We know the EU is important; we demonstrate why and how in the following chapters. We also know that it can be made both comprehensible and interesting; our aim is to show how. If we succeed, it is in great part due to our team of star contributors, and support and publishing staff.

First, the contributors. One of the book's most distinctive and strongest qualities is its blend of academics and practitioners. All chapters were either co-authored or reviewed by both an academic and practitioner. We thank our team of authors for making this blend workable and even enjoyable. Special thanks are owed to the authors or co-authors who contributed to the first four editions: Alexander Stubb, Laura Cram, Lynn Dobson, Lykke Friis, David Martin, John D. Occhipinti, Michael E. Smith, Michael Shackleton, Rory Watson, Albert Weale, Andrew Geddes, Marlene Gottwald, and the late, great Sir Neil MacCormick. We also continue to be in the debt of Elizabeth Bomberg who was the lead editor of the first three editions. Elizabeth did more than anyone to establish this book's credentials as the first one to assign to inquiring minds trying to make sense of this strange and often baffling political beast.

A second batch of thanks goes to the editorial and production team. As always, we are in considerable debt to series editor Helen Wallace, who has offered not only excellent substantive guidance but also unflagging and essential encouragement in the production of this and past volumes. Thanks also to the editorial and production team at OUP, especially Francesca Walker (née Mitchell), who demonstrated patience and skill in seeing the project through, and Aishwarya Panday for efficiency and precisions during the production process.

Third, our readers. The advantage of doing multiple editions is that we are able to benefit from the feedback from the last one as we plough ahead with the next one. We've profited enormously from comments offered by reviewers of the first four editions, by practitioners in Brussels, and by the many EU studies colleagues who have used this book in their teaching. An extremely useful range of comments, criticisms, and suggestions came directly from end users themselves—including students using the earlier editions in their courses at the University of Edinburgh.

Finally, amidst all the tumultuous change, there is always one constant: the support offered by our partners and families, and presumably those of our authors. Like last time, only more so: we could not have done it without you.

Daniel Kenealy, John Peterson, and Richard Corbett

Edinburgh and Leeds

LIST OF FIGURES

LIST OF BOXES

LIST OF TABLES

LIST OF ABBREVIATIONS AND ACRONYMS

ACP	African, Caribbean, and Pacific
AECR	Alliance of European Conservatives and Reformists
AKP	Turkey's Justice and Development Party
ALDE	Alliance of Liberals and Democrats for Europe
APEC	Asia Pacific Economic Cooperation
ASEAN	Association of South-east Asian Nations
CAP	Common Agricultural Policy
CEPOL	European Police College
CETA	Comprehensive Economic and Trade Agreement
CEU	Central European University
CFSP	Common Foreign and Security Policy
CIA	Central Intelligence Agency (US)
CoE	Council of Europe
COPS	European Political and Security Committee
CoR	European Committee of the Regions
Coreper	Committee of Permanent Representatives
CSDP	Common Security and Defence Policy
DG	Directorate-General (European Commission)
DUP	Democratic Unionist Party
EAF	European Alliance for Freedom
EaP	Eastern Partnership
EC	European Community
ECAS	European Citizen Action Service
ECB	European Central Bank
ECHO	European Community Humanitarian Office
ECHR	European Convention on Human Rights
ECJ	European Court of Justice
ECOFIN	(Council of) Economic and Financial Affairs
ECSC	European Coal and Steel Community
EDC	European Defence Community
EDF	European Development Fund

EEA	European Economic Area
EEC	European Economic Community
EEW	European Evidence Warrant
EFTA	European Free Trade Association
ELDR	European Liberal, Democratic and Reformist Party
EMS	European Monetary System
EMU	Economic and Monetary Union
ENP	European Neighbourhood Policy
EP	European Parliament
EPACA	European Public Affairs Consultancies Association
EPC	European Political Cooperation
EPP	European People's Party
ERF	European Refugee Fund
ERM	Exchange Rate Mechanism
ESC	Economic and Social Committee
ESDP	European Security and Defence Policy
ESFS	European Financial Stability Facility
ESM	European Stability Mechanism
ESS	European Security Strategy
ETUC	European Trades Union Confederation
EU	European Union
EULEX	European Union Rule of Law Mission
Euratom	European Atomic Energy Community
Eurostat	European statistical agency
FBI	Federal Bureau of Investigation (US)
FCO	Foreign and Commonwealth Office
FD	Framework Decision
FRG	Federal Republic of Germany
FTA	Free Trade Area
FYROM	Former Yugoslav Republic of Macedonia
GAERC	General Affairs and External Relations Council
GATT	General Agreement on Tariffs and Trade
GDP	gross domestic product
GMOs	genetically modified organisms
GNP	gross national product

IGC	Intergovernmental Conference
IMF	International Monetary Fund
IO	international organization
IR	international relations
JHA	justice and home affairs
MAXCAP	Maximizing the Integration Capacity of the European Union
MEP	member of the European Parliament
MEPP	Middle East Peace Process
MFA	Minister for Foreign Affairs
NAFTA	North American Free Trade Agreement
NATO	North Atlantic Treaty Organization
NGO	non-governmental Organization
NSS	National Security Strategy
OEEC	Organization for European Economic Cooperation
OLP	Ordinary Legislative Procedure
OMC	open method of coordination
OMT	Outright Monetary Transactions
OSCE	Organization for Security and Cooperation in Europe (formerly CSCE)
PCTF	Police Chiefs Task Force
PES	Party of European Socialists
PESCO	Permanent Structured Cooperation
PIS	Law and Justice Party (Poland)
PNR	Passenger Name Record
PTA	preferential trade agreement
QMV	qualified majority voting
REACH	Registration, Evaluation, Authorization, and Restriction of Chemicals
S&D	Progressive Alliance of Socialists and Democrats
SAP	Stability and Association Process
SCIFA	Strategic Committee on Immigration, Frontiers, and Asylum
SEA	Single European Act
SGP	Stability and Growth Pact
SIS	Schengen Information System
SME	Small and Medium-sized Enterprise
SNP	Scottish National Party
TEC	Treaty establishing the European Community

TEU	Treaty on European Union
TFEU	Treaty on the Functioning of European Union
TTIP	Transatlantic Trade and Investment Partnership
UK	United Kingdom
UKIP	United Kingdom Independence Party
UN	United Nations
UNICE	Union of Industrial and Employers' Confederations of Europe
US	United States
VIS	Visa Information System
VWP	Visa Waiver Program (US)
WEU	Western European Union
WTO	World Trade Organization

LIST OF CONTRIBUTORS

GRAHAM AVERY	St Antony's College, Oxford
RICHARD CORBETT	Member, European Parliament
DESMOND DINAN	George Mason University
FIONA HAYES-RENSHAW	Independent researcher, Brussels
NIKLAS HELWIG	Johns Hopkins University
DANIEL KENEALY	University of Edinburgh
BRIGID LAFFAN	European University Institute
JOHN PETERSON	University of Edinburgh
ALBERTA SBRAGIA	University of Pittsburgh
ULRICH SEDELMEIER	The London School of Economics and Political Science
FRANCESCO STOLFI	Macquarie University

NEW TO THIS EDITION

- A dedicated chapter on Brexit makes this the only introductory textbook to date to engage in depth with this unprecedented development in the EU.
- Fully updated throughout, reflecting the rapid pace of current events in Europe.
- Increased coverage of democracy and legitimacy highlights this key area of debate and contestation.

THE EUROPEAN UNION'S MEMBER STATES

* Member state until March 2019.

HOW TO USE THIS BOOK

This book is enriched with a number of learning tools to help you reinforce your knowledge, further your understanding, and develop your ability to think critically.

Summary

European governments responded to a series of do
challenges after World War II by establishing novel
order to accelerate political and economic integrati
from post-war reconstruction, to the Cold War, and t
largely by mutually compatible national interests. Fr
American influence, politicians responded by establ
nities in the 1950s and the European Union in the 199(
salience of **European integration** generated seer
lenges for the EU, touching on identity, **sovereignty**,

CHAPTER SUMMARIES
Identify the scope of the material to be covered and what themes and issues you can expect to learn about in each chapter.

BOX 3.1   How it really works: Who initiates po

The formal right to initiate proposals for policy or le
mission's most precious and fundamental powers. B
are diverse. In practice, most initiatives emanating
response to ideas, suggestions, or pressures from oth
priorities and action plans approved by the Europe
international obligations or new trade agreements. S
posals from the EP. A growing proportion are about
ous EU legislation, rather than legislating in new fields
years has been to simplify, consolidate, or repeal c

'HOW IT REALLY WORKS' BOXES
Further your knowledge of how the EU works in practice as these boxes connect theory with clear explanations of the reality. Additional boxes and tables provide you with extra information and examples to widen your understanding further.

BOX 3.5   Compared to what? The ECJ and the

The ECJ—like the EU more generally—is in many ways
body with no precise counterpart anywhere in Europ
parallels, as well as contrasts, can be drawn between
Court.
   The US Supreme Court exists to uphold the US (
has no such constitution. Yet even here the differe
it appears. The ECJ must uphold the EU's Treaties. I
cumulative impact of Court decisions that have inter
a 'quiet revolution' that effectively transformed the tre

'COMPARED TO WHAT?' BOXES
Contextualize your understanding of the subject and challenge yourself to think laterally by comparing the EU with other political systems.

BOX 7.1   Key concepts and terms

Bicameralism is from Latin *bi*, two + *camera*, cham
prises two chambers, usually chosen by different met
Democratic deficit was a term initially used to d
accountability inherent in national parliaments trans
to ministers meeting in the Council. It was considered
approve or reject EU legislation should compensate f
that the EP has such powers (in most policy areas),
precise meaning, often linked to the distance betwee
European Convention on Human Rights (ECHR)

KEY CONCEPTS AND TERMS BOXES
Reinforce your learning with helpful explorations of key terms and concepts.

DISCUSSION QUESTIONS

1. How can democratic accountability be as
   European level? Should it be via national p
   government's negotiating position, or via th

2. Does the relatively low turnout in European

3. Are fundamental rights sufficiently protecte

4. Should the European Commission emand
   the EP?

DISCUSSION QUESTIONS

Review your knowledge and develop your analytical and reflective skills with end-of-chapter discussion questions.

FURTHER READING

For a detailed account of the EP, see Corbett
Hix (2009) cover internal cleavages and votin
also offers a comprehensive programme for I
appraisal of the EP's links with the public, see
ations of the democratic credentials of the E
al democracy, see Siedentop (2000); Morave
Hoeksma (2010). For an interesting argument
not as a democracy but rather as a 'demoic
tinct peoples, see Nicolaidis (2013), a specia

FURTHER READING

Broaden your learning with guided further reading, where the authors highlight additional resources you may wish to read, and explain why these texts are helpful.

WEB LINKS

- The Institute for European Politics' (Berlin) we
  ful 'EU 28 watch' which offers a round-up of
  issues in all the member states: http://www.

- The best place to search for websites of the r
  al administrations is https://europa.eu/euro

- Other useful links can also be found on the I
  Commission, http://ec.europa.eu/index_er

WEB LINKS

Take your learning further with relevant web links to reliable online content.

GLOSSARY

Several of the terms below are defined and   Bicam
elaborated in more detail in the concept boxes   (chamb
of each of the chapters. Where this is the case, compris
the box number is provided.   ent met

GLOSSARY TERMS

Look up and revise key terms, which appear in colour throughout the text and are defined in a glossary at the end of the book.

APPENDIX: CHRONOLOGY OF EURO

1945 May   End of World War II in Europe
1946 Sep.   Winston Churchill's 'United States of
1947 Jun.   Marshall Plan announced
                Organization for European Economic
1949 Apr.   North Atlantic Treaty signed in Wash
1950 May   Schuman Declaration
1951 Apr.   Treaty establishing the European Coa

CHRONOLOGY

Revise key dates and developments in the history of European integration. This is provided in an appendix for easy reference.

ONLINE RESOURCES

This textbook is accompanied by online resources, which include questions and revision tools for students and additional teaching resources for registered lecturers.

For students:

-   Test your understanding and receive instant feedback with a range of multiple-choice questions

-   Revise key terms and test your knowledge of terminology from the book with our digital flashcard glossary

For registered adopters of the textbook:

-   Guide class debate with suggested seminar questions and activities

-   Adapt PowerPoint(R) slides as a basis for lecture presentations, or use as handouts in class

PART I

BACKGROUND

CHAPTER 1

Introduction

Daniel Kenealy, John Peterson, and Richard Corbett

Summary

The European Union (EU) is not easy to understand. Yet it is well worth the effort given the importance of the Union to the everyday lives of over 500 million EU citizens, and many more beyond its borders. This introductory chapter outlines the practical and analytical reasons for studying the EU. It then introduces some of the main conceptual approaches to understanding this unique and often baffling organization, how it functions, and why. Finally, the chapter sets out three broad themes that will tie together our analysis of the EU and how it works.

Studying the EU

The years since the last edition of this text was published (in 2015), have been turbulent ones for the EU. The impact of the global financial crisis, which crystallized towards the end of 2008, continued to be felt. Although daily turmoil within the Eurozone (comprising now 19 of the EU's 28 member states) that characterized much of 2010–12 seemed to be consigned to the past, the EU was rocked by new crises. The legacy of the earlier Eurozone crisis continued with ongoing questions about how to reform the institutions of the EU to enable it to better handle future economic crises. Turmoil in North Africa and the Middle East yielded a refugee crisis with which EU member states struggled to deal throughout 2015–16. Then, perhaps above all, the UK's vote to leave the EU ('Brexit'—see Chapter 10) and the election of Donald Trump as US president, with his unpredictable foreign policy and questioning of the US security guarantee to Europe via NATO, presented significant new internal and external challenges to the EU after 2016.

Meanwhile, the anti-EU parties that made unprecedented gains in the 2014 European Parliament elections remained present and active in Brussels, and gained domestic political support in Germany, France, Austria, Finland, and Greece. The institutions and member states of the EU faced what some called an internal 'values crisis', as governments in Hungary and Poland passed legislation and enacted policies that undermined some of the bedrock principles of the EU (see Chapter 4). Put simply, the second decade of the twenty-first century qualified as certainly one of— maybe even *the*—most challenging time(s) in the history of European integration.

Yet, the EU's defenders can plausibly argue that European integration remains the most successful experiment in international cooperation in human history. In the midst of some of its most difficult days ever, the Union was awarded the Nobel Peace Prize in 2012. Despite frequent commentary since (at least) 2010 suggesting that the EU was falling apart and destined to collapse, it continued to move forward with new and sometimes exciting policies and institutional reforms on the horizon.

BOX 1.1   What's in a name?

Even the question of what to call the EU can cause confusion. What became the European Union was originally established as the European Coal and Steel Community (ECSC) in 1951, followed by the (more expansive) European Economic Community (EEC, colloquially known as the common market) by the 1957 Treaty of Rome. Its remit was widened and its name shortened to European Community (EC) in 1992. That year's Maastricht Treaty created a European Union, consisting of the EC as well as two other 'pillars' of cooperation in the areas of foreign and security policy and justice and home affairs. The Lisbon Treaty formally merged all three pillars into a single legal entity, called the European Union, in December 2009. We use the label European Community (or EC) to refer to the organization in the pre-Maastricht period (see especially Chapter 2), but 'European Union' to refer to all periods—and the activities of all pillars—thereafter. As we will see, vocabulary in the EU can be a sensitive matter (see Box 11.1).

The EU is not easy to grasp (Box 1.1). To the uninitiated, its institutions seem remote, its remit unclear, and its policies perplexing. Such bewilderment is unsurprising as the EU defies simple categorization. It is less than a federal state, but clearly more than a standard international organization. Yet, it shares certain characteristics with both. The EU's development is shaped by an increasing number of players: at the time of writing, 28 (soon to be 27) member states, seven EU institutions including a Central Bank, two consultative bodies with legal status, an External Action Service, an Investment Bank, a clutch of agencies, and countless private interests, experts, foreign actors, and citizen groups try to influence what the EU does (or does not do). 'What the EU does' has expanded enormously since its origins. Originally concerned principally with establishing a common market, at first just for coal and steel, its policy remit has expanded to cover agricultural, monetary, regional, environmental, social, immigration, foreign, and security policy. And the list does not stop there (see Box 1.2).

BOX 1.2   The three pillars of the European Union

The 1992 Maastricht Treaty organized the activities of the EU into three areas, or 'pillars' (see Figure 1.1). When the Lisbon Treaty came into force in 2009, the pillars were collapsed into one common institutional structure and the EU as a whole

Figure 1.1 The three pillars of the European Union

Pillar 1 European Community	Pillar 2 Common Foreign and Security Policy	Pillar 3 Justice and Home Affairs [after 1997, Police and Judicial Cooperation in Criminal Matters]
Policy responsibilities internal market (including competition and external trade); related policies (environmental, cohesion, consumer protection, social); agriculture; economic and monetary union; immigration asylum, visas	**Policy responsibilities** common policy positions on foreign policy; common action to strengthen security of the EU; preserve peace; promote international cooperation	**Policy responsibilities** cross-border crime; criminal law; police cooperation
Decision-making style primarily supranational	**Decision-making style** primarily intergovernmental	**Decision-making style** primarily intergovernmental

→

was given a single legal personality. However, important differences between the 'non-existent' pillars persisted, especially for pillar 2. It remains the case that the EU cannot be fully understood without understanding the previous pillar system.

Pillar 1: European Communities—The first pillar was the biggest, incorporating the vast majority of EU responsibilities. It covered internal market policies as well as trade, agricultural, and competition policy among others. Eventually, it was extended to cover most immigration and asylum policy, and economic and monetary union (EMU). In this pillar the EU's common institutions (Commission, Council, Court, and Parliament) could act with a significant degree of autonomy from national governments.

Pillar 2: Common Foreign and Security Policy (CFSP)—In the second pillar, member states attempted to forge common positions and take joint action in areas of foreign and security policy. Decision-making was primarily intergovernmental (that is, between governments), by unanimity, and without a separate legal framework. Neither the Commission nor the Parliament had much direct influence.

Pillar 3: Justice and Home Affairs (from 1997, Police and Judicial Cooperation in Criminal Matters)—The objective of the third pillar was to increase cooperation on internal security, including the fight against international crime and the drugs trade. As in pillar 2, decision-making was essentially intergovernmental. Unanimity of member governments was required for virtually all important decisions.

Sometimes treaty reforms or specific decisions could shift policy responsibility from one pillar to another, changing the nature of decision-making. For instance, the 1997 Treaty of Amsterdam moved policy on visas, immigration, and asylum from the third to the first pillar, signalling a shift towards more supranational decisions in this area. A decade later the Lisbon Treaty (signed in 2007) abolished the separate pillars entirely, while keeping some of their special features.

The dramatic expansion of EU competences over time—especially into areas traditionally seen as the responsibility of elected national governments—has meant that debates about European integration have become wrapped up in larger debates about sovereignty, democracy, and the future of the nation state. To study the EU is thus to study a lot more than its institutions and their operations. Studying European integration means posing questions about legitimacy, democracy, law, state–society relations, international relations, bureaucracies, and much more. And the EU never stands still for long, making it a dynamic topic of study.

Why bother?

Although understanding the EU is a daunting intellectual challenge, there are (at least) three reasons why it has major pay-offs. First, on a practical level, no one can make sense of European politics without understanding an organization that has daily and powerful effects on European (and non-European) governments, markets, and citizens (Box 1.3). The way the Union works often lacks political drama. Yet, the EU is responsible for such practical, everyday things that make a tangible difference to European citizens as a cap on mobile roaming charges and a right to compensation when airline flights are delayed or cancelled. For students reading this book that are studying within the EU, but in a state other than that of which they are a national, the Union has been instrumental in establishing and securing that right to study.

BOX 1.3   The practical significance of the EU

The EU's practical impact is felt in a wide range of areas including:

- *Market*: The EU regulates the world's largest market, including around 508 million inhabitants (pre-Brexit)—the world's third largest population after China and India.
- *Legislation*: It is not easy to measure and estimates vary, but in most years something between 6 and 35 per cent of the domestic legislation enacted by the Union's member states originates from EU legislation.
- *Currency*: In 2002, 12 national currencies—some dating back 600 years—ceased to be legal tender and were replaced by the euro. By 2018, 19 countries and around 340 million consumers used this single currency.
- *Wealth*: The EU's net national income comprises approximately 22 per cent of global national income.
- *Trade*: Not counting intra-EU trade, the EU's share of world exports and imports accounts for around 15 per cent of all global trade, exceeding the share of the United States.
- *Aid*: The EU and its member states are the world's largest donors of development aid, accounting for around 57 per cent of all such aid globally.

While the wisdom or desirability of EU policies and actions are hotly contested, few would deny their practical importance.

Sources:
- https://europa.eu/european-union/about-eu/figures/living_en
- https://ec.europa.eu/info/business-economy-euro/euro-area_en
- https://data.worldbank.org/indicator/NY.ADJ.NNTY.CD
- http://ec.europa.eu/eurostat/statistics-explained/index.php/International_trade_in_goods
- https://www.oecd.org/dac/financing-sustainable-development/development-finance-data/ODA-2016-detailed-summary.pdf

---

In the last completed session of the European Parliament (2009–14), members of the European Parliament (MEPs) voted, among other things to:

- reject the Anti-Counterfeiting Trade Agreement, which sought to curb piracy on the Internet but that many activists claimed lacked safeguards to protect freedom of expression;
- to cap bankers' bonuses and introduce new, more stringent financial services regulations;
- to mandate that more information was provided for consumers on food products; and

- to support an EU tax on financial transactions, often called a 'Robin Hood' tax because it would take from the rich—such as banks—and potentially generate billions to tackle poverty.

At the more dramatic end, the EU has played a leading role over recent years in international action on climate change, fighting piracy off the Horn of Africa, and in negotiations over Iran's nuclear programme.

Second, as the most advanced experiment ever in multi-lateral cooperation (see Box 1.4), the EU is important analytically. Understanding the EU helps us frame questions about the future of the nation state, the prospects for international cooperation, the effects of **globalization** (see Box 1.5), and the proper role of governments in advanced industrial societies. Put another way, what makes the EU challenging to study—its dynamic character, complexity, and expanding activities—also makes it fascinating.

BOX 1.4   Constitutional, Reform, or Lisbon Treaty?

The Constitutional Treaty, the result of a special Convention on the Future of Europe (see Chapter 8), was unanimously endorsed and signed by government leaders in 2004. It was eventually abandoned . . . or was it? Debates persist even about the answer to this most basic of questions.

The Constitutional Treaty comprised three basic elements: institutional reform, a charter of fundamental rights, and the consolidation of existing treaties:

The primary **institutional measures** included:

- increased majority voting on the Council of Ministers (where each member state is represented), simplified to represent a double majority based on states and population;
- more legislative powers for the Parliament;
- a full-time president of the European Council (where heads of state and government are represented)—this post replaced the previous six-month rotation between presidents or prime ministers of member states;
- a smaller European Commission; and
- a new EU minister of foreign affairs.

The second section of the treaty codified a charter of fundamental rights (a wide-ranging statement of 'rights, freedoms principles' including the right to life, free expression, and the right to strike, binding on the Union's institutions and in the field of EU law (see Chapter 7).

The third part (by far the longest) consisted of a **consolidated** and amended version of all previous treaties. It formally designated the treaty as a constitution for the first time and gave the Union a single 'legal personality'. However, the term 'Constitutional Treaty' was a typical 'Eurofudge': yes, it had been prepared by a 'Convention' but it was finally agreed between member states as any treaty would be. At the same time it provided an exit clause for states wishing to leave the Union. Designed to streamline and bring the EU closer to its citizens, the treaty ended up

→

➤

stretching to 300 pages of text, not all of them comprehensible. (Thus the French government's decision to post copies of the entire text to all voters in advance of France's referendum was not a successful 'vote yes' strategy.)

Treaty change requires ratification by all member states. By mid-2007, 18 of the 27 had ratified the treaty. But voters in two founding member states—France and the Netherlands—had rejected the treaty in referenda held in 2005. An alternative solution had to be found.

In 2007, European leaders finally agreed to abandon the idea of a 'constitution' and instead amended the pre-existing treaties. They avoided all references to constitutional symbols such as a European flag or anthem, and dropped the idea of giving the title (EU) 'Minister of Foreign Affairs' to a more powerful foreign policy chief. But the new treaty maintained the bulk of the institutional reforms that were contained in the Constitutional Treaty. The treaty was initially referred to as the 'Reform Treaty'—after all, everyone is in favour of reform—but the designation was dropped when, like most treaties, it took on the name of the city where it was signed in late 2007: Lisbon. Eventually ratified by all member states by the end of 2009, Lisbon actually leaves the Union with two main treaties. The first is called Treaty on European Union (TEU) and contains the basic aims, principles, and instruments of the EU, as well as its provisions on foreign and security policy. The second is called Treaty on the Functioning of the EU, which contains detailed policy provisions and procedures. However, the two are often referred to in the singular as the Lisbon Treaty. Its close substantive resemblance to the Constitutional Treaty prompted debates about whether the original was a 'constitution' in anything but name and whether Lisbon was more than an ordinary 'treaty'.

Third, the EU is a political puzzle. On one hand, EU governments and institutions have transformed it from a common market of six countries into a peaceful, integrated Union of 27/8 states. The EU's economy is considerably bigger than that of the United States (even, by many measures, post-Brexit). EU trade with the rest of the world accounts for around 20 per cent of global exports and imports. It has its own currency and a fledgling foreign policy. A queue of applicant states waits at its borders.

Yet a growing number of citizens appear disillusioned with the EU, and not just in the traditionally more 'eurosceptic' states such as the UK. In 2005, citizens in two founding member states—France and the Netherlands—rejected a constitutional treaty designed to make the EU more efficient and bring it closer to its citizens (see Box 1.4). Eurobarometer (2007) surveys conducted after the onset of the Eurozone crisis revealed a marked fall in levels of trust in EU institutions (although that trend has begun to reverse in recent years) and a greater tendency to identify as a 'national' of a specific country than as 'European'.

Meanwhile, Brussels bureaucrats make easy targets for almost every ill. Populist political parties often gain electoral success through EU-bashing. The EU's institutions—the European Commission, the Council (representing national governments), and even the directly elected European Parliament—are viewed as remote and complex, or just not worth bothering about. The EU certainly is not a well-understood body, and it is difficult even for diligent students to see how (or if) it works.

This book addresses a central question: 'How does it work?' But the question has two separate meanings and constitutes what is known (in French) as a *double entendre*. One is, how does it do what it does: who are the main actors, and what are the main processes, dynamics, and explanations for what the EU does? But we also want to address the more rhetorical question: 'How (in the *world*) does it work?!' How can such a massive, complex, unwieldy amalgam of states, institutions, lobbyists, languages, traditions, legal codes, and so on possibly do much of the governing of Europe, let alone do so efficiently and legitimately? Why have sovereign states agreed to relinquish part of their **sovereignty** (see Box 1.5)? Why do European policies emerge looking as they do? Why does the EU elicit such strong demonstrations of support and antipathy? The primary purpose of this book is to address these questions in a lively and comprehensible way.

Each of our contributors is an expert with research, teaching, or policy-making experience (some with all three). Students need to understand both the formal rules of EU practice (what the treaties say, what EU legislation stipulates, and so on), and how it *really* works (how the treaties are interpreted, what informal rules guide action, and other such unofficial 'rules of the game'). A series of boxes entitled '*How it really works*' appear throughout the book and are designed to capture this dual dynamic. They illustrate how a particular actor, policy, or process actually works, regardless of the formal rules.

Most chapters also include a '*Compared to what?*' box. Their purpose is to place the institutions, structures and policies of the EU in a comparative perspective, and help the reader better understand the EU by underlining how it is like, or unlike, other systems of **governance** (Box 1.5). Finally, each chapter offers '*Key concepts*' boxes that define important terms, and also provide guides to further reading and useful Internet sites. All of these features are designed to bring the EU to life for our readers.

BOX 1.5   Key concepts and terms

Globalization is the idea that the world is becoming increasingly interconnected and interdependent because of increasing flows of trade, technology, ideas, people, and capital. Globalization is usually presented as reducing the autonomy of individual states, although whether its impact is essentially positive or negative, inevitable or controllable, are hotly debated questions (see Wolf 2004; Rodrik 2011).

Governance means 'established patterns of rule without an overall ruler'. Even though it has no government, the EU undertakes the sort of activities that have traditionally been the responsibility of governments. The EU is thus said to be a system of governance without a government (or an opposition).

European integration is the process whereby sovereign states partially relinquish, or pool, national sovereignty to maximize their collective power and interests.

Intergovernmentalism is a process or condition whereby decisions are reached

➡

---

by specifically defined cooperation between or among governments. Formally, at least, sovereignty is relinquished. The term intergovernmentalism is usually contrasted with supranationalism.

Multi-level governance is often used to describe the EU. It means a system in which power is shared between the supranational, national, and subnational levels. The term also suggests there is significant interaction and coordination of political actors across those levels. How they interact and with what effect helps determine the shape of European integration (see Hooghe and Marks 2001).

Sovereignty refers to the ultimate authority over people and territory. It is sometimes broken down into internal (law-making authority within a territory) and external (international recognition) sovereignty (see Krasner 1999). Opinions vary on whether state sovereignty is 'surrendered' to, or merely 'shared' or 'pooled' in the EU.

Supranationalism means above states or nations. Processes or institutions that are largely (but never entirely) independent of national governments make key decisions. The subject governments (in the case of the EU, the member state governments) are then obliged to accept these decisions. The **Court of Justice of the European Union** (Chapter 3) is a supranational institution. The term supranationalism is usually contrasted with intergovernmentalism.

Understanding the EU: Theory and Conceptual Tools

There is, and can be, no single theory of the EU. Some years ago, one of us (Peterson 2001) argued that EU theorists faced 'a choice'. That is, anyone seeking to theorize about European integration had to choose what they wanted to explain and at which level to engage with the EU to find the answer. For example, at one level of the EU remains a system of international relations in which states bargain, cooperate and compete to achieve their national interests. At another level, the EU is a political system that can usefully be studied using concepts and approaches from comparative politics and public policy. There is also an ever-expanding literature that adopts a constructivist approach, and focuses on how the rules of the game—formal or informal—are 'constructed' as different kinds of EU actor interact with one another at all levels of analysis.

When studying anything as complex as the EU, we need conceptual tools to guide us. Theories simplify reality and allow us to see relationships among the things we observe. When utilizing theories, it is important to specify what about the EU we are seeking to explain before choosing a theory that seems appropriate to the task.

Sketched below are some leading theoretical frameworks, including their key assumptions and insights. The chapters that follow use these insights to elaborate and explain how the EU works. Many of these theories have been developed and refined over many years. Readers are encouraged to explore them further through the suggested readings at the end of the chapter.

International relations (IR) approaches

Several classic theories of European integration draw from IR theory. The basic unit of analysis for most (not all) IR theories is the state. When applied to the EU, they are primarily concerned with explaining how and why states choose to form European institutions, and who or what determines the shape and speed of the integration process.

In 1958, after the establishment of the EEC, Ernst Haas published *The Uniting of Europe*, a classic work of neofunctionalist theory. Haas and other neofunctionalist scholars sought to explain how a merger of economic activity in specific economic sectors (starting with coal and steel) across borders could 'spill over' and provoke wider integration in related areas (Haas 1961, 1964; Lindberg and Scheingold 1970). One form of spill over was functional: for instance, a single EU market wasn't truly possible without a single EU environmental policy. Moreover, neofunctionalists posited that political spill over would supplement functional spill over. Political spill over referred to the possibilities created by new institutions at the European level. Actors at the national level (such as interest groups) would align their interests across borders and interact directly with EU institutions (say, the European Commission) and press for further integration. Through this process, a new field of political action—in addition to already existing national fields—would be created. Over time, and incrementally, interests and loyalties would gradually shift from the national to the supranational (Box 1.5) level.

Neofunctionalism appeared well suited to explaining the successful early years of integration. However, by 1965 the French president Charles de Gaulle was symbolic of the ongoing importance, to many, of state sovereignty and national interests. The mid-1960s were characterized by the so-called Empty Chair Crisis in which De Gaulle withdrew French participation from meetings of the Council of ministers (hence the empty chair) after he thought a variety of Commission proposals went too far in seeking to advance integration. Supranational institutions were weakened during this period. The nation state had seemingly reasserted itself. Neofunctionalist theory possessed a unidirectional logic (suggesting that integration could only go forward), which damaged its credibility as events of the 1960s and 1970s unfolded.

Dissatisfaction with neofunctionalism in the 1960s was reflected in Hoffmann's (1966) assertion that the nation state was 'obstinate, not obsolete', in Europe as well as globally. The phrase captured the notion that a logic of diversity among national interests might just as easily impede the development of European integration as further it. Interestingly, Hoffmann (1995: 1–6) identified himself as a realist.

Realism, a prominent theory within IR, has had surprisingly little to say about European integration (see Rynning 2005), despite the fact that E. H. Carr, one of its founding thinkers spent considerable time thinking about what an integrated Europe might look like after World War II (Kenealy and Kostagiannis 2013). In part this may be due to the dominance of a certain form of realism—often termed neorealism or structural realism (Keohane 1986)—in international relations. Neorealism's emphasis on the importance of the structure of the international system, on states as unitary and rational actors possessing fixed and often conflicting goals, and its pessimism about the positive impact of international institutions, jars with the complexity of the EU and its densely institutionalized mechanisms of interstate cooperation. Rosato (2011, 2012) has offered a realist account of European integration that identifies the Cold War threat posed by the Soviet Union as the key factor determining decisions by the original six member states (and then more member states later) to press ahead with integration. Rosato's highly provocative account has been criticized on both historical and methodological grounds (Moravcsik 2013).

An arguably more credible account is offered by Moravcsik's (1993, 1998) liberal intergovernmentalism. It contends that it is the preferences and power of EU member states that drive forward the integration process. The approach is 'liberal' because it assumes that economic interests, and not just security interests (as realists sometimes argue), motivate and drive European states. Liberal intergovernmentalism disaggregates the state and considers how national governments bargain with various domestic interest groups (especially economic ones) to produce a coalition of support broad enough to support its agenda. It is an 'intergovernmental' theory because, at the EU level, Moravcsik conceptualizes national governments as bringing their preferences to a bargaining table with the outcome being a reflection of the relative power of each member state. Moravcsik emphasizes national power, package deals, and the ability to make side-payments to reluctant partners. EU institutions and transnational alliances of interest groups are afforded little role, marking a key distinction between his approach and neofunctionalism.

Moravcsik's (1998) historically impressive work, *The Choice for Europe*, confines itself to major choices in the history of the EU—what Peterson (1995) calls 'history making decisions'. It does not account for much of what might be called the day-to-day activities of the Union. Along with other IR theories, it approaches the Union as a sub-system of international relations and one that is overwhelmingly dominated by states. Debates between variations of intergovernmentalism and neofunctionalism continue to animate academic debates about the nature of EU integration to this day (Bickerton *et al.* 2015; Schimmelfennig 2015; Biermann *et al.* 2017).

A comparative politics approach

Works drawing on comparative politics approaches have challenged the primacy of the state in shaping European integration. Foremost among them is the so-called new institutionalism (Hall and Taylor 1996; Pollack 2005), which emerged as part of a broader move in political science in the late 1980s and 1990s. What was new about institutionalism was that it brought 'back in' to the study of politics how institutions matter in determining outcomes, after a long period when they were neglected. It was applied fruitfully to the study of the EU to the point where, arguably, institutionalism became *the* leading theory of EU politics and policy-making (see Cowles and Curtis 2004).

Institutionalism insists that the EU's institutions are more than impartial arbiters in the policy-making process; they are key players with their own agendas and priorities (Armstrong and Bulmer 1998; Pollack 2009). Institutionalists contend that the Union's policies are not simply the results of bargaining between governments. Its institutions are unusually powerful compared to those of other international organizations. They thus play a key role in the formulation and adoption of EU policy. To illustrate, almost nothing can become EU legislation unless the Commission tables a proposal. The European Court of Justice (ECJ) has been able to shape EU integration even, at times, against the wishes of member states. The Parliament can kill off proposals that are supported by the governments of member states.

Many institutionalists focus on the impact of institutions over time and specifically how institutions, once established, can shape and even constrain the behaviour of the actors who established them (Pierson 1996, 2000). Political institutions and even policies, once established, can become subject to path dependency. Political actors often naturally stick with established institutions and policies as they increasingly learn how to operate with, and within, them. Institutions, and policies, are thus said to be 'sticky'; that is, once established, they tend not to change. Consider the EU's Common Agricultural Policy (CAP), which has persevered—with incremental adaptations—for many years despite intense criticism. The idea of starting again on a long, time-consuming, and expensive process of renegotiating the CAP has been resisted.

Obviously, institutions matter far more for institutionalists than they do for liberal intergovernmentalists. Perhaps inevitably, institutionalism is better at explaining developments after the fact than it is at offering predictive hypotheses. Still, its advocates are on strong ground in insisting that bargaining over the future of European integration and—especially—European policies is as much or more *interinstitutional* (that is, it occurs between the EU's unusually powerful institutions) than it is *intergovernmental* (between EU member states).

A sociological/cultural approach

One theoretical approach to the EU claims to be able to generate equally plausible explanations at all levels of analysis. Constructivism is strikingly diverse but at its core is an attempt to focus on the 'social construction' of the collective rules and norms that guide political behaviour (Eilstrup-Sangiovanni 2006: 393). At its most radical, a constructivist approach argues that reality does not exist outside of human interpretation and language. In the study of the EU, however, a less radical or abstract form of constructivism is prevalent (see Risse 2009). Constructivism shares neofunctionalism's concern with new arenas for socialization, transfers of loyalty, and processes in which actors redefine their interests as a result of interacting with the EU and its institutions (Haas 2004). Along with institutionalists, social constructivists suggest that informal rules and norms (such as reciprocity or good will) can shape or even determine the behaviour of political actors (Checkel 2006).

Of course, it is extremely difficult to show that abstract ideas or norms actually cause a change in behaviour, as many constructivists argue. Consider this example: during 2013–14 the idea emerged that the individual appointed as president of the European Commission should be the 'lead candidate' of the political party that won the most seats in the 2014 European Parliament elections. Some member states were staunchly opposed to that idea since choosing the Commission president had always been an intergovernmental decision taken by EU heads of state and government. And yet, ultimately, the idea prevailed and the lead candidate of the centre-right European People's Party—Jean-Claude Juncker—was appointed president (see Peterson 2017). A more cynical perspective might argue that those promoting the idea (such as the political party groups, leading MEPs) were simply seeking to advance their own interests and using the power of an idea, in this case the idea of a more democratic process of appointment, to attain their desired outcome.

Constructivists can, therefore, often correlate ideas with behaviour. But they have trouble proving that ideas matter more than interests (Aspinwall and Schneider 2000; Checkel 2004). Nevertheless, sociological/constructivist approaches to the EU offer insight into, for example, the extent to which EU Commission officials are socialized in a supranational way (Hooghe 2005; Kassim *et al.* 2013), or the extent to which actors can learn from prior interactions and alter their preferences accordingly (Checkel 2001). In recent years, sociological approaches to the EU have proliferated and offered new insights into the nature of political protests across the EU as well as which citizens are most likely to identify as 'European' (see Merand and Saurugger 2010; Risse 2010; Roche 2010). In response to the Eurozone crisis, there has been interesting research into the extent to which central bankers in the EU have become socialized by the EU's institutions or have remained more strongly influenced by their national cultures (van Esch and de Jong 2017).

A public policy approach

A fourth theoretical approach useful to those studying the EU is the policy network framework (Jordan and Schout 2006; Peterson 2009). Unlike neofunctionalism and liberal intergovernmentalism, this approach does not tell us much about the grand bargains struck between national governments, history-making decisions, such as treaty reform, that set the broad direction of European integration. But policy network analysis helps guide exploration of the behind-the-scenes negotiation and exchange that shapes EU policy day-to-day. A policy network is a 'cluster of actors, each of which has an interest or stake in a given EU policy sector and the capacity to help determine policy success or failure' (Peterson and Bomberg 1999: 8).

Policy networks at the EU level bring together institutional actors (from the Commission, Council, and Parliament) and other stakeholders such as representatives of private firms, public interest groups, technical or scientific experts, political campaigners, and national officials. Networks lack hierarchy. There is no one actor in charge. They rely instead on resource exchange. As a result, participants need to bring to Brussels (or Strasbourg) some valued resource with which to bargain. That resource could be information, ideas, money, constitutional-legal power, or political legitimacy. According to network analysts, bargaining and resource exchange among these actors, rather than strictly intergovernmental bargaining, determine the shape of actual EU policies. Research on such networks has spanned policy developments in spheres including energy, health, migration, and beyond (Kingah *et al.* 2015).

Different theories, different insights

Each of these theoretical approaches has a set of assumptions, strengths, and weaknesses (Table 1.1). No one theory can explain everything treated in this book. But each offers different insights about different key features of the EU: how integration evolves; the way policies are made; the role of different actors in the process; and so on. Readers need not master all these theories to use this book. Rather, these theoretical insights—and their application in subsequent chapters—are meant to encourage thinking about theory and its role in helping us understand and evaluate European integration and EU politics.

TABLE 1.1 Theories of European integration and the EU

Theory/approach	Proponents/ major works	Assumptions	Shortcomings
Neofunctionalism	Haas (1958)	Supranational institutions crucial; spillover drives integration	Cannot explain stagnation
Liberal intergovernmentalism	Moravcsik (1998)	Member states control integration	Too state-centric; neglects day-to-day policy-making
New institutionalism	Pollack (2009)	Institutions matter; path dependencies and sunk costs make institutions and policies 'sticky'	Over-emphasizes the power of the EU's institutions
Social constructivism	Checkel (2004)	Ideas matter; interests are constructed and not pre-determined	Methodological weaknesses
Policy networks	Peterson (2009)	Resource exchange within networks shapes policy	Cannot explain big decisions

Themes

To help the reader make sense of the EU, this text is held together by three common themes. Each highlights a key, distinctive feature of the EU as:

1. an 'experiment in motion', an ongoing process without a clear end-state;

2. a system of shared power characterized by growing complexity and an increasing number of players;

3. an organization with an expanding scope, but limited capacity.

We introduce each of these themes below.

Experimentation and change

Since its conception in the early 1950s, European integration has been an on-going process without a clear end-state (see van Middelaar 2013). In one sense its development has been a functional, step-by-step process: integration in one area has led to pressures to integrate in others. As neofunctionalists would point out, the EU has developed from a free trade area to a single market, and from a single market to an economic and monetary union. These developments, however, have not been smooth or automatic. Rather, the EU's development has progressed in fits and starts, the result of constant experimentation, problem-solving, and trial and error. European foreign policy—from the failed attempts of the 1950s (see Chapter 2), to the creation of a Common Foreign and Security Policy (CFSP) in the early 1990s and a Common Security and Defence Policy (CSDP) in the late 1990s—is a good example of this evolution. With no agreed end goal (such as a 'United States of Europe'), the EU's actors have reacted to immediate problems, but they have done so neither coherently nor always predictably.

The nature and intensity of change are also varied. Constitutional change takes place through intergovernmental conferences (IGCs)—special negotiations in which government representatives come together to hammer out agreements to adapt or alter the EU's founding treaties. The first (resulting in the 1951 Treaty of Paris) created the ECSC with six members. Most recently, the Lisbon Treaty (ratified in 2009) was designed to consolidate and streamline a Union of (then) 27 members, with the possibility of it growing still further to 30 or more (see Box 1.6). Less spectacularly, legislative change has taken place through thousands of EU directives and regulations. Finally, the EU's institutions, especially the European Commission and Court of Justice, and the member states, have themselves acted as instigators of change, through their interpretations of the treaties and of legislation as well as through informal agreements and practices supplementing them. The point is that change is a constant in the EU. This book explores its main sources and implications.

> **BOX 1.6   The treaties**
>
> When practitioners and academics use the term 'the treaties', they are referring to the collection of founding treaties and their subsequent revisions. The founding treaties include the Treaty of Paris (signed in 1951, establishing the ECSC) and two Treaties of Rome signed in 1957, one establishing the EEC and the other the European Atomic Energy Community (Euratom). The Treaty of Paris became void in July 2002. The Euratom Treaty never amounted to much. But the Treaty of Rome that established the EEC became absolutely central. It has been substantially revised, notably in the:
>
> - Single European Act (signed 1986);
> - Treaty of the European Union (TEU), more commonly termed the Maastricht Treaty (signed 1992);
> - Treaty of Amsterdam (signed 1997);
> - Treaty of Nice (signed 2001);
> - Treaty of Lisbon (signed 2007).

As Box 1.1 explained, the IGC leading up to the Maastricht Treaty not only revised the Treaty of Rome (which it re-named the treaty establishing the European Community), but also agreed the broader TEU (or Maastricht Treaty), which included two new pillars covering foreign policy and justice and home affairs (see Box 1.2). The Amsterdam and Lisbon Treaties subsequently collapsed the pillars into a single framework.

The EU's treaties are the basic toolkit of ministers, European commissioners, parliamentarians, and civil servants dealing with EU matters. Each piece of legislation is based on one of these treaty articles (of which there are more than 400). The treaties have grown increasingly long and complex. To improve the presentation, and facilitate the reading of the treaties, the articles were renumbered in the Amsterdam IGC of 1997. But the treaties are hardly an easy read. Even many legal scholars would agree that some of their language borders on the incomprehensible. The failed Constitutional Treaty of 2004 was intended to simplify the existing texts and make them more readable. The Lisbon Treaty made a more modest attempt at simplification, although the term 'constitution' was dropped.

Power sharing and consensus

Our second theme concerns power and how it is shared between different actors and across layers of government. The EU policy-making system lacks a clear nexus of power: there is no 'EU government', nor is there any 'opposition'. Instead, power is dispersed across a range of actors and levels of governance (regional, national, and supranational). Deciding which actors should do what, and at what level of governance, is a matter of ongoing debate within the EU. But, whenever possible, the Union seeks to act on the basis of broad consensus.

The three most important sets of actors are the member states, the EU institutions, and organized interests. Certainly, much about the evolution of the EU has been determined by the member states themselves, and in particular their different approaches to integration. Some member states want deeper integration, others do not, and this division continues to shape the speed and form of the integration process. Meanwhile, EU institutions have shaped its development as they vie for power with the member states, as well as among themselves. Finally organized interests—including representatives of sub-national levels of governance, private interests, and citizen groups—play an increasing role.

Part of what makes the EU unique—and certainly different from its member states—is that these actors exist in a complex web where there are established patterns of interaction but no overall 'ruler', government, or even dominant actor. Instead, actors must bargain and share power in an effort to reach an agreement acceptable to all, or at least most. This dynamic has been captured in the term multi-level governance (see Box 1.5), which suggests a system of overlapping and shared powers between actors on the regional, national, and supranational level (Hooghe and Marks 2001). EU governance is thus an exercise in sharing power between states and institutions, and seeking consensus across different levels of governance. Coming to grips with this unique and changing distribution of power is a key task of this book.

Scope and capacity

Our final theme concerns the expanding remit of the EU, and its ability to cope with it. The EU has undergone continuous (in a phrase used by insiders) 'widening and deepening'. The widening of its membership has been astonishing. It has grown from a club of six member states (West Germany, France, Italy, the Netherlands, Belgium, and Luxembourg) to nine (UK, Denmark, and Ireland joined in 1973), to 12 (Greece in 1981; Portugal and Spain in 1986), to 15 (Austria, Finland, and Sweden in 1995). Then in 2004 the EU jumped to 25 following the accession of ten mainly central and eastern European states. The accession of Bulgaria and Romania in 2007 took the EU to 27, with Croatia becoming the twenty-eighth (pre-Brexit) in 2013. Additional countries—the Former Yugoslav Republic of Macedonia (renamed North Macedonia in 2018), Montenegro, and Serbia plus Albania, Iceland, and Turkey—are candidate states. The institutional, political, economic, and even linguistic challenges that enlargement poses are immense (Box 1.7).

The EU has also 'deepened' in the sense that the member states have decided to pool sovereignty in an increasing number of policy areas, including, most dramatically, in sensitive policy areas associated with the Area of Freedom, Justice and Security (see Chapter 5). The sovereign debt crisis led the EU to become more actively involved in the sensitive area of national budgets and there are ongoing debates about the need to further develop Eurozone policies and institutions. Such developments mean that the EU is managing tasks that have traditionally been the exclusive preserve of the nation state.

> ### BOX 1.7   Lost in interpretation?
>
> Following the accession of Croatia in 2013, the EU boasted 24 official languages: Bulgarian, Croatian, Czech, Danish, Dutch, English, Estonian, Finnish, French, German, Greek, Irish, Hungarian, Italian, Latvian, Lithuanian, Maltese, Polish, Portuguese, Romanian, Slovak, Slovene, Spanish, and Swedish.
>
> The EU's translation service is the largest in the world by far (over twice the size of the UN's) and the cost of translation and interpretation is estimated to account for less than 1 per cent of the annual general budget of the EU. Divided by the population of the EU, this comes to around €2 per person. In 2016, the EU's Directorate-General for Translation's output was over 2.2 million pages, which was an increase of 11 per cent over the previous year. In Parliament alone, where interpreters in soundproof boxes attempt to translate words such as 'gobbledygook' (the word doesn't exist in Polish), and avoid confusing frozen semen with frost-bitten seamen (as occurred in one parliamentary debate), the cost and potential confusion is immense. But being able to communicate with your electors and fellow representatives in your own language is also seen as a fundamental right. After all, it is difficult for EU citizens to feel close to an institution that does not operate—at least officially—in their own language. In practice, most work of the EU is carried out in just three languages, English, French, and German. Meanwhile, the rising cost of translation has had one positive effect—it has forced practitioners to limit official texts to fewer than 15 pages.
>
> *Sources:* European Commission 2016; query to European Parliament Research Service, January 2018.

At the same time the EU continues to try to dispose of its image as 'economic giant, a political dwarf, and a military worm', a depiction attributed to the Belgian foreign minister Mark Eyskens. The EU is trying to stamp its authority on the international scene through its leadership on issues such as climate change and the Iranian nuclear programme. A CFSP has been developed that, according to the treaties, 'might lead to a common defence' (Article 24 TEU). These developments have challenged the EU's capacity—its practical and political ability to realize its ambitions. While the EU has taken on more members and more tasks, its institutional and political development has not kept pace. This mismatch—between the EU's ambitions on one hand and its institutional and political capacity on the other (see Hill 1993)—raises questions about the EU's future and ability to adapt. It also represents the third theme of the volume.

Taken together these three themes address:

- how the EU has developed and why (experimentation and change);
- who are the main players and how they interact (power sharing and consensus);
- what the EU does, and how it does it (scope and capabilities).

These three themes provide the glue necessary to hold together our investigation of the EU and how it works.

Chapter Layout

Any work on European integration that aims to be at all comprehensive is bound to cover a lot of ground, both theoretical and practical. In explaining how the EU works, it is necessary to look at the historical background of European integration, the major actors involved, the key policies and their impact, and the EU's global presence. This book's layout reflects this logic. Chapter 2 tells us 'how we got here' by providing a concise historical overview of the EU's development. The next part (Chapters 3–4) focuses on the major actors: the EU's institutions and member states. Part III focuses on policy and process. It provides an overview of key economic and related policies (Chapter 5), how policies are made (Chapter 6), and the wider constitutional and democratic issues arising from these policy processes (Chapter 7). Chapters in Part IV examine the EU's relations with the wider world. Chapter 8 covers EU enlargement and its policy towards states in its geographical neighbourhood. Chapter 9 focuses on the EU's growing role as a global actor. Although the UK remains, at the time of writing, a member state of the EU, the vote to leave the EU in June 2016 has created a significant challenge for the EU, and ongoing negotiations are seeking to establish the future of the EU–UK relationship. Chapter 10 focuses on 'Brexit' and considers its implications for the future of two unions: the UK and the EU. In chapter 11, a conclusion draws together the main themes of the volume and ponders how the EU might work in the future.

? DISCUSSION QUESTIONS

1. The EU can be seen as one of the most successful modern experiments in international cooperation, yet it is increasingly unpopular among its citizens. Why?

2. Which theory appears to offer the most compelling account of recent developments in European integration?

FURTHER READING

Some of the key themes introduced in this chapter are inspired by leading, general studies of the EU including Weiler (1998); Hooghe and Marks (2001); Jørgensen *et al.* (2006): and Wallace *et al.* (2015). Wiener and Diez (2009) feature a collection of works on European integration theory and practice. Good overviews of integration theory include Rosamond (2013); Eilstrup-Sangiovanni (2006); Pollack (2015); and the relevant chapters of Jones *et al.* (2012). Excellent recent additions to the literature are Van Middelaar (2013), written by the speechwriter to a former European

Council president, and Bickerton *et al.* (2015) and Börzel and Risse (2018), which offer novel theoretical interpretations of recent events. In the light of multiple crises faced by the EU some scholars have begun to think theoretically about the prospect of EU *dis*-integration (Webber 2014; Jachtenfuchs and Kasak 2017; Jones 2018).

Bickerton, C.J., Hodson, D., and Puetter, U. (eds) (2015), *The New Intergovernmentalism: States and Supranational Actors in the Post-Maastricht Era* (Oxford and New York: Oxford University Press).

Börzel, T. A. and Risse, T. (2018), 'From the Euro to the Schengen Crises: European Integration Theories, Politicization and Identity Politics', *Journal of European Public Policy*, 25/1: 83–108.

Eilstrup-Sangiovanni, M. (ed.) (2006), *Debates on European Integration: A Reader* (London: Palgrave).

Hooghe, L. and Marks, G. (2001), *Multi-Level Governance and European Integration* (Lanham and Oxford: Rowman and Littlefield Publishers, Inc).

Jachtenfuchs, M. and Kasak, C. (2017), 'Balancing Sub-Unit Autonomy and Collective Problem-Solving by Varying Exit and Voice: An Analytical Perspective', *Journal of European Public Policy*, 24/4: 598–614.

Jones, E. (2018), 'Towards a Theory of Disintegration', *Journal of European Public Policy*, 25/3: 440–51.

Jones, E., Menon, A., and Weatherill, S. (eds) (2012), *The Oxford Handbook of the European Union* (New York and Oxford: Oxford University Press).

Jørgensen, K. E., Pollack, M., and Rosamond, B. (eds) (2006), *Handbook of European Union Politics* (London: Sage).

Pollack, M. (2015), 'Theorizing EU Policy-Making', in H. Wallace, M. Pollack, and A. Young (eds), *Policy-Making in the European Union*, 7th edn (Oxford and New York: Oxford University Press): 12–45.

Rosamond, B. (2016), 'Theorizing the EU After Integration Theory', in M. Cini and N. Pérez-Solórzano Borragán (eds), *European Union Politics*, 5th edn (Oxford and New York: Oxford University Press): 79–96.

Van Middelaar, L. (2013), *The Passage to Europe: How a Continent Became a Union* (New Haven, CT, and London: Yale University Press).

Wallace, H., Pollack, M., and Young, A. (eds) (2015), *Policy-Making in the European Union*, 7th edn (Oxford and New York: Oxford University Press).

Webber, D. (2014), 'How Likely is it that the European Union will Disintegrate? A Critical Analysis of Competing Theoretical Perspectives', *European Journal of International Relations*, 20/2: 341–65.

Weiler, J. H. H. (1999), *The Constitution of Europe* (Cambridge and New York: Cambridge University Press).

Wiener, A. and Diez, T. (eds) (2009), *European Integration Theory*, 2nd edn (Oxford and New York: Oxford University Press).

WEB LINKS

- The EU's official website 'The European Union online' (http://europa.eu/) is a valuable starting point. It provides further links to wide variety of official sites on EU policies, institutions, legislation, treaties, and current debates.

- Precisely because the EU's website is so large, the Europa—Information Services website provides a nice index of where to find answers on the Europa website (http://europa.eu/european-union/index_en).

- You can also use the web to access the *Official Journal* (OJ), which is updated daily in several languages. The OJ is the authoritative and formal source for information on EU legislation, case law, parliamentary questions, and documents of public interest (http://eur-lex.europa.eu/).

- For pithier reporting, the *Economist* (www.economist.com) provides useful general articles, while *Politico* (www.politico.eu) offers insider coverage of EU policies and news.

- To follow current events and developments within the EU, the following sites are useful:

  - EurActiv reports EU current affairs with analysis, and has an easy-to-navigate system of 'dossiers', which provide an overview of different policy areas (http://www.euractiv.com).

  - EUobserver offers coverage of EU current affairs with a very useful email bulletin service (http://euobserver.com/).

  - Current debates and topics are also addressed in series of think tank websites. Some of the better known include the Centre for European Policy Studies (http://www.ceps.be); the European Policy Centre (http://www.epc.eu); the Centre for European Reform (www.cer.org.uk); and the Trans European Policy Studies Association (www.tepsa.be).

 Visit the Ancillary Resource Centre that accompanies this book for additional material: www.oup.com/uk/kenealy5e/

CHAPTER 2

How Did We Get Here?

Desmond Dinan

Summary

European governments responded to a series of domestic, regional, and global challenges after World War II by establishing novel supranational institutions in order to accelerate political and economic integration. These challenges ranged from post-war reconstruction, to the Cold War, and then to **globalization**. Driven largely by mutually compatible national interests, Franco-German bargains, and American influence, politicians responded by establishing the European communities in the 1950s and the European Union in the 1990s. Yet the increasing political salience of **European integration** generated seemingly insurmountable challenges for the EU, touching on identity, **sovereignty**, and **legitimacy**. At the same time, successive rounds of enlargement, which saw the Union grow in size from its original six member states, generated institutional and policy challenges that have shaped the contours of European integration.

Introduction

Continuity or change? Individual initiative or unstoppable momentum? Ideology or self-interest? Questions such as these help frame the debate about the origins and evolution of the European Union (EU). Specifically, to what extent do the vagaries of institutionalized economic, and political integration in the post-World War II period represent a decisive break from previous patterns of international relations? Has the EU been shaped more by human agency than by profound, impersonal forces? How important are ideas about European cooperation as opposed to material motives?

Historians have grappled with these and other questions, large and small, since the emergence of EU history as a sub-field of modern European history (see Box 2.1). Consensus remains elusive. Still, differences among historians are mostly of degree rather than of dogma. Antecedents of **European integration** existed well before the end of World War II. Economic, political, and strategic challenges in the post-war period facilitated the rise of European integration, which influential politicians helped to bring about. Often strongly sympathetic to European federalism, however vaguely understood, these individuals mostly operated within the framework of nation states. Without a realistic sense of what constituted the national interest, proponents of European integration would not have seen their ideas come to fruition.

BOX 2.1   Interpreting European integration

Historians have offered different interpretations of how European integration has developed and why. Alan Milward (1984, 2000) was a foremost historian of European integration. He argued that economic interests impelled Western European countries to integrate, but that national governments shared **sovereignty** only to the extent necessary to resolve problems that would otherwise have undermined their effectiveness, **legitimacy**, and credibility. Paradoxically, European states rescued themselves through limited **supranationalism**. Andrew Moravcsik (1998) has complemented Milward's thesis by claiming that national governments, not supranational institutions, controlled the pace and scope of integration. Moravcsik uses historical insights from a series of case studies from the 1950s to the 1990s to develop **liberal intergovernmentalism** as a theory of **European integration**. **Intergovernmentalism** generally is in the ascendant in the historiography of European integration, in contrast to the early years of the EC when **federalism** or the arguments of **neofunctionalist** scholars such as Ernst Haas (1958) and Leon Lindberg (1963) dominated academic discourse on the EC (see Chapter 1).

Post-War Problems and Solutions

One of the most pressing problems at the end of the World War II was what to do about Germany. The question became acute with the onset of the Cold War. As the Soviet Union consolidated its control over the eastern part of the country, the Western Powers—the United Kingdom (UK), France, and the United States (US)—facilitated the establishment of democratic and free market institutions in what became the (western) Federal Republic of Germany (FRG, or West Germany). The German question then became how to maximize the economic and military potential of West Germany for the benefit of the West while allaying the understandable concerns of Germany's neighbours, especially France.

The US championed integration as a means of reconciling old enemies, promoting prosperity, and strengthening Western Europe's resistance to communism. The Marshall Plan (see Box 2.2) was the main instrument of American policy. European governments wanted American dollars for post-war reconstruction, but without strings attached. For their part, the Americans insisted that European recipients coordinate their plans for using the aid. That was the extent of European integration in the late 1940s. The UK had no interest in sharing sovereignty. France wanted to keep the old enemy down and prevent (West) Germany's coal-rich Ruhr region from becoming a springboard to remilitarization. Few countries were willing to liberalize trade. Winston Churchill's famous call in 1946 for a United States of Europe belied the reality of politicians' unwillingness to change the status quo.

It was West Germany's rapid economic recovery, thanks in part to the Marshall Plan, which made the status quo untenable. The US wanted to accelerate German recovery in order to reduce occupation costs and promote recovery throughout Europe. A weak West Germany, the Americans argued, meant a weak Western Europe. France agreed, but urged caution. France wanted to modernize its own economy before allowing West Germany's economy to rebound. Indeed, France agreed to the establishment of West Germany only on condition that its coal production (a key material for war-making) remained under international control.

BOX 2.2   Key concepts and terms

The **Empty Chair Crisis** was prompted by French President Charles de Gaulle's decision to pull France out of all Council meetings in 1965, thereby leaving one chair empty. De Gaulle staunchly opposed the Commission's plans to extend the EC's powers generally and the application of the treaty provisions on the extension of **qualified majority voting (QMV)**.

➝

The **Luxembourg Compromise** resolved the empty chair crisis. Reached during a foreign ministers' meeting in 1966, the Compromise was an informal agreement (issued only in the form of a press release) stating that when a decision was subject to QMV, the Council would postpone a decision if any member states felt 'very important interests' were under threat, and would 'endeavour, within a reasonable time' to find a solution acceptable to all. Although France and the Five disagreed on what would happen if no such solutions were found within a reasonable time (continue discussions or proceed to a vote), in practice the compromise meant that **QMV** was used far less often, and unanimity became the norm.

The **Marshall Plan (1947)** was an aid package from the US of $13 billion (equivalent to almost 3 per cent of US GNP at that time) to help rebuild West European economies after the war. The aid was given on the condition that European states cooperate and jointly administer these funds.

QMV is the voting system most commonly used in the Council. Decisions require a high level of support but do not need unanimity. Further information is provided in Boxes 3.2 and 3.3.

The **Schengen Agreement** was signed by five member states in 1985 (Belgium, France, Germany, Luxembourg, and the Netherlands) and came into effect ten years later. It removed all border controls among its signatories, and now includes most member states as well as Iceland, Liechtenstein, Norway, and Switzerland. Ireland, the UK, Cyprus, Bulgaria, Romania, and Croatia are not in the Schengen area.

Subsidiarity is the idea that action should be taken at the level of government that is best able to achieve policy goals, as close to the citizens as possible: decentralized where possible, centralized where necessary. For example, local councils (of towns and cities) should handle rubbish removal, while the EU as a whole should make trade policy.

German resentment of French policy resonated in Washington. As the Cold War deepened, the US intensified pressure on France to relax its policy so that West German economic potential could be put at the disposal of the West. Yet the US was not insensitive to French economic and security interests. Instead of imposing a solution, Washington pressed Paris to devise a policy that would allay French concerns about the Ruhr region, without endangering West Germany's full recovery. Given its preference for European integration, the US hoped that France would take a supranational tack.

Originally, the US wanted the UK to lead on 'the German question'. The UK had already taken the initiative on military security in Europe, having pressed the US to negotiate the Washington Treaty (which founded NATO, the North Atlantic Treaty Organization). Yet the UK was reluctant for reasons of history, national **sovereignty**, and economic policy to go beyond anything but intergovernmental cooperation. Absent British leadership and under mounting American pressure, France came up with a novel idea to reconcile Franco-German interests by pooling coal and steel resources under a supranational High Authority.

The Schuman Plan

This idea became the Schuman Plan, drafted by Jean Monnet, a senior French civil servant with extensive international experience and American contacts. Monnet faced intense US pressure to devise a new policy towards West Germany but also believed in European unity and saw the Schuman Plan as a first step in that direction. More immediately, it would protect French interests by ensuring continued access to German resources, although on the basis of cooperation rather than coercion. The new plan bore the name of the French foreign minister, Robert Schuman, who risked his political life promoting it at a time when most French people deeply distrusted Germany.

The West German chancellor, Konrad Adenauer, endorsed the plan, which provided a means of resolving the Ruhr problem and rehabilitating West Germany internationally. Schuman and Adenauer trusted each other. They were both Christian Democrats, came from the Franco-German borderlands, and spoke German together. Aware of the UK's attitude towards integration, Schuman did not inform London of the plan. By contrast, the Americans were in on it from the beginning.

The Schuman Plan was a major reversal of French foreign policy. Having tried to keep Germany down since the war, France now sought to turn the inevitability of West Germany's economic recovery to its own advantage through the establishment of a common market in coal and steel. The Schuman Declaration of 9 May 1950, announcing the plan, was couched in the language of reconciliation rather than *realpolitik*. In fact the initiative cleverly combined national and European interests. It represented a dramatic new departure in European as well as in French and German affairs (see Box 2.3).

BOX 2.3 How it really works

Rhetoric versus reality in the Schuman Plan

Jean Monnet's drafting of the Schuman Plan in 1950 marked a diplomatic breakthrough on the contentious German question. More generally, the plan's proposal for a coal and steel community also advanced the goal of European unity. When outlining the proposal in the Schuman Declaration—a highly publicized initiative—Monnet emphasized the European and idealistic dimension of the proposal. Issued on 9 May (now designated as 'Europe Day'), the Schuman Declaration proclaimed that:

> World peace can only be safeguarded if constructive efforts are made proportionate to the dangers that threaten it . . . . France, by advocating for more

→

> than twenty years the idea of a united Europe, has always regarded it as an
> essential objective to serve the purpose of peace . . . . With this aim in view,
> the French government proposes to take immediate action on one limited
> but decisive point. The French government proposes that Franco-German
> production of coal and steel be placed under a common 'high author-
> ity' within an organization open to the participation of the other European
> nations . . . . [This step] will lay the first concrete foundation for a European
> federation, which is so indispensable for the preservation of peace.

But Monnet was also concerned to defend French national interests. He wanted
to ensure French access to German raw materials and European markets in view
of West Germany's economic resurgence. In a private note to Schuman some
days before the Declaration's release, Monnet explained that France had little
choice but to safeguard its interests by taking a new approach. On 1 May, Monnet
informed Schuman that:

> Germany has already asked to be allowed to increase its output [of steel]
> from 10 to 14 million tons [French output was 9 million tons at the time]. We
> will refuse but the Americans will insist. Finally, we will make reservations and
> give way . . . . There is no need to describe the consequences [of not giving
> way] in any detail. (quoted in Duchêne 1994: 198)

Instead of trying to block West Germany's advance, Monnet advocated a European initiative—the Schuman Plan—that also catered for French interests.

Participation in the plan was supposedly open to all the countries of Europe. In
fact, the list of likely partners was far shorter. The Cold War excluded Central and
Eastern Europe from the plan. In Western Europe, the UK and the Scandinavian
countries had already rejected supranationalism. Ireland was isolationist. Spain
and Portugal, under dictatorial regimes, were international outcasts. Switzerland
was resolutely neutral. That left the Benelux countries—Belgium, the Netherlands,
and Luxembourg—which were economically tied to France and West Germany;
and Italy, which saw integration primarily as a means of combating domestic communism and restoring its international **legitimacy**. Consequently, the European
Coal and Steel Community (ECSC), launched in 1952, included only six countries.
The ECSC soon established a common market in coal and steel products, with
generous provisions for workers' rights.

The European Defence Community

The same six countries ('the Six') signed a treaty to establish a defence community
in 1952. The rationale for both communities was the same: supranational institutions provided the best means of managing West German recovery. In this case, the

outbreak of the Korean War in June 1950, perceived as a possible precursor to a Soviet attack on Western Europe, made West German remilitarization imperative. France at first resisted, and then acquiesced on the condition that German military units were subsumed into the proposed **European Defence Community (EDC)**. Like the Schuman Plan, the plan for the EDC sought to make a virtue (European integration) out of necessity (German remilitarization). Although the EDC was a French initiative, most French people fiercely opposed German remilitarization. The EDC became the most divisive issue in the country. In view of the treaty's unpopularity, the government delayed ratification for two years, and the French parliament rejected the treaty in 1954.

Ironically, West Germany formed an army anyway, under the auspices of the Western European Union (WEU), an intergovernmental organization comprising the UK and the Six. West Germany joined NATO via the WEU in May 1955 and effectively regained full sovereignty. The intergovernmental WEU endured until it was folded into the EU, beginning in 2000. But the EDC was a bridge too far for European integration. At a time when the Six were setting up the ECSC, the launch of a similar initiative in the much more sensitive defence sector was too ambitious. Even if it had come into existence, in all likelihood the EDC would have been unworkable. Resistance to its implementation, especially from the far left and far right, would have been intense. Although ratified by the others, the EDC brought the idea of **supranationalism** into disrepute in France. The end of the affair allowed supporters of supranationalism to jettison the baggage of West German remilitarization and concentrate on first principles: economic integration.

By that time the ECSC was a fact of life, but its political and economic impact was slight. Despite what some observers (and neofunctionalist theorists) predicted, there was little 'spill over' from supranational cooperation in coal and steel to other sectors. Monnet, who was president of the High Authority, left office and returned to Paris in 1955 to lobby for a new initiative: an Atomic Energy Community (Euratom), organized along the same lines as the ECSC. Whereas Monnet saw Euratom as a further step towards European unity, the French government saw it as a means of bolstering France's nuclear programme for civil and military purposes. Not surprisingly, this idea held little appeal for France's partners.

The European Community

The relaunch of European integration after the EDC's collapse was due largely to changes in international trade relations in the mid-1950s. Thanks to liberalization measures in the Organization for European Economic Cooperation (OEEC) and the General Agreement on Tariffs and Trade (GATT), intra-European trade was on the rise. With it, prosperity increased. European governments wanted more trade, but disagreed on the rate and range of liberalization. The

UK favoured further liberalization through the OEEC and the GATT, as did influential elements in the West German government (notably Ludwig Erhard, the economics minister). The French were instinctively protectionist, although some prominent politicians advocated openness. The Dutch, with a small and open economy, wanted full liberalization and were impatient with progress in the OEEC and the GATT, where each member's veto power constrained decision-making.

The Dutch had proposed a common market for all industrial sectors in the early 1950s. The idea was to combine a **customs union** (the phased abolition of tariffs—taxes on imports—among member states and erection of a common external tariff, see Box 2.4) with the free movement of goods, services, and capital, as well as supranational decision-making in areas such as competition policy. The Netherlands revived the proposal in 1955, arguing that the international economic climate was more propitious than ever for the launch of a common market.

Successful negotiations to establish the European Economic Community (EEC or EC) in 1956, so soon after the collapse of the EDC, owed much to the leadership of politicians such as Paul-Henri Spaak in Belgium, Guy Mollet and Christian Pineau in France, and Konrad Adenauer in West Germany. Because of France's political weight in Europe and traditional protectionism, Mollet and Pineau played crucial roles. But their advocacy of the EC came with a price for the other prospective member states. In order to win domestic support, they insisted on a special regime for agriculture in the common market, assistance for French overseas territories (France was then in the painful process of decolonization), and the establishment of Euratom.

The negotiations that resulted in the two Treaties of Rome, one for the EC and the other for Euratom, were arduous. The UK chose not to participate. West Germany succeeded in emasculating Euratom and grudgingly accepted the EC's overseas territories provisions. In the meantime, Adenauer resisted Erhard's efforts to jettison the common market in favour of looser free trade arrangements, arguing that the EC was necessary for geopolitical as well as economic reasons. French negotiators fought what they called the 'Battle of Paris', trying to assuage domestic criticism of the proposed common market while simultaneously driving a hard bargain in the negotiations in Brussels.

The ensuing Treaty of Rome establishing the EC was a compromise. Its provisions ranged from the general to the specific, from the mundane to the arcane. Those on the customs union, calling for the phased abolition of tariffs between member states and erection of a common external tariff, were the most concrete. The treaty did not outline an agricultural policy, but contained a commitment to negotiate one in the near future. Institutionally, the treaty established a potentially powerful commission, an assembly of parliamentarians (of appointed, not elected, members) with limited powers, a council to represent national interests directly in the decision-making process, and a court of justice (see Chapter 3).

BOX 2.4   Compared to what?

Regional and economic integration

Economic integration in Europe has proceeded in a number of steps or stages. A similar trajectory has occurred in other regions of the world, although nowhere else has the level of economic cooperation that matches that found in the EU.

In a *free trade area (FTA)* goods travel freely among member states, but these states retain the authority to establish their own external trade policy (tariffs, quotas, and **non-tariff barriers**) towards third countries (that is, countries that are not part of the FTA). By allowing free access to each other's markets and discriminating favourably towards them, a free trade area stimulates internal trade and can lower consumer costs. But the lack of a common external tariff means complicated rules of origin are required to regulate the import of goods. One example of an FTA outside the EU is the European Free Trade Association (EFTA), which was established under British leadership in 1960 to promote expansion of free trade in non-EC Western European countries. The UK left EFTA to join the EC in 1973, but Iceland, Liechtenstein, Norway, and Switzerland are still members. Another FTA example is that Canada, Mexico, and the US signed the North American Free Trade Agreement (NAFTA) in 1992.

Regional organizations elsewhere have created closer economic ties, which may develop into FTAs. For instance the Association of South-east Asian Nations (ASEAN) was established in 1967 to provide economic as well as social cooperation among non-communist countries in the area. A wider forum for regional economic cooperation is found among Pacific Rim countries within APEC (Asia Pacific Economic Cooperation), which includes Australia, China, Indonesia, Japan, Mexico, the Philippines, and the US.

A *customs union* requires more economic and political cooperation than an FTA. In addition to ensuring free trade among its members, a customs union has a common external tariff and quota system, and a common commercial policy. No member of a customs union may have a separate preferential trading relationship with a third country or group of third countries. A supranational institutional framework is required to ensure that it functions. Customs unions generally create more internal trade and divert more external trade than do free trade areas. The six founding members of the EC agreed to form a customs union, which came into being in 1968, two years ahead of schedule. A customs union also exists in South America. Mercosur (the Southern Cone Common Market) was established in 1991 by Argentina, Brazil, Paraguay, and Uruguay.

A *common market* represents a further step in economic integration by providing for the free movement of services, capital, and labour in addition to the free movement of goods. For various economic and political reasons, the EC Six decided to go beyond a common market by additionally establishing a common competition policy; monetary and fiscal policy coordination; a common agricultural policy (CAP); a common transport policy; and a preferential trade and aid agreement with member states' ex-colonies. Not all of these elements were fully implemented. By the 1980s it was clear that the movement of labour and capital

→

→
was not entirely free, and a host of non-tariff barriers still stymied intra-Community trade in goods and services. The '1992 project' or **single market** programme was designed to achieve a true **internal market** in goods, services, labour, and capital.

   An *economic and monetary union (EMU)* is far more ambitious. It includes a single currency, a single monetary policy, and close coordination (if not unification) of fiscal policy. In the EU, plans to introduce EMU, outlined in the Maastricht Treaty, were successfully implemented in January 1999, with euro notes and coins circulating by January 2002. No other region in modern times has come close to this level of economic cooperation.

The Treaties of Rome were signed on 25 March 1957, and the EC came into being on 1 January 1958. Most Europeans were unaware of either event. Apart from the EDC, European integration had not elicited much of a reaction in terms of public opinion. Yet the ECSC and EC were highly significant developments. The Coal and Steel Community represented a revolution in Franco-German relations and international organization more generally, while the even more consequential EC had the potential to reorder economic and political relations among its member states.

Consolidating the European Community

The big news in Europe in 1958 was not the launch of the EC but the collapse of the French Fourth Republic and the return to power of General Charles de Gaulle. Events in France had a direct bearing on the EC. De Gaulle helped consolidate the new Community by stabilizing France politically (through the construction of the Fifth Republic) and financially (by devaluing the franc). On the basis of renewed domestic confidence, France participated fully in the phased introduction of the customs union, the cornerstone of the common market, so much so that it came into existence in 1968, 18 months ahead of schedule.

   De Gaulle also pushed for completion of the CAP. With a larger farming sector than any other member, France had most to gain from establishing a single agricultural market, based on guaranteed prices and export subsidies funded by the Community. France pressed for a generous CAP and had the political weight to prevail. Nevertheless, the construction of the CAP, in a series of legendary negotiations in the early 1960s, proved onerous. What emerged was a complicated policy based on protectionist principles, in contrast to the liberalizing ethos of Community policies in most other sectors (see Chapter 6). The contrast represented the competing visions of the EC held by its members, potential members, and the wider international community (see Box 2.5).

   Implementation of the customs union and construction of the CAP signalled the Community's initial success, obscuring setbacks in other areas such as the failure to implement a common transport policy. The customs union and the CAP had a major international impact. For instance, as part of its emerging customs union the EC developed a common commercial policy, which authorized the Commission to represent the Community in international trade talks, notably within the GATT. The CAP tended to distort international trade and irritate the EC's partners. It is no coincidence that the first transatlantic trade dispute was over the CAP (the so-called 'Chicken War' of 1962–3, sparked by higher tariffs on US chicken imports).

BOX 2.5   How it really works

British accession and competing visions of Europe

The integration of Europe is sometimes portrayed (not least in the popular press) as an inexorable process following some overarching agreed plan. But in practice integration has proceeded in fits and starts, the result of domestic and international pressures and competing visions of what the EU is or should be. The debates surrounding the UK's first application to join the EC illustrate very different visions of Europe competing for dominance during the Community's early years.

In a remarkable reversal of policy, the UK applied to join the EC in 1961. The UK wanted unfettered access to EC industrial markets, but also wanted to protect trade preferences for Commonwealth countries (former British colonies) and turn the emerging CAP in a more liberal direction. De Gaulle was unsympathetic to the UK's application. Economically, he wanted a protectionist CAP. Politically, he espoused a 'European Europe', allied to the US but independent of it. By contrast, the UK acquiesced in America's so-called Grand Design—espoused by the Kennedy administration in the early 1960s—for a more equitable transatlantic relationship built on the twin **pillars** of the US and a united Europe centred on the EC. Arguably, the Grand Design (at least in French eyes) disguised America's quest for continued hegemony in NATO. The US supported British membership in the EC as part of its Grand Design. By vetoing the UK's application in January 1963, de Gaulle defended the CAP and thwarted American ambitions in Europe. The episode suggests how international pressure, domestic politics, and competing visions of Europe have shaped the evolution of European integration.

The EC's fledgling institutions also began to consolidate during this period. The Commission organized itself in Brussels under the presidency of Walter Hallstein, a former top official in the German foreign ministry and a close colleague of Adenauer's. There were initially nine Commissioners, two each from the large member states and one each from the small member states (this formula would remain unchanged for nearly 50 years). The Commission's staff came initially from national civil services and from the ECSC's High Authority, which existed until it merged into the Commission in 1967. In the

Council of ministers, foreign ministers met most often, indicating the EC's predominantly political nature. The Council formed a permanent secretariat in Brussels to assist its work. Member states also established permanent representations of national civil servants in Brussels, whose heads formed the Committee of Permanent Representatives (Coreper), which soon became one of the Community's most powerful bodies. The Assembly, later known as the European Parliament (EP), tried to assert itself from the beginning, demanding that its members be directly elected rather than appointed from national parliaments. But the EP lacked political support from powerful member states. Working quietly in Luxembourg, the Court of Justice began in the 1960s to generate an impressive corpus of case law. In several landmark decisions, the Court developed the essential rules on which the EC legal order rests, including the supremacy of Community law (see Chapter 3).

Crisis and compromise

De Gaulle's arrival had a negative as well as a positive effect on the fledgling EC. De Gaulle openly opposed supranationalism. He and his supporters (Gaullists) had resisted the ECSC and the EDC. They tolerated the EC, but primarily because of its economic potential for France. In de Gaulle's view, states could and should form alliances and collaborate closely, but only on the basis of intergovernmentalism, not shared sovereignty. De Gaulle thought that the Community could be useful politically as the basis of an association of European states.

A clash over supranationalism arose in 1965 as, under the terms of the Rome Treaty, a number of decisions in key policy areas, including agriculture, were due to become subject to **QMV**. QMV is a key instrument of supranationalism because member states on the losing side agree to abide by the majority's decision. De Gaulle rejected this idea in principle, seeing QMV as an unacceptable abrogation of national sovereignty. Confrontation erupted in June 1965, when de Gaulle triggered the **Empty Chair Crisis** (see Box 2.2) by withdrawing French representation in the Council ostensibly in protest against Commission proposals to strengthen the EC's budgetary powers, but really in an effort to force other member states to agree not to extend the use of QMV. De Gaulle had a compelling practical reason to resist QMV: he wanted to protect the CAP against a voting coalition of liberal member states.

The crisis ended in January 1966 with the **Luxembourg Compromise** (see Box 2.2). The treaty's provisions on QMV would stand, but the Council would not take a vote if a member state insisted that its very important interests were at stake. The Luxembourg Compromise tipped the balance toward intergovernmentalism in the Community's decision-making process, with unanimity becoming the norm. This development had a detrimental effect on decision-making until the Single European Act (SEA) took effect in 1987.

The EC after De Gaulle

By 1969, when de Gaulle resigned, the EC was economically strong but politically weak. The Commission and Parliament were relatively powerless, and unanimity hobbled effective decision-making in the Council. De Gaulle had twice rebuffed the UK's application for EC membership, in 1963 and in 1967, after London decided by the early 1960s that, for economic reasons, it was better off inside the common market. Following de Gaulle's departure, British membership became inevitable, although accession negotiations were nonetheless difficult. Eventually, Ireland and Denmark joined the EC alongside the UK, in 1973.

The EC's first enlargement was a milestone in the organization's history. Unfortunately, it coincided with international financial turmoil and a severe economic downturn that slowed momentum for further integration. Moreover, the UK's early membership was troublesome. A new Labour government insisted on renegotiating the country's accession terms, much to the annoyance of France and West Germany. Based on the outcome of the renegotiation, a majority voted in favour of continued EC membership in the UK's first nation-wide referendum, in 1975. At the end of the decade a new Conservative government, under Margaret Thatcher, demanded a huge budget rebate. The UK had a point, but Thatcher's strident manner when pushing her case incensed other member states. The UK budgetary question dragged on until 1984, overshadowing a turnaround in the Community's fortunes after a decade of poor economic performance.

A difficult decade

Because of the UK's early difficulties in the EC and prevailing stagflation (weak economic growth combined with high inflation and unemployment) in Europe, the 1970s is generally seen as a dismal decade in the history of integration. Yet a number of important institutional and policy developments occurred at that time. On the policy side, the launch in 1979 of the European Monetary System (EMS), the precursor to the single currency, was especially significant. Concerned about America's seeming abdication of international financial leadership, and eager to curb inflation and exchange rate fluctuations in the EC, French and German leaders devised the EMS, with the Exchange Rate Mechanism (ERM) designed to regulate currency fluctuations at its core. The sovereignty-conscious UK declined to participate. By the mid-1980s, the inflation and exchange rates of ERM members began to converge, thus helping to keep their economies stable. The Lomé agreement of 1975, providing preferential trade and development assistance to scores of African, Caribbean, and Pacific countries, was another important achievement for the beleaguered Community, as was the launch of European Political Cooperation (EPC), a mechanism to coordinate member states' foreign policies (see Chapter 10). In terms of deeper integration, the expansion of EC environmental policy in the 1970s was even more important.

Institutionally, there was a gradual improvement in the Commission's fortunes, and the first direct elections to the EP took place in 1979, raising the institution's profile and enhancing the EC's formal legitimacy. The inauguration of the European Council (regular meetings of the heads of state and government) in 1975 strengthened intergovernmental cooperation. The European Council soon became the EC's most important agenda-setting body (see Chapter 3), while direct elections laid the basis for the EP's institutional ascension in the 1980s and 1990s. The Court of Justice continued in the 1970s to build an impressive body of case law that maintained the momentum for deeper integration.

By the early 1980s, the EC had weathered the storm of recession and the challenge of British accession. The end of dictatorial regimes in Greece, Portugal, and Spain in the mid-1970s presaged a second round of enlargement (Greece joined in 1981, Portugal and Spain in 1986). By that time the EC was more than a customs union but still less than a single market. A plethora of non-tariff barriers (such as divergent technical standards) hobbled intra-Community trade in goods and services, and the movement of people and capital was far from free. Intensive foreign competition, especially from the US and Japan, began to focus the attention of political and business leaders on the EC's ability to boost member states' economic growth and international competitiveness. This focus became the genesis of the single market programme, which spearheaded the EC's response to **globalization** and ushered in the EU.

The Emerging European Union

The single market programme for the free movement of goods, services, capital, and people emerged as a result of collaboration between big business, the Commission, the Parliament, and national leaders in the early 1980s. The European Council endorsed the idea on several occasions. But the initiative only took off when the Commission, under the new presidency of Jacques Delors, unveiled a legislative roadmap (a White Paper on the 'completion' of the internal market) in 1985. To ensure the programme's success, the European Council decided to convene an intergovernmental conference (IGC) to make the necessary treaty changes. Chief among them was a commitment to use QMV for most of the White Paper's proposals, thereby ending the legislative gridlock that had hamstrung earlier efforts at market liberalization.

As well as covering the single market programme, the SEA of 1986 brought environmental policy into the treaty, strengthened Community policy in research and technological development, and included a section on foreign policy cooperation. It also committed the EC to higher expenditure on regional development (cohesion policy), partly as a side payment to the poorer member states, including new entrants Portugal, Spain, and Greece, which were unlikely to benefit as much from market integration as were their richer counterparts. Institutionally, the SEA's most important provisions enhanced the EP's legislative role as a means of improving the EC's democratic accountability.

The single market programme, with a target date of 1992, was a success. Business responded enthusiastically to the prospect of a fully integrated European marketplace. 1992 unleashed a wave of europhoria. The EC was more popular than at any time before or since. Eager to remove barriers to the free movement of people even before implementation of the single market programme, France and West Germany agreed in 1984 to press ahead with the abolition of border checks. This pledge led to the **Schengen Agreement** (see Box 2.2) for the free movement of people, which gradually added other member states and formally became part of the EU under the terms of the 1997 Amsterdam Treaty.

Economic and monetary union

The popularity of the single market programme emboldened Delors to advocate EMU arguing, as did many businesses, that a single market would work better with a single currency. He had the strong support of German Chancellor Helmut Kohl, an avowed 'euro-federalist'. The Commission publicly justified EMU on economic grounds, but Delors and Kohl saw it primarily as a political undertaking. French President François Mitterrand also supported EMU, for both political and economic reasons. Prime Minister Thatcher opposed EMU vehemently, seeing it as economically unnecessary and politically unwise.

The European Council authorized Delors to set up a committee, composed mostly of Central Bank governors, to explore the road to EMU. The Delors Report of 1989 proposed a three-stage programme, including strict convergence criteria for potential participants and the establishment of a European Central Bank (ECB) with responsibility primarily for price stability. The report largely reflected German preferences for EMU. That was understandable, given West Germany's economic weight and obsession with inflation. Even so, opinion in Germany remained sceptical about EMU, with the politically influential West German central bank (Bundesbank) opposed to it.

Planning for EMU was well on track by the time the Berlin Wall came down in November 1989. By raising again the spectre of the German question, the end of the Cold War increased the momentum for EMU. Fearful of the prospect, however remote, that a reunified Germany would be rootless in the post-Cold War world, other leaders were determined to bind Germany fully into the new Europe, largely through EMU. Kohl was more than happy to oblige and cleverly exploited the concerns of Germany's neighbours to overcome domestic misgivings about EMU.

Maastricht and beyond

EC leaders convened two IGCs in 1990, one on EMU and the other on political union, meaning institutional and non-EMU policy reforms. Both conferences converged in the Maastricht Treaty of 1992, which established the EU with its three-pillar structure (see Box 1.2). The first pillar comprised the EC, including EMU; the second comprised the Common Foreign and Security Policy (CFSP), a direct response to the external challenges of the post-Cold War period; the third covered cooperation on justice and home affairs, notably immigration, asylum, and criminal matters. This awkward structure reflected several members' unwillingness to subject internal security and foreign policy to supranational decision-making. Thus the Commission and the EP were merely associated with Pillar 2 and 3 activities. Within Pillar 1, by contrast, the Maastricht Treaty extended the EP's legislative power by introducing the far-reaching co-decision procedure, which made the Parliament a legally and politically equal co-legislator with the Council of ministers (see Chapter 3).

The further extension of the EP's legislative authority, and the introduction of the principle of **subsidiarity** (see Box 2.2), demonstrated EU leaders' concerns about the organization's legitimacy. Those concerns were fully vindicated in tough ratification battles in several countries, including the UK, France, and Germany, but especially in Denmark where a narrow majority rejected the treaty in a referendum in June 1992. Voters approved the treaty, with special concessions for Denmark, in a second referendum, in May 1993, allowing the EU to come into being six months later.

At issue in Denmark and elsewhere was the so-called democratic deficit: the EU's perceived remoteness and lack of accountability (see Chapter 7). These concerns would remain a major challenge for the EU well into the twenty-first century. The resignation of the Commission under the presidency of Jacques Santer in March 1999, amid allegations of fraud and mismanagement, increased popular scepticism, although it also demonstrated the Commission's accountability to the EP (the Commission resigned before being sacked by the Parliament). Yet many Europeans were unenthusiastic about the EP: few understood exactly its role, and the turnout in EP elections was consistently low by the standards of national elections. For its part, the Commission undertook far-reaching internal reform, while EU leaders attempted to improve policy-making and delivery. Nevertheless, as illustrated by the negative results of several EU-related referenda since the Maastricht Treaty, and the strong support for anti-EU parties in the 2014 EP election, public opinion grew increasingly sceptical of the EU.

Hand-in-hand with public unease, the post-Maastricht period saw substantial EU policy development. The launch of the final stage of EMU in January 1999, in keeping with the Maastricht timetable, was one of the EU's most striking achievements. Euro notes and coins came into circulation in January 2002. The strengthening of the CFSP and the initiation of a European Security and Defence Policy (ESDP)— largely in response to the Balkan wars of the 1990s and uncertainty about US involvement in future European conflicts—was another important policy development. Reform of CFSP was an outcome of the 1997 Amsterdam Treaty, which nevertheless ducked increasingly pressing questions of institutional adjustment necessitated by impending enlargement.

Enlargement, constitution building, and crisis

Following the end of the Cold War, three militarily neutral countries (Austria, Finland, and Sweden) joined the EU in 1995. The newly independent states of Central and Eastern Europe soon applied as well, as did Cyprus and Malta. For the Central and Eastern European countries, the road to membership would be long and difficult, involving major political, economic, and administrative reforms. The slow pace of enlargement disappointed the applicant countries and their supporters in the US, who criticized the EU for being too cautious. The Union countered that enlargement, an inherently complicated process, was even more complex than (say) the expansion of NATO, in view of the applicants' history, political culture, and economic situations. Yet the EU's approach reflected a widespread lack of enthusiasm for enlargement among politicians and the public in existing member states. Negotiations with the Central and Eastern European applicants eventually began in 1998 (with the five front-runners) and in 2000 (with the five others). Cyprus also began accession negotiations in 1998 and Malta in 2000.

Eight of the Central and Eastern European counties joined in 2004, together with Cyprus and Malta; the other two, Bulgaria and Romania, joined in 2007. The EU reluctantly acknowledged Turkey as a candidate in 1999 and, no less reluctantly, opened formal accession negotiations with it in 2005. However, Turkey's unpopularity throughout the EU, specific issues such as the unresolved Cypriot question, and the increasingly authoritarian turn of President Recep Tayyip Erdoğan some years later, effectively derailed the country's membership prospects. Meanwhile, the EU acknowledged the 'European perspective' of the Western Balkans, suggesting that every country in the region stood a reasonable chance of eventually becoming a member (Croatia was first to join, in 2013).

As Chapter 8 explains, enlargement greatly altered the EU. The accession of so many relatively poor countries, with comparatively large agricultural sectors, was bound to have a major effect on the CAP and cohesion policy. The Union reformed both policies as part of its Agenda 2000 initiative, in anticipation of enlargement, but the results were patently inadequate. Further reform inevitably fuelled bitter budgetary disputes, such as the one preceding implementation of the 2014–20 financial framework.

The EU's institutions also required reform because of enlargement. Member states avoided this contentious question in the Amsterdam Treaty, agreeing instead to undertake an institutional overhaul in another IGC in 2000. That conference resulted in the Nice Treaty of 2001, which changed the modalities of QMV in anticipation of enlargement, but in a way that complicated rather than clarified legislative decision-making. In other institutional areas the outcomes of the 2000 IGC were equally disappointing. The messy compromises that were struck illustrated the growing difficulty of reaching agreement among member states on institutional issues, especially those that tended to drive a wedge between France and Germany, or between the small and large countries.

Appreciating the inadequacies of the Nice Treaty, the European Council decided in December 2001 to hold a convention of national and EU-level politicians to draft a new treaty that would supersede and supposedly simplify the existing treaties. That was the genesis of the Convention on the Future of Europe of 2002–3 and ensuing IGC, which resulted in the Constitutional Treaty of 2004. Among other things, the Constitutional Treaty altered the system of QMV, giving more power to the big member states; incorporated the previously negotiated Charter of Fundamental Rights into the EU's legal system; called for a standing president of the European Council; and provided for an EU foreign minister. Although it was ratified by most member states, voters in referenda held in the Netherlands and France, two of the EU's founding member states, rejected the Constitutional Treaty in spring 2005, for a variety of reasons mostly unrelated to the treaty itself, ranging from domestic political considerations to concerns about the consequences of globalization and fear of further enlargement. The results of the Dutch and French referenda were a severe blow to the image and prestige of the EU. But they did not derail the process of European integration, to which most European politicians (if not all their publics) remained committed, as was revealed in 2007 when EU leaders signed the **Lisbon Treaty**, which incorporated most of the changes in the unratified Constitutional Treaty. While apparently less far-reaching than the Constitutional Treaty, in fact the Lisbon Treaty, which came into effect in 2009, was another major milestone in the history of European integration.

Implementation of the Lisbon Treaty coincided with the onset of the euro crisis, which had a devastating impact on the EU's credibility, on relations among member states, and on public support for further integration. The weakness of EMU's fiscal foundations became abundantly clear as banking and/or sovereign debt crises engulfed the weaker **Eurozone** members. Germany, at the centre, enjoyed a boom in exports to the increasingly less competitive peripheral countries. As the banking and debt crises threatened the survival of the euro and exacerbated an economic recession, Germany's insistence on EU-wide austerity through radical deficit reduction alienated opinion in the worst-affected countries. Fissures in the EU widened between Germany and the rest; between the stronger and weaker Eurozone members; and between Eurozone and non-Eurozone countries. Although significant reforms of the governance of the Eurozone were introduced during the heat of the crisis, considerable work remains to be done. Debates persist about whether the Eurozone requires its own 'finance minister', whether a European monetary fund should be established and what its role would be, and whether a Eurozone budget (a common pot of money that could be used to assist Eurozone members that get into financial difficulty) ought to be created. Such debates are set to dominate the highest levels of EU decision-making throughout and beyond 2018.

The fallout from the chronic crisis fuelled pervasive euroscepticism, and boosted support for extremist parties in national elections as well as the 2014 EP election.

A huge influx of unregistered migrants into the EU, propelled by instability in North Africa and the Middle East, precipitated a political crisis in 2015-16. At issue were the porousness of the Schengen area's external borders; the unwillingness of Central and Eastern European governments to accept a share of the migrants, who were concentrated in Germany; and a controversial agreement between the EU and Turkey in March 2016 to staunch migration flows across the eastern Mediterranean. The migration crisis was grist to the mill of far-right, anti-EU parties, and further eroded confidence in the EU.

Adding to the pervasive sense of crisis was another festering problem: the UK's relationship with the EU. A combination of domestic political developments and party politics in the UK led David Cameron—Conservative prime minister from 2010 to 2016—to hold another referendum, more than 40 years after the 1975 referendum, on whether the UK should remain a member of the EU. The result of the June 2016 referendum stunned most informed observers: 'leave' won by 51.9 per cent to 48.9 per cent for 'remain'. Difficult negotiations on the terms of 'Brexit' duly began between the UK and the EU, in June 2017. According to the timetable for the negotiations, specified in the EU treaty, the UK would cease to be a member by the end of March 2019 (for a full discussion of Brexit, see Chapter 10). Brexit represented a profound shock to the EU system, which is predicated on the notion not only of 'ever-closer union', as called for in the pre-amble of the original EC Treaty, but also of ever-expanding union. The with-drawal of a big, influential member state raised a host of issues for the future EU, ranging from the budget to particular policies, to the informal weighting of national influence. Central and Eastern European countries regretted the depar-ture of a big member state traditionally sensitive to their interests, especially at a time of rising German power.

At the same time, eagerness to overcome the various crises, and to counter the anti-EU populism of far-right political parties, infused EU leaders with a renewed commitment to European integration. Internal and external circum-stances—economic growth within the EU; an uncertain geopolitical environ-ment outside it—set the scene for, among other things, Eurozone reform and closer cooperation on security and defence. The experience of treaty change in the 2000s meant that there was little enthusiasm for another 'grand bargain' among EU member states, but there was plenty of scope nonetheless for the consolidation and intensification of European integration. The partnership of Angela Merkel and Emmanuel Macron may prove significant in shepherding the EU through its current period of crisis, although it remains uncertain to what extent the contemporary EU can be driven by Franco-German bargains. Following his election, Macron brought forward ambitious proposals for reform-ing the EU but some of those proposals, particularly regarding the Eurozone, may struggle to win the approval of a Merkel-led government, not to mention other EU governments, in 2018 and beyond.

Conclusion

The history of the EU presents a fascinating puzzle: why did national governments, traditionally jealous of their independence, agree to pool sovereignty in a supranational organization that increasingly acquired federal attributes? The answer may be as simple as it is paradoxical: because it was in their national interests to do so. Political parties and interest groups did not always agree on what constituted the national interest, and governments themselves were sometimes divided. But at critical junctures in the post-war period, for various strategic and/or economic reasons, national leaders opted for closer integration.

This chapter has approached the history of European integration by focusing on national responses to major domestic and international challenges since the end of World War II, responses that gave rise to the EC and later the EU. France and Germany played key roles. The EC was a bargain struck (primarily) between them for mutual economic gain and to strengthen national security. Franco-German bargaining remained crucial for the intensification of European integration, notably with the launch of the single market programme and of EMU.

Yet the dynamics of Franco-German relations and leadership in the EU have changed, not least because of recent rounds of enlargement, which shifted the geopolitical balance of the EU eastward, in favour of Germany. As various negotiations on treaty reform have shown, France and Germany are often far apart on institutional issues, and increasingly differ on a range of core policy issues as well. Whereas a united Germany has grown more assertive in the EU, France has seemed unsure of its place in the world. Far from joining France and Germany in a tripartite leadership structure, or replacing France as Germany's favoured interlocutor in EU affairs, the UK never wholeheartedly embraced European integration and became distinctly semi-detached even before it decided to leave in its 2016 referendum.

Ideology—the quest for a united Europe—has not been a major motive for European integration. Some national and supranational leaders were (and remain) strongly committed to a federal EU, but managed to move Europe in that direction only when ideological ambition coincided with national political and economic preferences. The language of European integration, redolent of peace and reconciliation, provided convenient camouflage for the pursuit of national interests based on rational calculations of costs and benefits. Apart from spectacular episodes such as the Empty Chair Crisis, however, member states' perceptions of their national interests and of a common European interest generally converged. In the post-Maastricht period, by contrast, these perceptions have increasingly diverged, as was evident during the euro and migration crises.

Nevertheless, the history of European integration shows that countries can overcome institutional and policy differences for the sake of common economic and political interests. Over time, the context of European integration has greatly changed, but not necessarily its substance. With global challenges more pressing than ever before, arguably it is in the interest of all member states to manage the single market, make a success of monetary union, and increase the EU's effectiveness as an international actor. Member states may have little choice but to perpetuate European integration, while striving to strengthen the EU's democratic **legitimacy** and improve the EU's operation and output. Notwithstanding serious crises and the UK's departure, the EU is likely to survive, perhaps even thrive.

(?) DISCUSSION QUESTIONS

1. Are France and Germany bound to lead in Europe?
2. Why is the UK an outlier?
3. How significant have federalist aspirations been in the history of European integration?
4. Is the US a 'federator' of Europe?
5. What economic factors impelled European integration during various stages of its history?

(📖) FURTHER READING

Dinan (2014a) provides a thorough history of the EU, while Dinan (2014b) examines key developments in EU history and includes a chapter on the historiography of European integration. Van Middelaar (2013) offers a lively account of the trials and tribulations of European integration over six decades. For a neofunctionalist analysis of the EC's development, see Haas (1958). Milward (1984, 2000) is the most influential historian of European integration. Moravcsik (1998) blends political science and historical analysis to produce liberal intergovernmentalism and explain major developments in the history of the EU. Duchêne (1994) is excellent on Jean Monnet, and Gillingham (1991) provides an authoritative account of the origins of the ECSC. Gillingham (2003) describes the history of European integration as a struggle between economic liberalism and centralization, personified in the 1980s by Delors and Thatcher. Vanke (2010) provides a counterpoint to Milward and Moravcsik by emphasizing the importance of ideas and emotions—'Europeanism'—and not just economic interests in the history of European integration. Le Gloannec (2018) considers the EU as a geopolitical project.

Dinan, D. (2014a), *Europe Recast: A History of European Union*, 2nd edn (Basingstoke: Palgrave).

Dinan, D. (ed.) (2014b), *Origins and Evolution of the European Union*, 2nd edn (Oxford and New York: Oxford University Press).

Duchêne, F. (1994), *Jean Monnet: The First Statesman of Interdependence* (New York: Norton).

Gillingham, J. (1991), *Coal, Steel and the Rebirth of Europe, 1945–1955* (Cambridge and New York: Cambridge University Press).

Gillingham, J. (2003), *European Integration, 1950–2003* (Cambridge and New York: Cambridge University Press).

Haas, E. (1958), *The Uniting of Europe: Political, Social and Economic Forces* (Stanford, CA: Stanford University Press).

Le Gloannec, A. M. (2018), *Continent by Default: the European Union and the Demise of Regional Order* (Ithaca, NY: Cornell University Press).

Milward, A. (1984), *The Reconstruction of Western Europe, 1945–51* (Berkeley, CA: University of California Press).

Milward, A. (2000), *The European Rescue of the Nation-State*, 2nd edn (London: Routledge).

Moravcsik, A. (1998), *The Choice for Europe: Social Purpose and State Power from Messina to Maastricht* (Ithaca, NY, and London: Cornell University Press and UCL Press).

Vanke, J. (2010), *Europeanism and European Union: Interests, Emotions, and Systemic Integration in the Early European Economic Community* (Palo Alto, CA: Academica Press).

Van Middelaar, L. (2014), *The Passage to Europe: How a Continent Became a Union* (New Haven, CT: Yale University Press).

WEB LINKS

- The EU's official portal site has its own useful history page: https://europa.eu/european-union/about-eu/history_en

- The Florence-based European University Institute (EUI)'s European Integration History Index provides internet resources (in all languages) on post-war European history, with a particular emphasis on the EU: http://vlib.iue.it/hist-eur-integration/Index.html

 Visit the Ancillary Resource Centre that accompanies this book for additional material: www.oup.com/uk/kenealy5e/

PART II

MAJOR ACTORS

CHAPTER 3

The EU's Institutions

Richard Corbett, John Peterson, and Daniel Kenealy

Summary

No student of the EU can understand their subject without careful study of its key institutions and how they work. EU institutions are not just dry (and complex) organizations; they are dynamic organisms exercising a unique mix of legislative, executive, and judicial power. We begin by introducing the EU's five most important institutions. We outline their structures and formal powers—that is, what the treaties say they can do—but we also focus on how they 'squeeze' influence out of their limited treaty prerogatives. We then explore why these institutions matter in determining EU politics and policy more generally.

Institutions in Treaties and in Practice

What makes the EU unique, perhaps above all, is its institutions. This chapter explores the five that exercise the most power and influence: the European Commission, the Council of ministers, the European Council, the European Parliament (EP), and the European Court of Justice (ECJ). We draw analogies to their counterparts at the national level, but also show how they are distinct and unique. It is important to understand not just the formal powers conferred on the EU's institutions, but also how informal powers have accrued to them over time, and how incremental power shifts occur between rounds of treaty reform. The informal institutional politics of European integration are often lively and can have important consequences (see Chapter 6).

The European Commission

One of the EU's most powerful and controversial institutions is the **European Commission**. The EU's founders were faced with a challenge. If the member states wanted to pursue common policies in certain fields, should they hand over responsibilities to a common institution, and leave it to get on with it, which would pose major questions of democratic accountability? Or should policies be settled by agreement between national governments, thus risking endless intergovernmental negotiations and lowest common denominator agreements?

In the end they opted for a compromise: a common institution—the European Commission—was charged with drafting policy proposals (and implementing policies once agreed). But a separate institution—the Council—consisting of ministers representing national governments, would take (most) decisions on the basis of those proposals. This interplay of an institution charged with representing the common interest and those composed of representatives of national governments (Council) or citizens (Parliament) is the essence of what became known as the Community method (see Chapter 4).

Tasks and powers

The treaties allocated to the Commission other important tasks besides the right to propose policies. The Commission is charged with representing the general interest of the Union, and in this capacity, does a variety of jobs:

- it acts as guardian of the treaties (to defend both their letter and spirit), verifying the correct application of EU legislation;
- it can be given powers to implement EU legislation and manage its programmes;

- it is the competition authority for the **single market**, with powers to vet and veto mergers, even of companies located outside the EU;

- on the basis of Council mandates, it negotiates international trade and cooperation agreements.

Above all, nothing (or very little) can become EU legislation unless the Commission proposes it (although the Council and the Parliament can request it to draft proposals). All of these prerogatives make the Commission perhaps the most powerful international administration in existence (see Kassim *et al.* 2013). Many of its decisions are contentious. Perhaps controversy is unavoidable for an institution that is designed to act independently of the EU's member states and in the general, supranational interest of the Union as a whole.

The Commission's powers are not far short of those enjoyed, in the economic field, by national governments. But its capacity to act autonomously is more limited than that of a national government. To illustrate, it lacks powers that national governments have over armed forces, police, the nomination of judges, or foreign policy. The treaties limit both the Commission's powers and autonomy.

How the Commission is organized

'The Commission' rather confusingly refers to two elements of the same body: the political College of Commissioners (or executive Commission) and the administrative Commission (its permanent 'services'). The College is the powerhouse of the Commission. Each of the commissioners—one from each member state—is, like a minister in a national government, nominated by the prime minister or president of their country. Commissioners are not directly elected, but they are politicians rather than civil servants (most have held high office in national politics before becoming commissioners) and hold office only with the approval of the EP. The permanent civil servants (in French, the *fonctionaires*), who are recruited normally through competitive examination, work under the College's authority. Here we find a unique feature of the EU: its institutions recruit their own civil servants and do not rely (much) on national appointees.

The Commission president is elected by the EP on a proposal of the European Council, which itself is obliged to take account of EP election results in making that nomination (Corbett 2014; Dinan 2015). In other words, heads of government have to choose a candidate capable of commanding a parliamentary majority much in the same way that a head of state in a national context has to when nominating a prime minister. Several European political parties interpreted this requirement to mean that the European Council should choose as Commission president the nominee of the EP party with the most seats. Five parties duly proposed their own candidate ahead of the 2014 European elections. After the elections, the European Council indeed nominated the candidate of the 'winning' party (the centre-right European People's Party), the former Luxembourg prime minister, Jean-Claude

Juncker, although not without controversy as David Cameron, the (then) UK prime minister, strongly opposed this interpretation of the treaty provisions. Cameron was joined only by Hungary's Victor Orban in voting against Juncker in the first case ever of a Commission president being nominated via a qualified majority vote in the European Council (see Peterson 2017b).

Once elected by the EP, the president must then agree with each head of government on the nominee from each country for the remaining members of the College of Commissioners. It is then up to the president to distribute policy responsibilities—known as 'portfolios'—to individual commissioners (for transport, agriculture, and so on). The one exception is the EU High Representative for foreign affairs and security policy, who is also a vice president of the Commission.

The prospective Commission must then present itself to the Parliament for a vote of confidence. This vote is on the college as a whole—again, much like a vote of confidence in a government in a national context. However, prior to this vote, the EP holds public hearings for each commissioner before the parliamentary committee corresponding to their portfolio (which does not happen to ministers in most European countries). The Commission's fixed, five-year term is linked to that of the EP, which is elected every five years.

The distribution of portfolios can be controversial. Portfolios dealing with international trade, the internal market, competition policy, agriculture, regional development funds, and, in recent times, environment and energy are particularly sought after. In reality, how much an individual commissioner can shape policy is limited by the principle of collegiality: the entire College agrees all policy proposals. Once it takes a decision, if necessary by majority vote (but nearly always by consensus), it becomes the policy of all of the Commission. Moreover, key legislative and policy decisions have to be approved by other EU institutions. The Commission illustrates one of the ironies of the EU: its institutions are more powerful than they are autonomous.

The growing size of the Commission with successive enlargements has risked turning it from a compact executive into a miniature assembly. The 2009 Lisbon Treaty had provisions for a smaller commission but also allowed member states to vary its size, leading to a decision to stick with one commissioner per country. The move shows that there remains more concern for the Commission's legitimacy—with, for instance, one member of the College who speaks each country's language(s) and can appear in the national media—than with its efficiency.

Commissioners each have their own private office—or (in French) *cabinet*—of around seven personal advisers, although the president's *cabinet* is always larger. Cabinet officials are chosen by individual commissioners and may be drawn from inside or outside the Commission. They keep the commissioner informed about their own policy area(s) as well as wider developments in the Commission and Europe more generally. Most cabinets are composed largely of members of staff of the same nationality as the commissioner, but the head or deputy head of each must hail from a member state different from that of the commissioner. Member states are often accused of seeking to appoint their own national officials to Commission cabinets to ensure that their interests are not overlooked. Ever since new rules were imposed by President Romano Prodi (1999–2004), cabinets became more 'European'—with nearly all having at least three nationalities—and less male-dominated, with around 40 per cent of appointees being women (see Peterson 2017a: 129).

Controversy surrounding portfolio assignments and cabinet appointments shows that the defence of national interests in the Commission can never be entirely removed. Commissioners take an oath of independence when they are appointed, but never abandon their national identities. Indeed, many consider it to be an advantage that they bring knowledge of their respective countries to the Commission, even if they are not there to represent them—that job belongs to ministers in the Council.

The independence of commissioners can sometimes be a matter of contention. A commissioner who simply parrots the position of his or her national government would soon lose credibility within the Commission. However, one that too obviously ignores major national interests may be liable for criticism at home. Famously, the UK prime minister, Margaret Thatcher, despaired at the alleged failure of 'her' commissioner—Lord Cockfield—to follow the line of the Thatcher government. Thus, commissioners face a tough balancing act: they must be sensitive to the interests of the member state that (in Brussels speak) 'they know best', but must not undermine the independence of the Commission.

Most commissioners responsible for one or more Directorates General (DGs)—or services—that relate to their portfolio. These DGs, the equivalent of national ministries, cover the EU's main policy areas such as competition, the environment, or agriculture. A director general, who reports directly to the relevant commissioner, heads each. There are about 30 or so services that together make up the administration of the Commission.

The Commission is far smaller than is often portrayed in the popular press, where it is frequently characterized as an enormous body intent on taking over Europe. In fact, it has roughly as many officials (in policy-making posts) as work for a medium-sized national government department, such as the French Ministry of Culture, or a medium-sized city council. Of the Commission's approximately 33,000 officials, about one-tenth are involved simply in translating or interpreting into the 24 official languages of the EU.

In day-to-day work, the dividing line between administrative civil servants and commissioners is not always self-evident. While the College is ultimately responsible for any decisions that emanate from the institution, in practice many matters are handled much further down in the administration. Furthermore, the Commission's agenda is to a large extent set for it by the EU's Treaties or other commitments (see Box 3.1). In turn, some commissioners are more interventionist than others in seeking to influence the day-to-day functioning of 'their' DG, in much the same way as occurs in relations between ministers and civil servants in a national context.

BOX 3.1   How it really works: Who initiates policy?

The formal right to initiate proposals for policy or legislation is one of the Commission's most precious and fundamental powers. But the origins of its initiatives are diverse. In practice, most initiatives emanating from the Commission are a response to ideas, suggestions, or pressures from other sources. Some implement priorities and action plans approved by the European Council. Some arise from international obligations or new trade agreements. Some are in response to proposals from the EP. A growing proportion are about updating or amending previous EU legislation, rather than legislating in new fields. A particular effort in recent years has been to simplify, consolidate, or repeal old legislation, known as the 'REFIT' programme. In its 2017 work programme, the Commission announced 21 'key initiatives' (down, it claimed, from 23 per year in 2015 and 2016, and an average of 130 per year from 2009 to 2014), although these initiatives would require over 30 pieces of legislation. There would also be 18 proposals under REFIT and 16 proposals to repeal existing legislation.

The Lisbon Treaty added a new, direct source of proposals: one million EU citizens can sign a **European Citizens' Initiative** to invite the Commission to bring forward a legislative proposal. The Commission is not legally obliged to act, and at time of writing only four such initiatives (out of over 30 launched) have reached the one million threshold. But, for example, this route has led to legislative proposals concerning drinking water quality.

The major challenge for the Commission is stretching its limited resources to cover the wide range of tasks that member states have conferred upon it. At times, the Commission can be adept at making the most of the powers given to it. For example, the Commission was among the first institutions to conduct detailed research on climate change, which highlighted the necessity of new initiatives such as an emissions trading scheme and a stronger role for the EU. Thus, the Commission is not simply the servant of the member states but can sometimes 'squeeze' more prerogatives despite its limited competence.

The Council (of ministers)

The **Council** was created as the EU's primary decision-making body. The treaties state that it shall consist of 'a representative of each member state at ministerial level, who may commit the government of the member state in question and cast its

vote' and that it 'shall, jointly with the EP, exercise legislative and budgetary functions' and 'carry out policymaking and co-ordinating functions' (Article 16, Treaty
on European Union).

It is thus both a legislative chamber of states (as half of the Union's bicameral
legislative authority, together with the EP) and at the same time the body in which
the governments of the member states come together. They meet to resolve issues
of Union or foreign policy and coordinate domestic policies, such as macroeco-
nomic policies, that are primarily a national responsibility. It is in the Council that
national interests, as seen by the government of the day in each member state, are
represented and articulated.

The Council is a complex system. The treaties speak of only one Council, but
it meets in different configurations depending on what policy area is being discussed. For example, when agriculture is discussed, agriculture ministers meet;
when the subject is the environment, it is environment ministers, and so on. There
are altogether ten different configurations of the Council, with the General Affairs
Council (now largely comprising national Europe Ministers to relieve the burden
on foreign ministers, so the latter can concentrate on foreign policy) holding a
coordinating brief. The General Affairs Council is responsible for the dossiers that
affect more than one of the Union's policies, such as enlargement or the EU's budget
and for preparing meetings of the European Council.

The Council is aided by a secretariat of around 2,800 officials. It plays an important role in brokering deals and crafting compromises between member states.
Even with the help of the secretariat, the burden on EU ministers has increased
enormously. The agricultural, foreign, and economic ministers meet at least once a
month, others from one to six times a year.

Given their core function—representing member states—it is easy to conclude that the Council and its preparatory bodies are purely intergovernmental. But, as constructivists would note (see Lewis 2005), regular ministerial
meetings, informal contacts, and routine bargaining have provided the grounds
for continual and close cooperation among executives from different member
states. As a result, the Council has constructed a sort of collective identity that is
more than an amalgamation of national views. That identity has helped push the
Union forward.

Majority voting can be used in the Council in most areas of EU business. In
fact, votes rarely take place (see Box 3.2), although more often now than before
the 2004–13 enlargements. Council deliberations on legislation now take place in
public: they are web-streamed or televised (there is no physical public gallery).
Prior to the Lisbon Treaty, the Council legislated behind closed doors, which made
negotiations easier but left the Council vulnerable to the charge that it was the
only legislative body in the democratic world that enacted legislation without
the public being able to see how members voted. The Council still meets behind
closed doors on some non-legislative matters such as foreign policy and security
discussions.

BOX 3.2   How it really works: Reaching decisions in the Council

Qualified majority voting (QMV) (see Box 3.3 for its calculation) now applies to most areas of Council decision-making, and any national representative on the Council can call for a vote on any measure to which it applies. In practice, only a minority of decisions subject to QMV are actually agreed that way (see Wallace and Reh 2015: 83). Pushing for a formal vote too early or often creates resentment that disrupts the mood and effectiveness of the Council. Thus, whatever the formal rules say, decision-making in the Council—even accommodating 28 states— usually proceeds on the understanding that consensus will be sought, but equally that obstructionism or unreasonable opposition could be countered by a vote.

How is consensus achieved between 27/8 (now very disparate) states? Imagine a contentious item on the Council's agenda (say, dealing with work and safety regulations). Perhaps a majority of states support the initiative but some are opposed or ambivalent. Before proceeding to a vote, several attempts will be made to achieve some sort of consensus. Bargaining is most intense at the level of the Committee of Permanent Representatives, known by its French acronym **Coreper** (the committee in which member state ambassadors to the EU meet). Phone calls or informal chats between national representatives prepare the ground for subsequent meetings where agreements can be struck. Informal agreements might also be reached at the meals that are very much a part of both Coreper and Council meetings. Ostensibly a time for break and refreshment, these lunches provide opportunities for a delicate probing of national positions.

Similarly, a good chair can make use of scheduled or requested breaks in the proceedings to explore possibilities for a settlement. These breaks may feature off-the-record discussions or 'confessionals' between the chair and national representatives or among representatives themselves. Lubricating these discussions is the familiarity and personal relationships national representatives have built up over time. In the end, the objections of opposing states might be assuaged by a redrafting of certain clauses, a promise of later support for a favoured initiative, or the possibility of a derogation (or postponement) of a policy's implementation for one or more reluctant states. The point is that day-to-day practice in Coreper and the Council is characterized far more by the search for a consensus than by any straightforward mechanism of strategic voting.

Vice president of the Commission / High Representative for foreign and security policy

In 2010, a major innovation was the merging of two previously separate posts: the commissioner for external relations and the Council's High Representative for the Common Foreign and Security Policy (CFSP). The creation of the latter post in the late 1990s reflected the reluctance of member states to extend the Commission's role in external representation. France and the UK in particular were averse to the idea of the Commission representing the Union beyond its existing remit in trade, development, and humanitarian aid. Thus, the top civil servant of the Council, its secretary general, was designated High Representative for the CFSP. This division of labour, however, proved problematic and confusing. Non-EU countries were not always sure of to whom to turn in the first instance. In many situations, the Union had to be represented by both the High Representative and the external relations commissioner.

For these reasons, the Lisbon Treaty merged the two posts. Still called the High Representative—although now also a vice president of the Commission—the European Council chooses the appointee, with the agreement of the Commission president. The High Representative is charged with chairing meetings of the Council of Foreign Affairs Ministers. She (and to date it has always been a 'she') also has assumed authority for a new European External Action Service (EEAS), intended as something like an EU 'foreign ministry' (see Chapter 9).

Is the High Representative a Council cuckoo in the Commission nest or a Commission cuckoo in the Council nest? Some see it as a logical step towards bringing the tasks of the former Council High Representative fully into the Commission, ending the anomaly of foreign policy being different from other external policy sectors. Others see it as a smash-and-grab raid by the Council on the Commission's external representation role. The reality is an uneasy compromise, although one that potentially enables the Union's external relations to draw on both of its traditional methods in a more unified way. Batora (2013) theorizes the EEAS as sitting in the spaces between existing EU institutions creating 'a situation in which there are different and sometimes conflicting organisational principles and practices introduced' within the EEAS. The appointment of a sitting commissioner, the UK's Catherine Ashton, as the first incumbent was not without significance. Ashton had previously been commissioner responsible for trade, whereas her successor, Mogherini, had previously been Italy's foreign minister, bringing different experiences to the job. Many feel that Mogherini was more effective on the job—for example, chairing the successful multi-lateral talks to curb Iran's nuclear programme—while Ashton had the initial challenge of actually setting up the EEAS (see the symposium in the *Journal of European Public Policy* 2013c; and Juncos and Pomorska 2014). The political will of the EU member states will be crucial in determining whether the High Representative and the EEAS can close any gap between their capabilities and the expectations of them (Helwig 2013).

Interestingly, Mogherini's post—in identical guise—was labelled the EU 'minister of foreign affairs' in the Constitutional Treaty before that label was abandoned. Recycling the more anodyne title 'High Representative' for the post did not necessarily affect the likelihood of its holder becoming a high-profile figure representing the EU to the world. Vicere (2016: 557) contends that the post-Lisbon foreign and security policy architecture acts as an intergovernmental catalyst for greater integration, 'without greater empowerment of supranational actors'. However, the high representative is the most explicit case of seeking to combine the supranational and intergovernmental in one institutional post.

The Council presidency

Except for meetings of foreign affairs ministers, a minister from the member state holding the rotating 'Presidency of the Council' chairs the Council. Member states take turns chairing for six months each. Although often referred to in the media as the 'EU presidency', presidencies are, in fact, simply the chair of just one of the Union's institutions. Taking the presidency does not confer any additional powers on the holder. Rather, the presidency's job is to build consensus and move decision-making forward.

Holding the presidency places the country concerned in the media spotlight and can give it added influence. For instance, the presidency arranges meetings and can set the Council's agenda, determining which issues will be given priority. But holding the presidency also has disadvantages. The time required of national officials is daunting, especially for smaller states. Much can go wrong in six months, whether or not the country holding the presidency is responsible. Despite the media hype, the presidency's scope for action is limited and its agenda is largely inherited, or dictated by events.

Voting in the Council

The treaties provide, in most policy areas, that a qualified majority (see Boxes 3.2 and 3.3) can approve a Commission proposal, whereas unanimity is required to amend it—a crucial feature of the **Community method**. Some policy areas, however, require unanimity to approve any measure. Unanimity applies to sensitive matters such as taxation, anti-discrimination legislation, and non-legislative decisions on foreign and security policy and constitutional questions such as the accession of new member states (see Chapter 8). A simple majority, with one vote per member state, is used rarely, primarily for procedural questions. The chair of the Council decides whether and when to call for a vote (but must do so if a simple majority requests it). Even though consensus is always sought, and usually achieved (see Box 3.2), formal votes are sometimes needed. Even then, a qualified majority requires the support of a high threshold (see Box 3.3).

> **BOX 3.3**   Voting in the Council of ministers
>
> In nearly all cases, a qualified majority requires that a proposal secures the support of at least 55 per cent of the member states of the Council (at least 15 out of 27/8) and that they must represent, collectively, at least 65 per cent of the EU's population. However, a blocking minority (representing at least 35 per cent or more of the EU's population) must include at least four Council members in nearly all cases.

→

Prior to 2014, a different system of calculating a qualified majority applied, with a fixed number of votes given to each member state, ranging from three for Malta to 29 for the 'big four' (France, Germany, Italy, and the UK). It required roughly 74 per cent of the votes to approve a proposal. However, successive enlargements of the EU, adding mostly smaller or medium-sized member states, had led to a situation where—in theory—a qualified majority could be obtained by the representatives of a minority of the EU's population. Larger member states felt they were becoming under-represented in the system, which is primarily why it was reformed.

Coreper

Council decisions are preceded by extensive negotiation. Each EU member state has its own Permanent Representation ('Perm Rep') office in Brussels, headed by a permanent representative who has ambassadorial status. The national civil servants who staff the **Perm Reps** sit on all manner of preparatory working groups within the Council system. Much policy substance is thrashed out at these levels, particularly by **Coreper**. Composed of national ambassadors to the EU and their staffs, Coreper's job is to prepare the work of the Council and try to reach consensus or suitable majorities ahead of Council meetings. Items on which agreement is reached at Coreper are placed on the Council's agenda as so-called 'A points' for formal approval: if no minister objects they are nodded through. Coreper is split (confusingly) into Coreper II, made up of ambassadors, who deal primarily with the big political, institutional, and budgetary issues, and Coreper I led by deputy ambassadors, who deal with most other issues. Some sensitive or especially busy policy areas—such as security, economic and financial affairs, and agriculture—have their own special preparatory committees, composed of senior officials from the member states.

To the uninitiated (and many of the initiated), Coreper and its various working parties are shadowy and complex. National ambassadors and senior civil servants preparing Council meetings are assisted by numerous (around 140) working groups and committees of national delegates who scrutinize Commission proposals, put forward amendments, and hammer out deals in the run up to the Council meetings. The vast majority of Council decisions (around 70 per cent) are settled here, before ministers become directly involved (see Hayes-Renshaw 2017). Some see Coreper as a real powerhouse: 'the men and women who run Europe'. For others, including Coreper's civil servants themselves, their role is merely that of helping ministers. A civil servant's quote from some years ago remains apt: 'If ministers want to let Coreper decide, that is a ministerial decision' (*Economist*, 6 August 1998). And all decisions must go before the ministers, even if they nod them through.

European Council (of Heads of State or Government)

The **European Council** began in the 1970s as occasional informal fireside chats among heads of government (or, in the case of member states with executive presidents, such as France, heads of state). It became a regular get-together, and known as the European Council, in the mid-1970s (although the term 'summit' is still frequently heard). For a long time, the European Council was seen simply as the pinnacle of the Council system, comprising prime ministers rather than sectoral ministers. However, its composition is formally different—the president of the Commission is a member of the European Council alongside the heads of state or Government—and the very nature and dynamics of its meetings give it an unmistakably distinct character. The Lisbon Treaty formally made it a separate institution.

The European Council must meet at least four times a year, although six has been the norm in recent years. The treaties state that the European Council 'shall provide the Union with the necessary impetus for its development and shall define [its] general political directions and priorities'. Even prior to recognition of its role in the treaties, it became the major agenda setter of the Union. Initiatives such as direct elections to the EP, monetary union, successive enlargements, climate change strategy, and major treaty reforms have all been agreed or endorsed at European Council level. Meeting at 'the summit' of each member state's hierarchy guarantees that its conclusions, even when not legally binding, are acted upon by the Council, the member states and, in practice, the European Commission.

In the words of its own president, 'the European Council works by keeping out of day-to-day business which the other institutions do much better' (in the well-tested framework of the **Community method**), 'yet springing into action to deal with the special cases—changing the treaty, letting new members in the club, dealing with a crisis. In all these cases it draws upon the collective legitimacy of its members' (Van Rompuy 2012).

The European Council's other broad function is more mundane problem solving. Issues that cannot be resolved within Coreper or the Council are often settled at this elevated political level, at times through informal persuasion. At other times, European leaders strike package deals that trade off agreement on one issue (say regional spending) in exchange for concessions on another (say agricultural reform), deals that sectoral ministers cannot easily make. Serious deadlocks on the finances of the Union have often been resolved only through such deals in late-night sittings. The Lisbon Treaty also recognizes what has become, over time, an important role of the European Council: to nominate the president of the Commission and also the governor and board members of the European Central Bank (ECB).

The presidency of the European Council once rotated in tandem with that of the Council. With the Lisbon Treaty, it was agreed that heads of state or government would choose their own chairman for a two-and-a-half-year term (once renewable). The first such president, Herman Van Rompuy, took office on 1 January 2010, leaving his post of prime minister of Belgium (see Barber 2010). Donald Tusk suc-ceeded him five years later, leaving the post of prime minister of Poland.

A number of factors led to the creation of a 'permanent' and full-time president. Previously, the six-month term of office meant a new president every second or third meeting: a recipe for discontinuity and inconsistency. The preparation of European Council meetings—involving consultation of all heads of government—was, especially with successive enlargements, becoming increasingly onerous for any president or prime minister with their own national government to run. Also, the task of representing the EU externally at summit meetings on foreign policy issues, while at the same time representing their own country, was felt to be inappropriate.

Member states with an intergovernmentalist view of the EU saw the European Council president as a useful counterweight to the president of the Commission. Many French observers, given their domestic institutional system, see the presi-dent of the European Council as a sort of *président* of Europe, with the Commission president demoted to the status of a French prime minister: that is, devoted largely to internal affairs and even then deferring on major decisions to the president. Not all share that view. The first European Council president, Van Rompuy, described himself as being less than a *président* but more than a chairman: a facilitator, not a dictator.

The European Parliament

The EU is unique among international organizations in having an elected parlia-ment: the EP is the only directly elected multi-national parliament with significant powers in the world. The reasons for its unique status are twofold. Some saw the creation of a directly elected parliament as a means towards a more 'federal' system in which the Union would derive legitimacy directly from citizens instead of exclu-sively via national governments. Others simply saw the need to compensate the loss of national level parliamentary power, which is inherent in pooling compe-tences at European level.

To its admirers, the Parliament is the voice of the people in European decision-making. To its critics, it is an expensive talking shop. Both of these por-traits carry elements of truth. In contrast with most national parliaments, the EP cannot directly initiate legislation and its budgetary powers cover only spending, not taxation. The EP is dogged by image problems. Its housekeeping arrangements are clumsy and expensive: it is obliged by the member states to divide its activities between Brussels (three weeks out of four) and Strasbourg (for four days a month). The multiplicity of languages means that its debates lack the cut-and-thrust found in many national parliaments. Until 2014 there was no visible link between the out-come of the parliamentary elections and the composition of the executive, the situ-ation that voters are used to at the national level (our earlier discussion of Juncker's appointment to the post of Commission president in 2014 reflects how this dynamic has evolved). Turnout in EP elections is lower than in most national elections in Europe (although about the same as for mid-term, non-presidential, elections in the US).

But the EP exercises its legislative powers forcefully compared to national parliaments, which rarely amend or reject government proposals. Because no executive or any governing majority controls it, the EP can use its independence to considerable effect. Each successive treaty change has strengthened the role of the Parliament. The Parliament is a legal and political equal to the Council in deciding almost all legislation as well as the budget and ratification of international treaties. It elects the president of the Commission and confirms (and can dismiss) the Commission as a whole. Its members are able to network across the institutions and with national governments, interest groups, and non-governmental organizations.

The Lisbon Treaty caps the EP at 751 members with a minimum of six and a maximum of 96 seats per member state, degressively proportional to population. The members of the parliament (MEPs) sit in political groups, not in national blocs. Although there are over 150 national parties, they coalesce into eight groups, most of which correspond to familiar European political families: Liberals, Socialists, Christian Democrats, Greens, and so on. Of course, national allegiances do not disappear. Nonetheless, EP political groups have become more cohesive over time (Hix *et al.* 2009). The EP lacks the strict whipping system found in national parliaments, but positions taken by the groups—and the negotiations between them—are what count in determining majorities. And choices at stake when dealing with legislation are ultimately typical political choices: higher environmental standards at greater cost to those regulated, or not? Higher standards of consumer protection, or leave it to the market? On these subjects, there are nearly always different views within each member state, irrespective of the position taken by their ministers in the Council. These various views are represented in the Parliament, which contains members from opposition parties as well as governing parties in every member state. There is a considerably higher degree of pluralism in the Parliament than in the Council.

The leaders of each political group, along with the Parliament's president, constitute the Conference of Presidents, which sets the EP's agenda. But, like the US Congress, the detailed and most important work of the Parliament is carried out in some 20 standing committees, mostly organized by policy area (such as transport, agriculture, or the environment) and some cross-cutting (such as budgets or women's rights). The committee system allows detailed scrutiny of proposals by members who are, or become, specialists.

The powers of the EP

The Parliament's powers fall under four main headings: legislative, budgetary, scrutiny, and appointments. The Parliament's legislative powers were originally very weak, having only the right to give an opinion on proposed legislation (see Box 3.4). After successive treaty changes the EP now co-decides nearly all EU legislation in what amounts to a bicameral legislature consisting of the Council and the Parliament. What is now, revealingly, called the Ordinary Legislative Procedure (OLP) requires that both agree a text in identical terms before it can be passed into law. Similarly, international treaties or agreements are subject to the consent procedure: the Parliament has the right—in a yes or no vote—to approve or reject the agreement. When it comes to budgetary matters, the Lisbon Treaty also provides for a sort of co-decision.

BOX 3.4   How the European Parliament 'squeezes' power

The EU's Parliament has tended to make the most of whatever powers it has had at any given moment. Even when it was merely consulted on legislation it developed techniques, such as the threat of delay, to make its influence felt. In budget negotiations the EP uses its power to sign off—or not—on the annual budget selectively but effectively.

Similarly, the EP has stretched its powers to oversee the Commission. Formally, the Parliament has only a collective vote of confidence in the Commission before it takes office and no right to hire or fire individual commissioners. Yet, for example, in the parliamentary confirmation hearings of 2004 the EP objected to Italian commissioner-designate Rocco Buttiglione's statements that homosexuality was 'a sin' and that women 'belonged in the home' (Peterson 2017a: 120). These comments caused widespread consternation, especially as his portfolio was to include civil liberties. As it became clear that Parliament might vote to reject the entire Commission, president-elect Barroso formally withdrew the team on the eve of the vote and came back a few weeks later with a new College from which Buttiglione had been dropped. Note that the Parliament did not have *de jure* power to sack Buttiglione, but in practice, it did just that. It did the same to other candidates in 2009 and 2014.

Of course the EP's threats must seem real. For that to happen, it needs solid majorities. Such unity is not easy to come by in such a large and diverse institution with 751 members from a vast array of parties and backgrounds. Thus, despite its ability to 'squeeze' power, the Parliament does not always get its way.

The Parliament also exercises scrutiny of the Commission (and to a degree other institutions and agencies). Its oversight is exercised via its right to question (through written questions or orally at question time), to examine and debate statements or reports, and to hear and cross-examine commissioners, ministers, and civil servants in its committees. The Parliament also approves the appointment of the Commission and, more spectacularly, can dismiss the College (as a whole) through a vote of no confidence. The latter is considered to be a 'nuclear' option—a strategic, reserve power that requires an absolute majority of all MEPs and a two-thirds majority of all votes cast. As in most national parliaments, which do not make daily use of their right to dismiss the government, its very existence is sufficient to show that the Commission must take due account of Parliament.

This power effectively was exercised only once, when it resulted in the fall of the Commission under the Presidency of Jacques Santer in 1999. Even then, the Commission resigned prior to the actual vote, once it was clear that the necessary majority would be obtained. One upshot of this episode was a treaty change to allow the president of the Commission to dismiss individual members of the Commission (which the EP cannot do). Thus, if the behaviour of a particular commissioner gives rise to serious parliamentary misgivings (as the former French prime minister Edith Cresson's did in the Santer Commission; see Peterson 2017a: 114), the president of the Commission can take action to retain the EP's confidence. Besides the Commission, the Parliament also elects the European ombudsman and is consulted on appointments to other EU posts (see Box 3.8).

In short, the EP's powers have grown significantly since direct elections were first held in 1979 (Hix and Høyland 2013). However, some still question its ability to add legitimacy to EU decision-making. Its claim to represent the peoples of Europe is undermined by relatively low turnouts for its elections (around 43 per cent in recent EP elections). In the 2014 election, voters elected an unprecedentedly high number of Eurosceptic MEPs, who question the very existence of the EU, with such parties topping the poll in some member states (including France and the UK). The relative lack of citizen engagement, combined with the Parliament's image—accurate or not—as a 'gravy train' does not help. Ultimately, the Parliament's future role is tied up with larger questions of democracy and power in the EU (see Chapter 7).

European Court of Justice

At first glance, the ECJ seems neither a particularly powerful nor controversial institution. It is located in sleepy Luxembourg and is currently comprised of 28 (27 post-Brexit) judges (one from each member state) plus nine Advocates-General who draft Opinions for the judges. The General Court (previously known as the Court of First Instance), a lower tribunal created in 1989 to ease a growing workload, supports the ECJ. By 2010 the General Court had dealt with nearly 17,000 cases. The ECJ and the General Court are collectively referred to as the Court of Justice of the European Union (CJEU). The ECJ's profile is generally low, apart from within European legal circles.

Simply put and according to the EU treaties, the role of the ECJ is to ensure that 'in the interpretation and application of the treaties, the law is observed'. The Court is thus powerful: it is the final arbiter in legal disputes between EU institutions or between them and member states or between citizens and EU institutions. The Court ensures that the EU institutions do not go beyond the powers given to them. Conversely, it also ensures national compliance with the treaties and the legislation that flows from them. The ECJ even has the right to fine member states that breach EU law.

The Court is sometimes accused of having a pro-integration agenda, a reputation that derives mainly from landmark decisions it made in the 1960s. In practice, the

Court has to interpret the texts as they have been adopted. Significantly, its members are not appointed by EU institutions, but by member states. The ECJ therefore differs from the US Supreme Court, whose members are appointed by American federal institutions (see Box 3.5).

BOX 3.5   Compared to what? The ECJ and the US Supreme Court

The ECJ—like the EU more generally—is in many ways *sui generis*: an international body with no precise counterpart anywhere in Europe or beyond. But interesting parallels, as well as contrasts, can be drawn between the ECJ and the US Supreme Court.

The US Supreme Court exists to uphold the US Constitution, whereas the EU has no such constitution. Yet even here the difference may not be as stark as it appears. The ECJ must uphold the EU's Treaties. For some legal scholars, the cumulative impact of Court decisions that have interpreted the treaties amount to a 'quiet revolution' that effectively transformed the treaties into a constitution insofar as they constitute the basic rule book of the EU (see Weiler 1998).

One difference is jurisdiction, or the power to hear and decide cases. The jurisdiction of the US Supreme Court is vast. It can hear all cases involving legal disputes between the US states. Even more important is its power to hear cases raising constitutional disputes invoked by any national treaty, federal law, state law, or act. The ECJ's jurisdiction is far more confined. Its rulings on trade have had a fundamental impact on the single market and the EU more generally. But many matters of national law and most non-trade disputes between states fall outside its remit. Moreover, the ECJ cannot 'cherry pick' the cases it wants to hear, as the US court can. Finally, recruitment, appointment, and tenure differ. Following nomination by the president and confirmation by the Senate, US Supreme Court justices are appointed for life. Their appointments are highly politicized. In contrast, the member state governments appoint judges to the ECJ with little publicity. They remain relatively unknown for their six-year renewable term.

Still, we find parallels between the two. The rulings of both the ECJ and Supreme Court take precedence over those of lower or national courts. Lower courts must enforce these rulings. Like the US Supreme Court in its early decades, the ECJ's early decisions helped consolidate the authority of the Union's central institutions. But perhaps the most interesting similarities involve debates surrounding these courts' powers and political role. In the case of the US Supreme Court, concerns about its politicization and activism are well known, especially in its rulings on abortion, racial equality, and campaign spending (see Martin 2010). In the EU too, concerns about the Court's procedure, its ability to push forward or limit integration, and the expansion of its authority have propelled the Court into the heart of political debates about the future of the Europe. Debate about its role featured in the 2016 EU referendum in Britain, despite some confusing it with the quite separate (non-EU) **European Court of Human Rights**. Thus, whatever their differences, both the ECJ and US Supreme Court raise fundamental questions about the proper limits of judicial activism and the role of courts in democratic societies more generally.

EU law is qualitatively different from international law in that individuals can seek remedy for breaches of the former through their domestic courts, which refer points of European law to the EU Court. The process allows national courts to ask the ECJ for a preliminary ruling on the European facet of a case before them. The national courts, in judging cases, use such preliminary rulings. This method has shaped national policies as diverse as the right to advertise abortion services across borders, roaming charges for mobile phones, and equal pay for equal work. If the Court has a pro-integration agenda; it is primarily to integrate national courts into a cooperative system for applying EU law. Otherwise, what would be the point of EU law?

Its critics sometimes claim that the Court has, in effect, become a policy-making body (see Weiler 1998: 217). Its defenders point out that it can only rule on matters referred to it, and then only apply texts adopted by legislators. Certainly, the Court's role in the 1960s was crucial in giving real substance to the EU legal system. Three landmark decisions stand out. In the 1963 *Van Gend en Loos* case, the Court established 'direct effect': the doctrine that EU citizens had a legal right to expect their governments to adhere to their European obligations. In 1964 (*Costa v ENEL*), the Court established the 'supremacy' of EU law: if a domestic law contradicts an EU obligation, European law prevails.

Later, in the 1979 *Cassis de Dijon* case, the Court established the principle of 'mutual recognition': a product made or sold legally in one member state—in this case a French blackcurrant liqueur—cannot be barred in another member state if there is no threat to public health, public policy, or public safety. This principle proved fundamental to the single market because it established that national variations in standards could exist as long as trade was not unduly impeded.

These judgements took place in a period normally characterized as one of stagnation and 'Eurosclerosis', when political integration seemed paralysed. Scholars who take inspiration from neofunctionalist thinking often cite evidence from this period to undermine the intergovernmentalist claim that national governments alone dominate the rhythm of integration (see Chapter 1). But the Court's power is limited: it must rely on member states to carry out its rulings. The powers of the Court—and how they should be wielded—remain contested in EU politics.

Also contested is the relationship between the main institutional players—Commission, Parliament, Council, European Council, and Court—which is constantly changing. Power shifts across and between institutions not only as a result of formal treaty changes, but also due to changes in practice, the assertiveness of the various actors, agreements between EU institutions, and Court judgements. For instance, the ability of the Council to impose its view has declined as the bargaining power of Parliament has increased. The European Council's growing power to set the EU agenda has usurped the Commission's traditional and legal right of initiative. The establishment of a full-time president of the European *Council* challenges the primacy of the president of the *Commission*.

Both formal and informal institutional change has contributed to a blurring of powers among core institutions. This blurring does not mean that the formal rules do not matter. Rules and treaty provisions serve as the basis of authority from which the institutions can and do act. But formal powers are only starting points: knowing how the institutions exploit, compete for, and ultimately share power is also crucial for grasping how the EU works (see Box 3.6).

BOX 3.6   How it really works: Turf wars!

Relations between EU institutions are both consensual and conflictual. Cooperation is unceasing because of the shared recognition that all institutions must compromise and work together to get a policy through or decision agreed. Even those final decisions that rest with one institution usually involve proposals from or consultation with another.

Yet interinstitutional rivalry is also fierce. Each institution usually guards its prerogatives (to initiate policy or control budgets) jealously. **New institutionalist** scholars such as Armstrong and Bulmer (1998) and Pollack (2009) have underlined the importance of this dynamic. Perceived attempts by one institution to encroach on another's 'turf' often elicit heated responses or fierce demonstrations of institutional loyalty. For example, in 2010, the Commission disliked the fact that the European Council had set up a Task Force, chaired by the European Council's president, to make proposals on the reform of economic **governance** procedures—something the Commission felt should be its job. Although represented on the Task Force, and broadly in agreement with its emerging recommendations, the Commission insisted on tabling them as its own legislative proposals to Parliament and Council one week before their final approval by the Task Force.

Why Institutions Matter

Examining its institutions and how they work is essential to understanding the EU. First, it gives us a starting point from which to examine the EU's policy process. Second, it helps us to identify the diversity of actors involved and to understand how they together determine the shape and speed of integration. Finally, it reminds us that there are many interesting questions still to be answered about European integration. Is it heading towards a European federal state? Or a looser, more intergovernmental body? Or a multi-tiered system? How democratic or efficient will it be? Who or what will determine the pace and shape of integration?

More particularly, the EU's institutions help illustrate the three central themes of this book: (1) that the EU is an experiment in motion; (2) the importance of power sharing and consensus; and (3) the capacity of the EU structures to cope with the Union's expanding size and scope. The very fact that powers are wielded at a level beyond the nation state, albeit with the involvement of their governments, remains controversial in some countries and was highlighted by Leave campaigners in the 2016 UK referendum (see Chapter 10).

Experimentation and change

The EU's institutional system has evolved considerably since the establishment of the European Coal and Steel Community in 1951. As we have seen, the institutions have adapted over time. The founding treaties, and subsequent changes to them, formally mandate some of their tasks. Others have emerged as more informal experiments in cooperation. A variety of pressures have combined to encourage task expansion and the reinvention of institutions over time. In particular, gaps in the capacity of the EU to respond to events and crises have resulted in an ad hoc expansion of the informal powers of the institutions. For example, the need for common action on the environment meant that informal environmental agreements predated formal competences introduced by the treaties. Sometimes member states agreed on the need to establish informal cooperation in new areas, but were not initially ready to be legally bound by the treaties, as in the gradual expansion of the powers of EU institutions focused on justice and home affairs (see Chapter 5). Studying the institutional dynamics of the EU allows us not only to understand the extent to which the EU is subject to experimentation and change, but also to pose questions about where this process might be headed.

Power sharing and consensus

Scholars of European integration have long and fiercely debated where power lies in the EU. Do the EU's institutions drive the integration process forward? Or do national governments remain in control? Neofunctionalists and intergovernmentalists have taken up the two sides of this debate, respectively. Both sides can cite changes in formal EU rules to buttress their case.

For example, as the Parliament has gained powers and member states have accepted more proposals on the basis of QMV, it could be claimed that supranationalism is on the rise. Equally, as the European Council has come to dominate high-level agenda setting, and some EU states have opted out of certain policies (such as monetary union), it could be said that intergovernmentalism is holding strong. In recent years, as the EU has responded to, among other things, the Eurozone crisis, researchers continue to debate whether we have entered a period of a 'new intergovernmentalism' (Bickerton *et al.* 2015) or not (Schimmelfennig 2015). But depicting integration as a pitched battle between EU institutions and the member states misses the point. Dividing lines are often within each of the above. Competition is fierce, but so, too, is the search for consensus. Enormous efforts go into forging agreements acceptable to all.

The overall trajectory of integration is thus a result of to-ing and fro-ing between a rich variety of actors and external pressures. This image is quite neatly captured in Wallace's (2000) description of EU governance as a pendulum, swinging some-times towards intergovernmental solutions and other times towards supranation-alism, but not always in equal measure. In this system, power is often a product of how well any institution engages with other actors—lobbyists, experts, govern-ments, and other international organizations—at different levels of governance. Focusing on the institutions and how they cooperate or compete with each other and other actors helps us to begin to make sense of the EU as a complex policy-making process.

Scope and capacity

The step-by-step extension of the scope of the EU's activities is one thing. Its capacity to deal with those subjects that fall within its remit and to cope with successive enlargements is another. Have the institutional structures originally conceived for a Community of six member states been sufficiently adapted to deal with the demands of a EU of 27/8 or more (see Box 3.7)? In most policy fields, the EU has managed to avoid decision-making gridlock following each successive enlargement, although arguments continue as to whether enlargement has been at the cost of having to settle for lowest common denominator solutions. Certainly in areas that require unanimity within the Council, the EU now is vulnerable to slow, cumbersome decision-making and even total blockage at the instigation of one or another member state.

BOX 3.7   Enlargement's institutional impact

Enlargement has brought both opportunities and headaches to the EU's institu-tions. The impact has varied across institutions, with some adapting more smooth-ly than others. The EP, despite real linguistic challenges (see Box 1.7), seems to have had the least difficulty absorbing new members (see Donnelly and Bigatto 2008). Decisions are based on majority votes and the EP has shown that it is still able to deal with difficult legislation even with more than 700 MEPs. Moreover, the quality of MEPs from new (that is, post-2004) states generally has been high, with many having held important positions (including presidents and prime ministers).

In the Commission, new and generally younger officials from states that recent-ly joined the EU hold out the prospect of revitalizing and renewing the institution with fresh ideas and reform-minded Europeans (see Kassim *et al.* 2013: 245–72). However, a college of 28 (27 post-Brexit) commissioners has resulted in a less cosy and, arguably, more **intergovernmental** and less collegial body (see Peterson 2008). With one per member state, its membership is now like that of the Council. Finding a sufficient number of responsible and interesting portfolios of relatively equal importance has proved difficult.

The Council and European Council have felt the effects of enlargement most keenly, especially where unanimity is required or desired. Since 2004, the

→

→

Council has found it increasingly difficult to push through important decisions in areas such as foreign policy, police cooperation, and migration. National vetoes are not necessarily more common in an enlarged EU (see House of Lords 2006; Hagemann and De Clerck-Sachsse 2007; Kaeding and Stack 2015). But Council meetings are more time-consuming and not always as productive. On important questions, all or most member states still want to present their positions and may insist on lengthy interventions. The result is less time for real discussion and com-promise seeking, which is the essence of what makes the Council and European Council function. And a larger number of member states increases the chances of one or more outliers whose governments (or electorates) challenge the values and assumptions on which the EU is based.

The impact of enlargement on the institutions reflects its wider impact on the EU. It has brought a mix of logistical headaches, challenges, doubts, and crises. But it also offers fresh impulse, drive, and energy for a Union otherwise threatened by stagnation and inertia.

Strengthening European cooperation may appear to equate to empowering its institutions. Yet, policy cooperation has been extended in a variety of different ways that have widened the scope of the EU without necessarily expanding the powers of institutions. The careful exclusion of the ECJ, and the weaker role of the Commission and the EP, in most aspects of foreign and security policy are exam-ples. So is the gradual bonding together of European leaders outside the formal confines of the European Council but also not, strictly and exclusively speaking, as representatives of purely national interests (see Van Middelaar 2013). Finally, if there is one lesson to be learned from the study of EU institutions, it is their remarkable ability to adapt as new requirements are placed upon them. This chap-ter has tried to show that while the capacity of EU institutions may be limited, their ability to adapt is often impressive.

Conclusion

The EU's institutional system is complex. But so, too, is the diverse polity it helps govern. We have attempted to cut through this complexity by focus-ing on the powers of the institutions and how they are used. We have stressed the importance of both cooperation and rivalry between the institutions. Each institution may have its own agendas, but nearly all of the important decisions require some (and, usually, quite a large) measure of consensus spanning the EU's institutions and across member states within the Council (see Hodson and Peterson 2017). The institutions are as interdependent as the member states that make up the EU.

Moreover, EU institutions do not operate alone. Today they must deal with an ever-broader range of actors, especially because of the EU's enlargement (see Chapter 8), but also because organized interests have become increasingly active. Above all, understanding institutions helps us to explore broader questions of how and why the EU works the way it does.

BOX 3.8   Other institutions and bodies

Several other institutions and bodies carry out a variety of representative, oversight, or managerial functions in the EU. By far the most significant of these specialized institutions is the **ECA**. Based in Frankfurt and modelled on the fiercely independent German *Bundesbank*, the ECB is charged with a fundamental task: formulating the EU's monetary policy, including ensuring monetary stability, setting interest rates, and issuing and managing the euro (see Chapter 5). The ECB is steered by a governing council (made up primarily of national central bank governors) and headed by a president and executive board chosen by member states, although they cannot formally be removed by member states. The Bank's independence and power undoubtedly help ensure monetary stability but also have raised concerns about **transparency** and accountability. It must report to the EP several times a year. But its deliberations were until recently not made public and it enjoys considerable independence from other institutions or member states. While still a young institution, the Bank has already become an important, but also controversial player in EU politics (see Hodson 2015). Its remit was expanded in 2014 to include supervision of banks.

The **European Court of Auditors (ECA)**, with 28 members, is charged with scrutinizing the EU's spending and financial accounts. Acting as the 'financial conscience' of the EU, the Court has increased its visibility in recent years as public concern over mismanagement, and occasionally fraud, has mounted. Its annual and specialized reports consist mainly of dry financial management assessment. But it has also uncovered more spectacular and serious financial misconduct (see Laffan 2017).

Several smaller bodies not classified as institutions (therefore having fewer rights at the Court) carry out a primarily representative function (see Rowe and Jeffery 2017). For instance the **European Economic and Social Committee (EESC)** represents employers, trades unions, and other social or public interests (such as farmers or consumers) in EU policy-making. Chosen by the national governments, these representatives serve in a part-time function advising the Commission and other institutions on relevant proposals. Their opinions can be well researched but are not usually influential. The **European Committee of the Regions (CoR)** suffers from a similar lack of influence. Created by the Maastricht Treaty, the Committee must be consulted on proposals affecting regional interests (cohesion funding, urban planning) and can issue its own opinions and

→

→

reports. However, its membership is debilitatingly diverse (powerful regional ministers from Germany and Belgium sit alongside representatives from Irish local
councils). It has yet to exert the influence its proponents originally envisioned. But
perhaps its real role is as a channel of communication across several layers of
governance.

The EU ombudsman is empowered to receive complaints from any EU citizen or
any natural or legal person residing in the member states concerning instances
of maladministration in the activities of the Union institutions or bodies (other than
the Court in its judicial capacity). The EP chooses the ombudsman after each parliamentary election for the duration of its term of office.

The **European Investment Bank (EIB)** is the world's biggest, public, long-term
lending institution. It supports the development of infrastucture and economic
development projects. The EIB's shareholders are the member states. It borrows on
capital markets to finance capital projects. In 2016 it lent over €76 billion.

Last, but not least, are over 40 **European agencies** established by the EU to manage issues as diverse as air safety, police cooperation (Europol), authorization of
medicines and chemicals on the European market, food safety, or the supervision
of financial markets, including banks. They typically have a governing body appointed by the EU institutions and member states, and perform technical functions on a
pooled basis, avoiding the costs of duplicated efforts by member states, pooling
resources, or coordinating national efforts.

As the EU takes on new tasks, the burden on its institutions will increase. The EU's
growing role in areas such as migration, foreign and defence policy, food safety, and
climate change means that other agencies and bodies (including international ones
that transcend Europe itself) will join the institutional mix that helps govern EU
politics (see Box 3.8). Further institutional reform may prove both necessary and
inevitable to cope with the increasing size and policy scope of the EU. But given the
challenge of obtaining unanimous support for institutional change, institutional
reform—like so much else in the EU—is likely to be incremental and pragmatic
rather than spectacular or far-sighted.

? DISCUSSION QUESTIONS

1. Which EU institution is most 'powerful' in your view and why?

2. Why has the balance of powers between the EU's institutions shifted over time?

3. In what ways has enlargement affected the EU's main institutions?

4. Is the relationship between the EU's institutions characterized more by cooperation or conflict?

FURTHER READING

For comprehensive analysis of all of the EU's institutions, see Hodson and Peterson (2017). Helpful examinations of individual institutions include Kassim *et al.*'s (2013) analysis of the Commission; and Puetter's (2014) exploration of the roles of the European Council and Council of ministers; Corbett *et al.*'s (2016) account of the workings of the Parliament; and Weiler's (1998) provocative and thoughtful essays on the Court and EU's legal identity. Van Middelaar (2013) offers a perceptive treatment of how the EU's institutional system has developed over time.

Corbett, R., Jacobs, F., and Neville, D. (2016), *The European Parliament*, 9th edn (London: John Harper).

Hodson, D. and Peterson, J. (eds) (2017), *The Institutions of the European Union*, 4th edn (Oxford and New York: Oxford University Press).

Kassim, H., Peterson, J., Bauer, M., Connolly, S., Dehousse, R., Hooghe, L., and Thompson, A. (2013), *The European Commission of the Twenty-First Century* (Oxford and New York: Oxford University Press).

Puetter, U. (2014), *The European Council and hte Council* (Oxford and New York: Oxford University Press).

Van Middelaar, L. (2013), *The Passage to Europe: How a Continent Became a Union* (New Haven: Yale University Press).

Weiler, J. H. H. (1999), *The Constitution of Europe* (Cambridge and New York: Cambridge University Press).

WEB LINKS

- Most of the EU's institutions have their own website which can be accessed through the EU's official portal site, 'The European Union online' (http://www.europa.eu/).
- Here are the specific official websites of some of the institutions introduced in this chapter:
    - European Commission: http://ec.europa.eu/
    - Council of ministers: http://www.consilium.europa.eu/
    - European Parliament: http://www.europarl.europa.eu/
    - European Council: http://www.european-council.europa.eu/
    - European Court of Justice: http://curia.europa.eu/
    - European Court of Auditors: http://www.eca.europa.eu/
    - Economic and Social Committee: http://eesc.europa.eu/
    - European Committee of the Regions: http://www.cor.europa.eu/
    - European Central Bank: http://www.ecb.int/

- A nine-minute video on '10 things you need to know about the EU's institutions' is available at: https://media.ed.ac.uk/media/10+things+about+EU%21/1_80ra79kc
- Anyone brave enough to consider working as an intern or *stagiaire* in one of the EU's institutions can find out more at: http://ec.europa.eu/stages/
- For recent updates on institutional developments, especially in relation to treaty reform, see: http://www.euractiv.com/
- The London-based University Association for Contemporary European Studies (UACES) (http://www.uaces.org/) announces regular workshops and lectures on the EU institutions held in the UK and (occasionally) on the European continent.
- For information on conferences and lectures held in the US, see the website of the US European Union Studies Association (EUSA), which can be found at: http://www.eustudies.org

 Visit the Ancillary Resource Centre that accompanies this book for additional material: www.oup.com/uk/kenealy5e/

CHAPTER 4

Member States

Brigid Laffan

Summary

This chapter focuses on the European Union's (EU's) most essential component: its member states. It examines six factors that determine how a state engages with the EU: date of entry, size, wealth, state structure, economic ideology, and integration preference. We then explore how member states behave in the Union's institutions and seek to influence the outcome of negotiations in Brussels. We focus throughout on the informal as well as formal activities of the member states. The EU is a union based on law, which may be challenged from time to time by a member state. This dimension is explored by analysing the difficulties created for the EU by authoritarian populist governments. The final section explores the insights offered by theory in analysing the relationship between the EU and its member states.

Introduction

States are the essential building blocks of the EU. Without states there is no EU. All EU treaties are negotiated and ratified by the 'high contracting parties': that is, the governments of the member states. By joining the EU, the traditional nation state is transformed into a member state. This transformation involves an enduring commitment to participate in political and legal processes that are beyond the state but which also embrace the state. Membership of the Union has significant effects on national systems of policy-making, national institutions, and national identity, sovereignty, and democracy. Put simply, once a state joins the Union, politics may still begin at home. But they no longer end there. National politics, polities, and policies become 'Europeanized' (see **Europeanization** in Glossary; Box 4.1).

Member states shape the EU as much as the EU shapes its member states. The decision to join the Union is a decision to become locked into an additional layer of governance and a distinctive form of 'Euro-politics', which is neither wholly domestic nor international but shares attributes of both. This chapter explores this interactive dynamic. We tackle questions such as: what is the role of member states in the EU system? What is it about the EU that has led the member states to invest so much in the collective project? How do member states engage with the EU? What factors determine how any member state behaves as an EU member?

BOX 4.1   Key concepts and terms

Acquis communautaire is a French phrase that denotes the sum total of the rights and obligations derived from the EU treaties, laws, and Court rulings. In principle, new member states joining the EU must accept the entire *acquis*.

Demandeur is the French term often used to refer to those demanding something (say, regional or agricultural funds) from the EU.

Europeanization is the process whereby national systems (institutions, policies, governments, and even the polity itself) adapt to EU policies and integration more generally, while also themselves shaping the EU.

Flexible integration (also called 'reinforced' or '**enhanced cooperation**') denotes the possibility for some member states to pursue deeper integration without the participation of others. Examples include the **Economic and Monetary Union (EMU)** and the **Schengen Agreement** in which some member states have decided not to participate fully. The Amsterdam and Nice Treaties institutionalized the concept of flexible integration through their clauses on enhanced cooperation.

Tours de table allow each national delegation in a **Council of Ministers** meeting to make an intervention on a given subject. In an EU of 28 member states *tours de table* have become less common. If every minister or national official intervened for even five minutes on each subject, it would take nearly two-and-a-half hours.

Six Determining Features

The 28 (this number will fall for the first time when the UK leaves the EU, as currently scheduled, in March 2019) member states bring to the Union their distinctive national histories, state traditions, constitutions, legal principles, political systems, and economic capacity. A variety of languages (there are 24 official working languages in the EU) and an extraordinary diversity of national and subnational tastes and cultures accentuate the mosaic-like character of Europe. The enlargement of the Union (13 new states have joined since 2004) has deepened its pre-existing diversity. Managing difference is thus a key challenge for the Union. To understand how the EU really works, we must understand the multi-national and multi-cultural character of the EU and its institutions.

Classifying the member states—including how and why they joined and how they operate within the EU—is a good first step towards understanding the member states' relationship with the EU. Six factors are extremely important. No one factor determines the relationship between the Union and a member state, but together they provide a guide to understanding member states' engagement with the EU.

Entry date

It is useful to deploy the metaphor of an onion to characterize the expansion of the Union from its original six states to nine, ten, 12, 15, and finally to 28 or more states in the years ahead (see Figure 4.1). France, Germany, and the four other founding members form the core of the onion. What is now the EU was originally the creation of six states that were occupied or defeated in World War II. It is the creation especially of France, a country that needed to achieve a settlement with its neighbour and historical enemy, Germany. From the outset a key relationship in the EU was between France and West Germany. As explained in Chapter 2, the Franco-German alliance and the Paris–Bonn axis—now Paris–Berlin—has left enduring traces on the fabric of integration. The Elysée Treaty (1963) institutionalized very strong bilateral ties between these two countries. The intensity of interaction should not be taken as evidence of continuous agreement between France and Germany on major European issues. Rather, much of the interaction has worked to iron out conflicts between them.

Close personal relationships between West German Chancellor Helmut Schmidt and French President Valery Giscard d'Estaing in the 1970s, and Chancellor Helmut Kohl and President François Mitterrand in the 1980s and early 1990s, were key to the most ambitious steps forward in European integration, including the creation of the European Monetary System (a precursor to EMU), the single market programme, and the euro. The Franco-German relationship was challenged by geopolitical change in Europe following the collapse of communism. German unification and the opening up of the eastern half of the continent altered

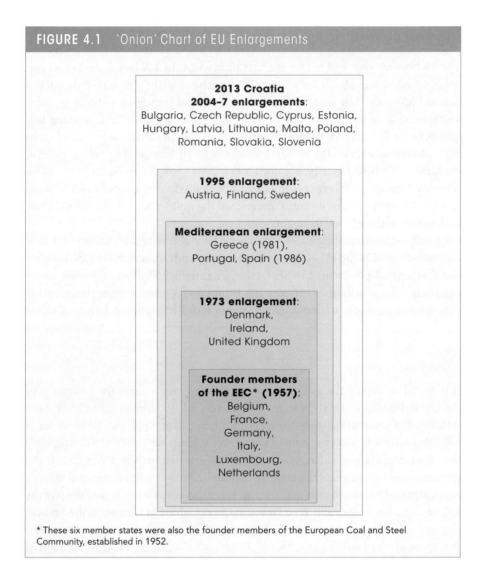

FIGURE 4.1   'Onion' Chart of EU Enlargements

2013 Croatia
2004-7 enlargements:
Bulgaria, Czech Republic, Cyprus, Estonia,
Hungary, Latvia, Lithuania, Malta, Poland,
Romania, Slovakia, Slovenia

1995 enlargement:
Austria, Finland, Sweden

Mediteranean enlargement:
Greece (1981),
Portugal, Spain (1986)

1973 enlargement:
Denmark,
Ireland,
United Kingdom

**Founder members
of the EEC* (1957)**:
Belgium,
France,
Germany,
Italy,
Luxembourg,
Netherlands

* These six member states were also the founder members of the European Coal and Steel
Community, established in 1952.

the bilateral balance of power, with Germany no longer a junior political partner
to France. The change was symbolically captured by the relocation of the German
capital to Berlin.

During the **Eurozone** crisis, the dynamic of the Franco-German relationship
was further tested as Germany became the pre-eminent state in the search for
policy solutions. The crisis led some scholars to speak of German hegemony
in the Union (Beck 2013; Bulmer and Paterson 2013). However, it is premature
to talk of the demise of the Franco-German partnership (see Schoeller 2018).
The victory of Emmanuel Macron in the 2017 French presidential elections and
the re-election of Chancellor Angela Merkel in September 2017 represented

a window of opportunity for a rebooting of the Franco-German relationship. President Macron campaigned on a strong European platform and immediately after the 2017 German election made a strong plea for a renewed partnership between Germany and France to launch a reform process within the Union. Macron was bold both in terms of rhetoric and prescription. Just how much of his ambition would be achieved depended on the response of especially Germany but also other EU member states. Yet, there was widespread consensus in Europe that the decision by the UK to leave the Union (see Chapter 10) placed a responsibility on the two large continental states to sustain and protect the Union.

The four other founder member states—Italy, Belgium, Luxembourg, and the Netherlands—see themselves as part of the hard core of the Union. All have played a significant role in the evolution of the EU. The Benelux countries (Belgium, Luxembourg, and the Netherlands) were traditionally at the centre of developments, often ready to push for deeper integration. They were all deeply committed to the Community method of law-making (institution-led rather than intergovernmental) and supportive of a strong, supranational Union. This dynamic, however, has changed in recent times. Since 2005 and the Dutch rejection of the Constitutional Treaty, Benelux cooperation has been at best lukewarm, at worst non-existent. For example, the 2007 EU summit that agreed the text of what would become the Lisbon Treaty featured a blazing row between the Belgian and Dutch prime ministers, with one attendee commenting: 'we thought they might come to blows' (*Financial Times*, 25 June 2007) over the issue of scrutiny rights for national parliaments.

Italy has oscillated between active involvement in EU diplomacy and a passive presence in the system. It has traditionally been enthusiastic about European institution building, but not consistently so (see Bindi with Cisci 2005). More generally, Italy's relationship with the EU and other member states is hampered not by a lack of enthusiasm but by endemic instability in its governing coalitions and its weak capacity for internal reform. The election in 2018 of a populist coalition government led by the 5-Star Movement and the League has added a euroscepticism to Italian input into EU politics that was absent in the past.

All states joining the EU after its initial formative period had to accept the Union's existing laws and obligations (or *acquis communautaire*; see Box 4.1), its institutional system, and way of doing business, all of which had been formed without their input. Thus for all latecomers, adjustment and adaptation to the EU was a process that began before their date of accession and continued well after membership. With the expansion of the Union's tasks, the burden of adjustment has grown for each successive wave of accession. As Chapter 5 demonstrates, the EU has taken on new policy areas over the years ranging from environmental policy to police cooperation (the *acquis communautaire* has grown to cover over 80,000 pages of legislation). This expansion has made it even more difficult for outsiders to catch up and adapt to membership (see Chapter 8).

Size

As in all political systems, size matters in the EU. The distinction between large and small states is often evoked in political and media discussions about representation in the EU. During the cumbersome negotiations on the Treaty of Nice, which focused on the reweighting of votes in the Council and the number of commissioners each state could appoint, tensions between large and small states escalated. Nice settled little, and battles between large and small states marked negotiations surrounding the 2004 Constitutional Treaty and its eventual replacement (the Lisbon Treaty).

In any event, a more nuanced approach to understanding the impact of size is warranted. The EU really consists of four clusters of states—large, medium, small, and very small (see Table 4.1). The first cluster contains six large states: Germany, the UK, France, Italy, Spain, and Poland. Together they make up about 70 per cent of the population of EU-28 (although even here we find dissent: Germany and France, are certainly seen as the 'big two', with Italy seen as less powerful, and some would dispute Spain's and Poland's categorization as large states). The forthcoming departure of the UK will reduce the Union's population by 65 million and the outcome of its 2016 referendum has already reduced the UK's influence and standing within the system. The next cluster consists of medium-sized states: Romania, the Netherlands, Greece, Belgium, Portugal, the Czech Republic, Hungary, Sweden, Austria, and Bulgaria whose populations range from seven to

TABLE 4.1 Clusters of member states by size			
Current member states (figure in brackets = approximate population in millions in 2017)			
Large	**Medium**	**Small**	**Very small**
Germany (81.2)	Romania (19.8)	Denmark (5.6)	Cyprus (0.8)
France (66.4)	Netherlands (16.9)	Finland (5.5)	Luxembourg (0.5)
UK (64.8)	Greece (10.8)	Slovakia (5.4)	Malta (0.4)
Italy (60.8)	Belgium (11.2)	Ireland (4.6)	
Spain (46.4)	Portugal (10.4)	Croatia (4.2)	
Poland (38.0)	Czech Rep (10.5)	Lithuania (2.9)	
	Hungary (10.0)	Latvia (2.0)	
	Sweden (9.7)	Slovenia (2.0)	
	Austria (8.6)	Estonia (1.3)	
	Bulgaria (7.2)		

Source: Eurostat, at http://ec.europa.eu/eurostat/tgm/table.do?tab=table&plugin=1&language=en&pcode=tps00001

20 million. The third cluster is one of small states: Croatia, Denmark, Finland, Slovakia, Ireland, Lithuania, Latvia, Slovenia, and Estonia, which all have populations of between one and six million. The fourth category, very small states, consists of Cyprus, Luxembourg, and Malta. Recent enlargements overwhelmingly have brought an increase of medium, small, and very small states (Poland being the exception).

Size has implications for power and presence in the Union's political and economic system. The power of large states is not just expressed in voting power in the Council. It manifests itself in political, economic, and diplomatic influence (see Wallace 2005: 38ff). Large states can call on far more extensive and specialized administrative and technical resources in the policy process than small states, and their diplomatic presence is far stronger throughout the world. The German chancellor, regardless of who holds the post, is usually the most powerful politician at European Council meetings. Small states, however, enjoy important advantages in EU negotiations. They tend to have fewer vital interests than larger states, their interests can be aggregated with much greater ease, and the potential for conflict and competing claims among different social groups is reduced. Luxembourg, for example, can concentrate all of its diplomatic energy on protecting its traditional industries, its liberal banking laws, and its presence in EU institutions.

Although size matters, it has little bearing on national approaches to substantive issues of EU policy. Instead, they are formed by economic considerations, domestic interests, and the proposed nature of the change. Thus, small states are unlikely to band together against the large states in substantive policy discussions. Their interests, just as those of the larger states, diverge. Coalition patterns in the Council have always consisted of a mix of large and small states in any particular policy domain.

However, small states do have a common interest in maintaining the EU's institutional balance and they can deploy a variety of strategies to cope with the structural disadvantage they face (Panke 2010). For instance small EU states can band together to oppose proposals that privilege a small group of larger states. They are keen supporters of procedural 'rules of the game' which protect their level of representation in the system. The key point here is that the multi-lateral, institutionalized, and legal processes of the Union have created a relatively benign environment for small states.

In the past, the EU successfully managed to expand its membership to include both large and small states without undermining the balance between them or causing undue tension. This balance began to shift in the 1990s. The 1995 enlargement and the prospect of further enlargement to the east and south heightened the salience of the small state / large state divide in the Union. The struggle for power—as reflected in number of commissioners, votes in the Council, or seats in the European Parliament (EP) each member state receives—figured on the EU agenda for well over a decade, from 1995 to 2009.

Wealth

The original EEC had only one serious regional poverty problem: the Italian Mezzogiorno (Italy's southern regions). As such, 'cohesion' (or regional development) was not an important concern. The first enlargement in 1973 to include the UK, Denmark, and Ireland increased the salience of regional disparities in the politics of the Union. The UK had significant regional problems, with declining industrial areas and low levels of economic development in areas such as Northern England, Scotland, Wales, and Northern Ireland. The Republic of Ireland had per capita incomes that were about 62 per cent of the EU average at the time. The Mediterranean enlargements in the 1980s to include Greece, Spain, and Portugal (all relatively poor states) accentuated the problem of economic divergence.

By the 1980s, the Union as an economic space consisted of a 'golden triangle', which ran from southern England, through France and Germany to northern Italy and southern, western, and northern peripheries. Although committed to harmonious economic development from the outset, the Union did not have to expand its budgetary commitment to poorer Europe until the single market programme in the mid-1980s. At that point, Europe's poorer states successfully linked the economic liberalization of the 1992 programme with an enhanced commitment to greater cohesion in the Union. This commitment manifested itself in a doubling of the financial resources devoted to less prosperous regions, especially those with a per capita income less than 75 per cent of the EU average (see Table 4.2). In addition, four member states whose overall **gross domestic product (GDP)** was low—Spain, Portugal, Greece, and Ireland—were granted extra aid (in the form of a cohesion fund) as a prize for agreeing to monetary union. Of the four states, Ireland was the first to lose its cohesion status.

With eastern enlargement in 2004 and 2007, and the accession of Croatia in 2013, the poverty gap between the member states grew considerably wider. Today GDP per capita in all new member states and candidate countries remains under the EU-28 average (see Table 4.2). Cyprus and Slovenia rank as the richest of the new members, while Romania and Bulgaria—the 2007 entrants—are the poorest. Most candidate countries are even poorer (see Chapter 8).

The promotion of economic and social cohesion will continue to resonate in the politics of integration well into the future. During the 2014–20 financial framework period, cohesion policy accounts for around a third of the total EU budget (see Chapter 5). After eastern enlargement, many of the former recipients of cohesion funds (including Spain and Ireland) were no longer eligible for many EU funds, which were now funnelled towards the newer and poorer member states.

Economic divergence has a significant impact on how the EU works. First, it influences the pecking order in the Union. The poor countries are perceived as *demandeurs* in the Union, dependent on EU subsidies. Second, attitudes

TABLE 4.2 Member states' gross domestic product in 2017

GDP per capita in purchasing power standards (PPS)

European Union average	100		
Luxembourg	267	Malta	95
Austria	126	Slovenia	83
Ireland*	177	Czech Republic	88
Netherlands	128	Portugal	77
Sweden	124	Slovakia	77
Denmark	125	Greece	67
Germany	123	Lithuania	75
Belgium	118	Estonia	74
Finland	109	Hungary	67
France	105	Poland	69
UK	108	Latvia	65
Italy	96	Croatia	59
Cyprus	81	Romania	59
Spain	92	Bulgaria	48

Notes: *Per capita PPS is not a good indicator for Ireland as the volume of foreign direct investment in the economy inflates it. Gross national income (GNI) is more reflective of actual wealth.

Source: Eurostat, at http://ec.europa.eu/eurostat/tgm/table.do?tab=table&init=1&language=en&pcode=tec00114&plugin=1

towards the size and distribution of the EU budget are influenced by contrasting views between net beneficiaries and net contributors. With the growth of the EU budget, a distinct 'net contributors club' emerged in the Union, led by Germany but joined also by the UK, the Netherlands, Austria, Sweden, Finland, and Denmark. The departure of the UK from the Union raises challenging issues for the future of the EU budget and its capacity to redistribute once the 2020 funding period ends. The net contributors are committed to controlling increases in the EU budget and limiting the budgetary costs of cohesion. As more states become net contributors, this club is set to grow. The poor countries as beneficiaries of financial transfers tend to argue for larger budgetary resources and additional instruments.

Third, relative wealth influences attitudes towards EU regulation, notably in environmental and social policy. The richer states have more stringent, developed systems of regulation that impose extra costs on their productive industries. They thus favour the spread of higher standards of regulation to peripheral Europe. By contrast, the poorer states, in their search for economic development, often want to avoid imposing the costs of high standard regulation on their industries. Overall, environmental and social standards have risen in Europe, particularly in peripheral Europe, but not to the extent desired by the wealthier states.

State structure

The internal constitutional structure of a member state has an impact on how it operates in the EU, and not just in terms of whether it has a Presidential or parliamentary-led system. The Union of 28 has three federal states—Germany, Austria, and Belgium. Others are unitary states or quasi-unitary, although the line is not always easy to draw. Unitary states can have subnational governments, self-governing regions, and autonomous communities. For example, Spain and the UK are in some ways de facto federations. Moreover, their devolution settlements are under considerable strain arising from the growth of both Catalan and Scottish nationalism. The subnational units in all three federal states have played a significant role in the constitutional development of the Union. The German Länder, in particular, insisted in the 1990s that they be given an enhanced say in German European policy. They have been advocates of subsidiarity (see Box 2.2) and the creation of the European Committee of the Regions. In the 1992 Maastricht Treaty, they won the right to send Länder ministers and officials to represent Germany in the Council of ministers when matters within their competence are discussed. Representatives of the German and Austrian Länder, representatives of the Belgian regions and cultural communities, as well as ministers of the Scottish government now sit at the Council table and can commit their national governments. The Brexit process is particularly difficult for Scotland as a majority of its electorate voted to Remain (62 per cent) and the exit of the UK has implications for the distribution of powers within the state (see Chapter 10).

In addition to direct representation, there has been an explosion of regional and local offices in Brussels from the mid-1980s onwards (Tatham and Thau 2014). Increasingly, state and regional governments, local authorities, and cities feel the need for direct representation in Brussels. Their offices act as a conduit of information from the EU to the subnational level within the member states. They engage in tracking EU legislation, lobbying for grants, and seeking partners for European projects. Not unexpectedly, there can be tension between national governments and the offices that engage in para-diplomacy in the Brussels arena (see Tatham 2013).

Economic ideology

Much of what the EU does is designed to create the conditions of enhanced economic integration through market building. The manner in which this economic liberalization has developed has been greatly influenced by the dominant economic and social paradigms of the member states. Different visions of the proper balance between public and private power, or between the state and market have left their traces on how the EU works. Hall (2014) has explored how different types of capitalism—export-led growth models in northern EU economies and demand-led growth models in southern EU economies—shaped both the nature of Eurozone economies in the years leading up to the crisis and subsequent policy responses.

All six founding member states might be regarded as adhering to a continental or Christian democratic model of capitalism. Yet, there are important differences amongst them. For instance, France traditionally has supported far more interventionist public policies than the German economic model would tolerate. But differences between France and Germany fade in comparison to differences between continental capitalism and the Anglo-Saxon tradition. The accession of the UK in 1973 and the deregulatory policies of successive Conservative governments brought the so-called Anglo-Saxon economic paradigm into the Union. The UK has been a supporter of deregulation and economic liberalization in the Union but not always of reregulation at Union level, particularly in the social and environmental fields. The UK's departure will alter the balance between different economic paradigms in the Union by reducing the weight of the economic liberals.

The Anglo-Saxon tradition, however, has always been somewhat balanced by the accession of the Nordic states with a social democratic tradition of economic governance and social provision, combined with a strong belief in market liberalization. The Anglo-Saxon economic model gained further ground with the 2004 and 2007 enlargements. The Eastern states generally favour a more liberal economic agenda. They were instrumental in pushing for a more liberal services directive in 2006. However, as Goetz (2005) argues, the new member states brought a diverse set of interests to EU policy-making and intra-regional cooperation between them is weak, making any notion of an 'eastern bloc' more myth than reality.

A battle of ideas continues in the Union, based on competing views about the right balance between state and market, the role of the EU in regulation, and questions of economic governance more generally. These differences were sharply exposed during the 2010 financial crisis when it became apparent that the public finances of a number of member states, notably Greece, Spain, Portugal, Cyprus, Italy, and Ireland, were on an unsustainable trajectory. In some cases, this situation arose because of problems in their banking systems. Following considerable disagreement, the (then) 16 euro member states (with Germany as primary paymaster) agreed to €500 billion of loan guarantees and emergency funding to address the Greek crisis. Following the intervention in Greece, three further member states were rescued: Ireland, Portugal, and Cyprus. Spain received assistance for its banking system and Italy came under very strong market pressure. One important result was unprecedented involvement by the President of the European Central Bank (ECB), Mario Draghi, who pledged in June 2012 to do whatever it took to support the euro (see Matthijs 2016). His intervention appeared to calm the financial markets and ended the acute phase of the euro crisis. Nevertheless, efforts to construct new rules and institutions to regulate systemically important banks and handle any future fiscal problems in Eurozone member states are ongoing (see Wolff 2017).

Integration preference

The terms pro- and anti-European, or 'good' European and awkward partner, are frequently bandied about to describe national attitudes towards the EU. The UK, Denmark, Poland, Hungary, and the Czech Republic are usually portrayed as reluctant Europeans (see Table 4.3). While not entirely false, such categorizations disguise several facts. First, attitudes towards European integration are moulded not just by nationality but also (and often more powerfully) by factors such as socioeconomic class, age, or educational attainment. Second, in all states we find a significant split between the attitudes of those who might be called 'the top decision-makers' and the mass public. A very high proportion of elites accept that their state has benefited from EU membership, and that membership is in their state's national interest. The wider public, in many states, does not share these sentiments. For instance, the comparative Table 4.3 illustrates the particular impact of the economic crisis. Although the percentage of EU citizens feeling that membership is a good thing for their country has increased across the Union since the depths of the crisis in 2011–12, certain countries (including Greece, Italy, and Romania) have seen a further fall in the number of citizens feeling that EU membership is a good thing (Eurobarometer 2016).

During the financial crisis, the decline in public support for the EU was particularly sharp in those states—Ireland, Spain, Greece, and Italy—that confronted a public finance crisis as well as in Germany, the member state that was asked to provide the most aid to those states. Most of the new member states were also characterized by a sharp decline in public support for the EU. Attitudes towards the EU in the UK were particularly salient as the 2013 pledge by Prime Minister David Cameron to hold an 'in or out' referendum on the question of membership led to UK voters opting to leave the EU in June 2016 (Chapter 10). The decision by a large and important state to choose exit from the Union over a seat at the table was a major shock to the EU.

Some states certainly are more enthusiastic about certain developments (say, enlargement or greater transparency) than others. But there is often an important difference between rhetoric and reality in EU negotiations. Some member states, including France and Germany, tend to use grandiose language in calling for deeper integration. However, around the negotiating table they are often the ones blocking an increase in qualified majority voting (QMV) on issues such as trade or justice and home affairs. Traditionally, the opposite was true for states such as the UK. British ministers and officials were inclined to language that makes them seem reluctant about European integration. Yet, in negotiations on, for example, trade liberalization, they were often in the forefront of more or closer cooperation. In short, member states' attitudes towards integration are far more nuanced than is implied by the labels 'pro' or 'anti' Europe. These are journalistic rather than academic terms.

TABLE 4.3 Public attitudes to EU membership

Member state	Per cent responding that EU membership is a 'good thing'*		
	2007	2011	2016
Netherlands	77	68	72
Ireland	76	63	74
Luxembourg	74	72	81
Spain	73	55	55
Belgium	70	65	65
Poland	67	53	61
Romania	67	57	53
Denmark	66	55	62
Estonia	66	49	66
Germany	65	54	71
Slovakia	64	52	54
EU AVERAGE	57	47	53
Slovenia	58	39	46
Greece	55	38	31
Portugal	55	39	47
Bulgaria	55	48	49
France	52	46	48
Italy	51	41	33
Malta	51	42	58
Sweden	50	56	64
Croatia	N/A	N/A	46
Czech Republic	46	31	32
Cyprus	44	37	34
Finland	42	47	60
UK	39	26	47
Hungary	37	32	47
Latvia	37	25	48
Austria	36	37	37

*Notes: *Question:* 'Generally speaking, do you think that (YOUR COUNTRY)'s membership of the European Union is a good thing, a bad thing, or neither good nor bad?' Note that this question has not been asked since Eurobarometer 75 in August 2011. In the figure for Cyprus, only the interviews conducted in the part of the country controlled by the government of the Republic of Cyprus are recorded.*

Source: Eurobarometer Report 67: Public Opinion in the European Union (Nov 2007), at http://ec.europa.eu/public_opinion/archives/eb/eb67/eb67_en.pdf; Eurobarometer Report 75: Public Opinion in the European Union (Aug 2011), at http://ec.europa.eu/public_opinion/archives/eb/eb75/eb75_publ_fr.pdf; Eurobarometer Report 86 (Sep/Oct 2016), as reported in http://www.europarl.europa.eu/pdf/eurobarometre/2016/parlemetre/eb86_1_parlemeter_synthesis_en.pdf.

An important feature of EU treaty change since the early 1990s has been the greater frequency with which states have been allowed to 'opt out' of certain policy developments. This dynamic in European integration is labelled differentiated integration
in the scholarly literature (Schimmelfennig 2015). For example, Denmark has opted
out of the euro, parts of the Schengen Agreement on the free movement of people,
and defence aspects of the Common Foreign and Security Policy (CFSP). Similarly,
the UK is not part of the euro, and neither it nor Ireland is a full participant in
Schengen. Of the newer member states, only Slovenia, Slovakia, Malta, Lithuania,
Cyprus, Estonia, and Latvia are thus far part of the Eurozone. Membership and
non-membership of the Eurozone became more significant as the euro states had to
engage in deeper policy integration to combat the euro crisis (see Box 4.2).

BOX 4.2   Rescuing the euro

The 2008 global financial crisis morphed into a Eurozone crisis in autumn 2009
when it became apparent that Greece had a serious public finance crisis.
Between December 2009 and May 2010, the euro states, particularly Germany,
struggled politically to come to terms with the consequences of the crisis and the
need to bail out Greece. Eventually, the situation within the Eurozone became sufficiently serious that Greece was rescued on 2 May. Full programmes for Ireland,
Portugal, and Cyprus followed. Spain avoided a full bailout but received support
for its banks. The Eurozone crisis underlined the deep interdependence among
member states in the single currency.

The crisis was one of the most serious every experienced in the EU. The Union's
laws, institutions, and policy capacity were stretched to the limit. During the crisis, Germany emerged as the dominant state as its support was necessary for
every rescue. German Chancellor Angela Merkel became the leading politician
in the EU. Policy developed along two tracks. First, there were bailouts for the most
troubled countries. They became 'programme countries' subject to very strict
conditionality from the so-called Troika: the Commission, ECB, and International Monetary Fund (IMF). Second, the Eurozone developed a range of new policy
instruments to prevent future crises from re-occurring and agreed very stringent
new laws to govern member state public finances. These laws were known as the
'Six Pack', 'Two Pack', and Fiscal Compact. Taken together, these laws amounted
to much stronger surveillance by the Commission and other member states of the
public finances and macro-economic management of each member state. In
addition, the Eurozone states agreed to establish a banking union bringing financial supervision under the control of the ECB.

The severity of the crisis pitted the creditor states in the North against the debt-
or states in the South (Ireland became an honourary member of Club Med). The
latter—Greece, Portugal, Spain, Italy, and Ireland—bore the brunt of the austerity
policies that were imposed. The crisis also created tension between the members
of the euro and those outside. For extended discussions of the crisis, see Authers
(2012); Marsh (2013); Pisani-Ferry (2014); Stiglitz (2016); and Varoufakis (2016).

When member states hold referendums on European treaties (of which there have been over 30) and on policy issues, there is often a blurring of the boundaries between domestic politics and the future of the EU. The Constitutional Treaty was the subject of four referendums in 2005 and was defeated in two held in France and the Netherlands. This round was followed by the defeat of the first referendum on the Lisbon Treaty in 2008 in Ireland. Three dramatic referendum defeats in as many years meant that the stakes in the second Irish referendum held in October 2009 were very high. Referendums have posed significant political tests for the EU over the last 30 years and are becoming an important political mechanism in European integration (Hobolt 2009; Box 4.3).

BOX 4.3   How it really works: Referendums

National referendums—or direct democracy—on European issues are a significant feature of how member states relate to the EU. In a national referendum on a European treaty or policy, the domestic electorate gets voice on an issue that has consequences for the EU as a whole. Since 1972 there have been 56 EU-related referendums in the member states, of which 62 per cent were on membership and ratification of a major European treaty. Since the coming into force of the Lisbon Treaty in December 2009, there have been nine referendums. This latter number highlights the fact that referendums are a growing feature of EU politics. Since 2009, only two of nine referendums were on the question of EU membership (Croatia 2012 and UK 2016) and only one on the addition of a new European treaty to the EU, namely, the 2012 referendum in Ireland on the Fiscal Compact. All of the others were on single issues. Two referendums were held in Denmark, one on the Patent Court that was carried and the second on opting-in to areas of EU justice and home affairs (JHA) policy that was defeated. Arising from a citizens initiative, the Netherlands held a referendum on the EU–Ukraine Association Agreement (2016), which was defeated. Following the 'No' vote the Netherlands and the EU entered talks on how manage the ratification process in the light of the negative verdict (on a somewhat arcane question). The most significant referendum of the nine was the decision by the UK electorate in June 2016 to leave the EU. This result triggered the Article 50 withdrawal process, which will lead to a UK exit in March 2019. For more on referendums in the EU, see Hobolt (2009).

Taken together, the six factors introduced in this section tell us a great deal about how the EU works. Styles of economic governance and levels of wealth have a major influence on national approaches to European regulation, and on just how much regulation each state favours at EU level. A hostile or favourable public opinion will help determine the integration preferences of particular states. How states represent themselves in EU business is partially determined by their state structure and domestic institutions. The point is that EU member states vary across several cross-cutting dimensions, there are different cleavages on different issues, and this mix is part of what makes the EU unique.

Member States in Action

Member states are not the only players in town, but national governments retain a privileged position in the EU. What emerge, as national interests from domestic systems of preference formation, remain central to how the EU works. But member states are not unitary actors. Rather, each consists of a myriad players who project their own preferences in the Brussels arena. National administrations, the wider public service, key interests (notably, business, trades unions, farming organizations, and other societal interests) all seek voice and representation in EU politics. A striking feature of European integration is the extent to which national actors have been drawn out of the domestic arena into the Brussels system of policy-making.

As Chapter 3 highlighted, the national and the European meet in a formal sense in the Council, the EU institution designed to give voice and representation to national preferences. On a midweek day, there are usually around 20 official meeting rooms in use in the Council building (named after the sixteenth-century Belgian philosopher, Justus Lipsius), apart from the month of August, when the Brussels system goes on holiday. Formal meetings are supplemented by bilateral meetings on the margins of Council meetings, informal chats over espressos, and by media briefings. Thus considerable backroom dealing, arbitrage, and informal politics augment the formal system of policy-making (see Chapter 6). In the evenings, national officials (from some member states more than others) frequent the many bars near the Rond Point Schuman, the junction in Brussels where several EU institutions are housed. The evening busses to Zaventem (the Brussels airport) are often full of national officials making their way back to their capitals after a long day in Council working groups. Those within earshot can pick up good anecdotal evidence of how the EU actually works when member state officials pick over the details of EU proposals.

All member states have built up a cadre of EU specialists in their diplomatic services and domestic administrations who are the 'boundary managers' between the national and the European. Most are at home in the complex institutional and legal processes of the Union, have well-used copies of the EU treaties, may read *Agence Europe* (a daily bulletin on European affairs) and *Politico.EU* every morning, and know their field and the preferences of their negotiating partners. The EU is a system that privileges those with an intimate knowledge of how the Union's policy process works and how business is conducted in the Council, the EP, and the Commission.

National representatives in Brussels seek to exploit their political, academic, sectoral, and personal networks to the full. With more member states, a widening agenda, and advanced communications technology, there has been a discernible increase in horizontal interaction between the member states at all levels—prime-ministerial, ministerial, senior official, and desk officer. Each prime minister and the French president has a Sherpa whose job it is to maintain contact with counterparts across Europe and to prepare for the multi-lateral and bilateral meetings of their political masters. Specialists forge and maintain links with their counterparts in other member states on a continuous basis. Deliberations are no longer left primarily to meetings at working group level in Brussels. Sophisticated networking is part and parcel of the Brussels game. Officials who have long experience of it build up extensive personal contacts and friendships in the system.

In addition to a cadre of Brussels insiders, many government officials in national capitals find that their work also has a European dimension. For most national officials, however, interaction with the EU is sporadic and driven by developments within a particular sector. A company law specialist may have intense interaction with the EU while a new directive is being negotiated, but may then have little involvement until the same directive is up for renegotiation.

The nature of EU membership demands that all member states must commit resources and personnel to the Union's policy process. Servicing Brussels—by committing time, energy, and resources to EU negotiations—has become more onerous with new areas of policy being added, such as JHA or defence. Once a policy field becomes institutionalized in the EU system, the member states have no choice but to service the relevant committees and Councils. An empty seat at the table undermines the credibility of the state and its commitment to the collective endeavour. Besides, the weakest negotiator is always the one who is absent from the negotiations.

Managing EU Business

All member states engage in internal negotiations and coordination, above all between different national ministries and ministers, in determining what their national position will be in any EU negotiation. The coordination system in most member states is organized hierarchically. National ministers and/or the heads of government will usually act as the arbiter of last resort.

In addition, all member states have either a minister or a state secretary of European affairs. The Ministry of Foreign Affairs plays an important role in all member states, and most central EU coordination takes place here. However, there are a number of member states, such as Finland, where the Prime Minister's Office takes the leading role. With the increasing prominence of EU policy in national administrations, more EU business is generally shifting to the offices of heads of government.

As discussed in Chapter 3, each member state also has a permanent representation in Brussels, a kind of embassy to the EU. In most cases it is the most important and biggest foreign representation the country maintains anywhere in the world.

It is, for example, usually much bigger than an embassy in Washington, DC, or Moscow or a representation to the United Nations. Although the official role of the permanent representation of each member state varies, they all participate actively in several stages of the policy-making process. In certain member states they are the key player in the whole process.

A Community of Values

Article 2 of the Lisbon Treaty codifies the values that are shared by EU member states. The rule of law and related values are fundamental to what it is to be a member state. This credo has been directly threatened by the election of illiberal Eurosceptic politicians to office in two member states. Since the election of Victor Orban as Hungarian prime minister in 2010, the EU has confronted the situation of a member state government openly challenging the foundational values of the EU by attacking civil society organizations and the Central European University (CEU). Developments in Hungary were followed by the election, in 2015, of the Law and Justice Party (PiS) in Poland, which returned to power a government that began to undermine the freedom of its judicial system, media freedom, and civil society organizations (see Sedelmeier 2014; more broadly, Diamond 2015; and Kochenov and Pech 2016). The EU and notably the Commission struggled to respond to having populist authoritarians around the table. In 2016 the Commission launched a dialogue under the Rule of Law Framework (the precursor to Article 7, which can lead to sanctions against a member state) because of the undermining of Poland's Constitutional Tribunal, its highest level court. The Commission also has taken infringement proceedings against the Hungarian government. Article 7 infringement proceedings have not, at the time of writing, been launched. Developments in Hungary and Poland pose an existential challenge to the EU as it is a Union based on law and all member states must trust their partners' political and legal processes. Serious undermining of the EU as a 'community of values' risks undermining the Union from within.

Explaining Member States' Engagement

We have looked at the factors that determine the engagement of different states in the EU, and at the member states in action. What additional purchase do we get from theory in analysing member states in the Union? The relationship between the EU and its member states has been one of the most enduring puzzles in the literature on European integration. From the outset, the impact of EU membership on statehood and individual states has been hotly contested. At issue is whether the EU strengthens, transcends, or transforms its member states. Is the Union simply a creature of its member states? Are they still the masters of the treaties? Or has the EU irrevocably transformed European nation states? The relationship between the

EU and its member states is a live political issue and not simply a point of contention amongst scholars. The theories and approaches introduced in Chapter 1 provide different lenses with which to analyse the member states in the Union.

Liberal intergovernmentalism provides a theoretical framework that enables us to trace the formation of domestic preferences in the member states and then to see how they are bargained in Brussels. It identifies the domestic sources of the underlying preferences and the subsequent process of interstate bargaining. The approach rightly concludes that the EU is an 'institution so firmly grounded in the core interests of national governments that it occupies a permanent position at the heart of the European political landscape' (Moravcsik 1998: 501). This approach is less helpful in tracing the impact of the EU on national preference formation or the cumulative impact of EU membership on its member states. Its focus on one-off bargains provides a snapshot of the Union at any one time rather than a film or 'moving picture' of how membership may generate deep processes of change (see Pierson 1996). Bickerton *et al.* (2015) claim to have adapted a 'new intergovernmentalism' that helps explain the 'integration paradox', whereby European integration has accelerated over the past 20 years without major transfers of power to supranational institutions.

Contemporary theorists who view the EU through the lenses of multi-level (Hooghe and Marks 2003) or supranational governance (Sandholtz and Stone Sweet 1998) emphasize how the national and the European levels of governance have become fundamentally intertwined. Similarly, Bartolini (2005) links the dynamics of European integration to state formation, concluding that the EU represents the latest stage in the emergence and adaption of the European nation state and state system. These approaches point to the influence of supranational institutions—notably the Commission, Court, and Parliament—on the EU and its member states. The EU may be grounded in the core interests of the national governments. But the definition of core interest is influenced by membership of the EU and its continuous effects at the national level. Put another way, the EU has evolved into a political system in its own right that is more than the sum of its member states. Becoming a member state is a step change from being a nation state.

The new institutionalism offers at least two crucial insights concerning member states in the EU political system. First, its emphasis on change over time captures the give-and-take nature of EU negotiations and the manner in which norms and procedures are built up gradually. Second, its concern with path dependency highlights the substantial resources that member states have invested in the Union (Meunier and McNamara 2007; Bulmer 2009). The costs of exit are very high and hence the decision of the UK to leave was a major shock both to the EU and to the UK as each attempts to disentangle itself from the other after 44 years of becoming increasingly intertwined. The EU's approach to managing diversity is to allow for differentiated integration, which may have a functional or territorial dimension, with different subsets of member states integrating in specific policy areas more than have all member states in the Union as a whole. Successive rounds of enlargement have led to increasing differentiation, which is intrinsic to the dynamic of integration.

A policy network approach captures the fragmented and sectorized nature of the EU. It highlights that the degree and nature of national adaptation differs from one policy area to another, and according to the different mix of players involved. Some policy fields, and the networks that preside over them, have been intensely Europeanized (agriculture) while others have not (transport). This approach helps us to gauge such variation and the varying involvement of different layers of government and public and private actors in different EU policy fields.

Finally, social constructivism helps us to analyse how national participants are socialized into the 'rules of the game' that characterize intergovernmental bargaining (Bulmer and Lequesne 2005: 15). For constructivists, national interests are not predetermined but are shaped (or 'constructed') by interaction with EU actors and institutions (see Checkel 1999). In fact, the very identities of individual players in EU negotiations are viewed largely as being constructed within those negotiations, and not fixed, leading constructivists to question whether national identities and interests are gradually being replaced by European ones.

BOX 4.4   How it really works: Decision gridlock?

Taking decisions in a big group is never easy. When the EU almost doubled its membership from 2004–7, many feared that the EU would face permanent gridlock. How did things actually turn out? Studies show that from 2004–6, the amount of legislation decreased compared to the rate prior to the 'big bang' enlargement (Hagemann and De Clerck-Sachsse 2007; Heisenberg 2007). Yet at the same time the EU was able to hammer out compromises at approximately the same pace as before. And the average time from a Commission initiative to an approved legal act remained approximately the same for an EU of 28 as it was for a Union of 15 (Settembri 2007).

However, enlargement has changed the political dynamic of the EU institutions and the role of member states within them. All the main institutions—the Commission, the European Council, the European Parliament, and the Council of ministers—are less cosy than before. There are simply more players around the table. The dynamic of working groups, committees, and the actual Council meetings has also changed. In Council meetings member states no longer have the ability to express their view on all issues all the time. It would simply take too long. Member states raise issues when they have a serious problem.

Every enlargement is preceded by a debate about the EU's capacity to integrate or 'absorb' new member states. The debate is focused on whether the EU's institutions, budget, and policies can accommodate a larger membership. Those who want to slow down enlargement often argue that the EU is not ready to take on board new member states before it has revised its own institutions and working methods. Previous enlargements, however, seem to indicate that while the EU is never fully prepared to enlarge, it manages just the same.

Conclusion

It is impossible to understand how the EU works without understanding its member states and their central role in the establishment and operation of the Union. In turn, the EU has altered the political, constitutional, economic, and policy framework within which the member state governments govern. Becoming a member state is transformative of statehood in Europe. Each enlargement is different and each enlargement has changed the dynamics of the EU (see Chapter 8). Many were afraid that the Union's decision-making would grind to a halt with the enlargements of the 2000s. Generally, it seems that these fears were unfounded. In fact, the pace of EU decision-making was not noticeably slower than before, despite (or perhaps because of) its expansion to 28 member states (see Box 4.4), although it was widely agreed that the Union needed new rules to streamline decision-making to avoid paralysis in the longer term.

All EU member states, along with states that aspire to join the EU, are part of a transnational political process that binds them together in a collective endeavour. Their individual engagement with the Union varies enormously depending on their history, location, size, relative wealth, domestic political system, and attitudes towards the future of the Union. Yet, all member states are actively engaged on a day-to-day basis in Brussels. National ministers, civil servants, and interest groups participate in the Commission's advisory groups, Council working groups, and meetings of the European Council. All member states engage in bilateral relations with each of their partners, the Commission's services, and the Council Presidency in their efforts to influence EU policy-making. In national capitals, officials and ministers must do their homework in preparation for the continuous cycle of EU meetings. National political parties interact with their MEPs. Brussels is thus part and parcel of contemporary governance in Europe. The member states are essential to how the EU works. Being a member of the Union, in turn, makes a state something rather different from an 'ordinary' nation state.

? DISCUSSION QUESTIONS

1. What are the most important features determining EU member state attitudes towards integration?

2. Which is more powerful: the impact of the EU on its member states, or the impact of the member states on the EU?

3. How useful is theory in explaining the role of the member states in the EU?

4. How different are EU member states from 'ordinary' nation states?

FURTHER READING

The literature on the member states of the Union is very diffuse. A good starting point is Bulmer and Lequesne (2012). Jones *et al.* (2012) contains a set of interesting chapters (18 to 22) on the member states and their various cleavages. Other comparative works include Zeff and Pirro (2015) and, specifically on the newer member states, Henderson (2007) and Baun *et al.* (2006). Grimaud (2018) examines the role and influence of the EU's smallest state—Malta—in the EU's decision-making process. Other country-specific studies include Closa and Heywood (2004), Papadimitriou and Phinnemore (2007), and Laffan and O'Mahony (2008). On the role, and importance, of Germany leadership within the EU, see Bulmer (2014) and on the interdependent histories of the EU and Germany, see Bulmer *et al.* (2010). The importance of the Franco-German tandem is evaluated by Krotz and Schild (2013) and Schoeller (2018). Classic discussions of the relationship between statehood and integration include Hoffmann (1966), Milward (2000), Moravcsik (1998) and Bartolini (2005). On the national management of EU business and the impact of the Union on national institutions, see Kassim *et al.* (2001) and Bulmer and Burch (2009). Saurugger (2014) explores the concept of Europeanization—the process through which the EU impacts the domestic level—in times of crisis.

Bartolini S., (2005), *Restructuring Europe: Centre Formation, System Building and Political Restructuring between the Nation State and the European Union* (Oxford and New York: Oxford University Press).

Baun, M., Dürr, J., Marek, D., and Šaradín, P. (2006), 'The Europeanization of Czech Politics', *Journal of Common Market Studies*, 44/2: 249–80.

Bulmer, S. (2014) 'Germany and the Eurozone Crisis: Between Hegemony and Domestic Politics', *West European Politics*, 37/6: 1244–63.

Bulmer, S. and Lequesne, C. (2012), *The Member States of the European Union*, 2nd edn (Oxford and New York: Oxford University Press).

Bulmer, S., Jeffery, C., and Padgett, S. (eds) (2010), *Rethinking Germany and Europe: Democracy and Diplomacy in a Semi-Sovereign State* (Basingstoke: Palgrave Macmillan).

Closa, C. and Heywood, P. S. (2004), *Spain and the European Union* (Basingstoke and New York: Palgrave).

Grimaud, M. (2018), *Small States and EU Governance: Malta in EU Decision-Making Processes* (Basingstoke: Palgrave Macmillan).

Henderson, K. (2007), *The European Union's New Democracies* (London and New York: Routledge).

Hoffmann, S. (1966), 'Obstinate or Obsolete: The Fate of the Nation-State and the Case of Western Europe', *Daedalus* 95/3: 862–915 (reprinted in S. Hoffmann (1995), *The European Sisyphus: Essays on Europe 1964–1994* (Boulder, CO, and Oxford: Westview Press).

Jones, E., Menon, A., and Weatherill, S. (2014), *The Oxford Handbook of the European Union* (Oxford: Oxford University Press).

Kassim, H., Peters, B. G., and Wright, V. (eds) (2001), *The National Co-Ordination of EU Policy: The European Level* (Oxford and New York: Oxford University Press).

Krotz, U. and Schild, J. (2013), *Shaping Europe: France, Germany and Embedded Bilateralism from the Elysee Treaty to Twenty-First Century Politics* (Oxford: Oxford University Press).

Laffan B. and O'Mahony J. (2008), *Ireland in the European Union* (Palgrave: London).

Milward, A. (2000), *The European Rescue of the Nation-State*, 2nd edn (London: Routledge).

Moravcsik, A. (1998), *The Choice for Europe: Social Purpose and State Power from Messina to Maastricht* (Ithaca, NY, and London: Cornell University Press and UCL Press).

Papadimitriou, D. and Phinnemore, D. (2007), *Romania and the European Union* (London and New York: Routledge).

Saurugger, S. (2014), 'Europeanisation in Times of Crisis', *Political Studies*, 12/2: 181–92.

Schoeller, M. (2018), 'The Rise and Fall of Merkozy: Franco-German Bilateralism as a Negotiation Strategy in Eurozone Crisis Management', *Journal of Common Market Studies*, advanced online access, doi: 10.1111/jcms.12704

Zeff, E. and Pirro, E. (2015), *The European Union and the Member States*, 3rd edn (Boulder, CO: Lynne Rienner).

WEB LINKS

- The Institute for European Politics' (Berlin) website features an enormously useful 'EU 28 watch' which offers a round-up of current thinking on EU policies and issues in all the member states: http://www.eu-28watch.org/

- The best place to search for websites of the member and candidate states' national administrations is https://europa.eu/european-union/about-eu/countries_en

- Other useful links can also be found on the homepage of the European Commission, http://ec.europa.eu/index_en.htm

 Visit the Ancillary Resource Centre that accompanies this book for additional material: www.oup.com/uk/kenealy5e/

PART III

POLICIES AND POLICY-MAKING

CHAPTER 5

Key Policies

John Peterson with Alberta Sbragia and Francesco Stolfi

Summary

European Union policies affect the lives of millions of people in Europe and beyond. Because of the variety of actors involved, variance in policy capacity in different areas, and the EU's constant evolution, policy-making is a challenging but fascinating area of study. This chapter describes some of the most important areas of EU policy-making. We begin by explaining how EU policy-making differs from national policy-making, and then describe the most important policies aimed at building the **internal market** and limiting its potentially negative impact on individuals, society, and the environment. We show how these policies are made and also why and how they matter.

Introduction: Policies in the EU

The EU sets policies in so many areas that it is difficult to think about national policy-making in Europe in isolation from Brussels. While the euro—the common currency used by 19 of the EU's 28 member states (as of 2018)—is perhaps the most visible manifestation of European integration, a diverse set of public policies affecting the everyday lives of Europeans are shaped by the decisions taken at the EU level. Agriculture, environmental standards, consumer protection, international trade, and the movement of goods, services, labour, and capital across borders are just some of the policies either made or affected by decisions taken in Brussels.

Yet the role of the EU should not be over-estimated. It is not a 'superstate' exercising control over all areas of policy. The Union is a selective policy-maker whose power varies significantly across policy areas. Most of the policies for which it is responsible are related to markets (see Box 5.1): some build markets, some protect producers from **market** forces, some try to cushion the impact of market forces.

The differentiated role of the EU across policy areas is not unusual if we compare it to federal systems, where power is shared between the national and subnational level (see Box 5.1). In such systems the national level may not be allowed to legislate in certain areas, leaving policy discretion to the constituent units. Canadians, Australians, and Americans, for example, take for granted that many decisions affecting their lives will be taken at the state or provincial levels. In the EU, citizens are becoming accustomed to such a system of differentiated policy responsibilities. Just as Washington lets each state decide whether to allow the death penalty within its borders, the EU does not legislate on Ireland's abortion policy, Sweden's alcohol control policy, or Spain's policy on bullfighting. Citizens of a federal polity accept that at least some unequal treatment comes with living in a federation. In a similar vein, it matters a great deal—and will continue to matter—where one lives within the EU.

However, the impact of the EU is such that its member states are, in many ways, much more alike now than they were 60 years ago. In certain policy areas, especially economic ones, member state governments as well as private firms either have had to engage in new activities (such as environmental protection) or alternatively change their traditional practices. To illustrate, at the time of writing the EU was set to propose that all plastic packaging in Europe be recyclable by 2030. And the introduction of the euro in 19 member states not only changed the landscape of monetary affairs but also made EU citizens aware of that changed landscape on an everyday basis.

The world of money and business has been changed by EU policies in very fundamental ways, but so have many related areas. Environmental protection, gender equality in the workplace, and occupational health and safety have all moved the EU towards a system in which many of the negative consequences of market activity are addressed in Brussels rather than in national capitals. This expansion in the EU's remit is the result not of some well-orchestrated plan but rather the product of constant problem solving, bargaining and experimentation (see Chapter 1). The crisis that engulfed the euro in the early 2010s is just one case amongst many where decisions made by the Union's institutions and member states under the pressure of events developing by the hour will probably have lasting consequences on the shape and nature of European integration.

BOX 5.1   Key concepts and terms

Benchmarking is the use of comparisons with other states or organizations (for instance on pension reform or employment practices) with the aim of improving performance by learning from the experience of others.

A **directive** is the most common form of EU legislation. It stipulates the ends to be achieved (say, limiting the emissions of a harmful pollutant) but allows each member state to choose the form and method for achieving that end. It can be contrasted with a regulation, which is directly binding and specifies means as well as end.

The **Eurozone** refers to the countries that are part of the **Economic and Monetary Union (EMU)**. EMU was launched in 1999 (with notes and coins entering into circulation in 2002) and included 19 member states as of 2018. All remaining new EU member states are expected to join once their economies are ready, with the exception of Denmark, which has an opt-out from EMU (the UK also has an opt-out but it is scheduled to leave the EU in March 2019).

Federalism is a constitutional arrangement in which the power to make decisions and execute policy is divided between national and subnational levels of government. In a federal system, both national and subnational units wield a measure of final authority in their own spheres and neither level can alter or abolish the other.

A **market** is a system of exchange that brings together buyers and sellers of goods and services. In most markets, money is used as means of exchange. Markets are regulated by price fluctuations that reflect the balance of supply and demand. To function properly, markets require the existence of law, regulation, and property rights. Virtually all markets are subject to some sort of regulation.

Non-tariff barriers refer to regulations, such as national standards or requirements (for instance, health and safety requirements) that increase the cost of imports and have the equivalent effect of tariffs. Often these regulations serve bona fide social purposes (such as the protection of the environment or of consumer health), but in practice also protect national producers from foreign competition.

Public policy is a course of action (decisions, actions, rules, laws, and so on) or inaction taken by government in regard to some public problem or issue.

This chapter introduces some of the EU's key policies. Since economic integration is at the core of what the EU does, we focus on economic and related policies. How open EU policies are to a large set of actors varies considerably. But a constant across policies is a preference for consensus building. While the remit of the EU has dramatically increased over time, one price of seeking consensus is that capacity remains limited in many policy areas compared to that of 'traditional' nation states.

Key Features of EU Policies

Differences between national and EU policies

EU policies differ in some important respects from policies decided at the national level. At a basic level, EU policies are different because it and its member states are structured and financed very differently. These varying financial structures lead to three main differences between national and EU policies:

- with a few exceptions, EU policies involve the spending of very little money, whereas national policy often involves spending a lot of it;
- the distance between those who formulate policy and those who actually execute it is far greater in the EU than it is in most of the national systems;
- the EU is active in a much narrower range of policies than are national governments.

We examine each of these differences in more detail below.

Money

One way to understand the EU's relative poverty in public finance is to compare its budget with the budgets of central governments in its member states. In 2017 the EU budget consisted of a little less than €158 billion of spending commitments. While that sounds like (and is) a lot of money, it pales by comparison to the national budgets of larger member states such as the UK (roughly €918 billion in 2017), France (about €1.1 *trillion* in 2017) and Germany (close to €1.2 *trillion* in 2017). It also pales when compared to the federal budget of the United States (around €3.3 *trillion* in 2017), which is over 20 times larger than the EU's budget.

The Union therefore relies on the power of law rather than money to carry out most of its policies. The EU's relative lack of money shapes what the content of policies can be. It has only a small number of policy areas that cost a great deal, whereas national systems typically have a large number of expensive policy areas, including those funding the welfare state. The Union could not, for example, finance health care for EU citizens or provide old age pensions or finance systems of public education. Overwhelmingly, the EU regulates economic activity: that is, it subjects it to rules and standards. However, in spite of the relatively small size of its budget, anytime the EU makes decisions about spending money, things inevitably turn contentious (Neheider and Santos 2011; see Box 5.2).

Legislation vs execution

In most national systems, a national government makes policy decisions and then has numerous ways of ensuring that those policies are executed 'on the ground'. Although that link is sometimes far from direct, it is far tighter in most national systems when EU policy is involved. Policy decided in Brussels faces several hurdles before it can be successfully executed on the ground.

BOX 5.2   How it really works: Budget bargaining

Unlike national governments, the EU cannot run a deficit; its revenues limit what it can spend. Various economic formulae are used to determine overall budget revenue (which comes mostly from customs duties (taxes on non-EU imports), value added tax, and national contributions) and budget allocation (who gets what?). Germany remains the 'paymaster of Europe', being by far the largest net contributor to the European coffers, followed by France and Italy.

On the expenditure side, two documents are important. First, the Financial Framework, decided by unanimity in the Council and with Parliament's consent, sets the overall expenditure level and how it is divided between various policy areas. Second, the annual budget, co-decided by majorities in Parliament and Council, determines the detailed amounts spent on every item each year within the ceilings.

Formulae aside, the EU's budget is a result of politics more than mathematics. Reaching a decision over the financial framework is usually highly contentious and a decidedly intergovernmental affair. Although the absolute amounts involved are not large—the overall EU budget equals only around 1 per cent of the member states' GDP—no government wants to appear weak in the eyes of its voters during budget negotiations. Moreover, the amounts involved can mean a great deal to strong domestic constituencies, especially in the case of the CAP.

The negotiations for the 2014–20 framework were especially acrimonious. For the first time, the long-term budget of the EU was reduced, by 3 per cent compared to the previous seven-year budget. Besides irritating France, which argued for increased spending to counter the effects of economic recession, the agreement was harshly condemned by the president of the **European Parliament (EP)** (Schultz 2013).

The battle of the 2021–7 budget was made no less bitter by the settling of the UK's 'divorce bill' in late 2017. The UK's departure created a funding gap of around €12 billion post-2020. And fists threatened to fly over Commission plans to link the receipt of EU funding to a 'functioning and independent judiciary' at a time when both Poland and Hungary were accused of judicial reforms that undermined the rule of law. The stakes were high: Poland was the largest recipient of EU cohesion funding and Hungary received around 3 per cent of its GDP from the EU budget, the highest of any member state.

The first step is known as 'transposition'. That is, laws (known as **directives**, see Box 5.1) adopted by the Council of ministers, and (usually) the EP, need to be 'transposed' into national legal codes before they can be executed by the member state's public administration or shape the behaviour of private actors in significant ways. The Commission enforces transposition to ensure it is timely and legislation is implemented correctly. Member states that fail to transpose directives properly can be taken before the European Court of Justice (ECJ). Although transposition has become increasingly timely, differences still exist among the member states. Interestingly, in this area the division between older and newer member states seems not to apply: the EU's Single Market Scoreboard—designed to encourage timely transposition of internal market legislation—shows on the latest available data (for 2016, Commission 2017) that the three best and the three worst performers include both new and old member states (Malta, Denmark, and Slovakia being the best; and Portugal, Cyprus, and Estonia the worst).

In sum, Union policies do not become 'policy' at the national level uniformly across member states. For example, a directive transposed in Finland shortly after its adoption in Brussels may not be transposed in France or Greece until several years later. These differences illustrate that while Brussels formulates and adopts policy, its actual impact is shaped by national systems of governance. National governments play a central role because they hold a monopoly of power in the actual execution of most policies adopted in Brussels. The EU has no administrative presence within the member states. While the Commission, has 'delegations' in all national capitals, and even some subnational ones, they are not tasked with monitoring the execution of EU law. The Commission thus relies on reports about violations from citizens, firms, and non-governmental organizations. Even then, it first tries to persuade errant governments, taking them to Court only as a last resort. But it does take member states to Court. For example, in July 2017 the Commission referred Slovenia to the Court of Justice for a failure to transpose directives concerning national budgetary rules into domestic law (Commission 2017).

Difficulties surrounding execution and monitoring mean that policies that affect a large set of actors are less likely to be executed uniformly than policies that affect a few. For example, environmental policy, which attempts to shape the behaviour of huge numbers of both public and private actors, is executed with a tremendous degree of variability across the Union. By contrast, the Commission's decisions about mergers and acquisitions are implemented uniformly. The number of firms affected by any single Commission decision is very small and a non-complying firm is very visible.

Jurisdiction

A third difference between EU and national policies concerns policy competencies (see Box 5.3). While certainly broader than other international organizations, the EU's policy remit is narrower than that of national governments. Health care, urban regeneration, family assistance, old age pensions, public health, industrial relations, child care, poverty alleviation, abortion, prison administration, and education, for example, generally are not subject to EU legislation because the Union lacks competence in these areas. Other areas remain under national control because of decision-making rules that apply. In taxation, for example, the decision-making rule is unanimity. The same was traditionally the case for energy policy, although pressures for a common EU energy policy are increasingly powerful and the Lisbon Treaty made EU competence 'clearer and more explicit, but . . . not wider' (Piris 2010: 319). But since the member states have been unable to agree on any single policy, those policy areas effectively remain under national control.

Recently, various 'soft' (that is, non-legal) measures such as **benchmarking** (see Box 5.1) or the 'open method of coordination' (OMC) of national policies—based on league tables that try to show best (and worst) practice—have been used to encourage national governments to address issues such as their pension burden. Generally, however, the welfare state and the direct provision of social services are primarily under national control.

Policies that have a moral or cultural dimension also remain under national control. Ireland's constitution banned abortion except when a mother's life is at risk, for example, and the EU did not have the power to tell the Irish either to change their abortion law or to keep it (although the Irish government held a referendum on the matter in 2018, which resulted in a majority vote to revoke the ban). The Swedish and Finnish alcohol control system has been under strain due to the ability of individual revellers to bring liquor in from other EU countries. But alcohol control policy in both Sweden and Finland is under national control.

BOX 5.3   The policy competences of the EU

Policy competence refers to the legal authority to act in particular policy areas. After the Lisbon Treaty, policy areas are divided into three categories depending on the degree of EU competence: (1) exclusive competence; (2) shared competence between the EU and the member states; (3) competence to support, coordinate, and supplement the actions of the member states.

1. The EU has exclusive competence in few, but important, policy areas: external trade in goods and services; monetary policy (for the Eurozone); customs; and conservation of marine resources.

2. Shared competences include agriculture and fisheries, justice, environmental policy, consumer protection, mergers and acquisitions, research, development aid, transport policy, energy, visas, asylum, and immigration.

3. Finally, policy areas exist where the member states are the main players, even if the EU is involved in general coordination or is engaged in specific projects. Education (think of the Erasmus programme), culture, sport, employment, public health, and research fall into this domain.

Some policy areas are difficult to place in one of these categories because lines between shared and member state competencies are blurred. For example, in foreign and security policies it is often unclear how much weight the EU has because member states must allocate the resources necessary to execute policy.

However, the EU often has important indirect effects beyond the immediate scope of its competencies. For instance, energy policy remains broadly under national control. However, the European energy market is being liberalized, as the EU requires national governments to allow consumers more choice of electricity suppliers. Similarly, the commitment of the EU to meet the Kyoto Protocol on climate change stimulated the creation of a European market where industrial producers trade carbon emissions permits, with the purpose of limiting overall emissions. Moreover, education remains under national control, but the EU has been a prime mover in encouraging university students to study in another EU member state. Commission programmes on student mobility have led to major changes in European universities' administrative structures and have encouraged them to embrace greater cross-national standardization in degree programmes (such as the length of time required to receive a degree). The lack of formal competence at the EU level does not mean that Brussels lacks influence in shaping the terms of debate within a policy area. The programmes that Brussels adopts, while not legally binding, are very important in providing incentives to national and subnational governments to carry out certain activities.

The primacy of economic integration

The EU's unique history and development has privileged some policy areas as important. As Chapter 2 explained, in the 1950s European states chose to defend each other within a transatlantic rather than a European organization (NATO includes Canada and the US). Defense and foreign policy were not central to the integration process and have become salient only recently (see Chapter 9).

By contrast, economic cooperation was viewed as a politically acceptable way of increasing integration while laying the groundwork for political cooperation in the future. Economic policy areas thus have been privileged from the beginning. The 1957 Treaty of Rome, by calling for a customs union and a common market (now referred to as a single or internal market), steered European integration towards liberalizing cross-border trade, a unitary external trade policy, and the free movement of capital, goods, services, and labour. The centrality of that effort symbolizes the importance that economic integration has within the EU (see Mariniello *et al.* 2015 for an overview of the development of the EU single market).

'Market-building' Policies

The focus on liberalization and creating a single market highlights the EU's concern with 'market building' and what is sometimes termed 'negative integration'. Building markets involves both *removing* barriers to trade and carrying out regulatory reform. So **negative integration** includes eliminating various tariff and **non-tariff barriers** (see Box 5.1) to trade, regulatory reform in economic regulation, and ensuring that competition among firms is encouraged. The goal is to facilitate cross-border economic transactions with the expectation that the resulting greater efficiency will lead to higher levels of prosperity (mostly through lower prices) for the citizens of Europe. This same aim is pursued globally within the World Trade Organization (WTO).

The political economy of EU member states has been profoundly affected by the privileging of economic policies (Sbragia 2001). Policies adopted in Brussels usu-ally 'pre-empt' national policies and the EU is said to have 'exclusive competence'. Monetary policy falls under this category, although it only applies to the members of the **Eurozone** (see Box 5.1).

In general, the negative integration that characterizes the EU is far more pene-trating than that found at the global (WTO) level or in other regional arrange-ments such as the North American Free Trade Agreement (NAFTA) (Söderbaum and Sbragia 2010). The EU's ambitions in 'market building' are serious and their scope very wide. The foundation of the single market is formed by the 'four free-doms'—freedom in the movement of capital, goods, services, and labour. However, a single market as envisaged by the founders of the Community does not occur simply by removing obstacles to trade. A whole host of interventions must be put into place to ensure that the hoped-for market will operate smoothly and efficiently. The construction of the European market has led to such widespread regulation from Brussels that Majone (1999) has termed the EU a 'regulatory state'. Whereas a welfare state engages in redistribution and spends a lot of money in providing social welfare (such as social security), a regulatory state primarily passes legisla-tion that regulates the behaviour of economic actors. The onset of the Eurozone crisis has led some observers to question whether the EU is now moving beyond a regulatory state because of new policy demands to help stabilize troubled Eurozone economies and to engage more actively in fiscal policy (Caporaso *et al.* 2015).

The development of a far-reaching EU regulatory regime has led to complaints from those affected by such regulation, negatively affecting the legitimacy of the EU among European voters (Schmidt 2013). Firms often complain that the EU over-regulates, fails to legislate fast enough to keep up with rapid technological change, or that a truly internal market does not exist. To illustrate, more than 80 per cent of the chairpersons of top (FTSE 100) British companies surveyed in 2014 backed the Conservative Party's determination to renegotiate the terms of the UK's EU membership, with most citing a desire for economic policy reforms (*Financial Times*, 28 July 2014). The battle cry of the Leave campaign ahead of the UK vote to leave the EU in 2016 was, tellingly, 'Take Back Control' (see Chapter 10).

Competition policy

One of the most important market-building powers given to the EU—the Commission specifically—is in competition policy. The Commission operates independently in this area, and the Council of ministers is not usually involved in policy decisions. In essence, competition policy—known as anti-trust policy in the US—is about encouraging competition among firms and battling monopolistic or oligopolistic practices or any privileging of national producers over those in other EU member states. The requirements can be tough and competition policy poses particular challenges for newer member states. Moving from economies that were largely under public control to ones in which the market is dominant has been difficult, and the rigour of the EU's competition policy has made that transition even more onerous.

The Commission has authority to rule on many mergers and acquisitions, fight cartels, and rule on the appropriateness of state aid given by national or regional authorities to firms. In this area, the Commission is an international actor as well as a EU actor, and its Directorate-General (DG) for Competition has become one of the most powerful, and controversial, competition authorities in the world (Aydin and Thomas 2012; Damro and Guay 2016). The Commission even has the power to sanction US firms with extensive operations in Europe even if American anti-trust authorities have approved them. To illustrate, the Commission vetoed the proposed merger between General Electric and Honeywell, fined Microsoft €780 million for abuse of dominant position and Intel a staggering €1.06 billion. In 2014 it issued a decision mandating that Google modify how it displays its search results, with the outcome that searches in Europe produce different results than searches done elsewhere in the world.

Trade associations and firms as well as national authorities and ministers (sometimes, prime ministers and presidents) lobby, especially informally, before decisions on specific competition cases. However, the Commission needs to engage in far less negotiation than is required in other policy domains and sometimes has turned a deaf ear to lobbying. In this area, DG Competition and the commissioner for competition are the central actors.

Commercial (trade) policy

The key goal of the Treaty of Rome was to create a common market across national borders. The objective required liberalizing national markets (that is, allowing imports to compete with domestically produced goods), which had been heavily protected for decades. Over time, national economies in Europe have become far more interdependent. Trade within the EU accounts for about two-thirds of the overall trade of the member states. However, trade with countries outside the Union is still very important for many EU member states.

The application of a single external tariff (applied to non-EU producers) in the late 1960s led to the decision that the European Economic Community (EEC; as the EU was then known) would speak with one voice in international trade negotiations. The Treaty of Rome gave the EEC competence in international trade negotiations in trade in goods. The Commission was granted the power to act as sole negotiator for the Community in world trade talks. That power was strengthened in the Treaty of Nice, which gave the Commission the right to negotiate (with certain exceptions) trade in services. However, the competence to *decide* the EU's position in international trade negotiations was given to the Council of the European Union, not the Commission acting on its own. So while the Commission is the negotiator, it is the Council, and thus ultimately the member states, that defines the Commission's negotiating mandate. Member states differ in their capacity to exert control over the EU's trade policy, often depending on the strength of their domestic administrative capacity (Adriaensen 2016). The relationship between the member states and the Commission is some-times conflictual, especially when powerful national constituencies see their interests threatened by trade liberalization. Moreover, the Commission itself is sometimes internally divided, with DG Agriculture, for instance, being more pro-tectionist than DG Trade (Conceição-Heldt 2011).

Economic and Monetary Union

At Maastricht, EU member states decided to create an EMU, with a common cur-rency and centralized responsibility for monetary policy. For the first time since the Roman Empire, Western Europe was to have a common currency. It was thought that a common currency would help keep a unified Germany tied to the project of European integration, increase economic efficiency in the EU and thereby raise standards of living, and develop a sense of European identity (see Marsh 2011). A common currency requires a single central bank in charge of monetary policy, and the European Central Bank (ECB) was created to run monetary policy with the goal of price stability (anti-inflation) as its top priority.

Part of the bargain that underpinned moving to a single currency by 1999 was an agreement that states wished to join the euro had to meet certain require-ments (informally known as the Maastricht criteria) on levels of inflation and interest rates, and the size of the government deficit and debt (the sum total of past annual deficits). EU heads of state and government took the decision, but finance ministers and a small group of national civil servants and central bank staff undertook the preparation that underpinned the decision. Private busi-nesses such as banks were not intimately involved, and the policy process was relatively closed.

The decision to move towards a single currency had profound implications for member states. The budget deficit requirements forced the restructuring of public finances in several Eurozone states. The desire to join the euro was so strong that some countries—such as Greece—resorted to questionable budget-ary tricks in order to qualify, which was the root of problems that triggered speculation at various points between 2012 and 2015 that Greece would be forced to leave the Eurozone. All member states of the EU are expected eventu-ally to join the EMU, except for Denmark and the UK, two states that possess formal opt-outs.

Eurozone members no longer have an independent monetary policy. The ECB, headquartered in Frankfurt, makes decisions about monetary policy that apply to all member states using the euro. National governments no longer control interest rates, which previously gave national governments (or national central banks) leverage over the direction of their economy. The ECB is mandated to privilege price stability and avoid inflation. But some actors—particularly those who would prefer it to adopt lower interest rates to stimulate the Eurozone economy and create more employment (often the position of the French government)—are critical of the bank. The ECB, however, has argued that job creation requires the adoption of more flexible labour markets and market liberalization. It has not tailored its interest rate policy to the wishes of the member states, nor to societal actors. The ECB has become an important, and very independent, actor in economic policy-making. The Eurozone crisis saw the ECB 'bolster its capacity to stabilize the euro without having its mandate formally enlarged' raising further questions of legitimacy (Scicluna 2017: 1).

Even after the creation of the EMU, stringent fiscal requirements remained, as EMU members committed to respect a Stability and Growth Pact (SGP), which includes financial penalties for states that violate it. After adoption of the euro, several member states found their macro-economic policies under scrutiny as they struggled to meet the budget deficit requirements. By 2003, four countries, including the three largest economies of the Eurozone (Germany, France, and Italy), were in breach of fiscal requirements set by the SGP. In the German case, the breach was attributed to ongoing problems of German unification, and in any case Germany's finances were in a good shape. However, France seemed to show a willful disregard of the SGP, as if to signify that respecting the SGP rules was beneath its status (Ludlow 2010). When the Commission recommended to the Council (meeting in its ECOFIN—Economic and Financial Affairs—format) the application of penalties mandated by the SGP, member states demurred.

In 2005 the SGP was modified to make it more flexible to allow fiscal leeway to countries in better financial shape. The reform, however, did not impart more discipline on the member states. The main problems were that the European statistical agency (Eurostat) was prevented from scrutinizing fiscal data provided by member states, thus opening the door to fraudulent accounts such as in the case of Greece. The imposition of fines proved politically difficult, so the deterrent power of the SGP was low. The crisis that began in 2010 when Greece revealed that its deficit was much higher than previously reported was one of the most severe in the EU's history. However, the ECB under its president, Mario Draghi, adopted a pro-active approach, calming the markets and giving troubled European economies room to address the crisis (Stolfi 2013). The response included the adoption by treaty (known as the Fiscal Compact) of more stringent rules with greater automaticity in imposing fines. The Commission recommendation is deemed to have been approved by the Council unless rejected by a qualified majority.

'Market-Correcting' and '-Cushioning' Policies

Policies to build markets have been a central feature of the Union's policy activity. But the EU has also been active in policy areas where the central goals might be viewed as 'market correcting' and 'market cushioning'. Market correcting policies, such as the Common Agricultural Policy (CAP) and cohesion policy, attempt to compensate for costs to particular groups imposed by the building of a single market and to limit inequality. Market cushioning policies, such as environmental, social, and justice and home affairs (JHA) policies, attempt to limit the potentially harmful effects of the market on the environment, human beings, and security.

Common Agricultural Policy

Perhaps the best-known policy designed to offset market forces is the CAP—for which the EU has almost exclusive competence. The CAP, with its system of agricultural support and subsides, has since its inception, been 'an integral part of the west European welfare state' (Rieger 2005: 182). However, reforms in past years have introduced new goals beyond supporting European farmers (Roederer-Rynning 2015).

The CAP is unique in the amount of money it receives from the EU budget (see Figure 5.1), the degree of power the Union exercises, and the amount of contestation it causes. Although the CAP created a market for agricultural goods within the Union, its market-correcting properties have been controversial outside the EU because non-European producers have found their goods subject to high tariffs when exported to the EU. Unsurprisingly, many countries find the EU's attitude, praising free markets and providing development aid, hypocritical when the Union does not open its own markets to the agricultural products from the developing world (Elgström 2007).

The CAP stirs up internal debate as well. The benefits of the CAP are distributed very unequally across member states. Although new member states depend much more on agriculture than do older members, the largest recipients are still older member states (see Table 5.1). However, some redistribution of agricultural funds from older to the newer member states has occurred: from 2007 the funds for farmers in older member states began to decline to make room for greater allocations for the farmers in newer states.

More generally, pressure from enlargement has spurred reform. The CAP has shifted away from supporting production, which in the past often led to over-production and waste, to supporting rural development and environmental protection (Grant 2010). However, the CAP remains a politically fraught policy area, where the interests of member states, European institutions, farmers, and other stakeholders continually collide (Daugbjerg 2012).

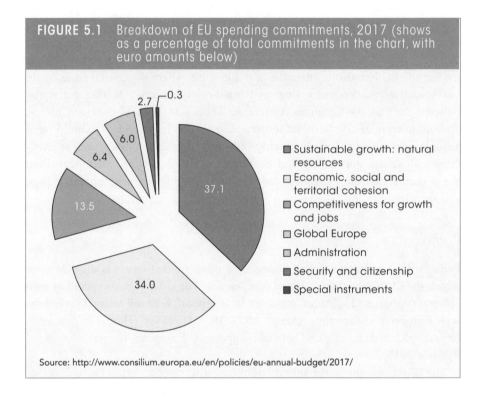

FIGURE 5.1   Breakdown of EU spending commitments, 2017 (shows as a percentage of total commitments in the chart, with euro amounts below)

Source: http://www.consilium.europa.eu/en/policies/eu-annual-budget/2017/

TABLE 5.1   CAP spending breakdown: top recipients

This table shows France is still the big winner from CAP spending, even increasing its share from the recent past. More generally, highly industrialized member states have also increased their share of CAP spending. The largest of the new member states, Poland, has seen its share decline.

Member state	Percentage of CAP expenditure (2009)	Percentage of CAP expenditure (2016)	Member state	Percentage of CAP expenditure (2009)	Percentage of CAP expenditure (2016)
France	13.3	16.0	Poland	9.0	7.6
Germany	11.3	10.7	United Kingdom	6.1	6.3
Spain	11.4	11.8	Greece	5.3	5.0
Italy	9.1	10.7	Romania	2.1	5.9

Source: Commission 2013a and 2016.

Cohesion policy

Cohesion policy was introduced to reduce inequality among European regions and compensate poor countries for the costs of economic integration. Cohesion policy—sometimes called the 'structural funds'—was introduced after the first enlargement (UK, Denmark, and Ireland), and has increased in importance over time. It now represents one of the most important areas for EU expenditure (see Figure 5.1).

The budget for cohesion policy represents approximately one-third of the EU's budget. The CAP, including funding for rural development and natural resources, has fallen from almost three-quarters of the total EU budget in 1985. But it still represents nearly 40 per cent of overall EU budget commitments. Every member state receives some funding as regions with specific problems (such as a declining industrial base) receive funding even if they are part of a wealthy member state, which makes the policy politically acceptable to all. Most funding is still spent in the regions with the highest need, where per capita GDP is below 75 per cent of the EU average.

The distribution of structural funding across many member states has rendered it one of the most visible EU policies, with road signs often advertising that a road or other public work has been financed with European funds. It also brings together actors across levels of governance: regional, national, and EU policy-makers are all involved in decisions surrounding the allocation of regional funds and their implementation. The interaction of actors from multiple levels of governance, and the sharing of power between them gives rise to the notion of the EU as a system of multi-level governance (Bache 2008) (see Chapter 1). Because regions in all member states have benefited from some form of regional spending, cohesion policy has escaped the intense controversy surrounding the CAP.

Still, enlargement has made cohesion policy more contentious, pitting net contributors against new recipients, or 'old' versus 'new' member states. Because the new member states are significantly poorer than old ones, the poorest regions of Europe are now all concentrated in the new member states. For instance, Poland is now by far the largest recipient of cohesion funds (Commission 2013a). With policies that appeared to neuter the media and politicize the judiciary, Poland's right-wing Law and Justice government elected in 2015 was scrutinized by the Commission to see if it was violating EU norms on democracy and the rule of law. The EU's Treaty offered the nuclear option (of Article 7) that could, if triggered, remove Poland's voting rights in the Council. But it had never been used and there was no precedent for turning off the cohesion-funding tap for political reasons.

Environmental and social regulation

Although the CAP and cohesion policy are probably the best known of the EU's policy areas outside of the single market, other policies have been initiated and become far more important over time. One such policy area is 'social regulation', designed to cushion the impact of the market on society. Occupational health-and-safety legislation is one area where the EU acted rather early.

On environmental policy the EU became active (especially in the area of pollution control) before many of its member states became environmentally conscious. Environmental policy was initially put on the agenda both because of its international salience and because it affected trade in goods such as automobiles. Over time, the focus was enlarged into areas that were not market-related, such as the protection of environmentally sensitive habitats.

EU regulation has significantly improved environmental standards in Europe (Holzinger and Sommerer 2011). In many areas of environmental policy, national governments are free to supplement EU legislation. Some do. In general, the Scandinavian member states, Austria, the Netherlands, and Germany are the most active in supplementing EU legislation. But most member states choose not to act unilaterally, thereby leaving the EU as the de facto primary actor.

Consumer protection is another area in which the EU is very active. A series of food scares and concern about genetically modified organisms (GMOs) has propelled this issue up the EU's agenda and led to the establishment of a Food Safety Agency. It has also caused conflict with the US, which is the largest producer of GMOs, and accuses the EU of using unscientific concerns as a way to shield European agriculture from foreign competition. Social regulatory policies related directly to the single market (such as regulations on product safety) pre-empt national policies, while other areas (such as hygiene standards) see the EU stipulate minimum standards that national governments can exceed if they so wish.

The EU has also been active on gender equality. National pension systems have had to be restructured to treat men and women equally. More generally, the EU has been a significant actor in the move towards equal pay (both in terms of income and benefits) in the workplace (Caporaso 2001). More recently, the EU passed laws against sexual harassment. While some member states already had tough laws, Spain, Portugal, Greece, and Italy had no laws that held employers responsible for harassment within the workplace; and Germany defined sexual harassment more narrowly than did the EU. Member states can adopt stricter definitions, but now European legislation provides a 'floor' for any national legislative activity.

Justice and home affairs policy

One area where cushioning the effects of a single market became a matter of urgency by the early 1990s was in internal security. The abolition of border checks created the danger that some of the prime beneficiaries of the single market would be organized criminals dealing in drugs, people-smuggling, and other illegal activities. Terrorists were always on the list, too, but by the early 2000s—following major attacks in London, Madrid, and the US—the EU had little choice but to develop extensive counter-terrorism policies.

It was perhaps ironic that internal security policy—or JHA in EU-speak—is the single policy area where the EU was most active after the mid-1990s. The irony stems from the stubborn refusal of member states over the course of years to subject internal security policy to the Community method, whereby the Commission has a monopoly on the right to propose legislation, the EP has the right to co-decide legislation or propose amendments, and the Council usually acts by a qualified majority. After all, ensuring the security of their citizens is job number one of national governments. Under the post-Maastricht pillar system, JHA was mostly subject to intergovernmental decision-making, not requiring a Commission proposal or agreement of the Parliament, with nearly all Council decisions requiring unanimity. Such cumbersome arrangements, however, proved inadequate to deal with problems arising from the abolition of checks at internal borders, including asylum-seeking and irregular migration. Over the course of a decade-and-a-half, the EU spent far more time and effort debating internal security than producing policy output.

The Lisbon Treaty abolished the pillar system. Qualified majority voting (QMV) was applied to key JHA policies, including police and judicial cooperation, with the EP given co-decision rights in many. The shift was, in retrospect, timely because the effect of the 2011 Arab spring followed by the intensification of the war in Syria was a tsunami of refugees coming to the EU: in 2015 nearly 1.3 million refugees applied for asylum in the Union, while close to 9,000 drowned trying to cross the Mediterranean in 2015–16. The result was an outright refugee crisis, with the EU resorting to extreme measures such as forcing a decision by QMV about how many asylum seekers member states would accept. With four member states (the Czech Republic, Hungary, Romania, and Slovakia) voting against the measure (and one, Finland, abstaining), the measure passed even as EU refugee sharing became politically untenable, leading to a legal war between the Commission and recalcitrant member states. JHA policy thus is revealed as an area where European policy cooperation is both essential yet elusive.

Comparing Policy Types in the EU

How can we make sense of all these policies? To start, note each category of policy has certain characteristics that distinguish it from others. While the categories are clearly not watertight, policies that fall within them do differ in significant ways along dimensions highlighted in Table 5.2. First, those policies that fall under *market-building* stimulate market forces and encourage regulatory reform. The emphasis on competition means such policies tend in practice to favour (although not require) privatization and the withdrawal of the state from areas in which it has protected national producers. Many policies in this category are regulatory. In general, they also tend to be made by the Community method in which the EU's supranational institutions are most active, the Union's competence is most comprehensive, and national activity is largely pre-empted.

TABLE 5.2   Policy types in the EU

Type	Level of EU competence	Key features	Primary actors	Examples
Market-building	Nearly exclusive; covering an extensive range of economic policies	Emphasis on liberalization and increasing economic efficiency; strong role for supranational institutions	Business actors; EU institutions; national finance officials; central bankers	Internal market policies (such as telecommunications or air transport); EMU
Market-correcting	Often exclusive but only in limited areas	Controversial; has redistributive implications; EP mostly excluded	Farm lobbies, national officials; Commission	CAP; cohesion policy; fisheries
Market-cushioning	Shared with member states	Significant implementation problems	Supranational institutions; sectoral ministers; public interest groups	Environmental protection; occupational health and safety; gender equality in the workplace

A variety of political dynamics, and range of political actors, also mark the creation of markets. The different theoretical approaches introduced in Chapter 1 shed light on these different dynamics. A few policy areas, such as energy and pharmaceuticals, feature what Peterson and Bomberg (1999: 81) describe as 'a relatively stable and cohesive policy network': policies are shaped by a tight and insular group of actors. Similarly, monetary policy is quite insulated from actors outside the central banking community. But most other areas related to trade do not exhibit such single-mindedness and networks of affected actors are often fragmented and internally divided.

Market-correcting policies differ from market-building policies in that they tend to protect producers from market forces. Most are redistributive—from consumers to farmers, or rich to poor regions. Because they are redistributive rather than regulatory, they tend to be difficult to change as the impact of any change is quite transparent. Market-correcting policies thus tend to be dominated by intergovernmental bargaining rather than by the EU's institutions. Liberal intergovernmentalists show how major decisions in these areas are dominated by national governments responding to strong societal actors (such as agricultural lobbies), with national ministers ultimately deciding when other considerations trump the demands of those lobbies.

Market-cushioning policies try to minimize the harm economic activities impose on nature and humans. These policies tend to be regulatory, impose demands on private actors, and fall under the 'shared competence' of the EU because both Brussels and national capitals typically co-govern in these areas. The role of institutions in propelling these areas forward, often with strong support from a variety of representatives of civil society, provides fertile ground for the new institutionalists' claim that 'institutions matter'. However, JHA policies may be the exception that proves the rule: they are matters of security policy (see Peterson and Geddes 2015). So while subjecting them to the **Community method** means they focus more on the rights of refugees (especially under the influence of the EP) than previously (see Acosta and Geddes 2013), EU decisions on refugee sharing still can come unstitched because security comes so close to the heart of national sovereignty. One recent study on theorizing EU internal security cooperation concludes that the empirical record points to the renewed importance of intergovernmentalism in European integration (Bossong and Rhinard 2016).

Conclusion

If institutions and member states are the skeleton of the EU, policies are its flesh. It is through its policies that the EU affects people's lives, within and beyond its own borders. The Italian retailer who can sell non-durum-wheat pasta against the opposition of the Italian authorities or the British holidaymaker who pays less for his or her mobile phone calls when holidaying in Spain are both feeling the influence of the EU in their daily lives. So does the American shareholder who sees the price of his or her Microsoft stocks affected by competition policy decisions of the European Commission or the Indian farmer adversely affected by high tariffs the EU imposes on agricultural products.

What makes studying EU policies enormously challenging—as well as fascinating—is that each policy has its own features and trajectory. But amidst all that variation, common themes also emerge. In particular, policies and policy-making in the EU reflect the three major themes of this volume:

1. experimentation as a driving force of European integration;

2. the astonishing array of actors and power-sharing and consensus-building among them; and

3. the contrast between the scope and the capacity of the EU.

The creation of the EMU was the result of dramatic experimentation. One of the main reasons for moving to a common currency was that the old status quo, with exchange rate agreements prone to collapsing, was no longer tenable. Yet monetary union was an untested course. As the former chief economist of the ECB argued,

European governments consciously chose to take a risk and make 'the big leap into monetary union' (*Financial Times*, 27 October 2006).

Different policy areas also show different levels of inclusiveness and power sharing. In some, such as competition policy and monetary policy, power is concentrated in a limited set of actors. In others, a larger set of actors is involved. Both environmental and cohesion policy involve a large number of actors at different levels of governance—including EU institutions, national governments, and private stakeholders—and exhibit a preference for consensus-building. But consensus comes at a price: decisions made by the EU, no matter how well thought out, seem to many Europeans to be made too far away from their control. Citizen control is still largely exercised through the democratic process in each member state rather than through participation in European decision-making. Although the Lisbon Treaty tried to address this concern, many Europeans still felt disconnected from the way decisions are made in the EU, as reflected in the UK referendum result in 2016 (see Chapter 10).

Finally, the policy capacity of the EU remains well short of any nation state, relying on a very limited budget and the national implementation of European legislation. At the same time, we have seen how the pressure of economic integration has led to expansion of the scope of the EU's policy remit, from policies directly related to market-building, to market-correcting and then market-cushioning policies. The Eurozone crisis continued this pattern, and European economic **governance** might well come out of it much more integrated than it was only a few years previously.

? DISCUSSION QUESTIONS

1. Why has the EU privileged economic policies over social welfare policies?
2. Why is the EU budget so much smaller than that of its major member states?
3. What implications does a single monetary policy have for the development of other types of policies within the EU?
4. What obstacles to the execution of EU policies exist that do not at the national level?
5. The CAP is often criticized on efficiency grounds. What environmental or social considerations can be brought to bear to support the CAP?
6. How has enlargement affected the EU's economic policies?

FURTHER READING

The definitive work on EU policies and policy-making remains Wallace *et al.* (2015). Another excellent, but more succinct review of policy-making in the EU is Nugent (2017). Quaglia (2010) analyses the governance of the financial services industry, and Bachtler *et al.* (2013) focus on cohesion policy. Wurzel *et al.* (2013) provide detailed coverage of developments in environmental policy in the EU and several member states. Jabko (2006) offers a provocative interpretation of the process of economic integration as a consistent strategy to achieve broader integration goals. Falkner *et al.* (2008) tackle the question of the (lack of) implementation of EU legislation by the member states. For a critical assessment of the impact of the EMU, see Hancke (2013). Quaglia (2007) describes central banking in Europe after the creation of EMU. A very clear explanation of the economics of the EMU is De Grauwe (2012). Pisani-Ferry (2014) offers a good discussion of potential policy developments triggered by the Eurozone crisis. The policy impact(s) of the EU's various recent crises are analysed by Dinan *et al.* (2017).

Bachtler, J., Mendez, C., and Wishlade, F. (2013), *EU Cohesion Policy and European Integration* (Farnham: Ashgate).

De Grauwe, P. (2012) *Economics of Monetary Union*, 9th edn (Oxford: Oxford University Press).

Dinan, D., Nugent, N., and Paterson, W. (eds) (2017), *The European Union in Crisis* (Basingstoke and New York: Palgrave Macmillan).

Falkner, G., Treib, O., and Holzleithner, E. (2008), *Compliance in the Enlarged European Union* (Aldershot: Ashgate).

Hancke, B. (2013), *Unions, Central Banks, and EMU: Labour Market Institutions and Monetary Integration in Europe* (Oxford: Oxford University Press).

Jabko, N. (2006), *Playing the Market* (Ithaca, NY: Cornell University Press).

Nugent, N. (2017), *The Government and Politics of the European Union*, 8th edn (Basingstoke and New York: Palgrave Macmillan).

Pisani-Ferry, J. (2014), *The Euro Crisis and Its Aftermath* (Oxford: Oxford University Press).

Quaglia, L. (2007), *Central Banking Governance in the European Union* (London and London and New York: Routledge).

Quaglia, L. (2010), *Governing Financial Services in the European Union* (London and New York: Routledge).

Wallace, H., Pollack, M., and Young, A. (eds) (2015), *Policy-Making in the European Union*, 7th edn (Oxford: Oxford University Press).

Wurzel, R., Zito, A., and Jordan, A. (2013), *Environmental Governance in Europe: A Comparative Analysis of New Environmental Policy Instruments* (Cheltenham: Edward Elgar Publishing).

WEB LINKS

- To locate EU publications covering policy, try the EU portal EUR-Lex (http://eur-lex. europa.eu/homepage.html). It is bibliographical in nature, but contains links to many full-text documents.

- For a record of EU legislation, search this site from the European Parliament: http://www.europarl.europa.eu/plenary/en/parliament-positions.html

- For full-text, non-EU documents see the websites 'European Integration Online Papers' (www.eiop.or.at/eiop/) and 'European Research Papers Archive' (http://eiop.or.at/erpa/).

 Visit the Ancillary Resource Centre that accompanies this book for additional material: www.oup.com/uk/kenealy5e/

CHAPTER 6

How Policies Are Made

Daniel Kenealy with Fiona Hayes-Renshaw

Summary

EU policies have a **direct effect** on the daily lives of millions of Europeans and those beyond, and it is important to understand how they are made and who is involved in the process. Most EU legislation is now adopted according to the **Ordinary Legislative Procedure (OLP)**, under which the Council and the **European Parliament (EP)** have equal powers. The basic policy-making rules laid down in the treaties have been supplemented over the years by formal agreements and informal understandings between the main actors in the decision-making institutions. The result is a highly complex process, involving large numbers of participants from each of the member states in a constant cycle of communication and negotiation at all levels. The process is followed closely by the international media and by interest representatives, who frequently try to influence the outcome. EU policy-making is open to criticism regarding its democracy, **transparency**, and efficiency, but it continues to deliver a rather impressive amount and array of policy outcomes.

Introduction

The EU has an impact on many aspects of the daily lives of citizens in Europe and beyond. It is responsible for the format and content of the labels on breakfast cereal, permitted pollution levels of modes of transport and the cost of roaming charges for mobile communications. On a daily basis people are speaking on Europe's behalf about nuclear security in international forums, imposing sanctions in Europe's name on foreign individuals or states and placing tariffs on the goods Europe imports. EU money is used to fund the building of roads and bridges in various parts of the Union and to assist development in far-flung parts of the world, such as Palestine and many countries in Africa. Yet the ways in which policies are devised, formulated, and adopted remain a mystery to most EU citizens.

There is a tendency in the member states to view EU policy-making as something that happens 'over there' in Brussels. 'There' is seen as a distant, unfamiliar, even threatening place, populated by antagonistic strangers with different interests and goals. In the UK's 2016 referendum on EU membership (see Chapter 10) much emphasis was placed, by Leave campaigners, on 'taking back control' of decision-making and law-making from Brussels. Appeals to lost sovereignty were common. People directly involved in the EU policy-making process are not always necessarily interested in revealing exactly how the policies are made in practice. It may be convenient, if the final policy outcome is unwelcome, to blame it on 'the EU' or 'Brussels'. On the other hand, if the policy outcome is likely to be popular within a certain community, many will rush to take credit for it. In particular, if the outcome is 'bad' for a given member state, the EU gets the blame. If the outcome is 'good', the member government claims responsibility.

How can we find out how policies are made? Since the EU is a law-based organization, the first place to look is in its constituent treaties, now thankfully consolidated in the 2007 Treaty of Lisbon. The basic policy-making rules can all be found there. But decades of decision-making at EU level have given rise to a range of conventions or accepted ways of doing things that have evolved through practice. Such conventions have been embraced as a means for increasing efficiency, democracy, transparency, or decision-making speed. Some are formalized in written texts, such as interinstitutional agreements or codes of conduct, thereby adding flesh to the bones of the basic rules. Other informal ways of doing things have not been codified but nonetheless need to be understood in order to gain a realistic picture of how EU decision-making operates in practice.

BOX 6.1   Key concepts and terms

Civil society refers to the broad collection of associations and groups (including private firms, trades unions, community groups, and non-governmental organizations (NGOs)) active between the level of the individual and the state. These groups generally operate independently of direct governmental control.

➔

→

A **European Citizens' Initiative** is a request addressed to the **European Commission** from at least one million EU citizens drawn from at least seven of the 28 member states to propose a specific piece of legislation in a policy area where the EU has competence to legislate.

Fonctionnaires or EU officials are international civil servants, who have successfully passed an entrance exam known as the 'concours' and are involved in policy-making in the EU's institutions.

The **legal basis** of an EU law is the treaty article or articles (cited in the legislation) which give(s) the EU authority to act in that area and lay(s) down the decision-making rules that apply.

Lobbying is an attempt to influence policy-makers to adopt a course of action advantageous, or not detrimental, to a particular group or interest. A lobbyist is a person employed by a group, firm, organization, region, or country to carry out the lobbying. Lobbyists in Brussels are increasingly referred to as interest representatives.

A rapporteur is a member of the EP who has been given responsibility for preparing a report of one of the Parliament's committees on behalf of the rest of its members.

Transparency refers to the process of making EU documents and decision-making processes more open and accessible to the public.

Trilogues (known as *trialogues* in French) are three-way meetings between key representatives of the Commission, the Council, and the EP, designed to advance negotiations and speed up budgetary and legislative decision-making.

How it Works *Formally*

If opponents of European integration are to be believed, intrusive laws made by faceless bureaucrats in Brussels increasingly and adversely affect the lives of EU citizens. However, the powers of the EU's institutions have been formally agreed by each of the member states and are clearly stated in the treaties. Even a quick read over these formal rules casts doubt on the eurosceptics' claims. Yes, decisions are now taken at European level in a large number of policy areas, involving the EU and its institutions to various degrees (see Box 6.2). But, rather than faceless bureaucrats, these institutions are made up of individuals from each of the member states, who are elected or appointed to their roles through transparent and accountable procedures. In fulfilling their respective roles in the legislative process, these individuals must follow strict rules and procedures that are open to scrutiny by a variety of observers.

BOX 6.2	A plethora of policies, processes, and procedures

The EU has much broader policy responsibilities than the original European Communities. Today, it is involved not only in trade, agriculture, and energy, but also foreign affairs, citizens' rights, and monetary policy, among other policy areas.

→

➡

However, the EU is not involved to the same extent in every area, because the ways in which it makes policy differ between policy areas, depending on where policy competence lies. In some policy areas, such as competition and external trade, most major policy decisions are taken at EU level, whereas in others, such as consumer protection or the environment, responsibility for major policy decisions is shared between the EU and national levels.

The majority of EU policy processes result in detailed legislation, but others produce such outcomes as an agreed budget or threshold (for example, the annual EU budget or total allowable catches in fisheries policy), rules set by the EU's institutions (such as the Commission's merger policy decisions) or coordinated national positions (such as the details of the Stability and Growth Pact or a joint statement on the crisis in Ukraine).

Most EU legislation is adopted by means of the **OLP**, under which the Council and the EP have equal powers to accept, reject, or amend legislation proposed by the Commission. The Treaty of Lisbon extended its scope and it now applies to 85 policy areas. The EP has more restricted rights under two special legislative procedures: the **consultation procedure** (which is used, for example, for certain measures in the **Common Foreign and Security Policy (CFSP)**) and the **consent procedure** (previously known as the **assent procedure**, which applies in a number of fields, including association agreements and the Multiannual Financial Framework). The consultation and consent procedures are also used for the adoption of certain non-legislative international agreements.

It is also possible for a group of like-minded member states (who must number at least one-third, currently nine of the 28) to act together in the interests of advanced integration in certain policy areas, using the EU's institutions and procedures. This is known as **enhanced cooperation** and has been used most recently in the areas of divorce (17 participating member states), patents (26 member states), and the establishment of a European Public Prosecutor's Office (20 member states). Ten member states have agreed, in principle, to consider an EU financial transactions tax but progress has been linked to developments in the Brexit negotiations, pushing any decision-making farther into the future.

The basic rules

The EU cannot unilaterally decide to get involved in a particular policy area. There are plenty of checks and balances to ensure that it does not over-step its assigned policy-making role. The first constraint is that the EU can only intervene in a given policy area if the member states have *empowered* it to do so: the Union can act only to the extent and following the rules laid down in the treaties. Policy competence may lie exclusively with the EU (as in external trade policy), or primarily with the member states (as in development cooperation). Sometimes, it is shared between the member states and the EU (as in transport policy). Every piece of EU legislation refers to one or more treaty articles as the authority for its involvement in that policy area (the so-called 'legal basis').

Second, the EU is required to respect two fundamental principles when it makes policy. The first is *subsidiarity*, meaning that the EU should only act in circumstances where its intervention is likely to be more effective than that undertaken by the member states individually. So the Union has competence in environmental policy where collective European action is required. But subsidiarity means that the EU is not involved in rubbish collection (although it may regulate landfills because of its wider environmental effects).

The second fundamental principle is *proportionality*. The EU's involvement is limited only to what is required to fulfill the objectives outlined in the treaties. Thus, it can be argued (albeit controversially) that the declared aim of consumer protection could be adequately achieved by providing information and advice to EU citizens rather than by imposing an outright ban on the use of all hormones in livestock farming.

Even clearing these initial hurdles does not imply a successful outcome for a proposal. Usually, a third basic rule is *shared legislative authority*. Policy-making in the EU allows for input from a wide variety of actors, many of whom have competing interests. Under the OLP, the European Commission—a body representing the general interest of the EU—proposes draft legislation. Two other institutions, composed of the representatives of the EU's citizens—the EP—and representatives of the governments of the member states—the Council—are designated as co-legislators (see Rasmussen 2012). This means that a new piece of legislation can only be adopted if both the EP and the Council agree to its content. Put another way, each institution has the power to ensure that a draft piece of legislation with which it disagrees cannot be enacted.

The principal actors

The Treaty of Lisbon describes the basic composition and powers of the main institutions and bodies that are directly involved in the EU's policy-making process (see Chapter 3). The European Commission—headed by a president who together with his fellow commissioners forms a 28-person college (27 after Brexit)—enjoys an almost exclusive right to initiate legislative proposals. The College acts collectively, formally by simple majority but usually by consensus.

The 751 (fewer after Brexit) members of the EP (MEPs) are directly elected by EU citizens, whose interests they represent. They have the power to adopt, amend, or reject the Commission's legislative proposals, working in conjunction with the Council and reaching agreement by majority. The Council is composed of ministers from each of the member states and exists to represent their interests. Like the EP, and in conjunction with it, the Council may decide to adopt, amend or reject draft legislation put forward by the Commission.

The Treaty of Lisbon also mentions the Economic and Social Committee (comprising economic and social actors from each of the member states) and the European Committee of the Regions (bringing together representatives of EU-wide regional and local governments), which are consulted for their specialist views in policy areas within their remit. A far more weighty and powerful institution is the

European Council: the heads of state or government from each of the member states. It sometimes becomes involved in the policy-making process, either at the beginning, when it may define political directions or priorities, or towards the end, if sensitive political issues are at stake. But the European Council—despite bringing together Europe's most powerful political leaders—does not have the power to take actual legislative decisions.

The key stages

Each chapter of the Treaty of Lisbon dealing with a specific policy area lays down the procedure according to which policy decisions are made. In most cases today, the legislative procedure in question is the OLP. On the face of it, the procedure is very simple:

- The Commission produces a draft piece of legislation and sends it to the EP and the Council.
- The EP and the Council discuss the draft separately in the course of one or two readings apiece, and may approve, amend, or reject the text.
- Only if Parliament and Council reach agreement on a mutually acceptable text is it adopted as a legislative act.
- If after two readings, agreement has still not been reached between the Council and EP, a joint conciliation committee is convened to try to find a compromise, which must then be endorsed by both in a third reading.
- If no agreement can be reached at this stage, the proposal is not adopted.

The treaty's description of the OLP demonstrates that it follows the three key stages of policy-making:

1. identifying specific goals in a given policy area (agenda-setting);
2. policy-makers discussing alternative ways of achieving them (negotiation);
3. reaching agreement on the end product (final decision).

By way of comparison, the UK government and civil service set the agenda by tabling draft legislation, which is examined, debated, and amended by the House of Commons and the House of Lords, who then decide whether to approve or reject it. In the EU, the agenda-setting role is attributed mainly to the Commission, while the EP and the Council are the principal players in the second and third stages (negotiation and final decision).

What Happens *in Practice*

The Treaty of Lisbon's provisions on policy-making provide us with a broad-brush understanding of the process as a whole. However, a more in-depth examination of what happens in practice adds finer detail that—in many cases—can change the overall picture. For example, the treaty suggests that the EU's three main legislative institutions—the Commission, the Council, and the EP—operate as a triangle, each one directly connected to the other two. The reality is that they can more correctly be visualized as three icebergs, whose tips are inhabited respectively by the commissioners, the ministers, and the MEPs. However, the (somewhat crowded!) iceberg tips are only the smallest, most publicized and visible part of far larger masses, which prove to be much more interconnected and close together beneath the surface of the water than above it. Exploring the less visible parts of the icebergs can help to identify the pivotal actors and key stages that are of paramount importance to those attempting to follow or influence the process.

The EU's policy-making remit has been subject to an impressive amount of expansion over the years, as has the membership of the Union. As a result, the institutions and other actors in the process have had to adapt. Today, the connections between the legislative actors at EU level are extensive, complex, and shape much of what happens on a day-to-day basis.

The adapted rules

The OLP requires a high level of agreement among the main institutional actors in order for new legislation to be adopted, securing both a qualified majority in the Council and a majority in the Parliament. Many different interests have to be reconciled at all stages of the procedure. The result is that a constant search for compromise has emerged as an important feature of the policy-making process, both within and between the institutions. This fact is evident in the ways in which the institutions now organize themselves and their respective work programmes in order to fulfill their legislative responsibilities. Written agreements co-exist with a number of tacit understandings about 'how things should be done' in order to ensure a harmonious working environment that encourages cooperation and facilitates agreement.

Interinstitutional cooperation and transparency are the first pre-requisites for an efficient policy-making process based on compromise and consensus. In the 1990s, early experience with the pre-Lisbon precursor to the OLP—the **co-decision procedure**—made it clear that, if agreement was to be reached within a reasonable amount of time, interinstitutional discussions and negotiations needed to get underway sooner rather than later, once the Commission had presented its proposal. Regular meetings, known as trilogues (see Boxes 6.1 and 6.3), were therefore scheduled between the key players in each of the three institutions, to assist in the search for compromises (Brandsma 2015; Roederer-Rynning and Greenwood 2016; Delreux and Laloux 2018). They constituted a relatively 'safe' forum for assessing the potential degree of support for proposed amendments or compromises before they were officially put to a vote. Over recent years, trilogues have come under some scrutiny. Some observers of the EU policy-making process have criticized the process for prioritizing speed and efficiency over inclusive and transparent decision-making (Box 6.3).

An interinstitutional agreement on better law making, published in 2003, updated in 2016, lays down how the Commission, Council, and EP coordinate their individual and joint legislative activities. They agreed to keep one another permanently informed about their work throughout the legislative process and to synchronize the handling of dossiers by their respective preparatory bodies. They also undertook to keep the public better informed at every stage, including by broadcasting political debates and votes on legislative proposals and publishing the results of their deliberations. This latter commitment entailed a significant cultural shift for the Council, which had a history of conducting its negotiations behind closed doors and avoiding votes where possible, preferring to adopt its positions by means of consensus (see Hillebrandt *et al.* 2014).

BOX 6.3   How it really works: Trilogues

Trilogues are three-way meetings between key representatives of the Commission, the Council, and the EP designed to advance negotiations and speed up decision-making. During the past three years for which figures are available the number of trilogues was 230 (in 2015), 153 (in 2016), and 247 (in 2017). *EUObserver* estimated that in 2013 there may have been as many as 1,000. Trilogues are not mentioned in the EU treaties. They have become an informal institution of the EU and are established as soon as the institutions agree their initial position on proposed legislation. They do not have a set format or a set composition but typically they bring together the *rapporteur* from the Parliament, the chairperson of the **Committee of Permanent Representatives (Coreper)** or the relevant Council working group, and an official from the Commission, often the person in charge of the dossier. The General Secretariat of the Council and the Secretariat-General of the Commission typically provide support. The purpose is to reach agreement between the Parliament and the Council on amendments to proposed legislation and also to secure the endorsement of the Commission. Any agreement reached in the trilogue is informal and must subsequently be approved through formal procedures in all of the relevant institutions.

While almost everyone involved in EU policy-making agrees that they are successful measured against the yardstick of efficiency, they have generated some criticism on the grounds of transparency. Trilogues are not minuted, meaning no official records are kept. They are less transparent that the standard scrutiny procedures involved in first and second readings and in conciliations. You can see from the figures in Table 6.1 that the number of dossiers concluded at second reading or in a conciliation committee has fallen markedly since 2004. This suggests that more legislation is being approved through the use of trilogues. Close observers of EU policy-making, and those who participate in it directly, disagree on the implications of trilogues. Some MEPs suggest that it cements the power of the Commission, while others argue that the Parliament can be a powerful player in the trilogue process if it presents a united, cross-party front. The UK House of

→

Lords (2009) claimed that trilogues 'make it harder for national parliaments to conduct effective scrutiny of EU legislation'. The debate about the impact of trilogues on the EU policy-making process looks set to continue.

TABLE 6.1   Stage at which agreement has been reached on dossiers concluded under the co-decision/Ordinary Legislative Procedure

Legislative period	Concluded at 1st reading	Concluded at 2nd reading	Concluded after conciliation	No agreement after conciliation	Total
1999–2004	146 (34.5%%%)	187 (44.2%)	88 (20.8%)	2 (0.5%)	**423**
(1 July 1999–30 June 2004)				(Takeovers & port services directives)	
2004–9	391 (78.8%)	80 (16.1%)	24 (4.9%)	1 (0.2%)	**496**
(1 July 2004–30 June 2009)				(Working time directive)	
2009–14	408 (86.3%)	55 (11.6%)	9 (1.9%)	1 (0.2%)	**473**
(1 July 2004–30 June 2014)				(Novel foods regulation)	
2014–17*	189 (83.3%)	38 (16.7%)	0 (0%)	0 (0%)	**227**
(1 July 2014–31 December 2017)					
Total	**1134** (70.0%)	**360** (22.2%)	**121** (7.5%)	**4** (0.2%)	**1,619**

Notes: *Figures are available up to the end of the Estonian Council presidency, on 31 December 2017. The term of the current (8th) European Parliament lasts until the 2019 elections. Broken down by EP legislative terms and corresponding Council Presidency periods.

Source: http://www.consilium.europa.eu/media/32583/180131-general-overview.pdf

Source: http://www.consilium.europa.eu/media/32583/180131-general-overview.pdf; author interviews with MEPs and Commission officials; Fox (2014); House of Lords (2009).

One rather controversial feature of EU policy-making concerns how interested parties can have input, whether in the form of consultation or lobbying. It is generally accepted that the Commission should be open to input from interested parties. To this end, it engages in widespread consultations in order to ensure that its proposed legislation will be both fit for purpose and likely to be acceptable to a majority of stakeholders. The information gathered during this process is important and useful to policy-makers who have to be aware of interests that need to be accommodated in any proposed legislation. There is little point in the Commission spending time producing a draft piece of legislation that proves either difficult to implement or incapable of dealing with the problems it has been designed to address. Similarly, MEPs and national government officials may consult interested parties when determining what position to take on a new Commission proposal.

Some interest representatives prepare amendments to be presented by MEPs in the EP's committee and plenary sessions. Others target national ministers and officials in an attempt to influence the position they will defend during discussions and votes on draft legislation in the Council. Research on lobbying in the EU echoes much of the research conducted on lobbying in national settings. Lobbyists often struggle to achieve their aims when a public policy issue is highly salient, grabs the public's attention, and involves a large policy network (see Woll 2013; Dur and Mateo 2014; Rasmussen 2015). However, as issues begin to lose salience, lobbyists can employ a range of tactics—some noisy, others quiet (see Culpepper 2011)—to try to shape the policy-making process in ways that meet their interests. On most issues, there is lobbying from a variety of viewpoints, sometimes diametrically opposed to each other.

Often it is the case that lobbyists water down legislative proposals, as opposed to blocking them altogether. For example, the EU adopted a revised Tobacco Products Directive in March 2014. The directive had a dramatic and controversial passage, involving the resignation of the responsible commissioner, John Dalli, over 'cash-for-access' allegations that were subsequently shown to be groundless, and a burglary at the Brussels offices of two anti-tobacco NGOs. The Tobacco Products Directive has been described as the most lobbied dossier in EU history. The tobacco companies employed a significant number of lobbyists (more than 160 by Philip Morris alone) and numerous third-party groups with links to the tobacco industry joined the effort. While the directive was passed, researchers have concluded that efforts by lobbyists to amend, or at least delay, the proposal were partially successful with, for example, the 'plain packaging and point of sales display ban removed during the 3-year delay in the Commission' (see Peeters et al. 2016). But crucially, the lobbyists failed to stop the legislation. Similarly, and more recently, it has been suggested that lobbying on behalf of the financial services industry was successful in watering down proposed directives for a European financial transactions tax (Kastner 2017).

Another more public feature of the OLP that has developed over the years is interinstitutional signalling to indicate what will or will not be acceptable to the relevant legislative partner. Thus, although the Procedure requires the Council to await the EP's first reading position before it adopts its own Common Position, ministers frequently issue a 'political agreement' to indicate which elements of the Commission's proposal (and the EP's proposed amendments) would or would not be acceptable to the Council. Similarly, the EP might choose, after adopting amendments, to postpone the final vote to establish its first reading position on a Commission proposal, in order to negotiate with the Council.

In line with its overtly democratic nature, voting in the EP has always been public. Decision-making within the Council has historically been more opaque, due to the so-called 'consensual reflex' that lingers throughout its various layers as a consequence (largely) of the EEC's original voting rules based on unanimity (Heisenberg 2005). For many years after majority voting rules were introduced, national officials and ministers still continued to try to reach agreements acceptable to as many members of the Council as possible, in an attempt to avoid publicly out-voting one or more of their colleagues. When votes were taken the voting records were not publicized (the chair would simply conclude that the necessary majority had been reached). Only since the introduction of co-decision has data on voting at ministerial level been made publicly available. Early analyses of this data demonstrated that the Council only registered negative votes or abstentions around 14 per cent of the time (Hayes-Renshaw and Wallace 2006: 259), rising to about 35 per cent in recent years (Miller 2013). The rest of the time it decides by consensus (see Novak 2013). In 2017, the Council voted a total of 88 times and on 60 of those occasions (68 per cent) no abstentions or negative votes were recorded. Of the remaining 28 votes, in only eight instances (9 per cent of all 88 votes) were any negative votes cast by member states (figures calculated from VoteWatch.Eu).

A variety of actors

When explaining the EU's policy-making processes, it is customary to use a kind of institutional shorthand to describe the main actors. As a result, we speak and read about 'the Parliament', 'the Commission', and 'the Council' as though they were single entities with a recognizable face and a given set of attitudes and characteristics. However, each of these institutions is made up of layers of individuals, each of whom possesses their own priorities and interests. This complexity must be taken into account if we are to gain a proper understanding of why the policy-making process operates in the way it does.

The principal actors are the College of Commissioners, ministers in the Council, and MEPs meeting in plenary in the EP. But most of the detailed policy-making work actually takes place elsewhere (usually lower down) within each of these institutions. Each commissioner and minister is assisted by a large number of aides and officials who do the preparatory work on draft legislation, often leaving just a small number of issues to be dealt with directly at formal meetings of the Commission and Council. Decisions in all three institutions involve the accommodation of competing interests, with the result that, more often than not, the single 'position' of each institution is only arrived at after a process of intense internal negotiation. In fact, internal debates within the Commission, Council, or EP may well continue

after the formal discussions with the other institutions have commenced. The negotiation of the 2011 Eurovignette Directive illustrates the point (see Dyrhauge 2014).

The detailed policy-making work in the Commission is carried out by officials (*fonctionnaires*) who are citizens of EU member states recruited centrally
by competitive examination. They are responsible for the detailed drafting of the
Commission's proposals and may attend meetings in the EP committees and Council
working groups when they are being discussed. Turf battles within the Commission
are not unknown, with the result that the 'Commission position' may not be supported with equal enthusiasm by all those bound by it. For example, a proposal to
ban or restrict the use of a pesticide may be energetically supported by Directorate-
General (DG) Environment, but only lackadaisically (if at all) by DG Agriculture.

The EP's detailed legislative work is done in its 20 or so specialized permanent
committees, and each MEP belongs to one or more of them according to his or
her policy interests or expertise. The committees vary in size but each contains
representatives of all the EP's political groups in proportion to their size. At committee meetings, the MEPs discuss the Commission's proposal in detail and agree
on a report (prepared by a *rapporteur*) that contains those amendments that have
attracted the necessary majority. The *rapporteur's* report is then sent to the EP plenary session, where the legislation is discussed and voted upon by all the MEPs,
whereupon it becomes 'the EP's position'. *Rapporteurs* (Box 6.1) enjoy formal and
informal agenda-setting powers and skillful MEPs can be influential in the role,
even becoming policy entrepreneurs in the process (Thierse 2017).

MEPs are accountable to their respective electorates. Thus, they try to ensure
that the interests of their constituents are protected when they vote on proposed
legislation. However, most MEPs also belong to one of the EP's political groups,
whose members try to vote together on draft legislation. The EP's position is therefore normally a compromise between different positions among the MEPs, some of
whom will have been out-voted in the committee or the plenary on details of the
position of importance to them.

The Council of ministers meets in ten main configurations and a number of sub-
formations, each one dealing with a specific policy area or set of related policy areas.
A member of the national government, who is authorized to speak and take decisions on
its behalf, represents every member state. The Environment Council consists of national
environmental ministers, the Foreign Affairs Council brings together foreign ministers,
and so on. The total ministerial membership of the Council is therefore very large (at least
300 people) and changes as a result of national elections, cabinet reshuffles or other real-
locations of responsibility in the member states. The Council's political approach is also
subject to change as left- and right-wing parties move in and out of power or governing
coalitions are formed or reformed at national level. Many different views co-exist in the
Council, requiring a constant process of negotiation in order to achieve 'the Council position'. A key figure in finding that position is the Council chair, occupied by the minister
from the member state that holds the Council presidency. This position rotates among
the member states every six months except in the Foreign Affairs Council, which is

chaired by the High Representative for foreign affairs and security policy (see Chapter 3) and does not normally deal with legislation. Council presidencies can be more or less successful in terms of their ability to set, or at least shape, the policy agenda (see Tallberg 2004; Thomson 2008; Smeets and Vennix 2014). The Council presidency's ability to determine what issues are discussed, when, and for how long, is thought to be a potentially useful power in the policy-making process (see Häge 2017), although in practice the short tenure means a largely inherited agenda.

The detailed preparatory work for Council meetings takes place first in one or more of its 150 or so specialist technical working groups. They are composed of officials from the relevant national ministries in the member states, who discuss the Commission proposal article by article, registering agreements and disagreements and suggesting amendments. Any provisions that cannot be agreed at working group level (usually the more political aspects of the proposals) are sent up to the more senior Coreper (see Bostock 2002 for a still insightful analysis). There they are agreed or sent back down to the working group or up to the ministers in Council for further discussion and/or agreement. A representative of the Commission attends all meetings in the Council hierarchy when a Commission proposal is being discussed. Officials from the Council Secretariat are also present, to take minutes and advise the presidency. The national civil servants who sit on these preparatory bodies negotiate on behalf of their member governments. But only ministers in the Council can take the final decision, which then constitutes 'the Council's position'.

Members of EU institutions do not operate in a vacuum when engaging in policy-making. The policy outcomes they produce affect countless people who need to be informed about them and who may have valuable contributions to make regarding their design. As a result, large numbers of people are engaged in finding out the state of play on dossiers under discussion and, more controversially, in trying to ensure that particular interests are either protected or are at least unharmed by proposed legislation. There is a large Brussels-based international press/media corps, which is only slightly smaller than the press delegations based in Washington or London. Fulltime correspondents, freelance journalists, and those employed by online services report, analyse, and comment upon the activities of the EU's policy-makers.

A large group trying to influence EU policy-making are the interest representatives (lobbyists). They work for and speak on behalf of companies, trade associations, NGOs, law firms, think tanks, academic institutions, churches, and local, regional, and municipal authorities. In 2011, in an effort to shed some light on their existence and activities, the Commission and EP amalgamated two previously separate registers and established a common Transparency Register for interest representatives. By the end of 2017 it had almost 12,000 registrants. However, given that the entries in the register are voluntary, the estimation by the Corporate European Observatory of some 30,000 interest representatives operating in Brussels is probably not wide of the mark. Exerting influence on EU policy-makers has become something of an industry. Those who do it best know how to focus their efforts on the most important individuals and stages—which are not necessarily the key ones mentioned in the treaties.

Fluid stages

The three key stages in the policy-making process—agenda setting, negotiation, and final decision—are not distinct phases but rather overlapping sequences (Pollack 2015). It can be difficult for outsiders to determine or predict the length of the process and also to identify the exact occasion on which key events in the process actually take place. EU policy-making is an intensely political process, and events such as an upcoming national or EP election, a changeover in the Council presidency or the appointment of a new European commissioner can have important implications for the adoption (or not) of proposed legislation.

The first (agenda-setting) stage can last a very long time, depending on the perceived need for the policy instrument in question and the urgency with which it is required. The Commission enjoys the right of initiative, and the 'power of the text' is an important one. Amending the text is a power possessed by the Commission, or by the Council and the EP but subject to strict voting rules in the latter two cases. However, the Commission is careful to do its homework before submitting a draft proposal. It holds wide-ranging consultations with a variety of actors (often with competing or even contradictory interests) to determine the best way to deal with an existing situation and to identify possible difficulties of implementation once the legislation has been enacted.

When the Commission publishes its initial proposal, it is sent at the same time to a variety of different bodies—the EP, the Council, the 28 national parliaments, and, where required, the European Committee of the Regions and the Economic and Social Committee. Their respective responses are subject to strict time limits. National parliaments have a period of eight weeks from the date of receipt of the proposal to indicate formally whether they think the principle of subsidiarity has been respected. Some national parliaments are able to use this process, in practice, to shape the position that their minister will take in the Council. There is no set time limit for the EP and the Council to complete their respective first readings, but the Council is expected to await the EP's position in order to take it into account when determining its own position. Second readings in the EP and the Council are subject to time limits, as is the conciliation process. Failure by the EP to amend or reject the Council's position by the deadline means it is accepted. Failure by the Council to act by the deadline means the proposed legislation goes to conciliation. Negotiation (the second stage) occurs throughout the process: between stakeholders and the Commission when the proposal is being drafted, between left-wing and right-wing political groups when the EP is trying to agree its official position, and often between the Council Presidency and a group of member states trying to block the adoption of a compromise. A draft piece of legislation is thus subject to intense scrutiny both within and between the institutions. These negotiations can continue for many months, if not years, before any key stages in the process are completed.

However, the (third stage) 'final decision', when it occurs, is often merely the rubber-stamping of agreements reached earlier in other forums. The final adoption of a piece of legislation, on the Council's side, takes the form of agreement on an agenda point at a ministerial meeting, with the agenda point normally passed without discussion and frequently by consensus, on a recommendation from Coreper. On Parliament's side, it will be a vote on the text as it results from the negotiations with the Council, though normally with a debate and—except if it is a third reading—Safter rejecting amendments tabled by groups or members opposed to the agreement (see Figure 6.1). Knowing when and where to intervene in the process is therefore very important for those trying to affect its outcome.

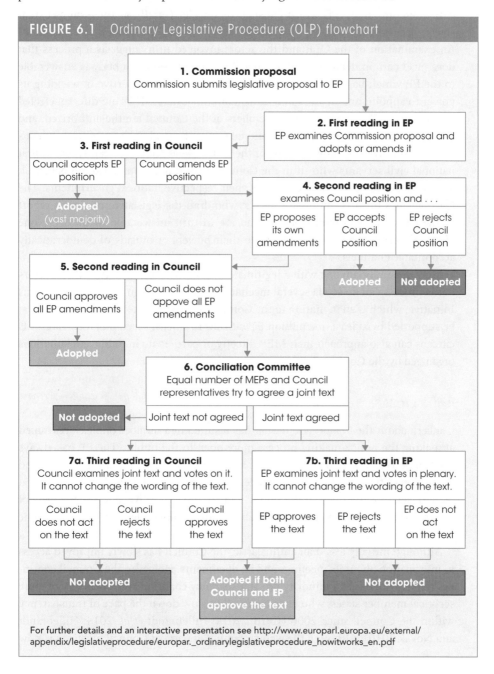

FIGURE 6.1   Ordinary Legislative Procedure (OLP) flowchart

For further details and an interactive presentation see http://www.europarl.europa.eu/external/appendix/legislativeprocedure/europar._ordinarylegislativeprocedure_howitworks_en.pdf

Assessing the Process

We have seen how the EU policy-making process works in practice. While a detailed examination of the process may enable us to understand *why* the process works in the way it does, it is worth asking whether the process can be viewed as transparent and efficient.

Before doing that, it is worth pausing to consider (briefly, as the issue is extensively discussed in Chapter 7) whether the policy-making process is *democratic*? An examination of the OLP, and the actors involved in it, suggests a process that does meet certain democratic standards. The Commission as a body is answerable to the EP, which has, in recent years, become increasingly assertive in wielding its power to appoint and dismiss individual commissioners. MEPs are directly elected by citizens of EU member states. Members of the Council are the authorized, and usually elected, representatives of national governments. For those officials operating at lower levels—below the tips of the icebergs—it should be remembered that national civil servants who sit in the Council's working groups speak on behalf of, and are answerable to, the members of their respective national governments. The *fonctionnaires* in the Commission's DGs, who draft the legislative proposals report to their respective commissioners, who are in turn answerable to the EP. None of the players operate without limits to their powers or outside of democratically accountable channels.

More generally, anyone with a legitimate message to convey to the official actors in the process can do so via several mechanisms. One is to sign a European Citizens Initiative, which is an invitation to the Commission to propose legislation that must be supported by at least one million EU citizens in at least seven member states. EU citizens can also approach their MEP directly or participate in public consultations organized by the Commission.

Is the process transparent?

Concern about the democratic deficit has resulted in a number of measures aimed at making the policy-making process more open to the public. The EP has always tried to be very open about its actions and modes of operation and has embraced the notion of transparency with considerable zeal. The Parliament's committee and plenary sessions are open to the public and are broadcast live, and the majority of its parliamentary documents are available in all 24 official languages in electronic format via a register.

Although initially less than enthusiastic, the Council has slowly improved access to information about its meetings and its documents. However, the Council continues to be divided into a minority pro-transparency coalition and a majority of more sceptical member states, who have managed to slow down the pace of transparency within the Council since 2006 (Curtin 2014; Hillebrandt *et al.* 2014; Hillebrandt and Novak 2016). Although the web-streaming of parts of Council meetings is now commonplace, the real negotiations continue to take place away from the cameras, lending credence to the view that most deals are still done behind closed doors in the interests of achieving public consensus.

Contrasting attitudes towards transparency within the EP and the Council are explained by the different nature of the policy-making process within both institutions. In the EP, debates in the committees and plenary are followed by a public vote, on which MEPs can be held to account by their constituents. In the Council, public votes by ministers reflect agreements reached elsewhere following detailed discussions behind closed doors among national officials in the preparatory working groups (see Miller 2013). It is significant that the conciliation and trilogue processes in the OLP, which bring together representatives of the Commission, the EP, and the Council, also take place behind closed doors. This practice is justified on the grounds that it is easier to reach agreement on controversial issues if the negotiations take place in private.

Is the process efficient?

Assessing the efficiency of the EU's legislative process has both quantitative and qualitative dimensions. It is relatively easy to produce figures on the number of legislative acts adopted each year, the stage in the process at which they are adopted, and the average length of time required to adopt them (see Tables 6.1 and 6.2). Undertaking a qualitative assessment is a more difficult exercise, because of the value judgements it is likely to contain about the process as a whole and the content of the output.

Generally, however, the output of the OLP is perfectly respectable (an average of 93 legislative acts adopted annually) and compares favourably to the output of many national systems. It is all the more impressive given the diversity of the actors and interests involved and the additional administrative steps required to accommodate the EU's 28 component systems. Trilogues (Box 6.3) have helped to make the process more efficient but, some argue, have come at the expense of transparency. Legislative output follows a certain rhythm, which is linked to both the EP's legislative term and the five-year life of each Commission. There are good reasons for this rhythm. A newly elected EP takes time to get itself organized—to decide on the composition and leadership of the committees and other organizational bodies, to agree on The appointment of *rapporteurs* for specific dossiers, and generally to get into a sustained tempo of work. Similarly, a newly appointed Commission must establish its priorities in legislative terms, and either continue or set in train a series of consultations and drafting exercises in order to produce proposals for legislative acts. Steering a legislative proposal through the various stages of the decision-making process in each of the institutions takes time (a minimum of 12 months). It also requires large amounts of coordination and communication at various levels both within and between the institutions.

As a result, the legislative output of the first year or so of the life of a new EP and Commission tends to be rather sparse. In contrast, the final year or 18 months of the EP's legislative term sees a sustained effort on the part of all the legislative actors to get as many procedures concluded as possible, if only because of uncertainty about their eventual fate in a new, unknown configuration of the EP after the European elections. This political reality explains the increased number of completed dossiers in the six months or so prior to the end of each legislative assembly's term.

Similarly, each Council Presidency period is marked by progress in the discussion and conclusion of procedures or, at least, agreement on the Council's stance on a particular dossier. Normally, agreements on Council positions reach a peak in the last month of the Presidency's term of office. Exit velocity is good for the Presidency's overall balance sheet, with legislative agreement viewed as one of the hallmarks of 'a good Presidency'. In qualitative terms, however, it is worth questioning the calibre of the legislative acts that are agreed, particularly if there is a suspicion that they were agreed under pressure of time. Sometimes, the EU is accused of producing poor-quality legislation or regulations that are difficult, if not impossible, to implement properly.

The procedural stage at which the final decision is reached between the Council and the EP is another means often used to assess the efficiency of the EU's legislative process. Since the introduction of the co-decision procedure there has been a steady increase in the number of dossiers agreed at an early stage in the process, and this increase has become more significant in recent years. At the same time, there has been a corresponding decrease in the number of issues that have been subject to conciliation. At face value, this shift suggests that the institutions are working well together to coordinate their positions in order to reach agreement without having to resort to additional readings. However, it is also likely that at least some of the dossiers included in these rather impressive totals were non-controversial and therefore had an easy passage through the process. It is also possible that the large number of dossiers ending up in conciliation in the early years of the co-decision procedure owed more to a high level of interinstitutional mistrust and

TABLE 6.2   Average length of time required to reach agreement under the co-decision / Ordinary Legislative Procedure

	1999–2004	2004–9	2009–14
1st reading	11 months	16 months	17 months
2nd reading	24 months	29 months	32 months
3rd reading (conciliation)	31 months	43 months	29 months
Total average length	22 months	21 months	19 months

Source: EP Activity Report on Codecision and Conciliation 14 July 2009–30 June 2014, at http://www.europarl.europa.eu/code/about/activity_reports_en.htm

the desire of the EP to flex its newly acquired legislative powers than to the divisive nature of the dossiers themselves.

It now takes an average of 17 months to reach agreement on the majority of dossiers adopted under the OLP. The general desire to avoid extra readings where possible has resulted in certain difficult dossiers now being agreed earlier in the process, thereby accounting for the increase in the average amount of time required for first- and second-reading agreements since the period 1999–2004. However, it should be remembered that, while strict time limits apply to the second-reading and conciliation (third-reading) phases of the procedure, no such limits apply to the first reading. It is therefore possible for either the EP or the Council to continue their internal first reading discussions on the dossier indefinitely with no legal or administrative consequences (apart perhaps from the irritation of those actors wanting a rapid outcome to the deliberations).

More positively, the lack of a time limit for the first reading gives the actors the opportunity to iron out difficulties and explore alternative solutions, which could lead to interinstitutional agreement at the end of the first reading. Taking a long time to reach an agreement may also be an indicator of the complexity of the dossier or of the initial distance between the positions of the various actors, which takes time to resolve. Time is often a valuable resource in all senses in EU policy-making. Inevitably, it frequently takes quite a lot of it to reach consensus on a policy result amongst 28 member states, three legislative institutions, and a vast number of affected interests, in Europe and beyond.

Theory and Practice

We have seen how EU policy-making takes place in practice. What light does theory shed? International relations approaches tend to focus on the broad development of European integration, rather than on how the Union makes policies. But neofunctionalists would highlight how the need for common European policy solutions has pushed integration forward via treaty changes to make collective action easier. For their part, liberal intergovernmentalists would insist that national EU governments still retain essential control—especially through the Council as well as the European Council—of what policies the EU actually produces.

Meanwhile, new institutionalists would argue that EU policy-making is now at least as much—if not more—about cooperation and competition between the EU's institutions than between European states. In particular, the EP has been empowered with each revision of the EU treaties. It has come into its own as a politically and legally equal co-legislator with the Council. Institutions truly matter in EU policy-making, especially because the EP and Commission are so much more powerful than their counterparts, if there really are any, in other international organizations.

Public policy scholars stand on strong ground in arguing that European policy-making is dominated by discrete policy networks; especially ones that are policy-specialized. Much of the EU's policy work is highly technical and requires specialist expertise, which creates barriers to entry to all but experts. Even at a more political level, each policy sector has its own Council, Commissioner, Commission DG, and EP committee. EU policies thus may be viewed as mostly a result of bargaining between (usually) a diverse collection of participants in sectoral policy networks.

Similarly, constructivists can claim to shed considerable light on EU policy-making. They find no shortage of evidence that the preferences—even the *interests*—of policy-makers are constructed in the course of bargaining at the EU level, as opposed to defined extrinsically and prior to negotiations in Brussels. The relentless search for compromise and consensus means that even when, say, a member state brings a strong position fixed in their national capital to EU negotiations, it almost inevitably is shaped and 'bent' in ways that make it possible to attract allies to adopt or block a policy decision.

Conclusion

In this chapter, we have looked at the formal rules that describe how the legislative process works in theory. We have also examined the ways in which these rules have been interpreted and implemented over the years in order to show how EU legislation is actually adopted in practice. We have seen how formal actors—the members of the EU's institutions—operate alongside and in close collaboration with a host of other participants drawn from a wide range of sectors of civil society. We have noted how the formal stages of the legislative process have been adapted to operate alongside other informal processes that can and do affect the final outcomes. We have, in other words, put some flesh on the bones of the process in order to build up a more accurate picture of its actual appearance—and hopefully to dispel a few myths.

There is no denying that the EU's policy-making process is complex. A very large number of official actors are involved at every stage of the process, operating in diverse forums, using a variety of languages and following complicated procedures. Their proceedings are monitored closely by a growing number of representatives of European civil society. Its members do their best, both publicly and behind the scenes, to have their interests taken into account when legislation affecting them is being prepared. A large European and international media corps publicizes and comments on the process. Each of the EU's institutions maintains a website with information on its activities in all the policy areas in which it is involved.

There is therefore no dearth of information about what is going on in the EU today. But there is no denying a lack of understanding about how the process actually operates in practice. Our description demonstrates that compromise and consensus are the key features of the process. In order to reach agreement at EU level, bargains must be struck not only between but also within the institutions in an ongoing process of negotiation. Some of these negotiations are played out in public, but the most difficult and sensitive discussions continue to take place behind closed doors. The most visible stages of the decision-making process are only one small part of a long and complex series of exchanges that are open to input from a much greater variety of actors, including ordinary citizens, than is immediately apparent. The process is still not as democratic or as transparent as many would like. But it continues to function and to produce a rather impressive amount of legislation that affects a growing number of realms of the daily lives of ordinary citizens in Europe and beyond.

DISCUSSION QUESTIONS

1. What are the most important differences between the formal rules for EU policy-making and more informal norms that have sprouted over time?

2. How do we explain the fact that the Council of ministers only takes a formal vote on proposed policy measures about 15 per cent of the time?

3. Does the increasing involvement of outside interests in the EU's decision-making process make for better policy?

4. Is democracy strengthened or undermined by the presence of non-elected interest groups in the EU decision-making process?

FURTHER READING

The definitive guide to policy-making in the EU remains Wallace *et al.* (2015). On the EP, including its political groups, see Corbett *et al.* (2016, especially Chapter 10). On the Council of ministers, see Hayes-Renshaw (2017). A special issue of the journal *West European Politics* (2011) contains interesting articles on the effects that changes in interinstitutional decision-making rules have had on politics and behaviour within the institutions. A special issue of the *Journal of European Public Policy* (2013b) reflects on 20 years of the co-decision/OLP process. There is a very wide literature on lobbying in the EU, with Greenwood (2017) the most up-to-date general text and Panke (2012) a strong overview. Van Schendelen (2013) is very readable and applies the work of Machiavelli to Brussels lobbying. Klüver (2013) develops an innovative quantitative methodology to study the influence of interest groups. Coen and Richardson (2009) remains a key work on EU lobbying that is both theoretical and case-study based. A special issue of the *Journal of European Public Policy* (2015a) is devoted specifically to interest representation in Brussels.

Coen, D. and Richardson, J. (2009), *Lobbying in the European Union: Institutions, Actors and Issues* (Oxford: Oxford University Press).

Corbett, R., Jacobs, F., and Neville, D. (2016), *The European Parliament*, 9th edn (London: John Harper).

Greenwood, J. (2017), *Interest Representation in the European Union*, 4th edn (Basingstoke and New York: Palgrave).

Hayes-Renshaw, F. (2017) 'The Council of Ministers: Conflict, Consensus and Continuity', in D. Hodson and J. Peterson (eds), *Institutions of the European Union*, 4th edn (Oxford: Oxford University Press): chapter 4.

Klüver, H. (2013), *Lobbying in the European Union: Interest Groups, Lobbying Coalitions, and Policy Change* (Oxford: Oxford University Press).

Journal of European Public Policy (2013b) Special issue on 'Twenty Years of Legislative Codecision in the European Union', 20/7.

Journal of European Public Policy (2015a) Special issue on 'Legislative Lobbying in Context: The Policy and Polity Determinants of Interest Group Politics in the European Union', 22/4.

Panke, D. (2012), 'Lobbying Institutional Key Players: How States Seek to Influence the European Commission, the Council Presidency and the European Parliament', *Journal of Common Market Studies*, 50/1: 129–50.

Van Schendelen, M. (2013), *The Art of Lobbying the EU: More Machiavelli in Brussels*, revised edn (Chicago, IL: University of Chicago Press).

Wallace, H., Pollack, M. A., and Young, A. R. (eds) (2015), *Policy-Making in the European Union*, 7th edn (Oxford and New York: Oxford University Press).

West European Politics (2011), Special Issue on 'Linking Inter- and Intra-Institutional Change in the European Union', 34/1.

WEB LINKS

- For a graphic explaining the OLP, see http://www.europarl.europa.eu/external/appendix/legislativeprocedure/europarl_ordinarylegislativeprocedure_howitworks_en.pdf

- Information on the state of play of all dossiers under discussion in the OLP can be found on the websites of EUR-Lex http://eur-lex.europa.eu/collection/legislative-procedures.html) and the EP (http://www.europarl.europa.eu/oeil/home/home.do). The EP's conciliations and co-decision website (http://www.europarl.europa.eu/ordinary-legislative-procedure/en/home/home.html) contains much useful and interesting information and statistics on dossiers now subject to the OLP.

- The website of the EUI Observatory on Institutional Change and Reforms contains links to the main documents introducing changes to the co-decision procedure (http://www.eui.eu/Projects/EUDO-Institutions/DocumentsonLegislation.aspx).

- www.Votewatch.eu is an excellent source of information on voting in the Parliament and the Council.

- The Commission's and the EP's Transparency Register, which is constantly being updated, can be viewed (at http://www.ec.europa.eu/transparencyregister). See www.lobbyfacts.eu for further information about interest representation in the EU and specifically about groups who have signed up for the Transparency Register.

- The websites of the main Brussels-focused think tanks include the Centre for European Policy Studies (http://www.ceps.eu/); the European Policy Centre (http://www.epc.eu/); the Centre for European Reform (http://www.cer.eu/); and Bruegel (http://www.bruegel.org/).

 Visit the Ancillary Resource Centre that accompanies this book for additional material: www.oup.com/uk/kenealy5e/

CHAPTER 7

Democracy in the European Union

Richard Corbett

Summary

With so many decisions taken at European Union (EU) level, what are the implications for democracy? All EU member states are (indeed, have to be, as a condition for membership) democratic. But when they take collective decisions through European institutions, the individual choices available to national democracies are naturally constrained. To what extent do democratic procedures at the European level compensate for this narrowing of choices at national level? Is there a 'democratic deficit'? How, anyway, do we measure 'democracy'? National democratic systems are diverse, but do have some common features: can we evaluate the EU using them as a yardstick?

Democracy Beyond the State?

Economic, environmental, and other forms of interdependence mean that national authorities alone cannot adequately deal with a growing number of problems. Many require concerted international action at various levels. But traditional methods of international cooperation are slow, cumbersome, and frequently opaque. They involve negotiations among ministers (and, in practice, mainly officials) representing their countries. In most cases, nothing can be agreed without consensus—thus creating a bias towards weak, lowest-common-denominator agreements. When an agreement *is* reached, it is (perhaps) submitted as a fait accompli to national parliaments on a take-it-or-leave-it basis. The quality of democracy on such issues is low. Such are the working methods of the World Trade Organization (WTO), the International Monetary Fund (IMF), the World Bank, the United Nations (UN, including on climate change), North Atlantic Treaty Organization (NATO), and regular summits such as the Groups of 8 or 20 (G8 and G20) and countless other structures.

The EU purports to be different. It is not (always) in hock to the lowest common denominator. It has an elected Parliament, directly representing citizens and bringing into the process representatives of both governing and opposition parties in each country. Decisions on legislation are taken in public. It has an independent executive, the European Commission, headed by commissioners who are politically accountable to the Parliament. It has a common Court to ensure uniform interpretation of what has been agreed. It has safeguards to ensure that it respects fundamental rights. It has more developed mechanisms than any other international organization for informing, and sometimes involving, national parliaments. So, can we say that 'the EU not only forms a Union of sovereign democratic states, but also constitutes a democracy of its own' (Hoeksma 2010)? Can democracy work at all on an international basis?

Some argue that democracy can only work when there is a demos, that is, a common feeling of belonging to the same community (see Moravcsik 2002). A demos is usually held to involve speaking the same language and having a shared past and similar expectations about behaviour and values. Others argue that this view of democracy is tribalist and point out that if speaking a common language is a requirement, then Switzerland, India, Canada, South Africa, and many others cannot be categorized as democratic. Debates around 'demos' and decision-making will continue, but most agree that, as some decisions *are* taken at European level, it should be done in as transparent, accountable, and democratic a way as possible.

The EU's basic rulebook is set out in the treaties. They lay down its field of competences, the powers of its institutions, how to elect or appoint people to those institutions, and the details of its decision-making procedures. Some scholars argue that the treaties can therefore be described as a *de facto* constitution (see Weiler 1998; Box 11.1). But, an attempt to rewrite those treaties and formally label them as a 'constitution' failed in part because of reticence in some countries to the idea of the EU being a state-like federation. Opinions diverge as to what the nature of the EU should be and how far its democratic accountability should flow through democratically chosen governments in each county or, alternatively, through the directly elected Parliament. Or perhaps it should flow through both, with a dual democratic legitimacy, represented by its bicameral legislature: the Council representing the governments of the member states, whose democratic legitimacy is conferred on the national level, and the European Parliament (EP), directly elected by citizens. It is not a question of whether national governments *or* the EP best represent EU citizens: both are needed to sustain the EU's claim to be democratic.

Caveats, however, apply. First, the EU does not operate by simple majoritarian rule. The adoption of legislation by a qualified majority vote in the Council may indeed achieve more than the lowest common denominator consensus that applies in traditional international organizations. But it still requires a hefty majority: as we saw in Chapter 3, a qualified majority must comprise at least 65 per cent of the represented population in the Council. And in the Parliament, members of the European Parliament (MEPs) do not represent citizens equally, as the ratio of member to population is considerably lower in the smaller member states. This point was highlighted by the German Constitutional Court in its 2009 ruling on the Lisbon Treaty in which it held that, for that very reason, the EP could not be compared to a parliament representing a single people. Second, democratic choice of the executive is not as visible in the way that citizens are used to in a national context (see Hix 2008; Chevenal and Schimmelfennig 2013; Hurrelmann 2014). Neither by direct election nor through parliamentary elections does the electorate determine the political composition of the Commission—or at best, only for its president (and for the others, via nominations by elected national governments). Do these caveats render the EU undemocratic? Is there a **democratic deficit** in the EU (see Box 7.1)?

BOX 7.1   Key concepts and terms

Bicameralism is from Latin *bi*, two + *camera*, chamber. When a legislature comprises two chambers, usually chosen by different methods or electoral systems.

Democratic deficit was a term initially used to denote the loss of democratic accountability inherent in national parliaments transferring their right to legislate to ministers meeting in the Council. It was considered that giving the EP the right to approve or reject EU legislation should compensate for this transfer of power. Now that the EP has such powers (in most policy areas), the term has taken on a less precise meaning, often linked to the distance between EU institutions and voters.

European Convention on Human Rights (ECHR) is completely separate from the EU and its Court of Justice. It is an international treaty drafted in 1950 by the

→

➜ then newly formed **Council of Europe (CoE)**. All (the now 47) Council of Europe member states are party to the Convention. Any person who feels his or her rights, as defined in the Charter, have been violated by a state can appeal to the **European Court of Human Rights**. Judgements finding violations are binding on the state(s) concerned.

Charter of Fundamental Rights of the European Union: the EU has its own Charter of Rights that binds the EU institutions, and with which EU law must comply. Adopted initially as a political declaration by the EU institutions in 2000, it was given treaty status by the Treaty of Lisbon. It obliges EU institutions to respect the rights contained in the ECHR and others.

To shed more light on this discussion, we evaluate the democratic credentials of the EU by asking whether it matches some key features common to many modern democratic systems:

1. Representation: is legislation adopted by representative assemblies?

2. Are powers separated?

3. Is the executive democratically accountable?

4. Are fundamental rights guaranteed?

5. Do competing political parties offer voters genuine choice?

Legislating through Representative Assemblies

Under the Union's **Ordinary Legislative Procedure (OLP)**, proposals need to be approved by directly elected representatives in the Parliament and indirectly elected representatives in the Council. The budget is similarly subject to the approval of both, as are almost all international agreements entered into by the Union. This dual requirement involves a scale of parliamentary scrutiny not found elsewhere beyond the level of the nation state. And, as we saw in Chapter 3, the EP is not a rubber stamp, subservient to the executive through a governing majority party or a coalition. David Farrell, a leading academic expert on legislatures and parliamentarians, has described it as one of the most powerful legislatures in the world. We also saw (in Chapter 2) that it has not always been thus. Originally, the EP was merely a consultative body of seconded national parliamentarians, with final decisions being taken behind closed doors in the Council. After the first direct elections in 1979, it took three decades and successive revisions of the treaty to change this state of affairs. Public perceptions have lagged behind, and the Parliament is still seen by many as a toothless tiger.

The EP is also sometimes held to be inadequate in another respect. It is not just the approval of legislation, but also the right to initiate it, which is held to be an important democratic criterion. After all, people are elected to parliaments having made promises to their voters: at least some of those promises require initiating or repealing legislation. But in the EU, there is a gap insofar as the EP cannot (except in a few specific cases) itself table proposals for adoption.

Yet this difference must be nuanced. Parliament and Council both have the right to request the Commission to put forward a legislative proposal. If it does not, both have ways and means to make life difficult for the Commission. Conversely, in national parliaments, which in most (but by no means all) cases do enjoy a right of legislative initiative, it is almost invariably the government that initiates proposals. It is in the give-and-take of debate and discussion between the legislature and the executive that ideas and initiatives emerge. This dynamic is not so different at EU level.

How representative are the Parliament and the Council?

Where the Parliament is concerned, the question of representation is often linked to electoral turnout. Turnout in the most recent EP elections has been around 43 per cent, or about the same as for mid-term US Congress elections (that is, when there is no presidential election). By one view, it is normal that turnout is lower than for national parliamentary elections in European countries—less is at stake. But turnout for EP elections has also fallen—by nearly 20 percentage points over a 30-year period. This decline (accentuated by the accession of new member states, several of whom have a low turnout in all elections) is not actually less than the decline in turnout in national parliamentary elections in most countries. Declining participation is a challenge for democracy at all levels, not peculiar to the European level, even if the latter does have special features (see also Box 7.2).

> **BOX 7.2   Compared to what? Referenda in EU member states**
>
> An alternative to representative democracy is direct democracy: the organizing of referenda to settle issues. National traditions diverge enormously, with referenda being (almost) unknown in most member states, or at least reserved only for constitutional changes. There is no provision under the treaties to allow for EU-wide referenda, even on 'constitutional' changes to the EU system. Occasional proposals to introduce them come up against the opposition of countries that do not have referenda as part of their national traditions. Even if member states did agree, the question remains: by what majority should decisions be taken? Just a simple majority of those voting, or also a majority (or more) of states as well?
>
> Some member states have organized national referenda on European issues. Most countries acceding to the EU did so, with only Norway deciding not to join.
>
> →

> Some have had referenda on treaty changes: two frequently (Ireland and Denmark, because of national constitutional requirements) and four (France, Luxembourg, the Netherlands, and Spain) occasionally. The UK coalition government in 2010 introduced legislation to require a national referendum for any future treaty change that transferred powers or competences from the UK to the EU. Most famously of all, in 2016, the UK Conservative government led by David Cameron, held an advisory referendum on UK membership of the EU. A majority of 51.9 per cent of voters (37 per cent of the electorate) voted to leave the EU (Curtice 2017).
>
> Previously, debates on the merits of referenda on treaties had featured during the ratification stage of the proposed EU Constitution in 2005. Most member states considered that it required detailed scrutiny and a vote by their national parliament. Four held national referenda: two approving it (Spain and Luxembourg) and two rejecting it (France and Netherlands). Although the grand total of the votes in the four countries showed a majority in favour—and every parliamentary vote approved it—the need for every single member state to ratify individually caused the Constitutional Treaty to fall.

Even on a low turnout, European elections do result in all the main strands of public opinion being represented in the EP. A transnational parliament highlights that most policy choices at European level have political, not national, dividing lines, with the different sides of an argument present in every member state. MEPs come from parties of the left and of the right and even from parties who are opposed to the very existence of the EU. Because EP elections frequently fall mid-term in national political cycles, they often result in a larger share of the seats going to opposition parties and smaller parties than would be the case in most national elections. EP elections thus can perhaps be dismissed as little more than a protest vote, but the results matter: they elect a wide variety of parties and thus have the effect of balancing the Council, whose members come exclusively from governing parties. The Parliament thus enhances pluralism and ensures that EU decisions are not left exclusively to ministers, diplomats, and bureaucrats.

In the Council, member states' representatives (ministers) cast a number of votes related to their size, unlike in many federal systems where the 'chamber of states' often gives equal representation to all states irrespective of size. This proportionality can be seen as making the Council more representative of citizens. Yet, the fact that Council representatives must cast all their votes on behalf of their member state as a bloc could be viewed as distorting the representation of the people. However it is viewed, the weighted bloc vote is a feature the Council shares with the German *Bundesrat*, with which it also shares a number of other structural similarities (see Box 7.3).

BOX 7.3   Compared to what? The Council and the German *Bundesrat*

	Council	Bundesrat
Composition	Ministers from member state governments; preparatory meetings by permanent representatives (ambassadors) of member states in Brussels	Ministers from state (*Länder*) governments; preparatory meetings by permanent representatives of states in Berlin
Voting	Each member state's vote weighted by size and cast as a bloc	Each state's (*Land*) vote weighted by size and cast as a bloc
Majorities required	Usually, threshold higher than simple majority (qualified majority or unanimity)	To disagree with *Bundestag*, threshold usually higher than simple majority (absolute majority)
Reconciliation with elected chamber	Conciliation Committee with EP	Conciliation Committee with *Bundestag*

As we saw in Chapter 3, what had originally been the key aspect of this weighted bloc vote, namely a fixed number of votes, disappeared in 2014. The new system features a double majority based on one vote per state on the one hand, and a vote weighted by population (still cast as a bloc) on the other. Thus, the two traditional representational features found in bicameral federal systems—equality of states in one chamber and equality of citizens in the other—will both be found in a single chamber in the EU: the Council. Meanwhile, representation in the Parliament is digressively proportional, over-representing smaller states.

Nonetheless, the Parliament and Council between them can test the acceptability of proposals from the point of view of both a majority of component states and the majority of the component population, with states represented as such in one chamber, and citizens in the other. They perform these functions in the context of a consensual, rather than an adversarial, style of political system. High thresholds are needed, notably in the Council, to adopt any legislation, budget, or policy. All in all, the EU system involves a greater number of representative channels than can be found anywhere else in the world above the level of the nation state.

Involving national parliaments

Also unique are the Union's provisions for helping *national parliaments* scrutinize the participation of their government in EU institutions. In certain cases, national parliaments may intervene directly themselves independently of their national government. The treaty lists a number of ways in which national parliaments 'contribute actively to the good functioning of the Union'.

One notable innovation in the Lisbon Treaty is a Protocol 'on the Application of the Principles of Subsidiarity and Proportionality'. It contains a new procedure allowing national parliaments to send, within eight weeks of receiving a legislative proposal, a reasoned opinion to the EU institutions stating why they consider that the draft does not comply with the principle of subsidiarity (that is, it goes beyond the remit of the EU). If such reasoned opinions come from enough national parliaments (roughly one-third), then the Commission must review the draft. It must then justify its decision to maintain, amend, or withdraw its proposal. Employing a football analogy, this procedure is known as the *yellow card*. Alternatively, if such reasoned opinions come from more than half of EU parliaments, then a special vote must take place in the Council and in the EP, either of which can immediately kill off the proposal (by a simple majority in the EP or by a majority of 55 per cent of the members of the Council). This is known as the *orange card* procedure, as it was proposed by the Dutch (whose football team wears orange), and is not quite a red card. These procedures are an important safeguard to prevent over-centralization of powers, even if they are rarely needed: in the first seven years of operation of the procedures, only three proposals triggered even a yellow card.

But the very existence of these procedures means that more national parliaments are paying close attention to European legislation—and in practice to its substance—rather than just checking subsidiarity. More may start holding committee hearings of their country's minister before Council meetings, as is already standard practice in the Nordic countries, or send comments on the substance of proposals directly to the Commission (there are currently some 200 such submissions per year). Also, parliaments confer among themselves, exchanging documents through an electronic exchange system (IPEX), or meeting together at committee level or in inter-parliamentary conferences.

National parliaments are also involved in the process of future treaty change. Any intergovernmental conference to revise the treaty must (unless the EP decides otherwise) be preceded by a Convention composed of members of national parliaments, the EP, the Commission, and a representative of each government. And, of course, in most member states, national parliaments must ultimately ratify such treaty changes.

The treaty provisions involving national parliaments are thus quite numerous. In truth, most national parliaments have little time to devote to the fine-grained detail of EU issues. Unlike the EP, most are in a classic government/opposition structure where governing majorities mean that there is, in practice, little scope to amend government texts or reverse their policies. National parliaments also have less time, expertise, and staff to devote to European matters than does the EP, which works full time on EU affairs. National parliamentary procedures, practices, and timetables all diverge. Nonetheless, national parliaments are able to scrutinize and sometimes take part in EU decision-making to a degree that simply does not exist in other international organizations. In sum, the involvement in the adoption of legislation of both a dedicated EP and national parliaments means that the EU's credentials measured against this particular yardstick of democracy are substantial.

Separation of Powers

Most democracies operate a separation of powers, although the separation of the legislative, executive, and judicial functions is not always clear. Indeed, many speak of a 'sharing' of powers across institutions, with checks and balances, rather than a separation of powers (Neustadt 1991). In particular, the executive and the legislative functions have tended to merge in most European democratic systems (although they remain more distinct in presidential systems, notably in the Americas).

Some European countries blur this distinction completely. The UK and Ireland, for instance, actually require members of the government to be simultaneously members of the legislature (even if this sometimes just means appointment to the UK House of Lords or the Irish Senate). By contrast, in France, a parliamentarian who becomes a minister must resign his or her seat for the duration of his or her ministerial mandate. Either way, it is the norm in most European countries for the executive to have a majority in Parliament, which, through the party system and other mechanisms, is usually compliant to the wishes of the executive. The separation between these two branches thus becomes less than clear. Only the judicial function remains clearly separate.

In the EU, the separation between the executive and the legislature is in some ways more distinct. Commissioners may not simultaneously be MEPs. In the EP there is no compliant governing majority for the executive. Thus, in adopting legislation, a majority has to be built anew for each item through explanation, persuasion, and negotiation. The EP's role is thus more proactive than that of most national parliaments in Europe.

The Council (of Ministers) is the institution that muddies the waters. It is, of course, a co-legislator with the EP. However, it is also empowered to act as an executive in specific cases. When acting on macro-economic policy or foreign affairs, it is fulfilling an executive rather than a legislative function, albeit one that consists largely of coordinating national executives rather than constituting a European one.

The European Council (of heads of state and government) does not directly act as an executive, or as a legislature (indeed it is precluded from exercising a formal legislative role by the treaty). Yet it influences both. Formally, it is the strategic body, charged with defining the 'the general political directions and priorities' of the Union. Informally, as a meeting of the most powerful political figures of the member states and the Union, it is often called upon to settle thorny political questions that can be of an executive, legislative, or constitutional nature. It also nominates or appoints a number of key posts in the Union. Its own president has a representational role in addition to his main task of preparing and building consensus. The European Council could be considered as a sort of collective 'head of state' of the Union in that its political role is similar to that of heads of state in national semi-presidential systems (see Chapter 3).

As for the judicial function, the European Court of Justice (ECJ) is composed of judges 'chosen from persons whose independence is beyond doubt'. They must take an oath to 'perform their duties impartially and conscientiously'. The deliberations of the Court are secret, so individual judges cannot be pressurized about judgements. We never know how any judge voted on any case unless they reveal how they voted in their memoirs.

Interestingly, the Court's members are appointed neither by the EU's executive nor by its legislature. Instead, they are appointed by the member states. The Court thus differs from the US Supreme Court, whose justices are appointed by federal authorities (president and Senate), not by the states. The only common European element in the appointment procedure of the members of the ECJ was introduced in the Lisbon Treaty. Appointees are now scrutinized by a panel chosen by the Council and consisting of seven former judges of the Court (or of national supreme courts) or eminent lawyers.

The appointment of individual judges therefore depends more on the government of the member state from which they originate than on the European executive or legislature. If there is any political consideration in their appointment, it is at the member state level and diffuse: each national government nominates only one judge. Another method used in many democracies to lessen political pressure on judges is to appoint them for a lengthy term of office, or even for life, as in the US Supreme Court. Judges in the ECJ are appointed for a (renewable) six-year term of office.

The Court has exercised an important independent function, ensuring that the institutions respect the law, though it can only do so when a matter is referred to it. The independence of the judiciary is clear. It has both struck down acts of the Union's political institutions and ruled against member states when they have failed to apply European law. Overall, the Union system is characterized by a separation, or sharing, of powers, which is at least as distinct as is the case in most of its member states.

Executive Accountability

The relationship between the outcome of European parliamentary elections and the composition of the executive is not as visible as it is in most European national parliamentary elections. But, the view that the Commission is 'unelected', unlike national governments that are, is simplistic. For example, the people do not elect the UK government: technically, the head of state (an unelected one at that) appoints a Prime Minister who appoints a government but crucially the government must enjoy the confidence of the directly elected House of Commons. Similarly, the European Commission must enjoy the confidence of the EP. The EP has always had the right to dismiss the Commission. In the 1990s, it acquired the right to approve the appointment of the Commission, and indeed to elect its president. In fact the EP took such votes even before such procedures were laid down formally in the treaties (see Table 7.1). The grilling that candidate commissioners receive from EP committees at their confirmation hearings prior to their confirmation goes well beyond what ministers have to face in most European countries.

Despite all this, few citizens would consider the Commission to have an elected mandate. They might if the College of Commissioners were composed to reflect a majority party or, more likely, a majority coalition, in the EP. Yet a Commission thus composed is unlikely to emerge in the short-to-medium term: most governments want to nominate as the commissioner from their country a member of their own political 'family'. What *has* begun to change is that the vote on the president of the Commission is becoming more political and linked to the outcome of elections. That vote is increasingly important, as the president's pre-eminence within the Commission has grown.

The change to the treaties brought in by Lisbon refers to the 'election' of the president of the Commission by the Parliament. This vote is, as before, on a proposal of the European Council but the latter must now 'take into account the results of the European elections' in making its nomination. This provision potentially makes the

TABLE 7.1 Election of Commission President by the European Parliament

	Incoming Commission presidents	Parliamentary votes
July 1992	Jacques Delors (third term)	278 votes for, 9 against
July 1994	Jacques Santer	260 votes for, 238 against (23 abstentions)
May 1999	Romano Prodi (for unfilled portion of Santer term)	392 in favour, 72 against (41 abstentions)
September 1999	Romano Prodi (full 2000–5 term)	426 in favour to 134 against (32 abstentions)
July 2004	Jose Manuel Barroso (first term)	431 in favour to 251 against (44 abstentions)
September 2009	Jose Manuel Barroso (second term)	382 in favour to 219 against (117 abstentions)
July 2014	Jean-Claude Juncker	422 in favour to 250 against (47 abstentions)

> **BOX 7.4**   Compared to what? How are heads of executive chosen?
>
> *Commission president*: elected by EP by an absolute majority on a proposal of the European Council, which must take account of the results of European parliamentary elections.
>
> *German chancellor*: elected by the *Bundestag* by an absolute majority on a proposal of the Federal president.
>
> *UK prime minister*: appointed by the Queen in light of advice as to who can secure a parliamentary majority in the lower chamber (House of Commons), but with no formal vote in parliament.
>
> *US president*: chosen by an electoral college, whose members are elected in each state, normally as a function of which presidential candidate they support.
>
> *French prime minister*: chosen by the directly elected president, without requiring a vote by parliament. However, the lower chamber (*Assemblée*) may dismiss the government by an absolute majority.
>
> *Swiss government*: college of seven (with annual rotation of the president among them), elected by the two chambers of the parliament (and comprising members of all major parties).
>
> *Swedish prime minister*: nominated by the speaker of the parliament and serves unless opposed by an absolute majority of (single chamber) parliament.
>
> *Italian prime minister*: nominated by the president whose **cabinet** then requires approval by both chambers of the parliament (simple majority).

nomination similar to that of a head of state choosing a candidate prime minister who is capable of enjoying a parliamentary majority (see Box 7.4).

As a result, European political parties have started nominating their candidates for Commission president ahead of European elections. Even before Lisbon, ahead of the 2009 elections, the European People's Party (centre-right) was very clear that, in the event of it having the largest number of seats in the EP, it would expect the nominee for Commission president to come from its ranks. The Greens actually nominated Daniel Cohn-Bendit as their candidate, in the unlikely event that they would obtain a parliamentary majority. This momentum continued in 2014, when the five main European political parties named their candidate for Commission president ahead of the elections, and televised debates were held between these candidates ahead of the elections (Dinan 2015; European Parliament 2015). The public attention this generated, however, varied from country to country. Nonetheless, despite some misgivings from some of its members, the European Council proceeded to nominate the candidate of the largest party, Jean-Claude Juncker, who was duly elected by the EP. Early analysis suggests that this new system has not transformed European democracy in any significant way (Christiansen 2016).

In practice, no single party ever wins a majority of seats in the EP. Some bargaining and coalition forming is inevitable. But this kind of negotiation also occurs in most member states. The spectacularly direct link between the outcome of a parliamentary election and the designation of a prime minister seen (usually) in the UK is the exception rather than the norm. But the outcome even in, say, the Netherlands is that the public sees that the executive—usually consisting of a coalition of parties—that eventually emerges is connected to an election and reflects its pattern of votes.

If this practice of naming candidates for the position of Commission president becomes established, the link to the elections will still apply only to the *head* of the Commission. The other commissioners nominated by each national government will reflect national political balances. Does this 'halfway house' mean the Union is not comparable to a national democracy and can never be? Not necessarily. Take the case of Switzerland, which for over half a century has been governed by a coalition of the four largest parties, with an annually rotating president. Is such a collegiate system undemocratic? Does the lack of a direct relationship between the outcome of the parliamentary elections and the governing coalition render elections meaningless? Most Swiss would seriously object to their country being described as undemocratic. Yet the composition of the European Commission too is always (in political terms) a coalition of at least the three main political parties in Europe (the Juncker Commission has 14 Christian Democrats, eight Socialists, five Liberals, and, initially, one Conservative). The Commission would appear to be edging towards a hybrid of Swiss-style collegiality in its overall composition, but with a more majoritarian approach to designating its president.

If so, it is part of a long-term trend. Before 1994, commissioners were simply designated by the member states to serve a four-year period without further ado. The Maastricht Treaty changed the term of office to five years to coincide with the cycle of European parliamentary elections, and provided for a vote of confidence by Parliament on the Commission as a whole. From 1999, the Amsterdam Treaty required a decisive parliamentary vote on the designation of the president. The Lisbon Treaty characterized this vote as an election and required the European Council to make its nomination taking account of the EP election result—further implying that the parliamentary majority is what will be decisive.

What of the president of the European Council? From December 2009 this post became a full-time and longer term position, and thus vital for the dynamics of the European Council. The president's role as a facilitator and broker of deals at the highest political level is crucial, but he or she has no formal powers to take decisions as an individual, other than setting the agenda and convening meetings.

Certainly, it can be a confusing post for the public to understand. The press sometimes uses the term 'president of Europe' in some cases (and in some countries) for the president of the European Council and in other cases (and other countries) for the president of the Commission. With one chairing the day-to-day executive with a right of initiative, and the other chairing the strategic body laying down the Union's priorities and settling key issues, the difference between the two presidents will not always be clear to average Europeans. Nor indeed for third countries: both presidents represent the Union at external summit meetings.

But above all, the two presidents have quite different forms of democratic legitimacy. That of the Commission president (elected by the EP and linked to majorities resulting from its elections) is likely to be more visible than that of the president of the European Council (elected by the heads of state or government of the member states). Suggestions that one or both should be directly elected are unlikely to get very far and would in any case likely cause further problems in the relationship between the two. Even with the best will in the world, some degree of uncertainty about these respective 'presidential' roles is likely to continue. The possibility of merging them, as has been done at the level of the High Representative (who is both a vice-president of the Commission and chair of the Council (of foreign ministers)), may return to the agenda. But it is unclear that it would ever gain sufficient support.

Finally, to the extent that the Council (of ministers) has an executive role, to whom is it accountable? Collectively, to no one—though most decisions require EP approval. But individually each of its members is accountable through a national government to a national parliament. Given that the Council's main 'executive' tasks are essentially about coordinating national policies (foreign policy, defence, macro-economic coordination), this member-state-based accountability may be considered appropriate. In any event, the Council must additionally justify itself in EP debates and answer parliamentary questions.

To sum up, accountability of the executive is present in the EU even if it is complex. For the main executive body (the Commission), a system close to what is found in most national contexts—that is, accountability to a Parliament—has been established. However, the system is not well known to citizens and the link between the results of parliamentary elections and the composition of the executive is not very visible. As for executive functions exercised elsewhere, they are either in an institution that is deliberately independent (the Central Bank), or else through institutions (Council and European Council) whose members are accountable individually to separate parliaments.

Respecting Fundamental Rights

Democracy is frequently defined as rule by the majority. But in modern times, it is increasingly seen as going hand-in-hand with respect for minorities and for the rights of individuals. Governments and even elected parliaments can be challenged in the courts should they fail to respect fundamental rights.

This feature can also be found in the EU. Initially it was exercised via case law: the ECJ acknowledged that the Union had to respect the fundamental rights that are common to the constitutional traditions of the member states. The Court recognized that all member states had signed the ECHR (of the Council of Europe) and that it should be a source of law for its own deliberations. The Maastricht Treaty after 1992 entrenched this case law in the treaty itself.

With the Lisbon Treaty, the Union obtained its own Charter of Rights (see Box 7.1), intended both to make those rights already contained in the ECHR visibly applicable to the Union but also to complement them with other rights. The Charter was framed in such a way as to be binding in the field of EU law. In other words, it binds the EU institutions, and member states when applying European law. It means that decisions or acts of the Union can be struck down by the Court should they fail to respect the rights contained in the Charter.

Furthermore, the Lisbon Treaty provided for the Union itself to accede to the ECHR. Although this has not yet occurred, it will give plaintiffs the right to appeal to the European Court of Human Rights should they fail to gain satisfaction from the ECJ, much in the same way as in member states an appeal can be made against the final judgement of a national court. In other words, the EU's legal system will be subject to the same external yardstick as member states' legal systems. Thus, in relation to the formal criterion of respecting fundamental rights, the EU system and procedures measure up well.

Political Parties

Besides the constitutional requirements for democracy to function effectively, a functioning system of political parties is a practical need. As we have seen, the EP provides a pluralistic forum, with over 150 national political parties converging into political groupings. But to offer choice to the electorate in elections, and to channel and aggregate policy demands into workable programmes, party structures beyond Parliament are needed. One of the main points of debate about democracy in the EU is about whether pan-European democracy is impossible in the absence of pan-European parties (see Lindberg *et al.* 2008). In the European context, such parties have evolved as federations of national parties, but they are looser groupings than are parties in most national European contexts (see Box 7.5).

BOX 7.5   European political parties

European political parties are cross-national and can reach beyond the EU. They are linked to but distinct from the political groups in the EP. Three existed before the first direct elections to the EP:

- the Party of European Socialists (PES), comprising parties affiliated to the Socialist International;
- the European People's Party (EPP), comprising Christian Democrats and other centre-right or conservative parties; and
- the Alliance of Liberals and Democrats for Europe (ALDE), previously the European Liberal, Democratic and Reformist Party (ELDR), comprising a variety of liberal and allied parties.

➡

→

Two more emerged between 1979 and 2004 (and MEPs from these two parties currently sit in the same Group in the Parliament):

- the European Green Party;
- the European Free Alliance, comprising regionalist and nationalist parties such as the Scottish, Flemish, Basque, Corsican, Sardinian, Catalan, and Welsh nationalists.

A number of other (usually smaller) European political parties were created following the adoption of a system for financing such parties in 2004. Some on the right or far right have been through several configurations, and regroupings, as alliances have shifted, and some folded. For example:

- the Party of the European Left (which includes a number of Communist or former Communist parties);
- the Alliance of European Conservatives and Reformists (AECR, notably including (pre-Brexit) the UK Conservatives);
- Movement for a Europe of Liberties and Democracy (Eurosceptic national conservatives);
- the European Alliance for Freedom (EAF) (far right, ultra-nationalists);
- the Alliance of European National Movements (far right, ultra-nationalist);
- Europeans United for Democracy (formerly EU Democrats) (Eurosceptic).

The recognition and the development of these parties have been incremental. The Treaty of Maastricht introduced a new article referring to the importance of European political parties. Later, they were granted legal personality and—crucially—access to funding, provided certain conditions are met, such as being represented in a sufficient number of member states (at least one-quarter) and respecting the principles of the EU (such as liberty, human rights, and so on), although they do not have to support the existence of the Union itself. They also must publish their accounts and have them independently audited, as well as publish the names of any donors contributing more than €500. Parties may not accept donations of more than €12,000 from any single donor, nor accept anonymous donations. Money provided from the EU budget for European parties may not be passed on to national parties.

The main parties are active in a growing number of areas. They organize regular congresses, composed of delegates from the respective national parties and involving their EP Group. Their leaders can hold 'summits' with leaders of their national parties (often prior to European Council meetings), sometimes involving fellow party members in the Commission and their EP Group leader. They adopt common manifestos for European elections. Their decision-making tends in practice to be by consensus among the national member parties, which means that the content of their policies tends towards the lowest common denominator. Their visibility is limited. They are generally unknown to the public, except in the broadest sense that—for the Socialists, Liberals, Greens, and Christian Democrats—national voters may be aware that they are part of a larger European grouping and that they work together in the EP. Only a sophisticated minority of voters will actually be aware of the common manifestos on which they stand in European elections.

However, even without such awareness, their activities can lead to a degree of convergence around common positions of corresponding parties. The parties do certainly play a role in the 'division of spoils' in terms of securing prominent positions at European level, and not just within the EP. For example, it was quite clear at the time of the choice of president of the European Council and High Representative in 2009, and again in 2014, that these posts were to be shared between the EPP and the Socialists.

Parties also play a role in the choice of president of the Commission, as we have seen earlier in the chapter. The further development of this role provides an opportunity for European political parties to become more visible, as well as offering the electorate a choice of personalities and not just of policies. In short, European political parties do play a role, not just in representation but also in policy formation and in the choice of key political office holders. That role remains limited and rather invisible to the bulk of the electorate. However, it has been developing and expanding, albeit slowly.

Conclusion

The EU requires that its member states be democratic and respect fundamental rights. The EU even has a procedure for suspending a member state that ceases to fulfil this requirement. Developments after 2017 in Hungary and Poland, for the first time, raised questions about how the EU ought to handle the existence of member states that might not be upholding and practicing appropriate democratic standards (see chapter 4). Whether the EU *itself* fulfils these criteria is a more complex question. It has given rise not only to much debate, but also to many of the treaty amendments of the last 30 years.

We have seen that the EU system does fulfil fundamental democratic norms, but in a way that is more complex and less visible to the public than is the case at national level. Like any political system, it has its own idiosyncrasies. Inevitably, its detailed functioning is different from what people are familiar with within their national system (themselves diverse). Those differences and complexity give rise to misunderstandings and can also be exploited by its opponents.

Nonetheless, the EU is unique in how far it goes to try to apply democratic principles at a level above the nation state. How successful it is, remains open to debate (see Habermas 2008). One of the arguments deployed by the Leave campaign in the 2016 UK referendum was that it is insufficiently democratic (and some even argued that democracy can only exist at national level). A study by Duina and Lenz (2017) concluded that the EU, at the very least, was one of the most democratically legitimate regional economic organizations. There is no doubt that this debate itself is one of the features of the EU that make it so fascinating.

DISCUSSION QUESTIONS

1. How can democratic accountability be assured for those matters dealt with at European level? Should it be via national parliamentary scrutiny over their own government's negotiating position, or via the EP, or both?

2. Does the relatively low turnout in European elections matter?

3. Are fundamental rights sufficiently protected at European level?

4. Should the European Commission emanate from a parliamentary majority in the EP?

5. Are referenda in individual member states an appropriate way to ratify EU treaties or to settle membership?

FURTHER READING

For a detailed account of the EP, see Corbett *et al.* (2016). Hix *et al.* (2007) and Hix (2009) cover internal cleavages and voting patterns in the EP. Hix (2008) also offers a comprehensive programme for EU democratic reform. For a critical appraisal of the EP's links with the public, see Hug (2010). For different evaluations of the democratic credentials of the EU and the challenges of transnational democracy, see Siedentop (2000); Moravcsik (2002); Bogdanor (2007); and Hoeksma (2010). For an interesting argument that the EU should be evaluated not as a democracy but rather as a 'demoicracy'—that is a polity of multiple, distinct peoples—see Nicolaidis (2013), a special issue of the *Journal of European Public Policy* (2015b), and Cheneval and Nicolaidis (2017). More recent work connects the concept of 'demoicracy' to questions about political boundaries within the EU, see *Journal of European Integration* (2017). Glencross (2011) offers interesting insights on ways to legitimize the EU. Corbett (2002) assesses the impact of having an elected parliament on the process of integration. For an interesting examination of alternative futures by a leading European intellectual, see Habermas (2008).

Bogdanor, V. (2007), *Democracy, Accountability and Legitimacy in the European Union* (London: Federal Trust for Education and Research).

Cheneval, F. and Nicolaidis, K. (2017) 'The Social Construction of Demoicracy in the European Union', *European Journal of Political Theory*, 16/2: 235–60.

Corbett, R. (2002), *The European Parliament's Role in Closer EU Integration* (Basingstoke and New York: Macmillan).

Corbett, R., Jacobs, J., and Neville, D. (2016), *The European Parliament*, 9th edn (London: John Harper Publishing).

Glencross, A. (2011), 'A Post-National EU? The Problem of Legitimising the EU without the Nation and National Representation', *Political Studies*, 59/2: 348–67.

Habermas, J. (2008), *Europe: The Faltering Project* (Cambridge and Malden, MA: Polity).

Hix, S. (2008), *What's Wrong with the European Union and How to Fix It* (London: Polity).

Hix, S. (2009), *What to Expect in the 2009–14 European Parliament: Return of the Grand Coalition?* (Stockholm: Swedish Institute for European Policy Analysis).

Hix, S., Noury, A., and Roland, G. (2007), *Democratic Politics in the European Parliament* (Cambridge and New York: Cambridge University Press).

Hoeksma, J. (2010), *A Polity called EU: The European as a Transnational Democracy* (Amsterdam: Europe's World).

Hug, A. (2010), *Reconnecting the European Parliament and its People* (London: Foreign Policy Centre).

Journal of European Integration (2017), Special Issue on 'European Boundaries', 39/5.

Journal of European Public Policy (2015b), Special Issue on 'Demoicracy in the European Union', 22/1.

Moravcsik, A. (2002), 'Reassessing Legitimacy in the European Union', *Journal of Common Market Studies*, 40/4: 603–24.

Nicolaidis, K. (2013), 'European Demoicracy and Its Critics', *Journal of Common Market Studies*, 51/2: 351–69.

Siedentop, L. (2002), *Democracy in Europe* (Harmondsworth: Penguin).

WEB LINKS

- Websites of the institutions: see Chapter 3.
- Voting behaviour in the EP: http://www.votewatch.eu/
- European People's Party: http://www.epp.eu/
- Party of European Socialists: http://www.pes.org/
- European Liberal Democrats: https://www.lidems.org.uk/alde
- European Green Party: http://europeangreens.eu/
- COSAC: http://www.cosac.eu/en/

Visit the Ancillary Resource Centre that accompanies this book for additional material: www.oup.com/uk/kenealy5e/

PART IV

THE EU AND THE WIDER WORLD

CHAPTER 8

EU Enlargement and Wider Europe

Ulrich Sedelmeier with Graham Avery

Summary

The European Union (EU) has enlarged many times, and many countries still aspire to join. The EU has extended the prospect of membership to countries in the Balkans and Turkey and has developed a 'neighbourhood' policy towards other countries, some of which may want to join in future. Enlargement illustrates the success of the European model of integration. It has also provided the EU with a powerful tool to influence domestic politics in would-be members. But enlargement also poses fundamental challenges. It has implications both for how the EU works (its structure and institutions) and for what it does (its policies). The EU has become lukewarm about further enlargement, which raises questions about its continued ability to use its transformative power to promote stability, prosperity, and good **governance** in would-be member states.

Introduction

The EU's process of enlargement goes to the heart of important questions about the nature and functioning of the Union. Why do countries wish to join? How does the EU decide its future shape and size? How should it interact with its neighbours? How committed is the EU to further expansion?

It is often said that enlargement is the EU's most successful foreign policy tool. The EU has indeed used enlargement to promote prosperity, stability, and good governance reforms in neighbouring countries. It has set demanding conditions for membership: would-be members have to carry out far-reaching reforms before they are allowed to join. The success of accession conditionality (see Box 8.1) gives enlargement a special place among the EU's external policies.

But enlargement is much more than foreign policy: it is the process whereby outsiders become insiders, and shape the development of the EU itself. In accepting new members, and deciding the conditions under which they join, existing members define the EU's future composition and collective identity. In that sense, enlargement could be described as a constitutive policy (Sedelmeier 2015): when the EU makes choices about new members, it determines its own future.

Widening versus deepening

The prospect of enlargement poses basic questions both for applicant countries and existing members. Before applying, countries need to analyse how membership will affect them. What will accession (see Box 8.1) mean in political and economic terms? What will be the costs and benefits? What should be the country's long-term aims as a member? This kind of reflection raises questions of national strategy and identity.

A recurrent theme in the development of the EU has been the tension between the 'widening' of its membership and the 'deepening' of integration between its members (Wallace 1989; Kelemen *et al.* 2014). Each time the EU contemplates a further expansion, its members are compelled to address fundamental questions about the purpose and the future of European integration.

BOX 8.1   Key concepts and terms

Absorption capacity refers to the EU's ability to integrate new members into its system.

Accession is the process whereby a country joins the EU and becomes a member state.

Benchmarks in accession negotiations are conditions for opening and closing 'chapters' related to specific EU policies.

Candidate countries refer to those countries whose application for membership the EU has confirmed, but which are not yet members.

→

> **Conditionality** refers to the fact that the EU makes the accession of a country dependent on its compliance with certain requirements for membership.
>
> **European Economic Area (EEA)** is an arrangement that extends the EU's **single market** to Norway, Iceland, and Liechtenstein.
>
> **Screening** occurs at the start of negotiations when the applicant and the Commission examine the **acquis** to see if there are particular problems to be resolved.
>
> **Variable geometry**, also known as multi-speed Europe or differentiated integration, is the idea that not all EU member states need to take part in creating common rules in some policy areas.

When considering who should be new members, the EU has to reflect on how the membership of this prospective member will affect its set of common policies and the functioning of it institutional set-up, as well as the prospects for changing, or agreeing new, common policies and institutions in the future. Debates on the future of European integration regularly accompany enlargement, although for countries trying to join the EU the 'widening versus deepening' debate can seem introspective. But the potential impact of enlargement on the Union's capacity to take decisions is an important question. The EU is attractive to non-members not only because its current policies are beneficial for them, but also because the Union is effective in taking decisions and developing policies. To expand without safeguarding its effectiveness would be an error. Enlargement policy is thus linked with wider debates on, and presents an occasion for, institutional reform.

Have successive enlargements weakened the EU? Although the arrival of new members requires a period of 'settling in', it is often followed by the development of new policies and strengthening of the institutional framework. For example, the EU's structural funds and a more ambitious cohesion policy resulted from the accession of Greece, Portugal, and Spain; poorer countries needing financial aid. Later it was feared that the accession of Austria, Sweden, and Finland—countries that had pursued neutrality or non-alliance—would put a stop to the EU's Common Foreign and Security Policy (CFSP). But in practice these countries have viewed the CFSP's development more favourably than some of the older members.

From time to time older members complain that it was easier to take decisions when the EU was smaller. But arguably successive increases in size have allowed the EU to develop more substantial and effective policies, internally and externally, than would have been possible with a smaller group. The process of widening has often accompanied or driven deepening: 'more' has not led to 'less'.

Enlargement as soft power

The success of enlargement in helping to drive political and economic change in Central and East European countries offers a good illustration of the EU's 'soft power' (Nye 2004) or 'external governance' (Schimmelfennig and Sedelmeier 2004;

Lavenex 2004). The EU's external pressure through accession **conditionality** (see Box 8.1) was a powerful transformative factor for policy-makers in those countries to pursue domestic reforms in the pre-accession period (Schimmelfennig and Sedelmeier 2005a; Vachudova 2005; Epstein and Jacoby 2014; Grabbe 2006, 2014). As countries in post-Communist transition, they were receptive to western political and economic models, and needed sustained external assistance.

Conditionality was not employed in earlier enlargements. When the Commission proposed in 1975 that Greece's membership should be preceded by a period of preparation, member states rejected the idea. In the 1990s, Austria, Sweden, and Finland, which already had a high degree of economic integration with the EU through a free trade agreement and **EEA** membership (see Box 8.1), were able to join swiftly after the Council decided to start accession negotiations. The principle of conditionality was developed for the countries of Central and Eastern Europe, as existing members were apprehensive that taking in so many new countries that had just emerged from Communist authoritarian political systems and planned economies without adequate preparation could impair the EU. These concerns led the EU in 1993 to define the membership criteria for the countries of Central and Eastern Europe.

These membership requirements (known as the 'Copenhagen criteria' as they were announced at a European Council meeting in Copenhagen, see Box 8.2) have become the standard template for enlargement. They require a wide-ranging assessment of a country's political, economic, and administrative standards that go further than any examination made by the EU of its existing members (although member states can be sanctioned for failure to respect the Union's basic principles). Crucially, the membership criteria relate not only to a country's ability to comply with the EU's common rules and the body of EU law. Conditionality also includes political criteria relating to democracy, human and minority rights, and good governance, where the EU demands high standards of new members that do not apply to existing members. The different demands for would-be members can be seen as double standards. However, the different treatment is only temporary. After joining, an applicant country becomes a member like others. That the leverage gained through conditionality is effective only in the pre-accession period raises questions about the sustainability of conditionality-induced political changes and what the EU can do about 'democratic backsliding' after accession.

BOX 8.2   Criteria for membership

Treaty provisions

The Treaty on European Union (TEU) states:
Article 49 [extract]:
   Any European state which respects the values referred to in Article 2 and is committed to promoting them may apply to become a member of the Union. . . . The

→

> → conditions of eligibility agreed upon by the European Council shall be taken into account.
>
> *Article 2:*
>
> The Union is founded on the values of respect for human dignity, freedom, democracy, equality, the rule of law and respect for human rights, including the rights of persons belonging to minorities. These values are common to the Member States in a society in which pluralism, non-discrimination, tolerance, justice, solidarity and equality between women and men prevail.
>
> ## Copenhagen criteria
>
> The European Council at Copenhagen (1993) stated that membership requires that the candidate country has achieved:
>
> • stability of institutions guaranteeing democracy, the rule of law, human rights and respect for and protection of minorities;
>
> • a functioning market economy as well as the capacity to cope with competitive pressure and market forces within the Union;
>
> • the ability to take on the obligations of membership including adherence to the aims of political, economic and monetary union.
>
> It added another criterion for enlargement:
>
> • The Union's capacity to absorb new members, while maintaining the momentum of European integration, is also an important consideration in the general interest of both the Union and the candidate countries.

An institutional paradox

The enlargement process gives specific insights into the functioning of the EU's institutions. The mode of operation for enlargement is essentially intergovernmental. The Council adopts all decisions on enlargement by unanimity. While majority voting in EU decision-making has been extended in many areas, no one has ever suggested extending it to enlargement. Accession negotiations take place in an intergovernmental conference organized between the member states and the applicant state. The result is an Accession Treaty, signed and ratified by sovereign states.

The roles of the European Parliament and the Commission in the process of enlargement are limited. The Parliament has the right to approve or reject enlargement, but only at the end of the negotiation process, when it votes on a yes/no basis without being able to modify the Accession Treaty. During accession negotiations, Parliament is informed regularly, but has no seat at the table.

The Commission's status in accession negotiations is not the same as in external trade negotiations where it acts as spokesperson (see Chapter 9). In accession conferences the Council Presidency, rather than the Commission, presents EU positions, even on matters where the Commission has competence. Formally the Commission is not the EU's negotiator, although it may be mandated by the Council to 'seek solutions' with applicants. Nevertheless, in practice the Commission plays an extremely influential role in the process of enlargement. In fact, it exercises more influence over applicant countries than after they become members. The Commission's influence stems from its role in monitoring the progress of applicant countries in respect of the criteria for EU membership. Its annual 'Regular Reports' on each country provide the benchmarks for decisions on the conduct of enlargement. It is the Commission that presents proposals to the Council for 'common positions' to be taken by the EU side, and it is thus in a position to act as an intermediary with the applicant countries. It can (and should) take account of the future interests of the EU as a whole by making proposals that reflect the views of the future members as well as existing members.

Within the Council, enlargement is handled in the General Affairs Council, not the Foreign Affairs Council. One upshot is that the EU's High Representative for foreign and security policy has no role in accession negotiations. The fact that the Commission, not the European External Action Service, manages Enlargement policy shows that it is not considered primarily as foreign policy.

How the EU Has Expanded

The first applications for membership were made by the United Kingdom (UK), Denmark, and Ireland in 1961, soon after the European Communities came into existence. The contested nature of enlargement was reflected in two vetoes of the UK's accession by French President De Gaulle, but the three countries eventually joined in 1973. Over time, the number of EU member states has quadrupled (see Box 8.3), its population has tripled, and its official languages have increased from four to 24. Especially since the end of the Cold War, enlargement has been a permanent item on the EU's agenda. Multiple countries are either already in accession negotiations or have formally applied for membership (see Box 8.4).

BOX 8.3 Chronology of enlargement			
	Application for membership	**Opening of negotiations**	**Accession**
UK	1967	1970	1973
Denmark	1967	1970	1973
Ireland	1967	1970	1973
Greece	1975	1976	1981
Portugal	1977	1978	1986

Spain	1977	1979	1986
Austria	1989	1993	1995
Sweden	1991	1993	1995
Finland	1992	1993	1995
Hungary	1994	1998	2004
Poland	1994	1998	2004
Slovakia	1995	2000	2004
Latvia	1995	2000	2004
Estonia	1995	1998	2004
Lithuania	1995	2000	2004
Czech Republic	1996	1998	2004
Slovenia	1996	1998	2004
Cyprus	1990	1998	2004
Malta	1990	2000	2004
Romania	1995	2000	2007
Bulgaria	1995	2000	2007
Croatia	2003	2005	2013

Notes: The UK, Denmark, and Ireland first applied in 1961, but negotiations ended in 1963 after France vetoed their admission.Norway applied twice (1967, 1992) and completed negotiations, but Norwegians twice said 'No' in referenda (1972, 1994). Switzerland made an application in 1992 but suspended it in the same year after a 'No' in a referendum on the EEA. Iceland made an application in 2009 and negotiations began in 2010, but were suspended in 2013 by its government. In 1990 enlargement took place without accession when East Germany joined the German Federal Republic.

Despite the large number of countries wishing to join, the path to membership is not easy. Conditionality requires extensive, and often very difficult, domestic reforms before negotiations on accession can begin. And even if they are eventually started, the negotiations are arduous (see Boxes 8.5 and 8.7): there is no guarantee that they will end in agreement, or by a certain date, and the bargaining is inevitably one-sided. The EU insists that applicant countries accept all its rules (known as the *acquis*), and allows delays in conforming to EU law in specific issue areas (transitional periods, see Box 8.1) only in exceptional cases. Moreover, the member states often insist on transition periods during which the new members will not fully enjoy the benefits of membership, for example with regard to free movement of labour or receipts from the EU budget (see Schneider 2008). Yet new members generally accept even such one-sided accession treaties since they are still much better off inside the EU than outside, and they benefit much more from EU membership than the current members benefit from their accession. This asymmetry in the intensity of preferences for enlargement between the EU and **candidate**

countries explains why the EU has much more bargaining power in accession negotiations. The EU has never invited others to join its club—in fact it has tended to discourage them. In this sense, the EU's strategy for enlargement has been reactive rather than pro-active. The Union has grown because of its attraction for neighbouring countries, not as the result of an expansionist strategy.

BOX 8.4 Prospective members

	Application for membership	Candidate status	Opening of negotiations
Turkey	1987	1999	2005
Macedonia (FYROM)	2004	2005	
Montenegro	2008	2010	2012
Albania	2009	2014	
Serbia	2009	2012	2014
Bosnia-Herzegovina	2016		
Kosovo			

Notes: This list includes all countries currently considered by the EU to be in the accession process. When the EU decides that an applicant country has made sufficient progress, it may award it the status of 'candidate'. Until then, it has the status of 'potential candidate', as Kosovo had at time of writing (despite not being recognized as a state by some EU members).

Why countries want to join . . .

The demand for accession reflects a mixture of self-interest and identity politics (Schimmelfennig and Sedelmeier 2002, 2005b). Countries apply to join the EU if they consider membership to be in their political and economic interest. In the case of the UK, its application was motivated by the prospective benefits of the common market for trade and economic growth. But its leaders also realized that the original six members were on the way to creating a European system from which the UK could not afford to be excluded politically. Ireland and Denmark, due to their close economic relations with the UK, tied their application to the UK's. For the UK (and Denmark), the economic incentives trumped a long-standing opposition to European supranational integration. In the UK, these contradictory dynamics continued to coexist uneasily until the narrow rejection of EU membership in the 2016 referendum (see Chapter 10).

BOX 8.5 The path to membership

Start. A country submits an application for membership to the Council of the European Union:

1. The Council considers whether the country satisfies the conditions of Article 49 (see Box 8.2).

→

→

2. The Council asks the Commission for an Opinion.
3. The Commission delivers its Opinion to the Council.
4. The Council confirms the applicant country's status as a candidate.
5. The Council decides to open accession negotiations, conducted in an intergovern-
    mental conference between the EU member states and each applicant individually.
6. The Commission screens (see Box 8.1) the 34 chapters of the *acquis* with the appli-
    cant.
7. Individual chapters in the negotiations are opened when the Council decides that
    the applicant has met the relevant benchmarks (see Box 8.1).
8. The applicant presents its position for that chapter; the Commission proposes a 'com-
    mon position' of the EU, the Council approves it, and presents it to the applicant.
9. After agreement is reached on each chapter, it is closed when the EU decides that
    the applicant has met the relevant benchmarks.
10. When all chapters are closed, the EU and the applicant agree on a draft treaty of Ac-
    cession.
11. The Commission issues an Opinion on the treaty.
12. The European Parliament gives its consent.
13. The member states and the applicant(s) sign the treaty.
14. The signatory states ratify the treaty according to their national procedures, which
    may include a referendum.
Finish. The treaty comes into force, and the applicant country becomes a member
state.

The applications from Greece, Portugal, and Spain were made in different circumstances. After emerging from right-wing totalitarian regimes, these countries saw
EU membership as a confirmation of their return to democracy. In contrast to the
UK, identity politics—the sense of being accepted back into the European family of
democracies—were an important driving force for accession, rather than merely the
prospect of access to the common market and significant transfers from the budget.

When Austria, Sweden, and Finland applied for membership in the late 1980s
and early 1990s, the balance of economic rationale and identity politics mirrored
more closely the UK's. These countries applied, despite longstanding reserva-
tions about European integration, to ensure unrestricted access to the newly created single market. The end of the Cold War had made redundant their traditions
of neutrality, and thus domestic obstacles to EU membership were lifted. The EU's
concerns that their primarily economically motivated accession would become
an obstacle to further integration and foreign cooperation resulted in the creation of the **EEA** in 1994 (see Box 8.1) as an alternative framework to membership, but a framework that gave them access to the single market. Since the EEA
obliged them to accept EU rules without having a say in deciding them, the
three countries never considered it more than a temporary step on their way to
full membership—although it turned out to become precisely that for Norway,
which had also been engaged in EU accession negotiations. After its population

voted in 1994—repeating the result of a 1972 referendum—against EU membership, Norway (with Iceland and Lichtenstein) decided to remain in the EEA. The economic benefits of the single market, and the exclusion of agriculture and fisheries from the EEA were sufficiently large to outweigh the political assymmetry of hte EEA.

BOX 8.6 Compared to what? EU and NATO—a double race to membership

After the end of the Cold War, most of the countries of Central and Eastern Europe wanted to join the North Atlantic Treaty Organization (NATO) as well as the EU. NATO is a transatlantic military alliance created in 1949 in face of a perceived threat from the Soviet Union. Its members are committed to mutual assistance under Article 5 of the NATO Treaty, which says that 'an armed attack against one or more of them in Europe or North America shall be considered an attack against them all'. NATO now has 29 members:

• US, Canada;

• 22 EU states (all except Austria, Cyprus, Finland, Ireland, Malta, Sweden);

• Norway, Iceland, Turkey, Albania, Montenegro.

Most other European states, including Russia and Sweden, have an association with NATO but are not full members.

For the countries of Central and Eastern Europe, concerned about Russia's future intentions, NATO offers hard security in the military sense, including its nuclear 'umbrella'. In contrast, the EU offers **soft security** in the sense of membership of its political and economic union. For these countries NATO is easier to join than the EU because:

• NATO has less demanding membership requirements, mainly concerning the organization and equipment of troops;

• NATO's leading member, the US, pressed for its enlargement.

The result of the double enlargement is that the membership of the two organizations now largely overlaps, which makes it easier for them to work together. But the NATO/EU relationship is not simple, and there remains a basic asymmetry (see Chapter 9). NATO, unlike the EU, includes the US. NATO has the military tools to deal with the results of insecurity, while the EU has tools of civilian crisis management as well as those needed to address causes of insecurity, relating to the promotion of economic integration and good governance.

When the countries of Central and Eastern Europe escaped from Communism and Soviet domination, they turned to the EU for economic assistance and membership. Like Greece, Spain, and Portugal, they wanted to rejoin the European family, and to consolidate their return to democracy. For their transition from central planning to market economy, the EU's standards offered a convenient template. Uncertain of Russia's future role, they wanted EU membership for security in addition to NATO membership, which they pursued at the same time (see Box 8.6).

BOX 8.7 How it really works: Joining the EU individually or together

Although enlargement may involve a single country (as in the cases of Greece and Croatia), the EU usually prefers to have a group of countries joining in a single wave of accession. Even when the EU negotiates with a group of countries at the same time, each accession negotiation is separate. The EU insists that it treats each applicant country on its own merit, according to the principle of 'differentiation': the path to membership depends on individual progress in meeting the criteria. Differentiation also allows the EU to create competition between applicant countries that puts pressure on individual candidates to accept concessions made by other candidates for fear of being left behind. Such competition further increases the asymmetric nature of accession negotiations, in which the EU is in a far stronger bargaining position. It helped to push the Central and East European countries towards membership together in 2004, despite significant obstacles in the negotiations, and on terms that were highly favourable to the existing member states.

Applicants often demand a target date for membership. But the EU does not concede one until the end of negotiations, since the promise of a date weakens the conditionality of the process.

. . . and when the EU decides to let them in

As we saw in the initial applications of the UK, the EU does not always respond positively to accession requests. Just like candidate countries applying for membership, member states inside the EU are influenced by a combination of self-interest and identity politics when deciding whether to let an applicant country join (Schimmelfennig and Sedelmeier 2002). Moreover, since enlargement requires a unanimous decision in the Council, the member states least interested in enlargement generally determine whether and under what conditions accession takes place. Usually they also extract concessions from the new member states and from other member states that are keen to see enlargement happen (see Box 8.7).

Enlargement is generally considered beneficial to the EU, since it enlarges the Union's market and increases the effectiveness of common policies. At the same time, a larger membership can make decision-making more difficult, especially if preferences become more diverse. It can also create problems for the sustainability of certain EU policies that require significant budgetary resources, such as agriculture or regional policy. In general, enlargement is easier when candidate countries are rich, as in the 1995 enlargement, rather than poor, as in the southern and eastern enlargements. Smaller countries are easier to absorb (as was the case in 1995 with Austria, Finland, and Sweden) than bigger countries. Bigger countries have the advantage of more significant markets, but they can also put more serious pressure on EU policies if they are poor and have a large agricultural sector (such as Poland). Concerns by individual member states about economic competition has also been an important factor delaying accession, such as concerns of French farmers about Spanish agricultural products in the case of the southern enlargement.

Apart from material self-interest, considerations of identity also play a role, both as a driving force and an impediment of enlargement. De Gaulle's veto of the UK also reflected doubts about the European vocation of a country considered too Atlanticist to be fully committed to European integration. Conversely, arguments about Greece as a cradle of European civilization by then French president Giscard d'Estaing convinced other member states to overrule the Commission's opinion that Greek membership should be preceded by a preparation period.

The case of eastern enlargement presents a particularly interesting example of the role of identity politics. Although these new members made significant concessions in accession negotiations that reduced the costs of enlargement for the insiders (Schneider 2008), they were temporary. Those concessions cannot fully explain why there was no veto from member states such as Portugal, Spain, or Ireland— that compete with the newer eastern members for agricultural and regional funds— and where geographical distance greatly reduces both the economic opportunities of enlargement and the risks of non-enlargement. One explanation is that the EU's pan-European identity and rhetoric of re-uniting the continent in a community of democracies served as a constraint on openly self-interested opposition to enlargement. Many governments were reluctant about enlargement but felt that they could not legitimately object to a policy to which they had rhetorically committed themselves (Schimmelfennig 2003; Sedelmeier 2005). Since the eastern enlargements have been the most challenging so far, they deserve a more detailed discussion.

Recent enlargements

The disintegration of the Soviet bloc in 1989 was a seismic shock, creating risks of instability in Europe. Civil war broke out in ex-Yugoslavia, and such strife could have occurred elsewhere if events had unfolded differently. But the countries of Central and Eastern Europe succeeded in charting a route to democracy, stability, and prosperity by making far-reaching economic, social, and political reforms. The prospect of EU membership served to guide them through a peaceful 'regime change' in which the process of Europeanization—the domestic process of adapting to the EU's rules, norms, and policies—played a key role (see Chapter 4; and Vachudova 2005; Schimmelfennig and Sedelmeier 2005a; Grabbe 2006, 2014; Epstein and Jacoby 2014).

Faced in the early 1990s by many new aspirants for membership, the EU responded cautiously. At first, it concluded 'Europe Agreements' on aid, trade, and foreign policy consultations with countries of Central and Eastern Europe, but initially refused to promise membership. At the Copenhagen summit in 1993, the Union eventually accepted that these countries could join once they fulfilled the 'Copenhagen criteria' for membership (Box 8.2).

Accession negotiations opened with the first six countries in 1998 and six more in 2000 (including, Cyprus and Malta as non-post-Communist countries), reflecting differences in the pace of alignment with EU requirements. The main problems were:

- free movement of labour: the EU allowed old members to maintain restrictions on workers from new member states for up to seven years;
- agricultural policy: the EU insisted on a period of 12 years for introducing direct payments to farmers in the new member states; and
- regional fund and cohesion policy: the EU restricted the level of payments to the new, much poorer, members (see Avery 2004).

The enlargement to Central and Eastern Europe was an extraordinary episode in the history of European integration. It shifted the EU's scale of activity to a continental level. Eastern enlargement helped the transition both to democracy and market economies in post-Communist states and united a Europe divided during the Cold War between east and west. In awarding the Peace Prize to the EU in 2012, the Norwegian Nobel Committee cited enlargement, declaring that it had 'helped to transform most of Europe from a continent of war to a continent of peace'.

However, despite its many successes, eastern enlargement has also contributed to a marked cooling in the EU towards further enlargements—an 'enlargement fatigue'. With the enlargements of 2004 and 2007 and the financial crisis of 2008, the question of 'absorption capacity' (see Box 8.1) has again become an element in the debate. This notion, introduced at Copenhagen in 1993 (see Box 8.2), is vague but refers to the need to ensure that enlargement does not jeopardize the EU's ability to 'maintain the momentum of European integration'. However, the claim of a limited absorption capacity is also a convenient cover for much deeper reluctance about enlargement among many member state governments due to domestic opposition that populist parties tap into and galvanize.

Public opinion, particularly among the older member states, is more resistant to enlargement. It is often blamed for, or exacerbates, problems arising from other causes such as globalization or government cuts to public services. In particular the influx of workers from the newer member states has been perceived as causing social problems in some of the older member states.

The persistence of governance problems—such as corruption, maladministration, and weak judiciaries—in the new members generally, and especially in Bulgaria and Romania, led to a widespread perception in the EU that their accession had been premature and that the accession criteria should be applied more rigorously. One result was the EU's 'New Approach' to accession negotiations in 2012, under which the chapters on fundamental rights, justice, freedom, and security are treated as a priority. Moreover, future accessions may be subject to referenda in existing member states.

More generally, the EU's more cautious approach to enlargement has led to a weakening of membership prospects for current candidate countries. The decreased credibility of the incentive of membership—that candidate countries are not sure if the EU will accept them even if they have met all the accession criteria—has triggered a vicious circle. The EU has lost leverage over domestic reforms through accession conditionality and a slowdown and even reversal of domestic reforms in candidate countries has in turn rendered the prospect of membership more remote. How the EU's waning commitment to enlargement has affected the accession prospects of individual candidates varies depending on a range of domestic factors both in existing EU member states and in prospective members.

Prospective Members

The EU officially considers several countries as prospective members: Turkey and the Western Balkan countries. Others—Iceland, Norway, and Switzerland—have applied for membership in the past. Although the treaty says that 'any European state' may apply to become a member (see Box 8.2), other European countries are at present discouraged from applying, including some successor states of the Soviet Union that are subject to the EU's Eastern Partnership (EaP) (see 'The Eastern Partnership').

Balkan countries

In southeast Europe about 20 million people remain outside the EU:

- Albania: 3.6 million;
- Bosnia-Herzegovina: 4.5 million;
- Former Yugoslav Republic of Macedonia (FYROM): 2.1 million;
- Kosovo: 1.8 million;
- Montenegro: 0.7 million;
- Serbia: 7.3 million.

A glance at the map (Figure 8.1) shows that the EU surrounds these countries—known as the Western Balkans. They are at different stages on their way to potential EU membership (see Box 8.4). At a summit at Thessaloniki in 2003, the EU's leaders recognized all the countries of the Western Balkans as prospective members, and the Union now provides financial and technical help through its pre-accession programmes.

   These countries are trying to make the political and economic reforms necessary to join the EU, but have—to varying degrees—difficult legacies of Communism, ethnic conflict, and recent statehood. With the exception of Albania, for most of the twentieth century the region was united in Yugoslavia. The disintegration of the Yugoslav federation in the 1990s led to civil war and ethnic conflict, especially in Bosnia and in Kosovo, then part of Serbia. The conflicts, were eventually ended through interventions by the UN and NATO, but problems of contested frontiers, inter-ethnic

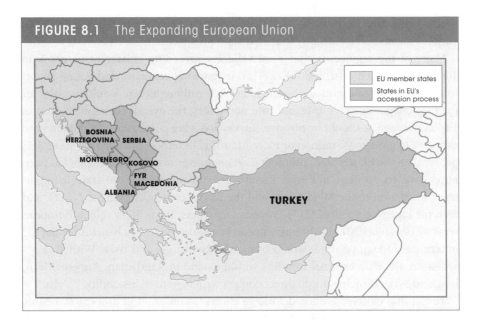

FIGURE 8.1   The Expanding European Union

tensions and fragile statehood persist. The question of Kosovo's international status is not fully resolved, with its independence from Serbia not recognized by all EU members. A European Union Rule of Law Mission (EULEX) supervises Kosovo's government. Bosnia is still under external tutelage: a UN High Representative, who is also an EU special representative, supervises it. Coupled with problems of poor governance, corruption, and crime, the region suffers from political dependency on external actors. But domestic reforms, and EU membership itself, require autonomy and a functioning democracy.

The region poses the biggest test yet of the EU's transformative power. Can conditionality and pre-accession instruments be used as successfully as they were in Central Europe? Given the more difficult legacies that make adjustments to EU conditionality more demanding and often politically contentious, the decreasing credibility of the membership promise makes it less likely that the EU can encourage good governance and reconciliation between communities. Although Croatia succeeded in joining the EU in 2013, and Serbia has begun to normalize its relations with Kosovo and started accession negotiations, as has Montenegro, the signs are not encouraging. A general backsliding has occurred in democracy and good governance, most notably in (the Former Yugoslav Republic of) Macedonia, which the Commission repeatedly recommended for accession negotiations after 2009, only to see them blocked by Greece over the dispute about the country's name.

Turkey

Turkey's 'European vocation' was proclaimed as early as 1964 in its Association Agreement with the EC. Its application for membership dates from 1987. But as Redmond (2007) recounts, the path towards membership has been long, and remains difficult. Despite the fact that accession negotiations opened in 2005, Turkey's membership currently looks a distant prospect.

Many of the arguments that were valid for preceding enlargements apply to Turkey. As Barysch *et al.* (2005) explain, its growing economy and young labour force would bring benefits to the single market. Although there would be costs for the EU's budget in agriculture and cohesion policy, the overall economic impact of Turkey's accession should be positive. Turkey has a big population: 78 million now, expected to grow to 90 million or more in future. In terms of income per head, it is poorer than the EU average, although its economic growth in recent years has been impressive. Its position on Europe's southeastern flank gives it geostrategic importance in relation to the Middle East and the Black Sea region; being in NATO, and with the biggest army of NATO's European members, it has a key role in European security (see Tocci 2011). Although Turkey's membership offers benefits for the EU in terms of foreign policy, it would bring new challenges and risks. With Turkey's accession, the EU's external frontiers would extend to Azerbaijan, Armenia, Iran, Iraq, and Syria, bringing it into direct contact with regions of instability.

The EU has closely monitored Turkey's efforts to conform to European standards of democracy, human rights, and rule of law. Especially between 1998 and 2005, progress was made towards meeting the Copenhagen criteria, although remaining problems included Turkey's treatment of its Kurdish minority, and its restrictions on freedom of speech and of the press. The increasingly autocratic turn under President Recep Tayyip Erdogan and his religious-conservative Justice and Development Party (AKP), especially after a thwarted coup in 2016, has led to major steps backwards on the EU's political conditions. There is a sense that EU membership is no longer a serious goal for the AKP government.

Even before this deterioration in relations, Turkish membership has always been highly contested in the EU. Public opinion in the EU is very negative (Toshkov *et al.* 2014: 14–16), influenced by fear of an influx of Turkish migrant workers but also by identity-related factors (Toshkov *et al.* 2014: 23): the idea that Turkey is different and not European in geographical or cultural terms. Turkey's difference is often linked in political discourse to the majority of Turkey's population being Muslim, but it has been a secular state since the 1930s.

Cyprus is a further thorn of contention. Since Turkey intervened militarily in 1974, the Turkish Republic of Northern Cyprus—not recognized by the rest of the international community—has been separated from the south. Hopes of reuniting the two parts of the island were dashed in 2003 when the Greek Cypriots in the south voted against a UN plan that was accepted by the north. As a result, the enlargement of 2004 brought a divided island into the EU. Turkey's refusal to recognize the Republic of Cyprus has also prevented it from implementing the Customs Union between the EU and Turkey in relation to Cyprus, which has created further problems for EU–Turkey relations.

These problems put a question mark over Turkey's bid for EU membership. Although accession negotiations formally continue, progress has been slow and several chapters are blocked by objections from France and Cyprus. Negative public opinion has resulted in an opposition to Turkish membership from mainstream political parties in France, Germany, and Austria (among others). Some member state governments are not unhappy that the deterioration of democracy and declining interest in EU membership in Turkey makes Turkish accession a distant prospect. Yet the diminishing prospect of membership means that the EU's ability to influence domestic developments in Turkey is also greatly diminished.

Norway, Switzerland, and Iceland

It is sometimes forgotten that membership applications have been made by Norway, Switzerland, and Iceland (see Box 8.3). Oil-rich Norway negotiated and signed two Accession Treaties, but did not join after its people said 'No' twice in referenda. This divisive experience has made its politicians reluctant to re-open the question of EU membership. As a member of the EEA (Box 8.1), it has access to the single market and participates in other EU policies. The EEA is the closest form of relationship that the Union has ever made with non-member countries.

In Switzerland, the French-speaking part of the population is broadly in favour of the EU, while a majority of German-speakers are opposed. Switzerland's application for EU membership was suspended when its citizens voted 'No' to joining (what eventually became) the EEA in a referendum in 1992. Since then Switzerland has pursued its interests through bilateral agreements with the EU.

Iceland, as a member of the EEA, decided to apply for EU membership in 2009 after a banking crisis showed its vulnerability as a small country (see Avery *et al.* 2011). Accession negotiations began in 2010, but were suspended by Iceland's new government in 2013, even before discussions began on the EU's common fisheries policy, the main obstacle to membership for Iceland. However, small, rich countries like these easily fulfil the conditions for membership and are thus ideal applicants for the EU. If they decided to apply again, they would be accepted readily as candidates.

Wider Europe

European Neighbourhood Policy

With its expansion to Central and Eastern Europe, the EU encountered a series of new neighbours to the east. It already had a Euro-Mediterranean Partnership with countries to the south, and was obliged to rethink relations with the countries of Eastern Europe that were formerly in the Soviet Union. Newer EU members such as Poland and Hungary did not want to see their accession lead to the erection of new barriers to countries with which they had cultural, social, and economic links. The result was the development of the European Neighbourhood Policy (ENP) covering 16 countries: Morocco, Algeria, Tunisia, Libya, Egypt, Israel, Jordan, the Palestinian

Authority, Lebanon, and Syria in the south; and Armenia, Azerbaijan, Georgia, Moldova, Ukraine, and Belarus in the east (see Figure 8.2).

The ENP's aim is to extend stability, prosperity, and security, and create a 'ring of friends' by developing political links and economic integration with the EU. Its main instrument is a series of Action Plans negotiated with each partner country and backed by financial and technical assistance. These plans cover political dialogue, economic and social reform, trade, cooperation in justice and security, transport, energy, environment, education, and so on. They require the neighbours to adopt and implement European regulations and a large part of the *acquis*: the system is modelled on the EU's Accession Partnerships with future members (Kelley 2006). Crucially, the ENP lacks the big incentive of the enlargement process: the 'golden carrot' of EU membership. For Eastern European states such as Ukraine, the fact that the policy is 'accession-neutral' has been a disappointment.

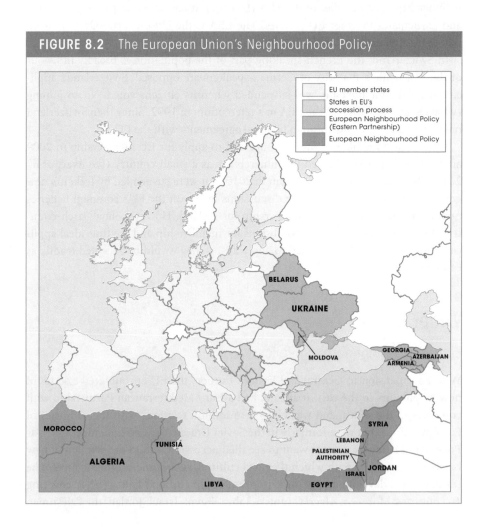

FIGURE 8.2   The European Union's Neighbourhood Policy

The Eastern Partnership

The ENP has been diversified to take account of the different situations and interests of the countries concerned. On the initiative of France, relations with the countries of the EU's southern neighbourhood were deepened through the creation in 2008 of the 'Union for the Mediterranean'. An initiative from Poland and Sweden led to the creation in 2009 of the EaP with Armenia, Azerbaijan, Belarus, Georgia, Moldova, and Ukraine to the east. Although it offers improved political cooperation, economic integration, and increased financial assistance, in practice, the EaP does not add much additional incentive for domestic reforms. The main innovation is the conclusion of Association Agreements—which in the past have been precursors to the accession process—and visa facilitation. But accession remains off the table.

Despite the ENP's declared aims, the EaP has had limited success in promoting democracy, good governance, and prosperity in Eastern Europe. However, although it offers financial aid and long-term benefits, it demands reforms that are too difficult and costly without the incentive of EU membership. Belarus still has an autocratic regime, while Ukraine has experienced a series of political and economic crises. Nevertheless, the EU continues to be attractive: the decision of Ukraine's President Viktor Yanukovych at the end of 2013 to pursue closer ties with Russia, rather than an Association Agreement with the EU, led to popular protests and the fall of his government. Russia's response, with its annexation of Crimea and support of dissidents in Eastern Ukraine, caused Ukraine to ask for support from the west and seek membership of the EU and NATO. To date neither organization has responded positively.

The region remains one where the EU and Russia are engaged in a competition for influence. Russia fears that closer relations with the EU may lead to former Soviet countries joining NATO. The adoption of European standards of governance may pose a threat to Russia's own political and economic system. Armenia withdrew from negotiations for an Association Agreement in order to join Russia's Eurasian Economic Union, although the EU signed a new Partnership Agreement with Armenia in 2017. Russia's invasion of Georgia in 2008, in response to an attempt by Georgian forces to re-assert control over its Russian-backed separatist regions Abkhazia and South-Ossetia, and Russian actions in Eastern Ukraine in 2014 have shown that it is prepared to use force to control its neighbours and redraw frontiers.

What Limits for EU Expansion?

The EU has used the prospect of membership successfully to extend stability and prosperity to neighbouring countries. Its reluctance to offer membership unequivocally, even once its conditions are met, has limited its ability to do so in southeastern Europe and Post-Soviet Eastern Europe. Does the EU have to decide how far its expansion can continue and where its final frontiers lie? The EU already has different frontiers for different policies, as is the case for the euro and Schengen. In this sense, the EU is already a multi-frontier system. But problems arise as some perceive differentiated integration as leading to an exclusionist 'core-group'. All members, and all applicants, want full rights in decision-making; there is no market for 'second-class' membership.

The founding EU treaties say that 'any European state may apply to become a member' (and subsequent treaties have added a reference to the liberal democratic values listed in Article 2 of the TEU; see Box 8.2). But what are the geographical limits of the European continent? To the north, west, and south, seas and oceans define it, but to the east there is no clear boundary. Although the Ural Mountains and Caspian Sea are often invoked as natural frontiers, some geographers consider Europe as the western peninsula of the Asian landmass—a subcontinent rather than a continent.

In any case, different geographical, political, and cultural concepts of Europe have prevailed at different times. Asia Minor and Northern Africa were within the political and economic area of the Roman Empire, but much of today's EU was outside it. Other historical periods are cited as characterizing Europe in cultural terms, such as the experience of the Renaissance or the Enlightenment. It is sometimes suggested that the EU is based on shared liberal democratic values specified in Article 2 rather than geography. But if this argument were correct, we would expect like-minded states in distant parts of the world—such as New Zealand—to be considered as future members. While the emphasis on identity is important, what a 'European identity' entails is contested. For some, Christianity is a defining element of European identity. Yet the drafters of the Constitutional Treaty explicitly rejected a Polish proposal for a reference to God in its preamble. All these examples show how difficult it is to arrive at an agreed definition. The European Commission (1992) has taken the view that:

> The term 'European' has not been officially defined. It combines geographical, historical and cultural elements which all contribute to the European identity. The shared experience of proximity, ideas, values and historical interaction cannot be condensed into a simple formula, and is subject to review by each succeeding generation. It is neither possible nor opportune to establish now the frontiers of the European Union, whose contours will be shaped over many years to come.

One way to establish which countries are considered European is to look at the Council of Europe (CoE), founded in 1949 before the creation of the European Communities. It has a wider membership than the EU (see Box 8.8) and thus provides an indication of the limits of Europe. All EU members are members of the CoE, and can hardly refuse to consider other signatories as 'European'. This suggests the following list of potential members of the EU (including two states not currently CoE members*):

- Albania, Bosnia-Herzegovina, Kosovo*, Macedonia (FYROM), Montenegro, Serbia;

- Turkey;

- Iceland, Norway, Switzerland;

- Armenia, Azerbaijan, Belarus*, Georgia, Moldova, Ukraine;

- Russia.

BOX 8.8   Other Europeans

Not all European states are in the EU. The other main intergovernmental organization in Europe is the CoE, which is concerned with human rights, social and legal affairs, and culture. It has 47 members:

- 28 EU states;
- Albania, Bosnia-Herzegovina, Macedonia (FYROM), Montenegro, Serbia;
- Turkey;
- Iceland, Norway, Switzerland;
- Armenia, Azerbaijan, Georgia, Moldova, Russian Federation, Ukraine;
- Andorra, Liechtenstein, Monaco, San Marino.

We should add two potential members: Belarus, which would be accepted as a member of the CoE if it became more democratic, and Kosovo, which would be accepted if the problem of its international recognition was solved.

Looking at the list in relation to membership of the EU, we should leave aside the last four, which as mini-states have little interest in joining. So we have a total of 17 states that are in the CoE but not in the EU.

Of this list of 17, the EU already considers some as potential members. Could it eventually embrace all the others? Could the final limits of the EU be set at 45 countries? That is unlikely: no state is obliged to apply, and the EU is not obliged to accept applicants. Meanwhile states may leave the EU, and new states may be created. In any case, an attempt by the EU institutions to decide the ultimate limits in advance would not give a clear answer. Such a decision would require unanimity, and existing member states have differing views on future membership. Those sharing borders with non-members often wish to bring them into the EU for reasons of stability and security. Poland, for example, wants its neighbour Ukraine to be a member of the EU. But others such as France are more restrictive, especially on the inclusion of Turkey. In fact, a discussion of the 'limits of Europe' can easily become a debate on 'should Turkey join?'.

What are the prospects for countries such as Ukraine, which are presently in the framework of the EaP? They are far from meeting the Copenhagen criteria, and EU membership is unrealistic for them for many years. But Russia's actions in Ukraine have driven it towards the west for political support and financial assistance. Such actions have also strengthened the case for using the leverage of prospective EU membership to encourage the long-term reforms needed to rebuild the Ukrainian state and economy. Prudence argues for keeping open the prospect of EU enlargement to all European states. Aspirant countries can modify their behaviour significantly in the hope of obtaining membership. To define the EU's ultimate borders now would demotivate those states that were excluded, and diminish the EU's leverage over those included. Thus a strategy of 'constructive ambiguity' is likely to prevail in the EU's enlargement policy.

Finally, what of Russia? It too is a European country, but its geographic expanse and population of 140 million mean that Russia joining the EU would be more like the EU joining Russia. Most crucially, its political trajectory in recent years has moved it away from European values, not towards them.

Evaluating Enlargement

Has enlargement been a success story for the EU? At the beginning of this chapter we saw that enlargement is not only foreign policy, but also a constitutive policy, in the sense that each accession reconfigures the EU's composition. So what are the criteria for evaluating the success of enlargement policy? The evaluation needs to be twofold: a first set of criteria applying to the period before enlargement—the 'pre-accession' period—and a second to the period after accession, when applicant countries have become members of the EU.

The criteria for the pre-accession period are similar to those for foreign policy: enlargement policy is successful if it enhances security, stability, and prosperity for the EU and for the neighbouring countries concerned and if the EU can influence domestic democratic and good governance reforms in candidate countries. In this respect, enlargement policy was more successful with regard to the new members that joined between 2004 and 2013 than with current candidates and countries in the EaP.

An equally important test of enlargement policy concerns the period after accession. Here the conditions for a successful result may be defined as the harmonious integration of new members (without disrupting existing members, or the functioning of the EU's institutions and policies), a continuation and sustainability of pre-accession reforms, and the satisfactory continuation of the EU's development. Since there is no general agreement on the last criterion (what is a satisfactory development of the EU?) it is not surprising that opinions differ on enlargement. According to some, the supporters of expansion (typically, the UK) wanted to weaken the EU, while according to others the opponents of expansion (typically, the French) wanted to safeguard acquired positions and advantages. Although these caricatures are both false, evaluations of enlargement policy are coloured by pre-existing attitudes to enlargement that can differ widely within the EU.

What was the result of the increase from 15 to 28? It has not, as feared, paralysed the EU's decision-making, which seems to work as well, or as badly, as it did in the past (Best et al. 2008). Recent data show that enlargement had a rather limited impact on the EU's capacity to produce legislation, although it is extremely hard to disentangle the impact of enlargement from other developments

(Toshkov 2017). Nor has it led to an increase in 'variable geometry' within the EU, with more fields of policy having different memberships, as some commentators predicted (Schimmelfennig and Winzen 2017). Most new members, unlike some old members, have joined the Schengen system, and many of them have joined the euro.

By contrast, an assessment of the sustainability of pre-accession reforms and commitments after accession raises concerns. On the positive side, enlargement has not led to an increase of non-compliance with EU law (Börzel and Sedelmeier 2017). With the exception of the southern enlargement, new member states generally comply better with the *acquis* than older member states. This result is particularly the case for the eastern enlargement (Sedelmeier 2008) and confounded widespread concerns during the pre-accession period. However, this positive picture changes if we consider developments in areas covered by political criteria for accession. A deterioration of the quality of democracy and good governance is noticeable across Central and East European states (Vachudova 2009; Börzel and Schimmelfennig 2017). Most alarming is the fundamental challenge to pluralism and liberal democracy in Hungary and Poland. In both countries, the government has used a parliamentary (super)-majority to concentrate power, eliminated checks-and-balances by controlling the judiciary and the media, and stifled electoral competition. Although Article 7 TEU gives the EU the possibility to sanction countries that breach the values of Article 2 TEU, it requires unanimity (with the exception of the offending state) in the European Council. EU institutions have had little influence on redressing democratic backsliding (Sedelmeier 2014; Pech and Scheppele 2017). However, they have been more vocal in their criticism of Poland—where the party in government is not a member of the European People's Party (EPP), the European association of centre-right parties—than of Hungary, where the governing Fidesz party is sheltered from criticism by their colleagues in the EPP (Sedelmeier 2016; Kelemen 2017).

Leaving and Joining

States may leave the EU, as well as join it. In June 2016, citizens of the UK voted to leave the EU in a referendum (see Chapter 10). While Brexit negotiations are ongoing at the time of writing, it is worthwhile remembering that the frontiers of the EU had already changed for reasons other than accession. Parts of the territories of member states have gained independence—Algeria from France in 1962, Greenland from Denmark in the 1980s—and chose not to remain within the EC. In 1990, when East Germany (not a member state of the EU) and West Germany (a founding member state) re-unified, 16 million East Germans joined the EU.

National independence movements, which have made gains in Scotland, Catalonia, Flanders, and elsewhere, pose a question for which the EU has no precedent: the division of one of its member states into two states, both of which wish to remain in the EU. The TEU is silent on this question, and the Union itself has no explicit policy for such cases other than to respect the constitutional arrangements of its member states. However, it is clear that EU membership would not be automatic for a newly independent state: amendment of the treaty, requiring unanimity, would be needed (Avery 2014a, 2014b; Kenealy 2014; Kenealy and MacLennan 2014).

Conclusion

The expansion of the EU has been remarkable in its scope and impact. But after increasing its membership from 12 to 28 states and its population by one-third in the period from 1995 to 2013, the EU will expand more slowly in future. In the medium term, it will limit expansion to countries of the Balkans, and possibly to Turkey, whose accession is currently a very distant prospect. In the longer term the EU may eventually accept other East European countries such as Ukraine. But in the meantime they remain in the framework of its ENP. The final limits of the Union will depend on developments in current members as well as in would-be new members and are likely to result from incremental political decisions, rather than from a long-term strategy.

? DISCUSSION QUESTIONS

1. Has the EU's enlargement to 28 members weakened its capacity for effective action? Has 'widening' stopped 'deepening'?

2. Turkey's application for membership dates from 1987: why is it so difficult for the EU to handle? Will Turkey ever succeed in joining?

3. The EU's basic treaty says 'any European state may apply for membership'. Should the EU try to decide where its frontiers would ultimately lie?

4. The EU's ENP aims to create a 'ring of friendly countries'. Can it ever be a substitute for joining the EU?

FURTHER READING

The enlargements of 2004 and 2007 are the subject of a voluminous literature, particularly on EU conditionality and reform in Central and Eastern Europe. For the evolution of the EU's policy and decision to enlarge, see Schimmelfennig (2003) and Sedelmeier (2005). The accession negotiations are described in Avery (2004). For conditionality and 'Europeanization', see Schimmelfennig and Sedelmeier (2005a); Vachudova (2005); Grabbe (2006); and Epstein and Sedelmeier (2009). A theoretical framework for explaining enlargement can be found in Schimmelfennig and Sedelmeier (2005b) and an overview of different enlargement rounds up to eastern enlargement in Preston (1997). On neighbourhood policy, see Weber *et al.* (2007) and Whitman and Wolf (2010). For analyses of enlargement and the EU's integration capacity, see Börzel *et al.* (2017). A good summary of developments, updated annually, can be found in the chapter on enlargement and neighbourhood policy in the *Journal of Common Market Studies Annual Review of the European Union*.

Avery, G. (2004), *The Enlargement Negotiations*, in F. Cameron (ed.), *The Future of Europe, Integration and Enlargement* (London: Routledge): 35–62.

Börzel, T., Dimitrova, A., and Schimmelfennig, F. (eds) (2017), 'European Union Enlargement and Integration Capacity', *Journal of European Public Policy*, Special Issue, 24/2.

Epstein, R. and Sedelmeier, U. (eds) (2009), *International Influence beyond Conditionality: Postcommunist Europe after EU Enlargement* (London: Routledge).

Grabbe, H. (2006), *The EU's Transformative Power: Europeanization through Conditionality in Central and Eastern Europe* (Basingstoke: Palgrave Macmillan).

Preston, C. (1997), *Enlargement and Integration in the European Union* (London: Routledge).

Schimmelfennig, F. (2003), *The EU, NATO and the Integration of Europe* (Cambridge: Cambridge University Press).

Schimmelfennig, F., and Sedelmeier, U. (2005a), *The Europeanization of Central and Eastern Europe* (Ithaca, NY: Cornell University Press).

Schimmelfennig, F. and Sedelmeier, U. (eds) (2005b), *The Politics of European Union Enlargement: Theoretical Approaches* (London: Routledge).

Sedelmeier, U. (2005) *Constructing the Path to Eastern Enlargement: The Uneven Policy Impact of EU Identity* (Manchester: Manchester University Press).

Vachudova, M. (2005), *Europe Undivided: Democracy, Leverage, and Integration after Communism* (Oxford: Oxford University Press).

Weber, K., Smith, M. E., and Baun, M. (eds) (2007), *Governing Europe's Neighbourhood* (Manchester: Manchester University Press).

Whitman, R. and Wolf, S. (eds) (2010), *The European Neighbourhood Policy in Perspective: Context, Implementation and Impact* (Basingstoke: Palgrave Macmillan).

 ## WEB LINKS

- The European Commission provides information and official documents on Enlargement at http://ec.europa.eu/enlargement/index_en.htm
- The European External Action Service provides information and official documents on Neighbourhood Policy at http://www.eeas.europa.eu/enp/

- The project website of the research consortium MAXCAP (Maximizing the Integration Capacity of the European Union; 2013–16) provides access to publications and resources on the EU's recent and future enlargements at http://userpage.fu-berlin.de/kfgeu/maxcap/index.html
- The project website of the research consortium EU-STRAT (2016–19) provides access to publications and a research database on the relationship between the EU and the countries in the European Eastern neighborhood at http://eu-strat.eu

 Visit the Ancillary Resource Centre that accompanies this book for additional material: www.oup.com/uk/kenealy5e/

CHAPTER 9

The EU as a Global Actor

John Peterson and Niklas Helwig

Summary

The European Union's (EU) ambitions to be a global power are a surprising by-product of **European integration**. Students of European foreign policy mostly focus on EU trade, aid, and the **Common Foreign and Security Policy (CFSP)**. But the extensive national foreign policy activities of its member states cannot be neglected. On most economic issues, the EU is able to speak with a genuinely single voice. It has more difficulty showing solidarity on aid policy, but is powerful when it does. The Union's external policy aspirations now extend to traditional foreign and security policy. But distinct national policies persist and the EU suffers from weak or fragmented leadership. Debates about European foreign policy tend to be about whether the glass is half full—with the EU more active globally than ever before—or half empty, and mainly about disappointed expectations.

Introducing European Foreign Policy

Jean Monnet once described European integration as a 'key step towards the organization of tomorrow's world' (quoted in Jørgensen 2006: 521). Yet, Monnet and the other founders of the original European Economic Community (EEC) had little or no ambition to create a new kind of international power. In fact, the EEC was initially given explicit external powers only to assist former European colonies in Africa and conduct international trade negotiations, since a common market with a customs union could not, by definition, exist without a common trade policy. Ultimately, both policies produced considerable political spill over. A commitment (demanded by France) in the Treaty of Rome to offer a small amount of foreign aid and work towards a free trade area with sub-Saharan African states evolved into a full-blown political 'partnership' with no fewer than 79 African, Caribbean, and Pacific (ACP) states by 2018. As for trade policy, spirited policy debates ensued almost immediately: trade agreements with whom? Should sanctions be imposed on oppressive or aggressive states? Member states soon felt the need to complement trade policy (and the external faces of other EC policies) with political criteria laid down in what was at first a separate, informal framework of 'political cooperation' and then later became a formal treaty objective of a common foreign and security policy.

The EU now aspires to be a global power: a major international actor that can, like the United States (US) or China, influence developments anywhere in the world, and draw on its full range of economic, political, and security instruments. It can be argued that 'foreign policy has been one of the areas in which European integration has made the most dynamic advances' (Tonra and Christiansen 2004: 545). Still, the EU is a strange and often ineffective global actor. Distinctive *national* foreign policies endure in Europe and show few signs of disappearing. The notion of 'European foreign policy', comprising all of what both the EU *and* its member states do in world politics, collectively or not, thus has gained prominence (see Carlsnaes 2006; Hill *et al.* 2017).

Debates about European foreign policy tend to be of the glass half full or half empty variety. To illustrate, the EU has used enlargement as a tool of foreign policy to transform dramatically the regions to its east and south (see Chapter 8). The Union is an economic superpower that packs a real punch in international economic diplomacy. It has gradually developed its Common Security and Defence Policy (CSDP) for crisis management or humanitarian intervention.

On the other hand, the EU suffers from chronic problems of disunity, incoherence, and weak leadership. European foreign policy can be undermined by all manner of rivalries: among its member governments, between EU institutions, and between them and national foreign ministries. The EU was entirely sidelined during the 2003 war in Iraq because it could not come even remotely close to agreeing a common policy (see Peterson 2003/4). The EU remained unable to respond effectively when the Libyan dictator, Muammar al-Gaddafi, threatened to instigate a bloodbath against his own people in 2011 (see Box 9.2). And it stood by almost helplessly as Russia annexed the Ukrainian region of Crimea in 2014 (see Box 9.4). Even when it can agree on a common policy, it relies overwhelmingly on its member states for the resources to execute it.

Sometimes, the same international event or issue can be used to defend either the half full or half empty thesis. Consider the dramatic developments of 2016, when the UK voted to leave the EU in a referendum and Donald Trump—an outspoken sceptic of globalization, free trade, and multi-lateral cooperation—was elected US president. With the UK and its foreign policy expertise and military power about to leave the EU and the Americans no longer a 'cheerleader' for European integration, Europe surely stood to lose global influence or even face a 'process of disintegration' (Kundnani 2017). Alternatively, Commission President Jean-Claude Juncker argued in his 2017 State of the Union address that faced with a choice to 'either come together around a positive European agenda or each retreat into our own corners', the EU was showing 'that Europe can deliver for its citizens when and where it matters' (Juncker 2017).

How it developed

The EU's international ambitions have their origins in the 1960s. In particular, American disregard for European preferences in Vietnam and the Middle East presented European countries with incentives to defend their interests collectively, and thus more effectively in foreign policy. According to a logic known as the 'politics of scale', the whole—the EU speaking and acting as one—is more powerful than the sum of its parts, or member states acting individually (Ginsberg 2001).

By 1970, a loose intergovernmental framework, European Political Cooperation (EPC), was created to try to coordinate national foreign policies. Linked to but independent of the European Community, EPC was very much dominated by national foreign ministers and ministries. Member governments identified where their national interests overlapped, without any pretension to a 'common' foreign policy. The European Commission was little more than an invited guest, and the Parliament largely excluded.

Nonetheless, EPC fostered consensus on difficult issues in the 1970s and 80s, including the Arab–Israeli conflict, apartheid in South Africa, and relations with the Soviet bloc (through what became the Organization for Security and Co-operation in Europe (OSCE); see Box 9.1). Europe was mostly limited to saying things—issuing diplomatic *démarches*—instead of doing things. But increasingly it backed up EPC positions with European Community actions using economic aid or sanctions (which, for instance, were applied to Argentina during the 1982 Falklands War).

EPC's perceived successes led to claims that Europe could become a 'civilian power' (see Galtung 1973). That is, the EC could emerge as an alternative to the two Cold War superpowers: it would uphold multi-lateralism, liberalism, and human rights and advocate peaceful conflict resolution. EPC was given treaty status and formally linked to the activities of the Community in the 1986 Single European Act.

Yet, the geopolitical earthquakes that shook Europe beginning in 1989 exposed EPC as too weak to foster collective action. The idea of strengthening foreign policy cooperation in a new 'political union' was given impetus by the dramatic transitions in Central and Eastern Europe, the Gulf War, the collapse of the Soviet Union, and war in Yugoslavia. Thus, the 1992 Maastricht Treaty grafted onto the EC a new Common Foreign and Security Policy (CFSP) a framework that allowed member states to formulate, decide, and represent policies collectively to the outside world. Over the following decades the EU developed institutions and instruments to try to make its foreign policy coherent and effective. One major addition to its toolbox was a **CSDP** in the early 2000s, under which member states contributed troops to civilian and military missions under an EU flag. Nevertheless, debates about whether and how effectively the EU was able to contribute to regional and global stability persisted, and still rage today.

> **BOX 9.1   Key concepts and terms**
>
> The **CFSP** was created by the 1992 Maastricht Treaty as a successor to the EPC mechanism. It has been revised by successive new treaties and given a Brussels-based Political and Security Committee to prepare foreign ministers' meetings and (by Lisbon) a 'new look' High Representative and the **European External Action Service (EEAS)**.
>
> The **CSDP** was created in 1999 to engage in the so-called '**Petersberg tasks**' (named after a German castle where an earlier summit devoted to defence was held): humanitarian and rescue missions, peacekeeping, crisis management, and the vaguely specified task of 'peacemaking'.
>
> The **EEAS** was established by the **Lisbon Treaty** and became active in 2010. It works under the authority of the High Representative and brings under one roof EU (Commission and Council) and national diplomats. The EEAS's task is to assist the High Representative in implementing the CFSP and other areas of EU foreign policy.
>
> The **OSCE**—brings together 57 (as of 2018) states from Europe and beyond in what is the world's largest regional security organization. It claims to take a 'comprehensive approach to security', extending especially to human rights. The OSCE works on the basis of unanimity and its decisions are politically, not legally, binding. It thus is criticized as toothless: for example, it failed to defuse the 2014 crisis in the Ukraine (both Russia and Ukraine are OSCE members).

The basics

The EU aspires to international power for two basic reasons. First, even the Union's largest states are medium-sized powers compared to, say, the US or China. All European states, especially smaller ones, seek to use the EU as a 'multiplier' of their power and influence. There is controversy about whether the Union is a truly global, as opposed to a regional power (Krotz 2009; Orbie 2009). However, its largest member states—France, the UK (until 2019), Germany, and Italy (the first two being members of the UN Security Council)—give the Union a 'pull towards the global perspective which many of the [other member states] simply do not have as part of their foreign policy traditions' (Hill 2006: 67). One upshot is that the prospect of an EU without UK input and military weight is troubling, even though it remains to be seen how London will be associated with the EU's international activities post-Brexit.

Second, the Union's international weight increases each time it enlarges or expands its competence. The 13 countries that joined after 2004 were all (besides Poland) small and (mostly) pro-American states with limited foreign policy ambitions. But EU membership allowed them to distance or defend themselves from the US on issues such as Russia or trade policy, while making the Union a potentially more powerful player on these and other international issues. Meanwhile, the EU has accumulated new foreign policy tools, such as the CSDP. It also created, via the Lisbon Treaty, new figures to represent the Union externally: a 'permanent' European Council president and a High Representative for foreign affairs and security policy who is also a vice-president of the Commission. Moreover, Lisbon gave birth to the EEAS, potentially a nascent EU foreign ministry. But whatever institutions it creates, the EU is powerful internationally above all because it presides over the world's largest single market of nearly 500 million consumers, or around 40 per cent more than the US.

Still, European foreign policy is hindered by three basic gaps. One is between task expansion, which has been considerable, and the integration of authority, which has been—at least prior to Lisbon—limited. Even before the creation of the EEAS, the total number of European diplomatic staff worldwide (EU plus national officials) was more than 40,000 diplomats in 1,500 missions. Yet, no single authority could give orders to this disparate collection of officials. No one claimed that the US—with around 15,000 staff in 300 missions—was weaker because it was so outnumbered (Everts 2002: 26).

The new High Representative was given authority over the EEAS, which at least promised to give the Union a figure who could direct the EU's own diplomatic corps, which often proved impossible in the past. However, in the first years after its establishment the EEAS struggled to 'demonstrate its relevance and added value' (Balfour and Raik 2012: 25). The High Representative was criticized for providing weak leadership (Helwig 2015). Those who see the EU as a global actor glass as half full noted that the new foreign policy machinery started to run more smoothly, especially after 2014, when the former Italian Foreign Minister Frederica Mogherini replaced the first post-Lisbon High Representative Catherine Ashton, who lacked previous foreign policy experience.

The gap between the EU's economic power and political weakness is a related but separate problem. Europe manages to defend its interests on matters of 'low politics'—economic, trade, and (less often) monetary issues—with a more or less single voice. External trade policy is made via the Community method of decision-making (see Chapter 3), which delegates considerable power to the

Union's institutions and sees the Council act by a qualified majority. The EU also has significant resources in aid and development policy. It has emerged as at least a potentially major power in international environmental diplomacy.

In contrast, the Union often fails to speak as one on matters of traditional diplomacy, or 'high politics', which touch most directly on national sovereignty, prestige, or vital interests. In this realm, most Council decisions must be unanimous. The CFSP created by the Maastricht Treaty was meant to cover 'all aspects of foreign and security policy'. However, there is no *single* EU foreign policy in the sense of one that replaces or eliminates national policies. In contrast to (say) EU trade policy, the CFSP relies overwhelmingly on intergovernmental consensus. This mode is especially engrained in the CSDP, where it remains difficult to envisage member states ever delegating to the EU power to decide life-and-death questions, such as whether to contribute military force to a 'hot' war. In short, the gap between the EU's economic power and political weight endures largely because the Community system remains more efficient and decisive than the CFSP system.

One final gap is between the world's expectations of the EU and its capacity to meet them (Hill 1998). In the early days of the post-Cold War period, European foreign policy-makers often oversold the Union's ability to act quickly or resolutely in international affairs. Nearly two decades later, the EU has a more realistic assessment of its impact on global stability and prosperity. Nevertheless, Mogherini (2016: 3) has been keen to highlight the potential of the combined weight of European states:

> As a Union of almost half a billion citizens, our potential is unparalleled. Our diplomatic network runs wide and deep in all corners of the globe. Economically, we are in the world's G3. We are the first trading partner and the first foreign investor for almost every country in the globe. Together we invest more in development cooperation than the rest of the world combined. It is also clear, though, that we are not making full use of this potential yet. A vast majority of our citizens understands that we need to collectively take responsibility for our role in the world.

These three gaps—between task expansion and integration, economic unity and political division, and capabilities and expectations—all contribute to a more general mismatch between aspirations and accomplishments. To understand its persistence, we need to unpack European foreign policy and consider it as the product of three distinct but interdependent systems of decision-making (White 2001):

- a national system of foreign policies;
- a Community system focused on economic policy; and
- the CFSP (including, with special provisions, the CSDP).

These systems remain distinct even if there is considerable overlap between them (see Table 9.1). For example, while the EU has exclusive competence on trade matters, development cooperation is a shared competence between national capitals and Brussels. The CFSP is governed under special institutional provisions.

TABLE 9.1	European foreign policy: Three systems			
System	**Key characteristic**	**Location (or treaty basis)**	**Primary actors**	**Policy example**
National	Loose (or no) coordination	Outside EU's structures	National ministers and ministries	War in Iraq
Overlap	*Some coordination of national and EU efforts*	*Coordination with EU with nuances (no funds from EU budget)*	*National ministers and ministries, Commission*	*Cotonou agreement*
Community	EU usually speaks with single voice	Articles 205–222, TFEU (formerly Pillar 1*)	Commission and Council	Commercial (trade) policy, e.g. EU–Canada trade deal
Overlap	*Turf battles*	*Article 29 TEU and Article 215 TFEU (formerly Pillars 1 and 2 *)*	*Council and Commission*	*Economic sanctions policy, e.g. against Russia since 2014*
CFSP	'Common, not single' policy	Articles 21–46 (formerly Pillar 2*)	High Representative; national ministers and ministries (especially of large states)	Nuclear diplomacy towards Iran

Note: *Pre-Lisbon Treaty.

Overlaps between the EU's external policy systems are, however, rife. Europe is the world's largest foreign aid donor, but only when the disparate and largely uncoordinated contributions of the Union and its member states are added together. EU environmental policy is made via the Community method. Even though EU's own diplomatic network contributed to the efforts to reach a deal, the landmark Paris Climate Agreement was pushed primarily by French leadership. Leadership of the CFSP sometimes falls to sub-groups of member states, as illustrated by the 'EU-3', with France, Germany, and the UK taking the lead on nuclear diplomacy towards Iran, but with the EU High Representative chairing a delegation that also included China, Russia, and the US, in another case of intersecting systems.

Such overlaps reflect how high and low politics often blur together. Disputes arising from Europe's dependence on Russia for energy, or the tendency of Chinese exporters to flood European markets, can touch on vital national interests and preoccupy diplomats and governments at the highest political levels. Meanwhile, the EU has a considerable track record in security and defence policy, which might be viewed as the ultimate expression of high politics. Blurred boundaries between both policy realms and systems for decision-making make European foreign policy an elusive subject that is far more difficult to 'source' or study than (say) Indian, Mexican, or South African foreign policy.

A National 'System' of Foreign Policies

Distinctive national foreign policies have not disappeared from Europe, even if the EU has become a more important reference point. France uses the EU to try to enhance its own foreign policy leadership of a Europe that is autonomous from the US. Germany has wrapped its post-war foreign policy in a European cloak in order to rehabilitate itself as an international power. Berlin has taken steps only lately to put its political weight on par with its economic power. Prior to its decision to leave the Union, the UK sometimes viewed the EU as useful for organizing pragmatic cooperation but also blocked proposed initiatives. Small states have considerably 'Europeanized' their foreign policies (Tonra 2001; Gross 2009) and rely on the EU to have a voice in debates dominated by large states. But all EU member states also conduct their own, individual, *national* foreign policy.

Whether national foreign policies in Europe form a true 'system', they are notable for:

- their endurance;
- their continued centrality to European foreign policy; and
- their frequent resistance to coordination.

The logic of foreign policy coordination differs markedly from the logic of market integration. Integrating markets often involves negative integration (that is, removing barriers to trade) and separate national policies can be tolerated as long as they do not impede free movement. A common foreign policy more often requires positive integration, with new EU institutions and structures potentially replacing national ones. If all member states do not toe the line on a specific foreign policy then it is hard to say that the EU has a *common* policy at all. Defenders of Europe's system of foreign policy coordination, including Chris Patten (2001), concede that Europe lacks a *single* foreign policy. However, they insist that the EU usually has a *common* foreign policy through which its member states and institutions act collectively. Each plays to its strengths and contributes policy resources to a (more or less) common cause. By this view, all member states increasingly tend to respect common EU policies and procedures.

Critics counter-claim that the war in Iraq showed how easily the EU is marginalized on matters of high politics. Decisions on whether to support the war were almost entirely made in national EU capitals, not Brussels. Similarly, in the case of the Libyan crisis in 2011, the decision to launch a robust military intervention took place mostly outside the EU framework (see Box 9.2). Nation states have long been primary sources of European foreign policy. They remain so, and this picture is unlikely to change anytime soon.

BOX 9.2   How it really works: The EU and the Middle East and North African region

Since the 2011 Arab Spring, the EU has been confronted with crises in the Southern Mediterranean, reaching from the Sahel region (including Mali) to (fragile) Libya, to (war-torn) Syria. A record level of refugees in Europe and increased human trafficking from African shores was the fallout with which the EU had to deal.

The Union's response to the 2011 Libyan crisis was widely criticized for being slow, incoherent, and ineffective. The first major post-Lisbon Treaty crisis began with high expectations that the EU could deliver a decisive response. While member states eventually agreed on the need for Libyan dictator Gaddafi to cede power, they remained at odds on the use of military force. Germany refused to support a UN Security Council Resolution (1973) authorizing the implementation of a no-fly zone over Libya, abstaining on the vote and withdrawing its military assets once a North Atlantic Treaty Organization (NATO) military action began. Although France and the UK eventually took the lead in implementing the no-fly zone, the NATO operation relied heavily on US military assets. Critics argued that the EU's defence policy—and the CFSP more generally—'died in Libya', fuelling the glass half empty argument. Yet, a more optimistic view saw the Libyan crisis as a lesson learned and an opportunity to address existing flaws and obstacles.

While Europe decided to act together with the US in Libya, it was destined to be a bystander in the war in Syria, which developed into a proxy-war that involved the US, Russia, Iran, and Turkey. Europe's humanitarian efforts were laudable, as donations by the EU and its member states reached almost €10 billion in 2017. Yet, the region was destined to remain a challenge for the EU for decades to come.

The biggest immediate challenge was the arrival of millions of refugees via the Western Balkans and Mediterranean with a peak in 2015. Following the EU's failure to agree a system to share refugees from the main arrival countries, Greece and Italy—as well as the preferred destination Germany—the Union focused on strengthening its outer borders. Deals with transit countries, including with difficult partners such as Turkey, Chad, Niger, and Libya, and an increase of military naval operations on the Mediterranean Sea, were criticized for jeopardizing European values, while failing to address the root causes of migration.

The Community System

The Community system for foreign policy-making consists of three main elements: external trade policy; aid and development policy; and the external dimension of internal policies, not least the internal market.

Commercial (trade) policy

The EU is the world's largest exporter and importer of both goods and services. It accounts for more than one-fifth of all global trade, and claims a higher share than the US. The EU is sometimes portrayed as a purveyor of a liberal trade policy, which emphasizes the benefits of the free market and limited government interference (see Cafruny and Ryner 2003; Young and Peterson 2014). Yet, all trading blocs discriminate against outsiders. More than half of all EU trade is internal trade, crossing European borders within a market that is meant to be borderless. EU member states are sometimes accused of acting like a protectionist club in which each agrees to take in the others' 'high-cost washing', or products that are lower in quality or higher in price than goods produced outside Europe, ostensibly to protect European jobs (see Messerlin 2001).

In practice, the EU is a schizophrenic trading power (see Young and Peterson 2014), mostly because it blends different national traditions of political economy. Generally, its southern member states are less imbued with free-market values than those in the north or east. One consequence is that it is sometimes harder for the EU to agree internally than it is to agree deals with its trading partners. The power of the Commission in trade policy is easy to over-estimate. However, the EU does a remarkably good job of reconciling Europe's differences on trade. When the EU can agree, international negotiations become far more efficient. There is capacity in the Community system for shaming reluctant states into accepting trade agreements that serve general EU foreign policy interests. For example, in 2001 the Union agreed to offer the world's poorest countries duty-free and quota-free access to the EU's markets for 'everything but arms' (see Faber and Orbie 2009), which France opposed but eventually agreed to accept. The EU generally claims that it offers the world's poorest countries a better deal than do most industrialized countries.

Europe increasingly finds itself facing fierce economic competition from emerging states such as China, India, and Brazil that have maintained higher economic growth rates than the EU in recent years. In the circumstances, EU trade policy has been accused of becoming aggressive, reactive, and defensive. The Union (and US) shouldered much of the blame for the breakdown of the Doha Development Round of world trade talks in 2008 (even though the obduracy of emerging states was at least as much to blame; see Young and Peterson 2014: 94). With multi-lateral trade negotiations at an impasse, the EU has sought bilateral preferential trade agreements (PTAs). Since the Doha stalemate, the EU has launched bilateral negotiations with the US, Japan, Malaysia, Vietnam, the Latin American MERCOSUR group, and others. It also has agreed free trade deals with Canada, Singapore, and—controversially—Ukraine. In fact, the EU's Comprehensive Economic and Trade Agreement (CETA) with Canada—an unusually 'deep' trade agreement that opened up (large) markets for public procurement and aligned some regulatory standards—offered the UK one possible model for its future relationship with the Union. However, CETA also exposed how the EU can be stymied by internal coordination problems: it was almost vetoed by a vote of the Walloon Parliament in Belgium.

Still, the EU has developed high ambitions in trade policy. In late 2017, the Commission agreed the main elements of an EU–Japan Economic Partnership, which was negotiated in parallel with a 'Strategic Partnership Agreement', which the EU advertised as 'a legally binding pact covering not only political dialogue and policy cooperation, but also cooperation on regional and global challenges, including environment and climate change, development policy and disaster relief, and security policy'.[1] A truly comprehensive EU–Japan agreement was a potential game-changer, especially as Donald Trump's America seemed to retreat into protectionism.

The Transatlantic Trade and Investment Partnership (TTIP) between the US and EU was frozen after President Trump came to office, even though it promised to create a lot of jobs and growth on both sides. It was hard to see how TTIP could ever be agreed with Trump in power, especially given staunch resistance by highly motivated elements of European civil society who mobilized against it even with President Barack Obama in the White House. That is to leave aside serious coordination problems on the US side, especially in getting state and local governments to buy into the TTIP negotiations (see De Ville and Siles-Brügge 2016; Young 2017).

An interesting question for students of European foreign policy is: how often does the EU use its economic power in the pursuit of foreign policy objectives? Agreements after 2010 to apply increasingly severe economic sanctions to Iran in response to its nuclear programme illustrate how the EU occasionally (in this case, after years of US cajoling) uses its economic power for political objectives. The same can be said for the PTAs the Union has agreed with developing countries and states on its borders as part of its European Neighbourhood Policy (ENP) (see Chapter 8).

Still, EU trade policy structures and behaviour challenge the idea of Europe as a 'civilian power'. The Lisbon Treaty states that trade policy 'shall be conducted in the context of the principles and objectives of the Union's external action' (Article 207). But responsibility is left in the hands of the commissioner for trade, not the High Representative. Damro (2010, 2014) characterizes the EU as 'Market Power Europe': an EU that defends its economic interests aggressively in individual trade disputes with little regard for broader foreign policy objectives. A less charitable portrayal is 'Parochial Global Europe' (Young and Peterson 2014): the EU's preoccupation with its own internal politics and policies, and staunch defence of its economic interests, hampers the Union's attempts to play a global role. It seems that the EU uses its (formidable) economic power quite rarely in pursuit of its wider foreign policy agenda.

---

[1] See https://eeas.europa.eu/headquarters/headquarters-homepage/19223/eu-japan-political-relations_en

Aid and development

The EU and its member states spend around €50 billion annually on development aid, or over half of the global total. Aid and access to the Union's huge market are frequently combined, along with other policy instruments, as in the cases of the EU's free trade agreements with Mexico and South Africa or the 2000 Cotonou Agreement agreed with ACP states. Market access or aid also may be part of political cooperation agreements designed to promote democracy or human rights. The EU's relations with its most important neighbours—such as Turkey, Ukraine, or Russia (Box 9.4)—are usually conducted through complex package deals involving trade, aid, and political dialogue.

The Union also has become the world's largest donor of humanitarian aid through the European Community Humanitarian Office (ECHO), located within the Commission. It announced the largest contribution of any donor to humanitarian aid in Afghanistan within days of the start of the 2001 war. ECHO also contributed more relief than any other donor after the 2004 Asian Tsunami and 2010 Pakistani floods.

Bad 'plumbing' often mars the EU's good deeds. ECHO was slammed for its lax spending controls by the Committee of Independent Experts, whose 1999 report sparked the mass resignation of the Santer Commission. For years, EU development funds helped prop up dictators who were overthrown in Egypt, Tunisia, and elsewhere in the 2011 Arab Spring. Even worse, the migration crisis increased the pressure on European governments to control migration flows (see Box 9.2). In its aftermath, the EU was criticized by non-governmental organizations for spending development money not only on economic growth, but also on measures intended to train and equip military and border forces in transit countries in Africa.

Externalizing 'internal' policies

In a sense, the EU has no internal policies: its market is so huge that every decision it makes to regulate it (or not) has international effects. When the Union negotiates internal agreements on fishing rights or agricultural subsidies, the implications for fisher(wo)men in Iceland or farmers in California can be immediate and direct. The ultimate act of externalizing internal policies occurs when the EU enlarges its membership, as it did when it almost doubled in size from 15 to 28 member states after 2004.

A rule of thumb, based on a landmark European Court decision (see Weiler 1998: 171–83), is that where the EU has legislated internally, a corresponding external policy competence for that matter is transferred to it. The Union has frequently taken this route in environmental policy, and now participates in several international environmental agreements. Where internal lines of authority are clear, the EU can be a strong and decisive negotiator. Its extraordinary commercial power sometimes makes headlines, for example when Apple was accused of accepting an illegal tax deal in Ireland worth €13 billion. When the Union seeks bilateral economic agreements, whether with China, Canada, or Cameroon, the Commission negotiates for the Union as a whole.

The Union's most important international task may be reconciling rules on its **single market** with rules governing global trade. The EU sometimes does the job badly, agreeing messy compromises on issues such as data protection or genetically modified foods that enrage its trading partners. External considerations can be a low priority when the Union legislates, and treated as someone else's problem. Most of the time, however, the internal market has offered non-EU producers better or similar terms of access than they were offered before the internal market existed (Young and Peterson 2014: 150).

Meanwhile, EU enlargement has been widely hailed as the most effective tool of European *foreign* policy, in terms of exporting both security and prosperity (Nugent 2004; Smith 2017). But it has also produced enlargement fatigue and rising concerns in longstanding member states about migration from less-developed newcomers. One result has been the ENP (see Chapter 8), a framework for cooperation with states on or near EU borders such as Ukraine or Belarus, which, in the Brussels jargon, do not have the 'perspective' of membership anytime soon. It is difficult to see how the powerful lure of actual membership could ever come close to being replicated by a policy that forecloses that possibility.

BOX 9.3   How it really works: Making foreign policy decisions

The Lisbon Treaty, on paper, brought significant changes to the way foreign and security policy is organized as it essentially put all EU policies under the umbrella of a single institutional system. It now incorporates the CFSP as well as internal security policy. However, as Piris (2010: 260) notes, leaving aside the High Representative, 'the Lisbon Treaty confirms that CFSP remains clearly subject to different rules and procedures from the other activities of the EU'. In particular, unanimity remains the norm. While **qualified majority voting (QMV)** on foreign policy was possible after the Maastricht Treaty, it was rarely used on matters that touched on national sovereignty. The glass thus remained half empty as nearly all important CFSP decisions required a consensus. Because it could not agree a unanimous position on Iraq (far from it), the EU was completely sidelined during the drift to war in 2003. The CFSP's annual budget is in the range of a paltry €150 million. After 13 countries joined the Union between 2004 and 2013, foreign policy by unanimity seemed even more impractical, if not impossible. Procedurally, it is clear how the CFSP works. Substantively, there is controversy about whether it works at all.

Or perhaps the glass is half full. As a consequence of the continuing de-stabilization efforts of Russia in Ukraine, the EU was able to agree a comprehensive sanctions regime against one of its largest trading partners. Unanimous decisions are difficult to agree, but they also send a strong message that the EU stands united. The EU's diplomacy (through the 'EU-3') on Iran, its participation in the Middle East Quartet (on an equal footing with the US, Russia, and the UN), a range of actions in Central Africa and the Balkans, and the (slow) maturation of the Lisbon foreign policy machinery suggest, for optimists, a steady integration of European foreign policy.

The CFSP and CSDP

The gap between the Union's growing economic power and its limited political clout was a source of increasing frustration in the early 1990s. Thus, a distinct system of making foreign policy was created with the CFSP at its centre. This new system overlapped with but did not replace the Community system. Over time, it incorporated a CSDP.

The CFSP unveiled in the Maastricht Treaty marked a considerable advance on the EPC mechanism. But it still disappointed proponents of closer foreign policy cooperation (see Box 9.3). The CFSP gave the Commission the right—shared with member governments—to initiate proposals. It even allowed for limited QMV, although it was always clear that most actions would require unanimity. Compliance mechanisms in the CFSP were not as strong as those on community matters, with the **European Court of Justice** mostly excluded. The CFSP (like the justice and home affairs policy initially) remained largely intergovernmental, although links to the Community system were gradually strengthened.

The 1997 Amsterdam Treaty's main foreign policy innovation was the creation of the High Representative for the CFSP (who also served, initially, as secretary-general of the Council). The High Representative was meant to help give the EU a single voice and the CFSP a single face. After his appointment to the post in 1999, former NATO Secretary General Javier Solana at times proved a skilful coordinator of different actions and instruments, whether sourced in Brussels or national capitals.

However, the EU continued to be represented externally by its so-called *troika*, with Solana joined by the foreign ministers of the state holding the Council presidency and the European commissioner for external affairs. There thus was no clear answer to the legendary (and apparently apocryphal) question asked by the US Secretary of State Henry Kissinger in the 1970s: 'What number do I call when I want to speak to "Europe"?'

It was also in the late 1990s when the EU made its first cautious steps into security and defence. Europe's two major military powers—France and the UK— kick-started EU military cooperation at a 1998 summit in St Malo. With the Bosnian crisis a recent memory, and the Kosovo crisis still to come, EU heads of state and government formally launched (what became) the CSDP at the 1999 Cologne summit. Given the CFSP's mixed record, as well as Europe's claims to be a civilian power, it seemed paradoxical to extend the EU system into the realm of defence. Most EU states had long accepted the supremacy of NATO on defence matters. Yet, the 1999 Kosovo crisis marked a turning point. The EU appeared timid and weak, as it had earlier in Bosnia. NATO took the lead in pushing both crises towards resolution, and the US military contributions dwarfed those of Europe. Thus, the EU responded with firmer commitments in the Treaty of Nice, which marked out the so-called **Petersberg tasks**—humanitarian and rescue missions, peacekeeping, and crisis management—as basic EU foreign policy goals. A new Political and Security Committee (known by its French acronym COPS) of senior national officials was

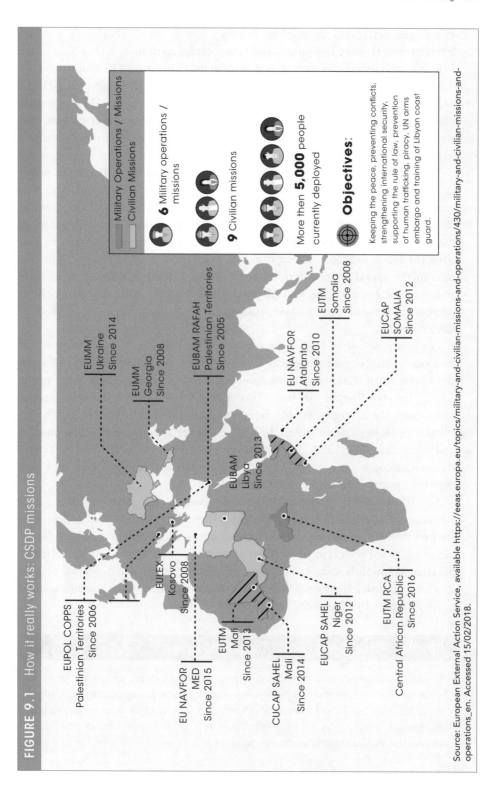

FIGURE 9.1   How it really works: CSDP missions

Military Operations / Missions
Civilian Missions

6 Military operations / missions

9 Civilian missions

More then **5,000** people currently deployed

Objectives:

Keeping the peace, preventing conflicts, strengthening international security, supporting the rule of law, prevention of human trafficking, piracy, UN arms embargo and training of Libyan coast guard.

EUPOL COPPS
Palestinian Territories
Since 2006

EUMM
Ukraine
Since 2014

EUMM
Georgia
Since 2008

EUBAM RAFAH
Palestinian Territories
Since 2005

EULEX
Kosovo
Since 2008

EU NAVFOR
MED
Since 2015

EUTM
Mali
Since 2013

EUBAM
Libya
Since 2013

EU NAVFOR
Atalanta
Since 2010

EUTM
Somalia
Since 2008

EUCAP
SOMALIA
Since 2012

CUCAP SAHEL
Mali
Since 2014

EUCAP SAHEL
Niger
Since 2012

EUTM RCA
Central African Republic
Since 2016

Source: European External Action Service, available https://eeas.europa.eu/topics/military-and-civilian-missions-and-operations/430/military-and-civilian-missions-and-operations_en. Accessed 15/02/2018.

created and designated the linchpin linking CSDP to the CFSP. The EU was also given its own Military Committee and crisis management unit. After 2001, for the first time military officers were seen at work in the EU's Council building.

Since its first military intervention in the Bunia region of Congo in 2002, the EU has launched over 30 civilian and military missions on three different continents (see Figure 9.1). Most—around two-thirds—have been purely civilian missions that channeled development aid or sent law enforcement officers or advisors to troubled regions, as opposed to military forces.

The 2009 Lisbon Treaty brought significant change to the EU's foreign policy architecture (Box 9.3). It introduced a new model High Representative, who combines the role of the previous High Representative with that of the commissioner for external affairs. The High Representative serves as a vice-president of the Commission and chairs EU Council meetings of foreign ministers, in perhaps the most audacious attempt ever to combine the supranational with the **intergovernmental** in one position (see Chapter 3). Doing so involves tricky compromises: for example, the High Representative has the (non-exclusive) right to propose CFSP initiatives without passing them through the entire College of Commissioners.

The first post-Lisbon High Representative Catherine Ashton spent most of her first year (2010) in post navigating a minefield of institutional bickering between the Commission, Council, and Parliament about the precise composition of the EEAS. One investigation concluded that 'Ashton proved to be a skilful negotiator, and despite the diverging views among the parties involved she managed to get the service off the ground within the first year of her appointment' (Vanhoonacker and Pomorska 2013: 1328). Still, by the end of Ashton's mandate (2014), diverse national attitudes towards the EEAS and more focus on internal problems than external strategy often undermined the CFSP.

Ashton's successor, Federica Mogherini, concentrated more on the role of Commission vice-president and highlighted the effects that EU's internal policies have on the EU's global role, such as functioning defence or energy markets. One of her most lauded achievements was formulation of the EU Global Strategy (see Box 9.5) that ambitiously sought to combine different EU internal and external policies in a joint approach. However, its implementation required member states to compromise, especially on planned reforms of the CSDP.

BOX 9.4   Compared to what? The EU and Russia

The EU's relationship with Russia is a classic glass half empty or half full story. A pessimist would stress the EU's dependence on Russia for energy, particularly after price disputes between Moscow and former Soviet republics or client-states led to repeated interruptions (or threats of them) in flows of Russian natural gas in the 2000s. The EU's concern for its energy security is often viewed as making it the

→

→

weaker partner. One upshot, according to this view, is that the Union is reluctant to speak truth to power about the erosion of Russian democracy, the 2007 cyber-war waged (apparently) by Russia on Estonia, and Russia's 2014 annexation of the Crimean region of Ukraine.

In practice, the EU and Russia are mutually and heavily interdependent. The EU relies on Russia to supply more than one-quarter of both its oil and natural gas. Russia relies on its sales of raw materials to the EU for most of its hard currency earnings, which fund nearly 40 per cent of Russia's federal budget. Around 60 per cent of Russia's export earnings come from energy sales, mostly to the EU.

Still, it is difficult to imagine that Russia and the EU could ever be 'partners'. Russia's intervention in Ukraine in 2014 followed the overthrow of a pro-Russian Ukrainian government by citizens motivated in large part by the rejection of an agreed EU–Ukraine trade deal by President Viktor Yanukovych. The contempt of the Russian President Vladimir Putin for the EU was reflected in his courtship of far right, Eurosceptic parties in Union member states. It occurred alongside a Cold War-style crackdown on domestic dissent in Russia amidst portrayals (ironically) of the new, post-Yanukovych Ukrainian government as dominated by 'fascists'. The words of a former EU diplomat remain appropriate more than a decade after they were uttered: 'Europe should clearly work for a comprehensive partnership with Russia, but . . . it is nonsense to suggest that this will be based on shared values' (Patten 2005: 178).

After Lisbon and the Global Strategy, the question remained whether the EU was a truly global actor or rather a facilitator for a joint approach of member states in global affairs. On key matters of international diplomacy, such as the crises in Ukraine (Box 9.4) and Syria, foreign ministers and heads of state and government continued to overshadow the High Representative. However, without consultation and preparation in Brussels, a united approach, such as on sanctions towards Russia, would have been impossible. On matters of international security, the EU has the potential to respond to crises in neighbouring areas such as Africa, where NATO has little to no role. Non-aligned European states find the EU provides them with a forum for security cooperation without requiring them to sign on to a mutual defence pact, as NATO does (see Bergman and Peterson 2006). Still, with some exceptions—such as its widely praised contribution to anti-piracy efforts on the east coast of Africa—the EU's international security operations in Africa, the Palestinian territories, Iraq, Afghanistan, Indonesia, and Libya have been relatively small and incidental compared to much larger operations under the auspices of the UN, NATO, or the US. In December 2017, 25 EU member states—all except Malta, Denmark, and the UK—agreed to establish Permanent Structured Cooperation (PESCO) of security and defence policy (European Council, 2017). PESCO was introduced in the Lisbon Treaty and allows for certain EU member states to strengthen cooperation in military matters (see Articles 42 and 46, Treaty on European Union (TEU)). The participating member states will work on a series of joint defence projects—for

> ## BOX 9.5   Insights: The EU Global Strategy
>
> In 2016 the EU High Representative presented a foreign and security policy strategy (Mogherini 2016) with the twin aims of reflecting member states' shared interests and mapping out ways to pursue them with the policy toolbox of the EU. Whether the document could be a blueprint to shape future EU policies was questionable, but it at least offered insights into European foreign policy thinking at time when external and internal crises challenged the EU's ability to act. 'Global' in the title was meant not only in terms of geographic reach, but also pointed to a broad set of EU instruments, including energy, counterterrorism, diplomacy, military and trade policies.
>
> A key concept that appeared throughout was 'resilience' against internal and external threats. The aim was to foster 'the ability [. . .] to withstand, cope, adapt, and quickly recover from stresses and shocks' (see Juncos 2016: 3) within the EU and its surrounding regions as well as around the world. Critics interpreted the focus on stability as a 'return to realpolitik' (Biscop 2016: 1) and wondered whether it implied that the EU had abandoned its focus on human rights and democracy for 'a defensive military orientation, for which the resilience concept stands as shorthand' (Bendiek 2016: 4).
>
> Another formulation in the Strategy that raised eyebrows was a call for 'strategic autonomy' of the EU. While it was framed more as the ability to react to threats and crises, it was quickly understood as a call of independence of Europe from the US security umbrella. With the EU missing key defence capabilities, let alone the existence of a credible nuclear deterrence, the latter remains unrealistic. Nevertheless, a tangible consequence of the Global Strategy was a bundle of CSDP reforms that aimed to foster defence research and industry across Europe and make EU deployments speedier. Whether (say) the creation of a billion-Euro European defence fund, military projects within the PESCO framework or closer coordination with NATO would lift EU defence to its feet remained to be seen. On a political level, the member states seemed to have understood that they needed to pull their military weight together in order to be leaders in a more contested international order in which US leadership was waning.

example a European Medical Command, a crisis response operation core, and cyber-security initiatives—throughout 2018 and beyond. Whilse critics suggested that the projects were too small to represent a step-change in CSDP, Donald Tusk and Jean-Claude Juncker hailed PESCO as a major development.

Theorizing the EU as a Global Actor

The expansion of the EU's foreign policy role confounds many international relations (IR) theorists, particularly those in the realist tradition. Most realists make two assumptions. First, power in international politics is a zero-sum commodity. Second, all alliances are temporary (see Mearsheimer 2001; Waltz 2002; Rosato 2011; 2012). On one hand, realists are often convincing in explaining why the EU is weak or divided on matters of high politics, such as Iraq or Russia. On the other hand, realists find it difficult to explain the EU's international ambitions and activities, or even why it does not collapse altogether. More generally, twenty-first century works of IR theory often barely mention the EU, or ignore it altogether (see Devetak *et al.* 2012; Burchill *et al.* 2013).

One consequence is that research on European foreign policy 'has come to resemble an archipelago' (Jørgensen 2006: 507), only barely connected to the study of IR more generally. Consider intergovernmentalist approaches to European integration, themselves derived from liberal theories of IR (Moravcsik 1998). Liberal intergovernmentalists assume that governments respond to powerful, domestic economic pressures. When governments agree policy deals that benefit national economic interests, they try to lock in those gains by giving EU institutions powers of enforcement. In contrast, governments face far weaker incentives to delegate foreign or defence policy powers to EU institutions, which explains why the EU's trade policy is far more integrated than the CFSP. Beyond that insight, however, only recently have intergovernmentalists begun to show interest in the EU's global ambitions. For example, Smith (2017) shows how attempts to enhance the Union's representation at the United Nations via the Lisbon Treaty were 'arrested' by the EU's internal intergovernmentalism.

In contrast, one of the oldest theories of European integration—neofunctionalism—may still have mileage. For example, Meunier (2017: 593) finds that the transfer of competence over foreign direct investment, which markedly increased the EU's clout in international economic diplomacy, occurred largely as a result of 'neofunctionalist Commission enterpreneurship'. Meanwhile, institutionalism—a theoretical cousin of neofunctionalism (see Haas 2001)—focuses on how the EU produces habits that eventually mature into institutionalized rules of behaviour (see Smith 2003; Menon 2011). The EU often creates new institutions—such as the High Representative or the Political and Security Committee—that develop their own interests, missions, and escape close intergovernmental control. Moreover, according to Smith's (2015: 127) glass half full view, 'a high degree of institutional learning' explains why 'the EU has come a *very* long way in terms of its foreign policy performance' since the 1980s and 90s (emphasis in original).

Yet, the leading theory of European foreign policy remains constructivism (see Bretherton and Vogler 2006; Meyer and Strickmann 2011; Keukeleire and Delreux 2014). Constructivists depart from realists and liberals in insisting that the interests and identities of EU member states are not fixed before they bargain with each other. Rather, they are 'constructed' through bargaining. Constructivists, in contrast to institutionalists, insist that ideas matter as much as (or more than) institutions in IR. Alexander Wendt (1992, 1999), perhaps the leading IR constructivist, portrays the EU as more than a temporary alliance because its member states assume a measure of common identity through shared ideas about the desirability of multilateralism, environmental protection, and so on. Many constructivists do not shy away from questions about what the EU *should* do in foreign policy, insisting on the importance of a 'normative power Europe' that stands up for its values and principles (Manners 2002, 2006; Forsberg 2011). Realists can be relied upon to scoff at such suggestions (Hyde-Price 2006).

Arguably, however, constructivism sets the bar too low. Its proponents can become apologists for EU inaction or incoherence in global politics by always falling back on the argument that Europe remains 'under construction' as a global actor. As much as constructivists insist the glass is half full, others—such as Toje (2010, 2011), who portrays the EU as a 'small power' analogous to Canada, Peru, or Switzerland—argue that it remains half empty.

Conclusion

When then British Prime Minister Tony Blair urged that the EU should become a 'superpower but not a superstate' in 2000, he provoked little controversy outside of his own country. The idea that the EU should take a lead in expressing European power internationally has become almost a mainstream view (see Morgan 2005; Peterson and Helwig 2017). The EU has come a long way from humble origins in foreign policy. But it remains an odd global power, which has difficulty living up to its ambitions. The EU has increased its potential international power each time it has enlarged but simultaneously increased the difficulty of reaching consensus. Yet, EU foreign policy is only as good as the quality of the consensus among its members, and it is often of poor quality in an enlarged EU of 28 (soon to be 27).

One reason why assessments of European foreign policy vary so widely is because it is unclear how the EU's success should be measured. There is no question that the Union is far more active internationally than its founders ever imagined it could be. In several policy areas, especially economic ones, it is a global power. No other international organization in history has even tried, let alone claimed, to have a 'common' foreign policy.

The Lisbon Treaty's institutional reforms aimed to move the EU closer to a truly common foreign policy (see Rogers 2009). Nearly a decade after its entry into force, the question of whether the EU will ever be an effective and global actor is as difficult to answer as ever. In the immediate aftermath of Lisbon's implementation, it seemed as if the EU's foreign policy was characterized by even *more* complex institutional interactions (Helwig 2013). Over the years, new informal leadership practices in EU foreign policy have emerged (Aggestam and Johansson 2017), and cases like the Ukraine crisis show that despite treaty changes the lead of member states remains indispensable.

Yet, while the EU was paralysed during the first half of the 2010s by institutional infights, the international environment became the challenge of the second half. With the UK leaving and an (often, apparently) leaderless US under Trump, the guarantor powers of the international order seemed to drop out as forceful partners of the EU. While Europe remained united in defence of, say—the nuclear deal with Iran, a two-state solution in the Middle East, and the rules enforced by the World Trade Organization (WTO)—it was unclear how much or effectively the EU could defend the liberal international order (see Peterson 2018).

The negative consequences of failing US leadership for the EU's ability to be a truly global actor cannot be over-estimated. Discussion of the different natures of US power and EU's international role is not new. The failure of hard (mostly) American military power to achieve US policy goals in Afghanistan or Iraq—let alone Iran or North Korea or the Middle East—rekindled questions about whether Europe's soft power might make it an alternative source of leadership in the twenty-first century (Rifkin 2004; Leonard 2005).

Yet, the Libyan crisis could be taken not only as an example where Europe was (again) reliant on US support and resources, but also one that exposed the limits of Europe's soft power approach (Menon 2011). Without US support on major international issues, such as the Iran nuclear deal or deterrence of Russian aggression in the Baltics, the Europeans often have little to show for themselves. Efforts to boost European military capabilities following the adoption of the EU Global Strategy were thus all the more pressing.

One of the EU's (now former) top diplomats argued that Europe will never maximize its soft power until it invests far more in hard power (Cooper 2004a). There is evidence that it has got the message, amplified by prodding from Donald Trump, to spend more on defence. There is no question that the EU faces powerful incentives—especially as it loses economic ground to states such as China, India, and Russia, and faces security challenges in its neighbourhood—to become more united in foreign policy. As Howorth (2007: 22) argues, 'The pressures for the EU to speak to the rest of the world with a single voice will become intense. The refusal to make collective EU choices in the world of 2025 will be tantamount to an abdication of sovereignty.'

It is easy to see why debates about Europe as a global actor are so lively. The EU remains an often uncertain and hesitant global power, but one that never stops trying to be more coherent and effective. It will no doubt continue to frustrate its partners, but sometimes show surprising unity, and to fascinate—probably as much as it confounds—students of international politics.

? **DISCUSSION QUESTIONS**

1. Define 'European foreign policy'. Explain why this term has assumed wide usage among those who study the EU's international role.

2. Why are member states reluctant to entrust the Commission with responsibilities for the political side of foreign policy, while they have done so for important areas of economic external relations?

3. Why does the EU have so much difficulty coordinating its different external policies, as its Global Strategy urges it to do?

4. How best to characterize the EU as a global actor? Civilian power? Normative power? Market power? Small power? Military power?

FURTHER READING

The best single source on Europe as a global actor is Hill *et al.* (2017). Useful overviews include Laïdi (2008); Toje (2010); and Smith (2014). Good historical treatments are available, told from the points of view of a practitioner (Nuttall 2000) and an academic institutionalist (Smith 2003). The effect of the Lisbon Treaty's institutional changes are examined by Vanhoonacker and Pomorska (2013) and Peterson and Helwig (2017). On EU external economic policy, see Young and Peterson (2014). The Union's contribution to the United Nations, as well as multi-lateralism more generally, is considered by Bouchard *et al.* (2013). On the idea of the EU as a 'civilian power', see Sjursen (2006b).

Bouchard, C., Peterson, J., and Tocci, N. (eds) (2013), *Multilateralism in the Twenty-First Century: Europe's Quest for Effectiveness* (London and New York: Routledge).

Hill, C., Smith, M., and Vanhoonacker, S. (eds) (2017), *International Relations and the European Union*, 3nd edn (Oxford and New York: Oxford University Press).

Laïdi, Z. (ed.) (2008), *EU Foreign Policy in a Globalized World: Normative Power and Social Preferences* (London and New York: Routledge).

Nuttall, S. (2000), *European Foreign Policy* (Oxford and New York: Oxford University Press).

Peterson, J. and Helwig, N. (2017) 'Common Foreign and Security Policy: Institutionalizing Europe's Global Role', in D. Hodson and J. Peterson (eds), *The Institutions of the European Union*, 4th edn (Oxford and New York: Oxford University Press): 307–33.

Sjursen, H. (ed.) (2006b), 'What Kind of Europe? European Foreign Policy in Perspective', Special Issue of *Journal of European Public Policy*, 13/2.

Smith, M. E. (2003), *Europe's Foreign and Security Policy* (Cambridge and New York: Cambridge University Press).

Smith, K. E. (2014), *European Union Foreign Policy in a Changing World*, 3rd edn (Oxford and Malden MA: Polity).

Toje, A. (2010), *The European Union as a Small Power: After the Cold War* (Basinstoke and New York: Palgrave).

Vanhoonacker, S. and Pomorska, K. (2013), 'The European External Action Service and Agenda-Setting in European Foreign Policy', *Journal of European Public Policy*, 20/9: 1316–31.

Young, A. and Peterson, J. (2014), *Parochial Global Europe: Twenty-first Century Trade Politics* (Oxford and New York: Oxford University Press).

 WEB LINKS

- A good place to start researching the EU's external policy role is the website of the Paris-based Institute for Security Studies (www.iss.europa.eu), which formally became an autonomous EU agency in 2002.

- Other specific areas of EU policy have their own, dedicated websites:

  - External relations and foreign and security policy: www.europa.eu/pol/cfsp/index_en.htm

  - Humanitarian aid: http://europa.eu/pol/hum/index_en.htm

  - Justice/home affairs: www.europa.eu/pol/justice/index_en.htm

  - Trade: http://europa.eu/pol/comm/index_en.htm

  - Development: http://ec.europa.eu/europeaid/index_en.htm

- The EEAS' site (https://eeas.europa.eu) has general information about EU foreign and defence policy, but the websites of national foreign ministries often reveal more.

- On the EU's relationship with the US, see http://www.euintheus.org and www.useu.be

- Weblinks on the EU's other important relationships include ones devoted to the Cotonou convention (http://www.acp.int/), EU–Canadian relations (www.canada-europe.org), and the Union's relationship with Latin America (http://aei.pitt.edu/view/subjects/D002022.html).

- To see how closely linked the EU's trade and aid policies are, see http://ec.europa.eu/trade/policy/countries-and-regions/development/aid-for-trade/.

- The European Council on Foreign Relations offers an annual assessment of European foreign policy in the form of a scorecard: http://www.ecfr.eu/scorecard/

 Visit the Ancillary Resource Centre that accompanies this book for additional material: www.oup.com/uk/kenealy5e/

CHAPTER 10

Brexit and the Future of Two Unions

Daniel Kenealy, John Peterson, and Richard Corbett

Summary

In June 2016, the United Kingdom (UK) held a referendum on continuing its European Union (EU) membership. The UK voted to leave the EU by a narrow margin, but one large enough for its new prime minister (after David Cameron, who called the referendum, resigned), Theresa May, to call 'Brexit' (the process of Britain *exiting* the EU) 'the settled will of the British people'. The result sent shock waves across Europe. This chapter seeks to explain how and why the Brexit vote occurred and what might happen—both to the UK and to the EU—as a result. Possible outcomes of the negotiations on Brexit are considered with a view to assessing their impact on the UK, the EU, and the future of **European integration**.

Introduction

On 23 June 2016, the UK held a referendum asking the question 'Should the United Kingdom remain a member of the European Union or leave the European Union?' With a 72.2 per cent turnout, the UK voted to leave the EU by a margin of 51.9 per cent to 48.1 per cent. The result sent shock waves through the UK political establishment and across Europe. In its immediate aftermath, concerns arose about a contagion effect: that other EU member states might stage similar referendums. Eurosceptic parties in several EU member states made such calls, but elections in 2017 that yielded pro-EU governments in the Netherlands, France, and Germany saw such threats recede. Within the UK, the fact that Scotland and Northern Ireland voted to remain in the EU created significant constitutional dilemmas.

The referendum also brought David Cameron's six years as UK prime minister to a sudden, crashing halt. Cameron had stunned political pundits by winning an unexpected majority in the 2015 UK general election. But he abruptly resigned the day after the referendum, saying that he was unable to be a head of a government whose primary task would be delivering 'Brexit'. The subsequent UK Conservative Party leadership election at times felt like something out of *House of Cards*. The former education and justice secretary under Cameron, Michael Gove, sabotaged his erstwhile partner in the cause of Brexit, Boris Johnson (former mayor of London), by repudiating Johnson's candidacy despite having initially managed the latter's bid to become prime minister.[1] Andrea Leadsom, who at first emerged as the most popular pro-Brexit leadership candidate, withdrew after a disastrous interview in which she suggested that being a mother meant she had a larger stake in society than her one remaining (childless) opponent: Theresa May. The result was that May, the UK's longest-serving home secretary since 1892, was crowned as Cameron's successor. The only thing that was certain about May's premiership was that Brexit would dominate it.

This chapter seeks to understand how and why Brexit happened and what might happen—both to the UK and to the EU—as a result. First, we consider the road to the referendum, exploring why Cameron decided to call it, how the campaign was fought, and why a majority of UK voters opted voted to leave. Second, the process of exiting the EU—commonly known as 'the Article 50 process', after the relevant article in the treaty—is discussed. We also explain the process of negotiating Brexit following the triggering of Article 50 in March 2017. Our third section identifies the major issues in the negotiations and considers a range of possible future relationships between the UK and the EU. The fourth section considers the potential impact of Brexit on the UK as well as the EU, whose leaders must consider a future

---

[1] At virtually the last moment in the leadership campaign, Gove withdrew from Johnson's campaign and announced his own candidacy to be party leader (and thus prime minister). The move effectively destroyed both of their chances, as Johnson stood down and Gove was eliminated in a second ballot of Conservative (sometimes called 'Tory') MPs.

without the UK that is littered with significant other challenges, from attacks on European values in Hungary and Poland, to a potential resurgence of troubles in the **Eurozone**, and to insecurity in the EU's near abroad.

The Referendum

When histories of David Cameron's premiership are written, they inevitably will dwell on the EU referendum, a gamble he made and ultimately lost.[2] Much like the previous cases of Anthony Eden and Suez, and Tony Blair and Iraq, Cameron's UK premiership is likely to be forever associated with one word: 'Brexit'. Why did Cameron call the referendum? Why did he lose it?

Why have a referendum?

This chapter is not the place to recount the history of the UK's post-war relationship with European integration and membership from 1973 (see Milward 2002; Wall 2012; Grob-Fitzgibbon 2016). The UK has often been termed an 'awkward partner' in European integration (George 1998). Successive UK governments opted not to sign up to the first efforts at integration in the 1950s: the European Coal and Steel Community (ECSC) and the European Economic Community (EEC). After joining what was then the EEC in 1973, UK governments secured opt-outs from a rich variety of policies and projects, including the euro and the border-free Schengen area. Perhaps as balm to the political shock of having a member state—for the first time ever—choose to leave the EU, some Brussels insiders were heard to say that 'the UK was never a *full* member anyway'. Yet, in some areas, such as the **single market** and EU-funded research programmes, the UK took a leading role.

To understand why the choice was made to hold the UK referendum in 2016, it is important to understand how Europe came to shape domestic politics, and in particular the internal politics of the Conservative Party. As a 2016 BBC documentary on Brexit put it, 'it was really a family row, one raging in the Conservative party' (BBC 2016a). Divisions within the Conservative Party about the UK's relationship with the EU were a powerful contributing factor in the downfall of Margaret Thatcher in 1990. They posed a serious challenge to John Major's government, with a slim parliamentary majority making the party's eurosceptic MPs disproportionately influential, during the 1992–7 parliament (see Young 1998: 412–71). In opposition during the years of the Labour premierships of Blair and Gordon Brown,

---

[2] The contrast between what future historians are likely to conclude about Cameron's political judgement and party management skills may be stark compared to one of his closest advisor's (C. Oliver 2016), whose Brexit memoir is useful and gripping if also hagiographic about Cameron's premiership.

it was still a highly divisive issue among Tories. Blair's ardent pro-Europeanism contributed to a shift by some Conservative MPs towards a firmer euroscepticism. But it was not a priority of many voters. In fact, after being elected leader of the Conservatives in December 2005, David Cameron told his party to stop 'banging on' about Europe. Nevertheless, the number of eurosceptic MPs in the Conservative parliamentary party rose following the 2010 general election (Heppell 2013).

As Conservative leader and later prime minister, Cameron tried to appease euro-sceptics within his party. Over time, he succeeded only in emboldening them. A first concession was when Cameron withdrew Conservative members of the European Parliament (MEPs) (against their will) from the European People's Party (EPP), the main centre-right and largest grouping in the European Parliament (EP). Conservative MEPs founded a new grouping, the European Conservatives and Reformists, which was avowedly anti-federalist, far less powerful than the EPP, and brought the Tories together with far right and (sometimes) overtly racist east European MEPs (see Lynch and Whitaker 2008; Bale *et al.* 2010). It meant that Conservative contacts and influence with mainstream centre-right parties across Europe were severely diminished.

In the 2010 UK general election, the electorate spared Cameron the fate of becom-ing beholden to the hardest eurosceptics in his parliamentary party. The hung parliament that resulted forced a coalition government with the pro-EU Liberal Democrats, which lasted until 2015. Yet the EU issue refused to go away. A signifi-cant number of Conservative MPs were increasingly vocal in calling for the UK to have a referendum on continued EU membership, and/or blaming the EU for a litany of domestic problems. Few Tory eurosceptics were placated by the 2011 European Union Act, which committed the UK government to holding a referendum on any future treaty that transferred powers to the EU. Many Conservative MPs were also concerned about the rise of the United Kingdom Independence Party (UKIP), a pop-ulist party that fused anti-immigration and anti-EU stances with calls for the UK to take back its **sovereignty** and control its borders (Ford and Goodwin 2014[3]). In short, the issue of the EU was threatening Cameron's party from within and without.

The issue came to a head as the Conservatives began to shift to a war footing ahead of the 2015 general election. To mollify the eurosceptic wing of his party, Cameron committed to holding an in/out referendum (UK Government 2013) following a renegotiation of the terms of the UK's membership of the EU, prob-ably never thinking he would have to deliver on it, as few thought that an overall Conservative majority was likely. But following their surprise victory, resulting in a single-party Conservative government, Cameron could no longer hide behind the Liberal Democrats.[4] Conscious that the EU issue could consume the entire 2015–20

[3] Notably, however, this book demonstrated clearly that UKIP was a potential electoral threat to *both* Labour *and* the Conservatives, perhaps over time more the former than the latter.

[4] In 2010 the Liberal Democrats campaigned on a commitment to a referendum 'the next time a British government signs up for fundamental change' in the UK–EU relationship which obviously had not occurred by 2015.

parliament, and mindful of the French and German elections in 2017, Cameron moved quickly into (re)negotiations with EU partners.

The result was a deal announced in February 2016 that Cameron claimed granted the UK 'special status' by, *inter alia*, giving it a symbolic opt-out from 'ever closer union', admitting that multiple currencies existed in the EU, and offering complicated formulas on limiting EU migration to the UK (see European Council 2016a). The concessions sought by the UK, and granted by the EU, were dismissed by hard-line eurosceptics as modest. In any event, the deal proved 'too complex' to be useful in the subsequent referendum campaign (Korski 2016). The deal will almost certainly end up a mere footnote in the history of European integration, given the result of the referendum.

The referendum campaign

There were two official UK referendum campaigns, *Stronger In* and *Vote Leave*. However, the leave side was supplemented by the efforts of *Leave.Eu*, an organization closely connected with senior figures and financial backers of UKIP. *Vote Leave* and *Leave.Eu* spoke to different audiences. Although the relationship between the two campaigns was at times fraught, their different pitches and tones were generally thought to have benefitted the leave effort (Bennett 2016).

Stronger In was an umbrella organization bringing together leading figures from the Conservative, Labour, and Liberal Democrat parties to urge a 'remain' vote. Cameron and George Osborne, the chancellor of the exchequer (the UK's equivalent of finance minister), were prominent figures in the *Stronger In* campaign. So were the first ministers of Scotland and Wales, and various senior Labour and Liberal Democrat MPs, as well as business and trade union leaders. In subsequently published campaign memoirs, the villain of the remain effort is most often Jeremy Corbyn, a lifelong eurosceptic who had been elected Labour leader by a grassroots campaign led by old school, anti-Blairite leftists. Corbyn was accused of being, much 'like [Theresa] May . . . only a tepid campaigner for staying in the [European U]nion' (Freedland 2017). But while May mostly kept quiet, Corbyn was accused of outright sabotage of remain efforts. Many Labour supporters clearly were confused by his campaign messaging: one poll during the campaign found that 45 per cent of Labour voters thought the Labour Party were either divided on Brexit or supported it (Goodwin and Heath 2016: 331),[5] whereas in fact the Labour Party conference had voted unanimously to campaign to remain. In the days following the referendum, Corbyn was subject to a vote of no confidence supported by over 80 per cent of Labour MPs.

A perhaps more decisive factor was *Vote Leave*'s major coup when Boris Johnson and Michael Gove, two senior Conservative politicians, confirmed that they would

---

[5] However, post-referendum polls confirmed that a clear majority (65 per cent of Labour's voters in the 2015 election) voted to remain in the EU (Moore 2016).

campaign for Brexit. They became the main faces of the Brexit campaign, along with the UKIP leader Nigel Farage. Farage's established brand of anti-establishment, beer-drinking, populist politics contrasted with the more measured public appearances and statements of Gove (as well as the German-born Gisela Stuart, a *Vote Leave* supporter and maverick Labour MP). Johnson brought his own inimitable style to proceedings.

Behr (2016) recounts how *Stronger In* decided, using polling and focus group evidence, to focus their campaign on the economic uncertainty Brexit would cause. In what might be a 'head versus heart' struggle—the heart saying leave but the head saying remain—*Stronger In* calculated that enough voters would ultimately vote for security and economic certainty. It was a similar playbook to that used by the campaign to keep Scotland in the UK during the 2014 independence referendum, that was often labelled 'Project Fear'. *Stronger In* failed to make a strong, positive case for EU membership, despite evidence that suggested doing so might have been a good strategy (Goodwin *et al.* 2015). The remain campaign seized on a forecast by the UK Treasury suggesting that Brexit would leave each household in the country £4,300 worse off. Osborne suggested that an emergency 'punishment' budget would be necessary in the wake of Brexit involving around £30 billion of spending cuts and tax rises. Neither claim came across as credible.

After focusing on economic insecurity, the remain campaign was left struggling to counter the Brexit campaign's more upbeat messaging. With a simple and effective slogan—'Vote Leave. Take Control'—and promising (fancifully) an extra £350 million a week for the UK's National Health Service from money that would no longer be sent to Brussels, the leave campaign captured the narrative as the campaign entered its closing stages. Gove himself famously insisted that 'people have had enough of experts', catching the mood of the moment and revealing pro-Brexit's 'scorched earth approach to evidence-based argument' (Behr 2016). One of the leave campaign's chief strategists recalled its core messages: the high cost of EU membership; the risk of Turkey imminently joining the EU (a preposterous claim); the risks of contagion by another Eurozone crisis; and the need to take control of the UK's borders. All were wrapped in a broader anti-establishment package that proved highly effective (Cummings 2017).

In particular, the remain campaign had no response on immigration. It failed even to point out that most migrants to the UK came from outside the EU, entirely under UK, not EU, rules, or that EU freedom of movement was not unconditional. Here, we see how 'campaigns can ride big waves but they almost never make them' (Cummings 2017). That is, underlying euroscepticism within UK society was the wave on which the leave campaign rode (see also Shipman 2016). It was difficult—maybe impossible—for Cameron suddenly to begin making a positive case for the EU after years of failing to do so, and often pandering to the eurosceptics. As Geddes (2016) succinctly puts it: '[t]he problem for Cameron was that, after years in which he had nothing positive to say about the EU, he then had become in a four month campaign an ardent advocate of the necessity of continued membership'.

The remain campaign failed not only to build a positive case for the EU but also for the UK's ability to shape outcomes and get what it wanted in Brussels (Korski 2016). Perhaps the primary flaws of the remain campaign were that all was bet on the idea that the economy would trump immigration and it failed to engage voters who felt they had little to lose from Brexit (C. Oliver 2016). Those voters, often labelled the 'left behind', proved crucial to the outcome.

Another important factor was the media landscape. Six of nine main UK national newspapers supported leaving the EU, in some cases with virulent headlines. Their dominance was even greater when the reach of each was factored in, producing overall coverage that was 'heavily skewed towards the Leave camp' (Levy *et al.* 2016).

Understanding the result

Analysis confirmed, but also added nuance, to the portrait of 'left behinds'—by globalization and neoliberalism—rebelling against economic change and a policy consensus supported by what has come to be termed 'the establishment'. Arguments about the economy, immigration, national identity, and sovereignty were all persuasive to different voters. As Curtice (2017: 13) puts it:

> the way that people voted in the EU referendum was related both to what they thought the instrumental consequences of leaving would be and to their sense of identity. The outcome . . . is best understood as the product of the interplay between both these forces.

Crucially, the referendum outcome was determined by those voters who felt that leaving the EU would make little difference to their lives: of those voters, nearly two-thirds voted to leave (Curtice 2017). The UK public's long-term (relative) lack of enthusiasm for the EU was exacerbated by higher levels of migration to the UK from the newer EU member states in Central and Eastern Europe and the impact of the 2008 financial crisis. In combination 'the two proved toxic for a public that had always been inclined to be sceptical about what had become one of the principal manifestations of globalization': the EU (Curtice 2017: 17).

Goodwin and Heath (2016: 324) identify deep divides within British politics that have simmered for many years and that cut across class, generational, and geographical lines. Especially for economically disaffected voters, the remain campaign's emphasis on economic risk simply did not resonate. Brexit voters held 'a more socially conservative outlook on Europe, immigration, and national identity that in recent years has become just as important as old disputes between labour and capital' (Goodwin 2016). This view is supported by figures showing that age and education levels were the two biggest indicators of how people voted in the referendum: the older you were, the more likely you were to vote leave, and the same if you had fewer educational qualifications (Curtice 2017). The rise of eurosceptic UKIP also helps us understand the story of Brexit. The party capitalized on 'changes to Britain's economic and social structure' and levels of support for Brexit were high in areas of the country where UKIP had performed strongly in the 2014 EP elections. The campaign was also bitterly divisive and 'less a traditional left-right battle, and more about identity and values'. It was a strong sign that the 'so-called "culture wars" of the US ha[d] arrived in Great Britain' (Swales 2016: 27).

Making sense of the broader context might well start with a process Norris and Inglehart (2016: 29) have described: 'the spread of progressive values has . . . stimulated a cultural backlash among people who feel threatened by the development'. A cross-national study of populist political parties suggests that a new political cleavage has emerged in western democracies between 'populism' (anti-establishment, nationalist, traditionalist) and 'cosmopolitan liberalism' (pluralist, multiculturalist, progressive) (Norris and Inglehart 2016: 34). It often cuts across the more familiar economic left-versus-right cleavage. As this new cleavage grows stronger, traditional party-political affiliations and alignments may be called into question and the west—including the EU—may become more prone to 'identity politics' of a kind most often associated with emerging states and young democracies in the recent past (see Chatterjee 2004). It is difficult to see how the EU would gain from such a development, or even survive it if there were a contagion effect from the UK to other member states. But, since Brexit is a political fact and any future contagion is unknown, diligent students of the EU need to know how a member state leaves the Union.

How to Leave the EU

The Union's treaties deal with the scenario of a member state seeking to leave in Article 50 Treaty on European Union (TEU). But this previously unused Article offers only a basic starting point (see Box 10.1). In this section we offer thoughts on the likely process and timeframes of the negotiations.

BOX 10.1 Article 50: The provision meant never to be used

Article 50 TEU was added through the 2009 **Lisbon Treaty**. Previously, there was no legal mechanism through which a member state could leave and the issue received little attention. Lord Kerr (who helped draft Article 50) stated that Article 50 was designed to cope with a member state that had lurched away from democracy and wished to 'storm out' of the EU (*Independent* 2017). Article 50 entered the political lexicon post-Brexit. It hands power to trigger the process of leaving to the member state wishing to depart. From the date of the UK's notification, the EU had two years to 'negotiate and conclude an agreement with that [departing] State, setting out the arrangements for its withdrawal, taking into account the framework for its future relationship with the Union'. If no agreement is reached within these

➡

two years, 'the treaties shall cease to apply to the State in question' (meaning it would leave without settling outstanding issues). But if there is an agreement, it sets the date of departure.

The wording 'taking into account' the framework for future relations is ambiguous. It makes clear that Article 50 does not itself define the future relationship. Yet, some measure of agreement must obviously exist as to what it will be in order to take account of it. UK ministers wanted to progress the withdrawal agreement and agreement on the UK's future relationship with the EU in parallel. But Article 50 suggests it is possible for a member state to leave without a final agreement on a future relationship.

The **European Council** sets the negotiating guidelines for the EU. Any final agreement is subject to a qualified majority vote in the Council as well as the approval of the EP. Article 50 thus creates a multi-level, complex negotiation featuring multiple players. Two years is a short time to untangle all the interdependencies, rights, and obligations that come with EU membership, let alone agree the future relationship between a departing member state and the EU. The timeframe can be extended, but only if all member states agree.

The negotiation process

Article 50 says little about the negotiation process other than that those negotiations will be conducted under guidelines set out by the European Council. The EU has experience of conducting negotiations with 'third countries' (which the UK is becoming) in external trade. The model by which the Council sets out a broad negotiating mandate and the Commission handles the day-to-day negotiation process is thus a familiar one.

Such a model has been adopted for Brexit. The European Council empowered the Commission to handle the negotiations on a day-to-day basis. Michel Barnier—former French foreign minister, EU commissioner, and MEP—was appointed as chief EU negotiator, working within the broad parameters set out by the European Council and more detailed negotiating directives set by the (ordinary) Council. Appointing the Commission as sole negotiator was not only a practical necessity—the expertise of the Commission services would be vital in detailed negotiations—it was also an indication of unity among the 27 remaining member states. Nonetheless, the latter, meeting within the Council without the UK, would retain ultimate control of what was agreed and would decide on the acceptability or otherwise of compromise deals as they emerged. A task force within the Council secretariat was set up, headed by Didier Seeuws (former chief of staff to European Council President Herman Van Rompuy) and the 27 would hear reports back from the Commission at several levels, from ministerial meetings, to Coreper (Committee of Permanent Representatives), to 'sherpas' (lead officials designated for this subject from each member state).

The EP appointed MEP Guy Verhofstadt—former Belgian prime minister—to be its lead on Brexit, with responsibility for linking the EP to the negotiators, attending some of the meetings, and expressing the views of the EP as defined in resolutions it would adopt. Verhofstadt was thus not a formal party to the negotiation but his views were likely to carry weight as the withdrawal agreement, and any future framework agreement, required the approval of the EP. Within the EP, Verhofstadt reported to a Brexit steering group (with a representative of each of the mainstream political groups in the EP) on general strategy and to the conference of committee chairs (of the 20 EP committees) on the details of the negotiations in specific policy areas relevant to those committees. In an initial resolution, Parliament placed particular emphasis on safeguarding the rights of citizens, especially EU citizens resident in the UK and vice versa (European Parliament 2017).

On the UK side, it might have been expected that the UK Cabinet Office—the department that sits at the centre, close to the prime minister—would have taken the lead, working closely with the Foreign and Commonwealth Office (FCO). Instead, May created two new departments: the Department for International Trade and the Department for Exiting the European Union (Owen and Munro 2016). The former took responsibility for laying the groundwork for, and then negotiating, new trade deals for the UK. David Davis—a veteran Conservative MP and former minister for Europe who had campaigned for Brexit—was appointed secretary of state for Brexit. Concern immediately arose that the UK civil service would be overstretched, lacked the expertise in sufficient numbers, and that the complexities involved in Brexit might detract from other areas of government business. That view was compounded by the resignation in January 2017 of Sir Ivan Rogers, the UK's permanent representative (ambassador) to the EU, and his complaints about poor preparation, ill-founded arguments, and muddled thinking (BBC 2017). Whitehall—a term for the UK government and the road on which the Cabinet Office is located—certainly faced 'capacity demands' as it approached Brexit (see Institute for Government 2017).

In March 2017, the UK government officially triggered Article 50, submitting notification of its intention to leave. Absent an extension of the two-year negotiation window, the UK would thus leave the EU, formally, at the end of March 2019. Given the need to ratify any EU–UK exit agreement before that date, the time for substantive negotiations was short, perhaps 12–18 months. The European Council authorized the opening of negotiations with the UK, nominated the Commission as the EU's negotiator, and adopted a set of negotiating directives in May 2017 (European Council 2017).

The likelihood of having to make unpopular choices during the negotiations with only a 12-seat majority in Parliament helps explain why Theresa May then called a snap UK general election, held in June 2017. Despite enjoying commanding poll leads, the Conservatives' campaign was widely regarded as poor and the result was a hung parliament, with May losing her majority. The prime minister had to agree a deal with Northern Ireland's Democratic Unionist Party (DUP) to continue to govern. The DUP's ten MPs would back May's government in key votes, including those pertaining to Brexit. The parliamentary arithmetic created by the 2017 election made May vulnerable to backbench rebellions, by both ultra-Brexit supporters and by pro-EU MPs who wished to see a softer form of Brexit pursued, with oversight of the process by the UK Parliament. Reliance on the DUP also raised questions about the Irish dimension of Brexit (as we shall discuss).

Most of those close to the Brexit process admitted that it would be virtually impossible to reach a Brexit deal by March 2019, the end of Article 50's two-year period, unless a transition period was agreed beyond 2019, during which the status quo would apply in many fields while the two sides continued to negotiate. In a speech in Florence in September 2017, Theresa May seemed to acknowledge that such a transition, for approximately two years, was necessary (UK Government 2017b). Nevertheless, the idea of remaining subject to EU laws, and its Court of Justice, remained a sensitive one in UK domestic politics, at least in the Conservative Party.

Can Article 50 be revoked?

One poll in early 2018 found that (excluding 'don't knows'), 58 per cent of UK voters favoured a second referendum, with increased backing from both sides of the debate, including 2016 leave voters (Guardian ICM survey 2018). Could the UK government tell the EU 'We've changed our minds?' Lord Kerr—former UK ambassador to the EU and the original author of Article 50—judged that it could be revoked (Open Britain 2017). For its part, the UK Supreme Court ruled in a case on Brexit that Article 50 'cannot be withdrawn' once invoked. But it did not adjudicate on a matter that would, in the event of a dispute, be for the EU's Court of Justice to settle.

The prevailing view in Brussels seems to be that Article 50 notification could be revoked. The two EU bodies to have pronounced on the matter—the EP and the European Committee of the Regions—agreed that it could be rescinded provided that it was done in good faith and not simply to gain more negotiating time (European Parliament 2017). The former head of the Legal Service of the Council agreed (Piris 2016). The president of the European Council, Donald Tusk, openly encouraged the UK to reconsider. Ultimately, if a departing member state changed its mind, it is hard to see from where a challenge would emerge.

What Might Brexit Look Like?

Since the UK referendum, debates about a 'soft' vs 'hard' Brexit have become commonplace. The terms refer to two ends of a spectrum, ranging from the UK maintaining many current rights and obligations, including membership of the EU single market and customs union, to leaving all areas of EU cooperation and having the same relationship with the EU as, say, Australia or the US. Some even contemplated leaving without any agreement. The type of Brexit to be delivered depends on a series of trade-offs between different issues: for example, free movement of EU citizens in exchange for unfettered UK access to the EU's single market. Up until our time of writing, the EU had been generally open and transparent about what the trade-offs could be, with the UK government adopting a far more secretive approach.

The key issues

The Brexit negotiations can, at the highest level, be broken down into two components. First is a deal that will settle the terms of the UK's departure from the EU. Second is an agreement on the future relationship between the UK and the EU. The EU made it clear from the start that progress had to be made on the first before commencing serious discussions on the second.

The European Council's (2017) guidelines for the negotiations advocated a 'phased approach' to Brexit, 'giving priority to an orderly withdrawal'. They also ruled out any cherry-picking of elements of EU membership that the UK found desirable while shedding ones that it found undesirable. The Council—echoed by the EP—was clear that exit negotiations had to come first. The first component of 'orderly withdrawal' involved settling the UK's budgetary liabilities. Upper estimates of that bill—covering ongoing liabilities and UK payments into pre-agreed EU-wide programmes (as well as pension liabilities for EU staff)— were around €60 billion, stretching to €100 billion according to press reports (Barker 2017). The precise amount and the methods by which it could be calculated were not the important point. The key was that the EU was prioritizing this thorny issue before serious negotiations about the future EU–UK relationship could begin.

The Council's guidelines also stressed the importance of early agreement on the rights of EU-27 citizens living in the UK, and vice-versa. At issue were the fates of far more than the four million people (three million EU-27 citizens and roughly a million UK citizens) living in other EU countries, but also those who had done so in the past, with many acquiring pensions, property, and families. The European Council made determining these rights—how long they would continue and under what status—an early priority. Others included the Irish border, UK military bases in Cyprus, international agreements to which the EU (and the UK) was party, re-location of UK-based EU agencies, and the jurisdiction of the EU's Court of Justice in settling any future disputes about EU law involving the UK.

Subsequent draft negotiating directives revealed other complex questions to be answered, such the UK's participation in and contributions to the European Investment Bank and the European Development Fund, which aids less-developed countries (European Commission 2017a). The negotiating directives were living documents, to be updated over time to direct (and constrain) the Commission as negotiations proceeded. By moving quickly, putting in place its negotiating team, and issuing clear guidelines, EU leaders set the framework of the Brexit negotiations.

Both EU and UK leaders expressed a desire for a close relationship after Brexit. Nonetheless, EU leaders made it clear that the UK could not have a post-Brexit relationship that was more beneficial than the status quo: if you leave a club, you cannot get better terms than its members. If it were possible to get a better deal by leaving the EU, then other member states might be tempted to do the same. EU leaders made it clear that the four freedoms—the free movement of people, goods, services, and capital—were indivisible.[6] The UK could not expect the same trading privileges if it did not permit EU-27 citizens to live and work in the UK. 'No cherry-picking' was repeated time and again by EU officials and politicians.

Hard versus soft Brexit

Given the EU's consistent and unified ban on 'cherry-picking', the UK government faced a trade-off between the economic benefits of single-market membership—the ability to trade goods and services with the EU freely—and being able to control migration to the UK by EU citizens. If it prioritized the latter it had to sacrifice the former. This position takes us into the distinctions between 'hard' versus 'soft' Brexit, terms that emerged in the aftermath of the referendum and quickly gained traction in UK political discourse.

Based on official statements by Theresa May, we can begin to understand the type of Brexit that she was envisioning (May 2016; UK Government 2017a). During the referendum campaign, May—at the time the home secretary—kept a low profile despite formally supporting the UK remaining in the EU. On assuming the premiership, her carefully balanced and triangulated position—trying to at once appease both hard-line eurosceptic members of her party and those in favour of a close ongoing relationship with the EU—became hard to sustain. May made clear that she wanted the UK to leave both the EU single market and the customs union (see Box 2.4). She also said that the UK would 'take back control of its immigration policy' (that is, end free movement—a personal priority for her after six years as home secretary), end the jurisdiction of the EU's Court of Justice in the UK, and not stay in 'bits of the EU'. Taken together, these pledges made softer forms of Brexit undeliverable (Box 10.2).

> **BOX 10.2   Hard versus soft Brexit: The available models**
>
> One way to think about the future of the UK–EU relationship is to consider existing models of relationships that the EU has with non-member states. These can be
>
> ➡

---

[6] Tusk has said: '[EU] Leaders made it crystal clear today that access to the single market requires acceptance of all four freedoms, including the freedom of movement. There will be no single market a la carte' (quoted in Cooper 2016).

→

arrayed on a spectrum from closer, institutionalized relationships to looser relationships principally focused on the free trade of goods. That spectrum runs from left to right in Table 10.1 and broadly maps on to the 'soft' versus 'hard' Brexit spectrum. UK government ministers insist that they are not seeking an 'off-the-shelf' model, but rather a bespoke relationship. EU officials have been largely resistant to that idea. The existing models most often identified are:

- The *EEA-EFTA (European Free Trade Association) states* (Iceland, Liechtenstein, and Norway) form an **internal market** with the EU member states. The four freedoms (movement of goods, services, persons, and capital) apply to these three states and EU laws and regulations relevant to the four freedoms are adopted, almost identically in substance, by these states. They also pay a significant contribution to the EU budget. However, EEA-EFTA states are not in a customs union with the EU, meaning they can strike their own trade deals with other states.

- *Switzerland*'s economic and trade relationship with the EU is governed through a set of more than 120 bilateral treaties. Switzerland has agreed to implement certain parts of EU legislation in exchange for accessing the relevant parts of the EU single market. Switzerland pays a contribution to the EU budget and allows the free movement of EU citizens to work in Switzerland. It is not in a customs union with the EU and so retains an independent trade policy.

- *Ukraine* has an association agreement with the EU. The economic component of the agreement is designed to increase the alignment of key sectors of the Ukrainian economy with the EU's regulatory standards. It thus restricts Ukraine's regulatory autonomy and grants a role to the ECJ in resolving any disputes arising from the agreement.

- *Turkey* has a customs union agreement with the EU, meaning that all industrial goods and processed agricultural products are traded without tariffs and that Turkey and the EU have a common external tariff for such goods with the rest of the world. Turkey's ability to pursue an independent trade policy is therefore limited. Turkey also has to align with several areas of EU law, significantly on industrial standards.

- *Canada* is outside of the EU's customs union and single market. It can enter into its own free-trade agreements and retains autonomy over its domestic regulations.

These models can be mapped on to the various 'red lines'—that is, non-negotiable positions—set out by Theresa May in her Brexit speeches, presented down the left-hand side of Table 10.1. If those red lines are taken at face value, then, as Martin Wolf of the *Financial Times* puts it: 'When everything impossible is ruled out, what is left is an agreement like that with Canada.' At the time of writing, UK ministers insist that they seek a 'Canada-plus' arrangement, with additional agreements that would allow for freer trade in services and, crucially, for the UK-based financial services sector.

TABLE 10.1 Mapping 'red lines'

Red lines as articulated by UK government	Models				
	EEA-EFTA (1)	Switzerland (2)	Ukraine	Turkey	Canada
No ECJ jurisdiction over UK laws	X		X		
No free movement of people	X	X			
No large contribution to EU budget	X	X			
Autonomy from the EU's regulations	X	X	X		
Independent trade policy				X	

'X'=breach of UK red line.
Source: Authors' figure, adapted from European Commission's (2018) depiction.

May's statements ruled out the possibility of the UK seeking to join Norway, Liechtenstein, and Iceland in the European Economic Area (EEA), an organization that brings them together with the EU in an internal market in which goods, capital, services, and people move freely. The three EEA-EFTA[7] states are not party to all EU policies, such as (for example) the Common Agricultural Policy and Fisheries Policy. As described in Box 10.1, they are free to complete free trade agreements with non-EU states, as they are not part of the EU's Customs Union. The EEA-EFTA option would give the UK some new freedoms but would not allow for the return of full control over immigration, or freedom from EU laws and regulations.

At the opposite end of the spectrum from EEA-EFTA membership (a soft form of Brexit), the hardest Brexit would be the UK 'crashing out' of the EU without agreeing a new relationship. May at one point insisted: 'no deal is better than a bad deal'. No deal would leave countless issues in legal limbo and mean a fall back onto World Trade Organization (WTO) rules for trade. The UK would have no preferential access to EU markets and would face significant tariffs on cars, other manufactured goods, and agricultural products. Independent analyses showed the loss to the UK of a shift to WTO-based terms to be significant (Dhingra and Sampson 2016; Oxford Economics 2016).

---

[7] They are termed EEA-EFTA states to differentiate them from the EU member states, all of which are also members of the EEA. EFTA brings together Norway, Lichtenstein, Iceland, and Switzerland (which is not a member of the EEA). These states are often termed as 'rule takers' because they have to comply with the vast majority of EU legislation but have no formal role in the decision-making process.

Unless the Brexit negotiations completely break down, there is no reason to expect such a dire outcome. In December 2017, the EU and UK reached agreement on a series of issues including citizen's rights, the UK's budgetary liabilities, and border issues between Northern Ireland and Ireland (European Commission 2017a, 2017b). These were the issues on which progress had been deemed essential in order for negotiations to proceed to the post-Brexit relationship between the EU and the UK. EU leaders then agreed that negotiations could proceed to the next stage. Subsequently, EU negotiators continued to maintain that the integrity of the single market could not be compromised and that the four freedoms were indivisible. The choice for the UK increasingly seemed to be between membership of the EEA—the softest form of Brexit (sure to be staunchly resisted by eurosceptic Conservative members of parliament (MPs))—and a free trade agreement similar to one between the EU and Canada. The UK government continued to articulate their preference for a relationship that was deeper than the EU–Canada deal, but which stopped short of continuing membership of the customs union and the single market.

In negotiations during—and likely beyond—2018, many other issues need to be addressed. For example, what arrangements will be made for fishing, balancing restricted access by EU-27 fishing fleets to UK waters with a continued ability to export UK fish to the EU? What solution for farmers if they are no longer part of the Common Agricultural Policy? What happens to the UK's participation in EU technical agencies for air safety, medicines, chemicals, and nuclear safety whose certifications are a requirement for selling in the European market? What about security cooperation and the UK's role in Europol? There are literally thousands of other issues that will require clarification at some point, ranging from the pet passport scheme (a quarter of a million Brits take a pet on holiday to the continent every year), to data protection rules, to emergency health care when travelling. On most of them, the intentions of the UK government were still not clear at the time of writing (more than 2 years after the referendum).

Finally, it is possible that the UK might continue to pay into the EU budget in order to secure participation in targeted schemes. Pan-European scientific and educational programmes (such as Erasmus) were often mentioned as candidates for future UK participation. So, informally, were financial services, despite Barnier's insistence on no 'cherry-picking' of the single market: 'There is not a single trade agreement that is open to financial services. It doesn't exist.'[8] The stakes in the sector are high, with 18 per cent of the City of London's workforce consisting of EEA citizens. In UK domestic politics, the issue of continued payments to the EU after Brexit is a highly sensitive one. Hard-line eurosceptics—well organized within the Conservative Party—oppose ongoing large payments.

[8] Quoted in *Politico*, 1–7, February 2018, p. 6.

The Future of Two Unions

Brexit raises significant questions for the future of two unions: the UK and the EU. Both may face existential crises, which Brexit compounds. Despite the UK going its own way, the fates of the two unions will remain intertwined. Theresa May, after becoming prime minister and seemingly embracing a harder form of Brexit, stressed that 'the British people voted to leave the EU, but they did not vote to leave Europe' (May 2017).

Brexit and UK constitutional politics

The UK's constitutional politics have been in flux since the Scottish National Party (SNP) won a majority of seats in the devolved Scottish Parliament in 2011, making a referendum on Scottish independence inevitable. The 2014 referendum resulted in a tighter vote than expected: 55.3 per cent voting 'No' to independence vs 44.7 per cent 'Yes'. Although the SNP lost the referendum, they 'won' the aftermath as their membership surged and the perception spread that they were the party that best stood up for Scotland's interests. The SNP went on to win 56 of Scotland's 59 seats in the 2015 UK general election. They also continued in government in Scotland following 2016 Scottish Parliament elections (Mitchell 2015; Cairney 2016).

The EU referendum boosted the SNP argument that Scotland's interests diverged from those of the UK, with 62 per cent of Scottish voters opting to remain in the EU. Within hours of the EU referendum result, Nicola Sturgeon—Scotland's first minister and SNP leader—said that a second independence referendum was 'highly likely' (BBC 2016b). After all, Scotland was being wrenched out of the EU against the will of its people.

In late 2016, the Scottish government produced a paper calling for a bespoke Brexit deal for Scotland. It proposed that the UK should join the EEA (a very soft Brexit) and, failing that, Scotland should be allowed to join the EEA while remaining in the UK (UK Government 2016). Sturgeon described the demand as compromise, but it was seen as virtually impossible given that membership in the EEA has always been for nation states only. By making the demand, the litmus test of May's reasonableness, the paper served its purpose and allowed the SNP to ramp up calls for a second independence referendum (Kenealy 2016).

In spring 2017, the Scottish Parliament voted to hold such a referendum. Perhaps mindful of polls showing that fewer Scots wanted a referendum than were prepared to vote 'Yes', May responded that 'now is not the time'.[9] For the prime minister,

---

[9] Because constitutional affairs are a reserved power in the UK's system of devolution, Westminster has to pass legislation permitting the Scottish Parliament to hold an independence referendum.

Brexit was the priority and its precise form had to be known before Scots could vote again on independence. At the time of writing the UK and Scottish governments were at an impasse. The result of the UK's snap general election in 2017 altered the dynamics, as the SNP's vote fell after their almost unrepeatable success in 2015. Nevertheless, Brexit remained tightly connected to Scotland's constitutional future (Mitchell and McHarg 2017).

Another constitutional issue, relevant to Wales and Northern Ireland as well as Scotland, is how repatriating powers from the EU would impact the UK's devolution settlements. In the late 1990s, certain powers were devolved to parliaments or assemblies in the UK's non-English regions, with other powers 'reserved' to the Westminster parliament in London (Bulmer *et al.* 2006). Leaving the EU meant powers returning to the UK for internally devolved policies including agriculture, fisheries, and areas of environmental protection. Whitman (2017: 7) noted 'substantial overlap between areas that have a high level of EU competence and those that come under the remit of devolved policy. So . . . where this overlap exists, to which authority should EU powers be repatriated after Brexit?'

UK ministers insisted that they wanted to see 'more devolution, not less' and gave an 'absolute guarantee' that the Scottish Parliament (and presumably the Welsh and Northern Irish Assemblies) would have more powers post-Brexit. However, the nature of those powers, and the process by which they would shift from the EU to devolved institutions, remained murky. Scotland's first minister accused the May government of a 'power grab' and demanded that all devolved powers exercised by the EU be returned to devolved institutions. The UK government argued that UK-wide frameworks might be necessary in some areas, such as agriculture, and that intergovernmental negotiations should determine how powers returning from Brussels were best deployed.

The UK system of intergovernmental relations—mechanisms by which Whitehall 'talks' to the devolved administrations—may be unfit for such purposes. The system has been widely criticized as not conducive to productive negotiation (House of Lords 2015; Paun and Munro 2015). New mechanisms that allowed devolved governments 'to be genuine participants in intergovernmental decision-making in the UK rather than "consultees"' (Whitman 2017: 9) might well be needed. As if Brexit were not challenging enough, its implications stretched well beyond a binary UK–EU negotiation.

Much as in Scotland, a distinct set of problems arose in Northern Ireland, which like Scotland also voted to remain in the EU (by 56 to 44 per cent). The status of the land border between the UK and Republic of Ireland—an EU member state—became one of the thorniest issues surrounding Brexit. It arose from the fact that 'a denser set of cross-border trade relations and economic interdependencies exists on the island of Ireland than exist between any other part' of the UK and EU (Doherty *et al.* 2017: 2).

A distinctive socio-political context also cast a shadow. Northern Ireland remained in transition to a post-conflict society, following the period known as the 'Troubles'.[10] Paramilitary activity in Northern Ireland has not entirely ended and the legacy of sectarian violence remains (see Gormley-Heenan and Aughey 2017). Devolution arrangements that mandate power-sharing between unionists and nationalists are 'a fundamental part of a larger peace agreement meant to bring about reconciliation between the two major communities' (Doherty *et al.* 2017: 3). An international treaty underpins devolution in Northern Ireland and assumes EU membership for both the UK and the Republic of Ireland. The Good Friday Agreement, which brought the troubles to an end, 'relies heavily on the "soft" border that is facilitated by the single market and customs union' (Whitman 2017: 12).

A hard Brexit—leaving the single market and with UK participation in the customs union unlikely—would mean some form of border between Northern Ireland and the Republic. The result would both disrupt economic relationships and also become a potential flashpoint for political violence. Citizenship issues are also distinctive, given that those born in Northern Ireland are eligible for Irish citizenship and thus, by extension, EU citizenship. In short, Northern Ireland will pose many distinct challenges for Brexit. Both the European Council and EP identified Northern Ireland as a priority area for the negotiations (European Council 2017; European Parliament 2017).

In the 2017 Northern Ireland Assembly elections, unionist parties for the first time failed to win a majority. Sinn Fein—the Irish nationalist party—called for a referendum on unification with Ireland. The political consequences of Brexit for Northern Ireland were thus far from certain. The situation was further complicated by the 2017 UK general election, a result of which was one Northern Irish political party—the DUP—entering into an agreement to support Theresa May's minority government. The run up to the December 2017 UK–EU agreement proved particularly fraught as the DUP delayed the announcement of a deal because of their concerns over the future of the Irish border.

Brexit and the EU's future

The UK's EU referendum was unwelcome in Brussels. It came when the EU was struggling with multiple crises (Peterson 2017). The Eurozone crisis that emerged

---

[10] The 'Troubles' refers to a 30-year period (1968–98) of violent conflict concerning the constitutional status of Northern Ireland. The conflict was predominantly a territorial one about whether Northern Ireland should remain part of the UK, or become part of the Republic of Ireland. On one side were the Unionists—overwhelmingly Protestant and the majority in Northern Ireland—who wanted to remain part of the UK. On the other side were Nationalists and Republicans—overwhelmingly Catholic—who wanted to become part of the Republic of Ireland. Over 3,600 people were killed during the conflict. The 1998 Good Friday Agreement brought the period to an end, although dividing lines between the communities of Northern Ireland remain to this day and devolution to Northern Ireland has remained volatile in the years since, with periods of direct rule by the UK government and periods where there was effectively no Northern Ireland government in office. For more information, see http://www.bbc.co.uk/history/troubles.

in Greece in 2010 continued to resurface. Conflicts in the Middle East and North Africa created large flows of refugees into the EU. The EU's attempts at closer ties with Ukraine were met by Russian annexation of Crimea and ongoing conflict in Eastern Ukraine. EU leaders were keen that Brexit did not monopolize their agenda.

A roadmap agreed by EU heads of state and government in Bratislava in late 2016 (European Council 2016b) sought to bind the EU-27 together after Brexit. The Commission followed up with a white paper on *The Future of Europe*, which set out five options (European Commission 2017b). At one extreme, the EU could focus on the single market and abandon plans to develop the governance of the Eurozone, advance social and employment policies, and forge ahead on security cooperation. At the other was a vision of more integration. Between the two were more realistic scenarios. In one, the EU would focus on 'doing less more efficiently', especially in foreign and defence policy and managing borders. In another, the EU would become more flexible, with select member states integrating in new policy areas, thus formalizing ideas of a multi-speed Europe, in which not all member states moved at the same pace. Both the Bratislava roadmap and Commission white paper reflected serious thinking about the EU's post-Brexit future.

Whatever that future, a UK departure will alter the balance of power within the EU, both in terms of votes in the Council and EP, and in the balance between economically more liberal member states and those who are more instinctively protectionist. The equilibrium between members of the Eurozone and those outside also will change. The fear that the departure of the UK might have a domino effect, triggering referendums in other member states, seemed unlikely, especially after the victory of mainstream parties and candidates in German Dutch and French elections in 2017. Yet, how Brexit will impact the future development of the EU remains, at the time of writing, unknown. What seems clearer is that leading figures within the EU—most notably the Commission president (Juncker 2017) and the French president (Macron 2017)—were keen to continue to develop bold new ideas about the future path of European integration.

Conclusion

By mid-2018, the mood in EU circles about Brexit was dark. Many thought that the May government had delusional expectations about the deal the UK might be offered. German insiders admitted that they took the UK vote to leave the EU personally, after trying over many years to be a bridge between the UK and the rest of the EU. French negotiators—relieved that the pro-EU Emmanuel Macron had won the spring 2017 presidential election—insisted that result would not mean giving the UK an easier ride in the Brexit negotiations, while also lamenting that De Gaulle had been right after all about the UK being an 'insular, maritime, [non-European]' nation (Havighurst 1985: 487). Commission officials involved in the negotiations grimly faced long hours of hard slog on Brexit that were—to their minds—entirely unnecessary, resulting from David Cameron's mismanagement of his own party, and distracting the EU from more important priorities. Verhofstadt (2017) estimated that 'a Brexit deal remains more likely than unlikely' because 'a no-deal scenario would be disastrous to us all'. All on both sides had strong incentives to make the negotiations succeed. But satisfying all who have a stake in them was a very tall order.

? DISCUSSION QUESTIONS

1. Why did David Cameron call a referendum of the UK's membership of the EU in June 2016?
2. How can we understand the outcome of the referendum?
3. What are the merits and drawbacks of various types of Brexit, from 'soft' to 'hard'?
4. What are the implications of Brexit for the future of the UK, and for the future of the EU?

📖 FURTHER READING

Most of what was published on Brexit by the time of writing consisted of memoirs of those involved in the 2016 referendum campaign or 'pop-up' analyses by journalists. The best of the former is C. Oliver (2016)—written by one of David Cameron's closest advisors—even if it presents Cameron's own political judgement (implausibly) as impeccable. Examples of the latter include Bennett (2016), Mosbacher and Wiseman (2016) and Shipman (2016). The three best academic sources thus far are Geddes (2016)—which is concise—Curtice (2017), on why the UK voted to leave, and Clarke et al. (2017), the first book-length study. An excellent set of academic articles is Wincott (2017).

Bennett, O. (2016), *The Brexit Club: the Inside Story of the Leave Campaign's Shock Victory* (London: Biteback Publishing).

Clarke, H. D., Goodwin, M., and Cowley, P. (2017), *Brexit: Why Britain Voted to Leave the European Union* (Cambridge: Cambridge University Press).

Curtice, J. (2017), 'Why Leave Won the UK's EU Referendum', *Annual Review of the Activities of the European Union—Journal of Common Market Studies*, 55 (Supplement S1): 19–37.

Geddes, A. (2016), 'Britain Beyond the European Union?', in R. Heffernan, C. Hay, M. Russell, and P. Cowley (eds), *Developments in British Politics*, 10th edn (Basingstoke: Palgrave Macmillan): 264–86.

Mosbacher, M. and Wiseman, O. (2016), *Brexit Revolt: How the UK Voted to Leave the EU* (London: Social Affairs Union).

Oliver, C. (2016), *Unleashing Demons: The Inside Story of Brexit* (London: Hodden & Stoughton).

Shipman, T. (2016), *All Out War: The Full Story of How Brexit Sank Britain's Political Class* (Glasgow: Harper Collins).

Wincott, D. (ed.) (2017), 'Studying Brexit's Causes and Consequences', Special issue of *British Journal of Politics & International Relations*, 19/3 and 4.

WEB LINKS

- One of us has produced a series of Brexit Briefings on how various sectors might be affected, available at: http://www.richardcorbett.org.uk/category/brexit-briefings/

Visit the Ancillary Resource Centre that accompanies this book for additional material: www.oup.com/uk/kenealy5e/

CHAPTER 11

Conclusion

John Peterson, Daniel Kenealy, and Richard Corbett

Summary

The EU is extraordinary, complex, and—in important respects—unique. This concluding chapter revisits three key themes that guide understanding of the EU. It then returns to the question: how can we best *explain* the EU and how it works? We review leading theoretical approaches, and identify what each approach claims is most important to explain about the EU, and why. Finally, we confront the question: 'Where do we go from here'? Does knowing how the EU works give us clues about how it might work in the future?

Introduction

This book has offered a *basic* introduction to how the European Union works. A vast body of work has emerged in recent years to satisfy those who wish to know more. Much that has been written about the EU may seem confusing or obfuscatory to the curious non-expert. We—together with our authors—have tried to do better and be clearer. For example, we have focused throughout on how the Union works in practice, not just in theory. We also have tried to show that the EU is not so exceptional that it resists all comparisons.

Yet, it does not take much study of the EU before one is struck (or becomes frustrated) by how complex and ever-shifting it seems to be. Most of our 'compared to what' exercises have ended up drawing contrasts—some quite sharp—between politics and policy-making in Brussels and these same processes elsewhere. There are very few analytical 'bottom lines' about how the Union works, except that it works quite differently from any other system for deciding who gets what, when, and how.

Three Themes

We have offered (Chapter 1) three general themes as guides to understanding how the EU works. The first is experimentation and change. The Union refuses to stand still: about the only thing that can be safely predicted about its future is that it is unlikely to remain static for long. The point was illustrated towards the end of 2017 by a clear will to rebound from the shock of Brexit with dramatic moves to upgrade EU defence capabilities and (French-inspired) proposals for more integrated governance of the euro.

Second, EU governance is an exercise in sharing power between states and institutions. Most of the time, its central goal is to seek consensus across different levels of governance. Getting to 'yes' in a system with so many diverse stakeholders often means resorting to informal methods of reaching agreement, about which the EU's treaties and official publications are mostly (or entirely) silent.

Third and finally, the gap between the EU's policy scope and its capacity—between what it *tries* to do and what it is *equipped* to do—has widened. The Union has been a remarkable success in many respects. But its future success is by no means assured. We briefly revisit each of these themes below.

Experimentation and change

Every chapter in this book, each from a different angle, has painted a picture of constant evolution and change. Few would deny that the EU has developed into more than an 'ordinary' international organization (IO). However, its development has not been guided by any master plan. Rather, it has evolved through messy compromises struck after complex political bargaining between member states (Chapters 2 and 4), institutions (Chapter 3), and organized interests (Chapter 6).

One consequence is that when the EU changes, it usually changes incrementally. Radical reform proposals tend to be scaled back in the direction of modesty in a system with so many different interests to satisfy. The unsuccessful attempt to establish a constitutional treaty for the EU proves the point, as does the Lisbon Treaty: it carried forward most of the institutional changes contained in the Constitutional Treaty while stripping out references to an EU flag, anthem, and the provocative designation 'EU minister for foreign affairs' (renamed, in the EU's familiar jargon, 'High Representative'). For many, the Constitutional Treaty simply went too far, at least in terms of symbolism (see Box 11.1). Similarly, efforts thus far to reform the institutional structure of the EU in light of the Eurozone crisis took several years to crystallize and represented a compromise between disparate national interests.

However, apparently unexceptional acts of fine-tuning, such as slightly increasing the European Parliament's power or sending an encouraging political signal to an applicant state, can sometimes gather momentum like a snowball rolling down a hill. Moreover, the EU's potential for wrenching and fundamental change, as illustrated by the launch of the single currency or dramatic decisions by the European Court of Justice (ECJ), cannot be denied. Perhaps because the EU is such a young political system, it is sometimes surprisingly easy to change its structure or remit. In recent years, it has created large bail-out funds, rewritten rules, and restructured the debts of struggling member states to keep the euro intact. Yet, the EU's mode of relying on compromises and incremental, modest changes often appeared inadequate in the face of a political and economic climate that led an incoming European Commission president to declare 'we are last-chance Europe' (quoted in *The Economist*, 25 October 2014).

The more general point is that the EU is a fundamentally experimental union (Laffan *et al.* 2000). Nobody argues that it always works like a smooth, well-oiled machine. It has become far more difficult to shift it in any particular direction as its membership has more than doubled in the space of just over a decade. Equally, almost no one denies that it is remarkably successful in coaxing cooperative, collective action out of sovereign states that regularly, almost routinely, went to war with each other a few generations ago. Increasingly, the Union is seen as a model or laboratory worthy, in some respects, of mimicry by other regional organizations in other parts of the world (Farrell 2007; Brown 2017; see also Box 2.4).

BOX 11.1 What's in a name?

The terms used to refer to the EU's artefacts often stir up controversy. A word can have different connotations in different languages or cultural contexts. Examples include:

Assembly or Parliament?

The designation of a European 'Parliament' was initially a term too far. The drafters of the original treaties prudently used the term 'Assembly'. The Assembly decided to call itself a parliament in the early 1960s. For a long time, some governments strictly avoided the term. However, in 1986, they agreed to amend the treaty to include the name **European Parliament**.

Commission or Executive?

Although many saw the Commission as an embryonic European government when what is now the EU was created, others did not. The authors of the treaty shied away from even describing it as an executive. In French, it is often referred to as the *Commission exécutive* to distinguish it from the *Commission parlementaire*, which is the French term for a parliamentary committee.

Constitution or treaty?

The treaties are sometimes described as the EU's Constitution, in that they lay down the EU's field of competence, the powers of its institutions and how the latters' members are elected or appointed. The ECJ has itself referred to them as a constitutional charter. However, the attempt to replace the treaties by a single text formally described as a constitution fell in 2005 when it failed to be ratified by France and the Netherlands. Arguments about that term featured in Dutch pre-referendum debates. Member states instead agreed to amend the existing treaties without formally labeling them as a constitution.

Federal or supranational?

The Schuman declaration, the basis for establishing the European Coal and Steel Community, referred to the ECSC as the first step towards a European federation. But this definition of the *finalité* of the Union has always been controversial. Definitions of 'federal' are highly divergent. The term '**supranational**' emerged instead.

Foreign minister or High Representative?

The merged post of vice president of the commission/High Representative was originally described as the EU minister for foreign affairs in the unratified Constitutional Treaty. The term was dropped in the Lisbon Treaty, although it is still used informally in Brussels.

Representative or ambassador?

The heads of the EU's representations in third countries have ambassadorial status, and are commonly referred to as ambassadors, though they are officially just representatives.

Why 'president'?

The EU gives the title 'president' to all kinds of functions that might have been named otherwise—at least in English. For Anglophones, it might make more sense to use 'speaker' of the Parliament, 'governor' of the Central Bank, 'chair' of the Council, and maybe 'prime commissioner'?

Sharing power and seeking consensus

A second theme that cannot be avoided when studying the EU is that power is distributed widely—between states, institutions, and organized interests. At the same time, consensus and compromise are highly valued. Enormous efforts are often required to strike agreements that are acceptable to all who have a slice of power to determine outcomes. Just being able to agree is often viewed as an achievement in itself. Once sealed, EU agreements are almost always portrayed as positive sum—that is, bringing greater good to a greater number of citizens than did the previous policy. Of course, nearly every policy creates losers as well as winners. But the perceived need to preserve support for the Brussels system means that heroic attempts are usually made to avoid creating clear losers.

It follows that coming to grips with how the EU works does not (just) mean mastering the treaties. The formal powers of institutions and member states, and formal rules of policy-making, are not unimportant. But they do not come close to telling the whole story, since informal understandings and norms are crucial in determining outcomes. Most of our investigations of 'how it really works' have accentuated the importance of unwritten rules that have emerged over time and through practice, almost organically—as opposed to being mandated in formal or legal terms. These rules and norms are then learned and internalized by EU policy-makers. For example, it is widely accepted in Brussels that formal votes in the Council should be avoided whenever possible, even if they have become more common—perhaps more necessary—in a radically enlarged Union. Still, the idea that consensus should be the ultimate aim, and that long negotiations and manifold compromises are an acceptable price to pay for it, is powerfully engrained. These norms often matter far more than what the treaties say about which state has how many votes, what constitutes a qualified majority, or where qualified majority voting (QMV) applies and where it does not. The post-2004 enlargements suggested that representatives of new states learn the rules of the game quite quickly. New EU member states were, for instance, able to lend their weight to a broad alliance supporting further liberalization of the services sector in 2006—not by threatening a blocking minority, but by constructively arguing their case.

Moreover, the EU is a uniquely multi-level system of governance. Even the most decentralized, federal nation-states—such as Germany or the US or Switzerland—have a government and an opposition. The EU has neither. As such, it often suffers (not least in foreign policy) from a lack of leadership. Rarely does one institution or member state, or alliance thereof, offer consistent or decisive political direction. Instead, grand bargains to agree quasi-constitutional change, as well as many more mundane agreements, result from a unique kind of power sharing across levels of governance, as well as between EU institutions and member states. What makes the Union unique is this diversity and mix of actors—regional, national, and supranational, public and private—the wide dispersal of power between them, and the need always to try to increase the number of 'winners'.

Scope and capacity

Third and finally, we have suggested that the EU's scope—both in terms of policy remit and constituent states—has grown much faster than its capacity to manage its affairs. Chapters 5 and 6—and perhaps especially Chapter 9—outlined the uneven yet unmistakable expansion of EU policy responsibilities. Chapter 8 focused on why, and with what consequences, the Union has continued to enlarge its membership and tried to improve its relations with countries in its near abroad. Chapter 9 showed how the EU has evolved, almost by stealth, into a global power. With no agreed-upon 'end goal', the Union has taken on new tasks and members, but without a concomitant increase in capacity, or tools and resources to perform its designated tasks. For instance, Chapter 3 highlighted the institutional limits of EU. Can the Commission, equivalent in size to the administration of a medium-sized European city, manage an ever larger and more ambitious Union? Perhaps the emphasis under the Presidency of Jean-Claude Juncker on being a 'political Commission' (see Peterson 2017)—particularly after his predecessor, José Manuel Barroso, sought a comparatively modest 'Europe of results'—marked a renewed commitment to the political purpose of further integration.

The Commission is far from alone in confronting a gap between scope and capacity. Can one Parliament adequately represent nearly 500 million citizens? Can 28 or more ministers sit around the Council table and have a meaningful negotiation? Can Brexit possibly end with a result that does not produce losers?

The gap between scope and capacity (institutional and political) raises broader questions about the Union's future. It seems risky to assume that the EU can continue to take on ever more tasks and member states (or even keep its existing ones), while retaining its status as the most successful experiment in international cooperation in modern history.

Explaining the EU

While seeking above all to describe how the EU works, we have also introduced—and tried to demystify—debates about what are the most important forces driving EU politics. Just as there is no consensus on the desirability of European integration, there is no consensus about what is most important about it. Social scientists disagree about what it is about the EU that most needs to be *explained*. The position they take on this question usually reflects their own approach to understanding the EU: as an international organization (IO)? A polity in its own right? A source of constructed identity? Or as a factory for public policies?

The process of European integration has generated a wealth of academic analysis. What is striking is the diversity of approaches and conclusions. It is also striking that different theories have ebbed and flowed as the EU has gone through different phases in its history. Perceptions also vary according to national, cultural, and/

or political backgrounds and predispositions, and it is not only politicians who write in a way that colours reality with their own hopes and expectations. It has been noted that lawyers tend to focus on the EU's legal system, with its several supranational features, while political scientists tend to focus on the EU's decision-making procedures and the interactions among national governments and between those governments and the EU's institutions. A similar trap awaits those who specialize in a particular aspect of the EU: an analysis of competition policy, with the dominant role in this area of the Commission, can produce a different impression from the study of EU foreign and security policy, far more dominated by the member states. Donald Puchala's (1971) analogy of blind men feeling an elephant and reaching different conclusions according to whether they are holding its trunk, touching its tail, or feeling its body, is a telling one.

We have seen how theory can help us frame interesting questions, and then decide what evidence is needed to answer them. If it is accepted that the EU is exceptionally complex, then it stands to reason that there can be no one 'best' theory of EU politics. What a former commission president, Jacques Delors, once called an 'unidentified political object' is a bit like other IOs such as North Atlantic Treaty Organization (NATO) or the United Nations, a bit like federal states including Germany and Canada, and a bit like the other leading system for generating legally binding international rules, the World Trade Organization (WTO). But it closely resembles none of them. It makes sense in the circumstances to approach the EU with a well-stocked tool-kit of theoretical approaches, and to be clear about what each highlights as most important in determining how it really works.

International relations approaches

International relations (IR) scholars bring important insights to the study of the EU. They can be relied upon to ask hard, stimulating questions about the nature of power in international politics, and the extent to which cooperation is possible or durable in the absence of any 'international government'. Students of IR add value—in two principal ways—to debates about the nature and significance of European integration.

First, approaching the EU as a system within a system—a regional alliance in the wider scheme of global politics—encourages us to ask why European states have chosen to pool a large share of their sovereignty. For neofunctionalists, the answer lies in the way that the choices open to states become narrower after they commit to free trade and thus to increase their economic interdependence (Börzel 2005; Jensen 2016). EU institutions, in alliance with interest groups, guide and encourage 'spill over' of cooperation in one sphere (the internal market) to new spheres (environmental policy). States remain powerful but they must share power with EU institutions and non-institutional actors in Brussels, as well as those in national and regional political capitals. For neofunctionalists, what is most important about the EU is how and why European integration moves inexorably forward. There are crucial differences between EU member states and ordinary nation-states in inter-national politics, because European integration is largely irreversible.

For intergovernmentalists, member states remain free to choose how the EU should work (Moravcsik and Schimmelfennig 2009; Cini and Borragàn 2016). The Union is built on a series of bargains between member states, which are self-inter-ested and rational in pursuing outcomes that serve their economic interests. Of course, conflict may arise in bargaining between states, whose preferences are never identical. Ultimately, however, the status quo changes only when acceptable com-promises are struck between national interests, especially those of the EU's largest states. EU institutions are relatively weak in the face of the power of its member states, which can determine precisely how much authority they wish to delegate to them to enforce and police intergovernmental bargains. For intergovernmentalists, what is most important to explain about the EU is how national interests are rec-onciled in intergovernmental bargains. European states are 'ordinary' states, whose national interests happen to be compatible often enough to produce unusually institutionalized cooperation. The EU 'occupies a permanent position at the heart of the European landscape' (Moravcsik 1998: 501), but only because member states want it that way. If any—witness the UK—decides it no longer wishes to be part of that landscape, then wrenching political change will occur. As such, much about European integration remains reversible.

A comparative politics approach

As the Union's policy remit has expanded, many comparativists have found them-selves unable to understand their subject—at least in Europe—without knowing how the EU works. In particular, new institutionalists have developed insightful analyses of how the EU works. Institutionalists view the EU as a system where cooperation is now normal and accepted. Policy-makers in Brussels have become used to working in a system where power is shared, in particular between its institutions. The bar-gaining required to make 'ordinary' EU policy is as much between institutions as it is between governments. Usually, it is contrasted with bargaining—viewed as primar-ily intergovernmental—in episodic rounds of treaty reform. Yet, some analysts view institutionalism as better than **intergovernmentalism** at capturing the essence even of negotiations that alter the Union's treaties (see Slapin 2008; Nugent 2017: 455–6). A key determinant of outcomes in any EU negotiation is the extent to which path dependency has become institutionalized and radical change is precluded.

Institutionalists share important assumptions with neofunctionalists, particularly about the need to view European integration as a continuous process (see Pierson 1996, 2004). But institutionalists tend to study the Union as a political system in its own right, analogous to national systems, as opposed to a system of IR. For them, institutions develop their own agendas and priorities, and thus load the EU system in favour of certain outcomes over others (Pollack 2009; Hodson and Peterson 2017). The EU is extraordinary, above all because it has such extraordinary institutions.

A public policy approach

Studying EU politics without studying what it produces—actual policies—is like studying a factory but ignoring the product it manufactures. We have seen (especially in Chapter 5) that most EU policies are regulatory policies, many of them highly technical. We have also seen how resource-poor the Union's institutions are. They have little choice but to rely on expertise and resources held beyond Brussels and/or by non-public actors. Advocates of policy network analysis insist that EU policy outcomes are shaped in important ways by informal bargaining, much of which takes place outside formal institutions or policy processes (Peterson 2009). By the time that ministers vote in the Council or members of the European Parliament (MEPs) vote in plenary, legislative proposals usually have been picked over and scrutinized line by line by a huge range of officials and, usually, lobbyists. Often, the proposal bears little or no relationship to what it looked like in its first draft. As we saw in Chapter 7, democratic controls are embedded in the EU more than in any other IO. But policy network analysis assumes that most policy details are agreed in a world far removed from the political world of ministers and MEPs.

Moreover, the EU is distinctive in its lack of hierarchy: it has no government to impose a policy agenda, so policy stakeholders bargain over what the agenda should be. No one actor is in charge, so stakeholders must work together and exchange resources—legitimacy, money, expertise—to realize their goals. For policy network analysts, what is most important to explain about the EU is its policies and who determines them. Making sense of policy outputs means investigating how sectoral networks are structured: are their memberships stable or volatile, are they tightly or loosely integrated, and how are resources distributed within them? The EU is, in effect, a series of diverse sub-systems for making different kinds of policy. What is common across the full range of EU activities is interdependence between actors: even those with the most formidable formal powers—the member states and EU institutions—are highly dependent on one another, and indeed on actors that have no formal power at all.

A sociological/cultural approach

For constructivists, the most important element of European integration that needs to be explained is how interests and identities are constructed. EU decision-makers are the same as anyone else: they are fundamentally social beings. But they are also different from most other political actors in that they interact intensively and extensively with actors whose national identity, language, and culture are different from their own. Brussels (along with Luxembourg and Strasbourg) is a truly multi-national crossroads and there is no other political capital in the world that features a more diverse cultural mix. In this sense, Brussels (along with other EU venues) is very different from the rest of Europe. One effect is to encourage a sort of disconnect between the EU and its citizens. But a European identity, which often seems barely to register with a majority of Europe's citizens, is very much in evidence among those who are closely involved in EU politics and policy.

Again, it is worth reiterating that constructivism is not a substantive theory of regional integration comparable to intergovernmentalism or institutionalism (see Risse 2009). It is a philosophical, even 'metaphysical' position that insists that social reality is constructed by human beings and reproduced in day-to-day practice. The main upshot is that we cannot explain how the EU works simply by calculating what is in the material interest of each member state, EU institution, or lobbyist. Nor can we assume that Brussels is a vacuum in which those interests are unchanging, unaffected by the informal rules of the game, or untouched by how those at the centre of the EU system view themselves as part of a major collective, political endeavour. Of course, European decision-makers are self-interested and egoistic. There is much about the European Union that does not work very well. But it produces far more collective action than any other system ever invented, or 'constructed', for the reconciliation of multi-national interests. The insights of constructivism are essential to explaining why.

No one approach has anything approaching a monopoly of wisdom on EU politics. All shed important light on key features of how the Union works. All downplay, even ignore, factors that others argue are important—or can be in the right circumstances—in determining who gets what. A first step in making sense of the EU is deciding what it is about this unidentified political object that is most important to explain.

Where Do We Go from Here?

When we ponder where the EU may be headed, we have to remember where it has been. For nearly 25 years the Union was preparing, negotiating, or ratifying a new treaty, modifying its basic treaties seven times between 1985 and 2007. By way of comparison, the US Constitution has been subject to fewer than thirty amendments over more than 225 years. Agreeing to reform the EU's institutions, disagreeing on the details, and then agreeing to try to agree again in a future intergovernmental conference (IGC) became routine. Then, the impact of the global financial crisis after 2008, and the emergence of the Eurozone crisis in 2010, triggered a flurry of activity by member states and EU institutions on monetary policy, fiscal policy coordination, and banking union (Box 4.3). The economic impact of the Eurozone crisis continues to pose a challenge to the Union and its members, and the policy responses to that challenge have, in themselves, triggered disagreements among member states. Against this backdrop, where does the EU go from here?

Debating the future of Europe

Sometimes it seems as if a debate on the future of EU is 'much of the same old'. The debates of the 1950s dealt with many of the same challenges that Europe faces today. Institutional reform, enlargement, policy remit, money, and external policy have always been on the EU agenda. The changes over the past 50 years might seem incremental in the short term. However, measured over time, the EU has actually experienced a radical metamorphosis from an institutionally weak and small club with a limited policy arsenal, separate currencies, and no foreign policy, to an institutional powerhouse of 28 (soon to be 27) members, a plethora of policies, a single currency and a central role in world politics. Whether the UK government under Theresa May was aware of it or not, the stakes involved in leaving the EU in 2019 and beyond were higher than ever in the Union's history.

The new millennium brought new themes to the European agenda. Peace, prosperity, and security remain the cornerstones of integration. But the agenda has shifted markedly towards economic reform, climate change, and energy. On one hand, the economic reform agenda resists simple solutions because a EU of 28 (soon to be 27) is far more economically diverse than ever before and Europe was hit hard by the post-2008 global recession. On the other hand, there were signs of fresh life in the integration process in the second decade of the 2000s, even given crises in the Eurozone, with EU measures such as the liberalization of services and fresh efforts to extend the single market important in the policy mix. The Union took a global lead on climate change by pledging to cut greenhouse emissions by 20 per cent by the year 2020 and encouraging the rest of the industrialized world to follow its lead. But it also was marginalized by emerging states at the 2010 Copenhagen summit. The Union remained far from a common energy policy. At the same time, it at least encouraged European citizens to see connections between energy security and environmental protection.

However, the second decade of the twenty-first century was mostly dominated by the EU's response to the Eurozone crisis. Since May 2010, when Greece stood on the brink of a sovereign default, the EU provided emergency assistance funding to four of its members (Greece, Portugal, Ireland, Cyprus). Through an intergovernmental treaty, euro members established the European Stability Mechanism (ESM), a permanent crisis resolution mechanism, in 2012. The ESM helps finance loans and other forms of financial assistance to euro members. It is an intergovernmental organization based in Luxembourg with a maximum lending capacity of €500 billion. A parallel series of measures, referred to as 'the six pack' and 'the two pack', were agreed in 2011 to try to strengthen the Stability and Growth Pact by enhancing surveillance of public spending and enforcement provisions. In 2013 a fiscal compact—signed by 25 of what were then 27 EU member states (the UK and the Czech Republic did not sign)—required member states to enshrine in national law a balanced budget rule.

Perhaps most dramatically the EU's member states have moved towards a banking union, involving a single supervisory mechanism for approximately 6,000 banks across the EU and a single rulebook with which all European financial institutions must comply. Still, much remains to be done to ensure that member states hit hardest by the Eurozone crisis find a path back to economic growth and that the highly complex banking union can operate effectively. The uptick in economic growth in the EU in 2017–18 alongside proposals—championed by French President Emmanuel Macron—to strengthen Eurozone governance thus had both retrospective and prospective logic.

How *will* it work?

We conclude with a few thoughts—not 'predictions'—about how the Union may evolve in the years to come. We have seen that there is no shortage of controversy about what is most important in determining how the EU really works. Be that as it may, it is useful to resort to models or visions of how the Union *should* work to stimulate thinking about different potential futures. These models are by no means mutually exclusive. On the contrary, the EU has always been a hybrid of the:

1. intergovernmental;

2. federal; and

3. functional.

An intergovernmental outcome to (say) the 2007 IGC would have meant a repatriation of competences, a weakening of the institutional triangle between the Commission, the Council, and the European Parliament, and a return to unanimous decision-making—with many decisions taken outside the current institutional framework. In some ways, the outcome was the opposite. The Lisbon Treaty extended qualified majority voting to some 30 new areas of policy. The pillar structure was eliminated. The EU was given a legal personality and all of its key institutions were strengthened (see Chapters 5 and 7). All member states realized that if the EU wanted to be a serious player on the international scene, strict intergovernmentalism was not an option. However, the response to the Eurozone crisis has saw member states—particularly Germany—come to the fore. The response to the crisis was a reminder of the importance of the Franco-German tandem, especially given the rift between them: in 2014, France submitted a budget that violated (again) the Stability and Growth Pact while Germany stubbornly insisted on fiscal rectitude.

A more *federal* Europe would have meant the adoption of something closer in form and substance to the Constitutional Treaty. Crucially, it would have been called a constitution—at least in some EU states—and have included constitutional symbols such as an anthem and flag, a president, and a foreign minister. But a truly federal EU, at least for ardent enthusiasts of the idea, would mean going beyond the Constitutional Treaty and giving the Union an elected government and a bicameral parliament. Arguably, a federal structure would be more transparent and democratic. Power sharing in most federal regimes is governed by the subsidiarity principle (see Box 2.2), with powers formally divided in a way that brings government as close to the citizen as possible.

Put simply, member governments and their publics remain unwilling to take a quantum leap to a federal state. The French and Dutch rejections of the Constitutional Treaty proved the case, which was further underscored by the results of the 2014 European Parliament elections. Then the UK voted to leave, causing arguably the biggest existential crisis in the EU's history. Many of the hallmarks of a federal state—a large central budget funded through direct taxation or giving the power of constitutional amendment to the legislatures of the constituent states (as opposed to their governments)—are unimaginable. There is no united political movement or **demos** pushing for a European federation.

Still, the history of the Union shows there can be **federalism** without a federation. The euro and European Central Bank are nothing if not federative elements. Thus, we find another apparent contradiction: the idea of a federal Europe—a nightmare to eurosceptics—is both a utopian pipe dream and a practical reality in some areas of policy. But if it ever arrives, a United States of Europe will not arrive in the near future. In some ways, political agreement on the Lisbon Treaty, as an alternative to the Constitutional Treaty, was a major setback to European federalists. Although significant steps forward have been taken in response to the Eurozone crisis, they remain far short of anything resembling a federation (at least, thus far).

A final, *functional* model of the future is a mix between the previous two. It is in essence what the Lisbon Treaty represented. More than either the inter-governmental or federal variants, the functional model favours continuity in European integration and is sceptical of radical change. It embraces a largely functional path of integration, which is practical and utilitarian rather than dec-orative or symbolic. It accepts that the EU does not yet (and may never) operate in policy areas such as childcare and many forms of taxation. It accepts that the Community method of decision-making, with powers shared between the EU's institutions, is inappropriate (at least initially) for some areas where European cooperation makes sense, including defence and border controls (see Chapter 9). The response to the Eurozone crisis demonstrated this functional logic. Member states played a crucial role in shaping the framework of that response, but the roles of the Commission and (perhaps most crucially) the European Central Bank were of crucial importance. The Commission played a leading role in putting flesh on the bones of the policy response, while the ECB was instrumental in calming financial markets and ensuring that countries such as Spain and Italy avoided having to draw on the ESM.

The functional model accepts a 'core Europe' in some areas of policy. As in the cases of Schengen or the Eurozone, some EU states may forge ahead with coopera-tive agreements that others choose not to support on the assumption that outsiders might become insiders later on (see Box 11.2). But the functional model also values power sharing for its own sake. It favours pragmatic cooperation extending to all EU members based on the institutional triangle between the Commission, Council, and EP—with the ECJ adjudicating disputes between them.

BOX 11.2   Two-speed Europe?

Debate about a 'two-speed Europe', a vanguard of countries that integrate further abound. The holding of Eurozone summits and the establishment of a fiscal compact with 25 participating states stimulated such discussions. Reality is more complex than the label 'two-speed Europe' would suggest. In practice, a striking variety of speeds and configurations exist. Some examples include:

- non-participation in defence cooperation: Denmark;
- non-participation in all aspects of Schengen: Ireland and the UK (prior to Brexit, but with the participation of Norway, Iceland, and Switzerland from outside the EU);
- no obligation to join the euro: UK and Denmark; no intention to join the euro soon: Sweden, Czech Republic;
- right to opt-in (or not) to measures in the field of freedom, justice, and security: Denmark, Ireland, UK (prior to Brexit);
- exemption from the single market rules regarding the acquisition of secondary residences on its territory: Denmark, and;
- exemption from the primacy of EU law regarding anything affecting abortion: Ireland.

Thus, we certainly do not find any straightforward group of slow states, nor an *avant-garde* group of leading member states. Instead, there is a variety of *arrière-gardes*, in each case rather small and with a different configuration, sometimes a single country. The general unity of the Union remains largely intact, even if the growing number of special situations regarding the UK was frequently commented upon even prior to Brexit, leading some to conclude that 'the UK was never a full EU member state anyway'.

A basic assumption underpinning this model is that the EU—warts and all—has worked to the further the greater good of European citizens. But form should follow function, not *vice versa* as in the federal vision. The functional model represents a path that has been followed from the earliest beginnings of European integration in the 1950s. It may well live on in the EU of the future simply because, in the past, it has worked: most say reasonably and some say remarkably, even if a minority says not at all.

Conclusion

The reality of European integration is naturally more complex than the simple models that we have outlined. French EU policy illustrates this point. On some federal projects—such as the euro—France has been instrumental. At the same time France has given intergovernmentalists cause for cheer by putting a halt to further European integration: in 1954 by blocking the European Defense Community, in 1966 by refusing to move to QMV, and in 2005 by rejecting the Constitution. Yet,

France has been a vocal advocate of the Common Security and Defense Policy and, more recently, further integration on the Eurozone, thus revealing its affinity for a Europe that is a more functional global actor.

The EU has always been a combination of these three models. It is more than an ordinary IO, but less than a state. It is likely always to be a multi-level system in which the supranational, national, and regional co-exist. It is a unique and original way of organizing cooperation between states, whose governments (if not always their citizens) genuinely see themselves as members of a political union.

The EU of the future will probably remain an experimental system, always in flux, with plenty of scope to be reformed and competing ideas about how to do it. It will continue to be, above all, an exercise in seeking consensus and trying to achieve unity, where it makes sense, out of enormous diversity. We can rest assured that how it really works will never match one vision of how it should work.

APPENDIX: CHRONOLOGY OF EUROPEAN INTEGRATION

1945 May	End of World War II in Europe
1946 Sep.	Winston Churchill's 'United States of Europe' speech
1947 Jun.	Marshall Plan announced
	Organization for European Economic Cooperation established
1949 Apr.	North Atlantic Treaty signed in Washington
1950 May	Schuman Declaration
1951 Apr.	Treaty establishing the European Coal and Steel Community (ECSC) signed in Paris
1952 May	Treaty establishing the European Defence Community (EDC) signed
Aug.	ECSC launched in Luxembourg
1954 Aug.	French Parliament rejects the EDC
Oct.	Western European Union (WEU) established
1955 May	Germany and Italy join North Atlantic Treaty Organization (NATO)
Jun.	European Community (EC) foreign ministers meet in Messina to relaunch European integration
1956 May	Meeting in Venice, EC foreign ministers recommend establishing the European Economic Community (EEC) and the European Atomic Energy Community (Euratom)
1957 Mar.	Treaties establishing the EEC and Euratom signed in Rome
1958 Jan.	Launch of the EEC and Euratom
1961 Jul.	The UK, Denmark, Ireland, and Norway apply to join the EEC
1962 Jan.	Agreement reached on the Common Agricultural Policy (CAP)
1963 Jan.	French President Charles de Gaulle vetoes the UK's application; de Gaulle and German Chancellor Konrad Adenauer sign Elysée Treaty
Jul.	Signing of Yaoundé Convention between EEC and 18 African states
1964 May	EEC sends single delegation to Kennedy Round negotiations on tariff reduction in General Agreement on Tariffs and Trade (GATT)
1965 Jul.	Empty Chair Crisis begins
1966 Jan.	Empty Chair Crisis ends with Luxembourg Compromise
1967 May	The UK, Denmark, Ireland, and Norway again apply for EEC membership
Jul.	The executive bodies of the ECSC, EEC, and Euratom merge into a commission
Nov.	De Gaulle again vetoes the UK's application
1968 Jul.	The customs union is completed 18 months ahead of schedule
1969 Apr.	De Gaulle resigns
Jul.	The UK revives its membership application
1970 Oct.	Council agrees to create Euopean Political Cooperation (EPC) mechanism Luxembourg's Prime Minister Pierre Werner presents a plan for Economic and Monetary Union (EMU)
1972 Oct.	Meeting in Paris, EC heads of state and government agree to deepen European integration
1973 Jan.	The UK, Denmark, and Ireland join the EC
Oct.	Following the Middle East War, Arab oil producers quadruple the price of oil and send the international economy into recession
1975 Feb.	Lomé Convention (superceding Yaoundé Convention) agreed between EEC and 46 African, Caribbean, and Pacific (ACP) states

Mar.	EC heads of state and government inaugurate the European Council (regular summit meetings)
Jun.	In a referendum in the UK, a large majority endorses continued EC membership
Jul.	Member states sign a treaty strengthening the budgetary powers of the European Parliament and establishing the Court of Auditors
1978 Jul.	Meeting in Bremen; the European Council decides to establish the European Monetary System (EMS), precursor to EMU
1979 Mar.	Member states launch the EMS
Jun.	First direct elections to the European Parliament
1981 Jan.	Greece joins the EC
1985 Jun.	The Commission publishes its white paper on completing the single market
1986 Jan.	Portugal and Spain join the EC
Feb.	EC foreign ministers sign the Single European Act (SEA)
1987 Jul.	The SEA enters into force
1988 Jun.	EC and Comecon (East European trading bloc) recognize each other for first time
1989 Apr.	The Delors Committee presents its report on EMU
Nov.	The Berlin Wall comes down
1990 Oct.	Germany is reunited
1991 Dec.	Meeting in Maastricht; the European Council concludes the intergovernmental conferences on political union and EMU
1992 Feb.	EC foreign ministers sign the Maastricht Treaty
Jun.	Danish voters reject the Maastricht Treaty
1993 May	Danish voters approve the Maastricht Treaty, with special provisions for Denmark
Nov.	The Maastricht Treaty enters into force; the European Union (EU) comes into being
Jun.	Copenhagen European Council endorses eastern enlargement
1994 Apr.	Hungary and Poland apply to join EU
1995 Jan.	Austria, Finland, and Sweden join the EU
1995 Mar.	Schengen Agreement implemented by seven EU member states
1995–6	Eight additional Central and Eastern European countries apply to join the EU
1997 Jun.	European Council agrees Amsterdam Treaty, which creates post of High Representative for the CFSP
Oct.	EU foreign ministers sign the Amsterdam Treaty
1998 Mar.	The EU begins accession negotiations with five Central and Eastern European countries, plus Cyprus
UK and France agree St Malo Declaration on European defence
Jun.	The European Central Bank (ECB) is launched in Frankfurt
1999 Jan.	The third stage of EMU begins with the launch of the euro and the pursuit of a common monetary policy by eleven member states
Mar.	The Commission resigns following the submission of a report of an independent investigating committee; the Berlin European Council concludes the Agenda 2000 negotiations
May	The Amsterdam Treaty enters into force
Dec.	The European Council signals 'irreversibility of eastern enlargement'; recognizes Turkey as a candidate for EU membership
2000 Feb.	The EU begins accession negotiations with the five other Central and Eastern European applicant countries, plus Malta

Dec.	Meeting in Nice, the European Council concludes the intergovernmental conference on institutional reform
2001 Feb.	EU foreign ministers sign the Nice Treaty
Jun.	Irish voters reject the Nice Treaty
2002 Jan.	Euro notes and coins enter into circulation
Feb.	Convention on the 'Future of Europe' opens
Oct.	In a second referendum, Irish voters approve the Nice Treaty
2003 Feb.	The Nice Treaty enters into force
Jun.	The Convention on the Future of Europe promulgates a Draft Constitutional Treaty
	The UK, Germany, and France (EU-3) launch a joint diplomatic effort to address the nuclear policy and programme of Iran
Oct.	An intergovernmental conference opens to finalize the Constitutional Treaty
2004 May	Cyprus, the Czech Republic, Estonia, Hungary, Latvia, Lithuania, Malta, Poland, Slovakia, and Slovenia join the EU
Jun.	The intergovernmental conference reaches agreement on the Constitutional Treaty
Oct.	National leaders sign the Constitutional Treaty in Rome
2005 May	French voters reject the Constitutional Treaty
Jun.	Dutch voters reject the Constitutional Treaty
	The European Council launches a year-long 'period of reflection' on the stalled Constitutional Treaty
Oct.	The EU opens accession negotiations with Turkey
2006 Jun.	The European Council decides to prolong the 'period of reflection' and calls on Germany to find a solution to the constitutional impasse during the country's presidency in the first half of 2007
	China, Russia, and the US join the EU-3 (forming the P5+1) to deal with Iran's developing nuclear programme
2007 Jan.	Bulgaria and Romania join the EU
	Slovenia adopts the euro
Jun.	European Council agrees mandate for new 'Reform Treaty' to replace Constitutional Treaty
Jul.–Oct.	Intergovernmental conference drafts the Reform Treaty
Dec.	National leaders sign the new treaty in Lisbon (the Lisbon Treaty)
2008 Jan.	Cyprus and Malta adopt the euro
Jun.	Irish voters reject the Lisbon Treaty
2009 Jan.	Slovakia adopts the euro
Oct.	In a second referendum, Irish voters approve the Lisbon Treaty
Dec.	The Lisbon Treaty enters into force
	The possibility of Greece defaulting on its soaring national debt causes its cost of national borrowing to soar and sparks crisis in the Eurozone
2010 Apr.–May	Greece applies for emergency support and concludes a loan agreement with the EU and IMF
May	EU leaders create the European Financial Stability Facility (ESFS) to make financial assistance available to troubled member states in the Eurozone. The EFSF is given capacity to offer up to €750 billion in loans, €250 billion of which will be contributed by the International Monetary Fund (IMF)
Nov.	Ireland agrees an emergency loan programme with the EU and IMF
2011 Jan.	Estonia becomes the 17th member of the Eurozone

Feb.	Eurozone finance ministers agree to establish a permanent emergency funding mechanism, the European Stability Mechanism (ESM)
Apr.	Portugal becomes the third Eurozone country to apply for an EU loan assistance programme
May	Portugal receives rescue package worth €178 billion
Jun.	EU leaders agree to a new €120 billion bailout of Greece, imposing further austerity measures as a condition; talk of Greece leaving the euro grows
Jul.	A second rescue package, worth €109 billion, is agreed for Greece
Aug.	ECB says it will purchase Spanish and Italian bonds as their yields rise to dangerous levels
Oct.	Opposition to austerity in Greece erupts into violence scenes outside of Parliament
Nov.	Greek and Italian prime ministers both resign and are replaced by technocrats
	Mario Draghi replaces Jean-Claude Trichet as president of the ECB
Dec.	Fiscal Compact agreed as an intergovernmental treaty between all EU states (except UK and Czech Republic) following David Cameron's veto
2012 Feb.	More protests in Greece as further austerity demanded in exchange for further rescue package
Mar.	Eurozone finally approves second rescue package, worth €130 billion, for Greece
May	Socialist Francois Hollande succeeds Nicholas Sarkozy as president of France
Jul.	Mario Draghi says that the ECB will do 'whatever it takes to preserve the euro'
Sep.	Mario Draghi announces plan to buy the bonds of struggling Eurozone economies, called Outright Monetary Transactions (OMT), against wishes of Germany
Oct.	The ESM is formally launched
Nov.	Cyprus formally requests emergency assistance
2013 Jan.	UK Prime Minister David Cameron delivers his 'Bloomberg' speech setting out his plans for renegotiating the UK's membership of the EU ahead of a planned referendum on UK membership in 2017
Mar.	Cyprus receives rescue package after controversy over its banking sector delayed the deal
Jul.	Croatia joins the EU
Nov.	P5+1 reach interim agreement with Iran over its nuclear programme
Dec.	Ireland becomes first country to exit its rescue programme
2014 Jan.	Latvia becomes 18th state to adopt the euro
Feb.	Ukraine's President Victor Yanukovych flees Kiev after weeks of domestic protest and violent clashes between police and protesters in Maidan Square; pro-Russian gunmen seize government buildings in the capital of the Crimea region of Ukraine
Mar.	A referendum is held in Crimea in which 97 per cent are reported to have voted to join Russia; the conduct of the referendum is widely condemned
	Vladimir Putin signs a law incorporating Crimea into Russia

May	Portugal exits rescue programme
	European Parliament elections see significant gains for eurosceptic and populist parties, including the UK Independence Party and the French *Front National*
	Donetsk and Luhansk declare independence from Ukraine after referenda
Jun.	The EU signs trade deal with Ukraine
Jul.	Malaysia airlines flight MH-17 is shot down over eastern Ukraine
	EU agrees economic sanctions on Russia
Sep.	The government of Ukraine, the anti-government rebels in Ukraine, Russia, and the Organization for Security and Co-operation in Europe (OSCE) sign a peace agreement in Minsk
Nov.	Jean-Claude Juncker becomes 12th president of the European Commission
Dec.	Donald Tusk succeeds Herman Van Rompuy and becomes the second president of the European Council
2015 Jan.	Mario Draghi unveils new ECB bond-buying scheme
	Anti-government rebels in Ukraine seize Donetsk airport
	Alexis Tsipras, leader of Syriza (Coalition of the Radical Left) party, becomes prime minister of Greece on a platform of renegotiating the EU rescue package
	Peace negotiations between Ukraine, the rebels, Russia, and the OSCE collapse
Feb.	Ukraine, Russia, Germany, and France agree to end hostilities in Eastern Ukraine at talks in Minsk
Apr.	P5+1 conclude a framework agreement with Iran regarding their nuclear programme
May	Commission proposes a relocation scheme for asylum-seekers across the EU, based on member state quotas
Jun.	Commission publishes 'Five Presidents Report' on EMU and Eurozone integration
5 Jul.	Greece defaults on a debt repayment to the IMF and votes against the terms of a new (third) financial rescue package
Jul.	P5+1 reaches a nuclear agreement with Iran
	Greek Parliament votes to support the reforms required by the terms of its third rescue package
Aug.–Sep.	Refugee crisis intensifies
Sep.	EU member states agree a plan to relocate asylum-seekers across the Union on a quota system, a policy that is deeply divisive among member states
Nov.	Terrorists kill 130 in suicide bombings and shootings in Paris, ISIS claims responsibility
Dec.	Serbia opens the first chapters of its EU accession negotiations
2016 Jan.	Schengen system challenged in Sweden, Denmark, and Austria as a result of the rise in asylum-seekers
	Commission launches investigation under rule of law mechanism into Polish government legislation
	Sanctions against Iran ended following completion of nuclear deal
Feb.	European Council approves €3 billion deal with Turkey aimed at stemming the flow of refugees

Mar.	Terrorist attacks by ISIS in Brussels kill 35 people
Jun.	UK votes to leave the EU (51.9 per cent to 48.1 per cent) in a national referendum
Jul.	ISIS terrorist attack in Nice kills 86 people
	Attempted military coup in Turkey is thwarted; a state of emergency is declared in the aftermath
Sep.	EU accepts application for membership from Bosnia Herzegovina, which was filed in March
Oct.	European Parliament ratifies the Paris Climate Change Agreement
	EU and Canada sign trade agreement
Nov.	Minsk talks between Russia, France, Germany, and Ukraine, aimed at resolving the conflict in Ukraine, fail to reach agreement
Dec.	Terrorist attack by ISIS at Berlin Christmas market kills 12 people
2017 Feb.	Greece's creditors agree to more lenient budget targets but refuse to consider formal debt relief as Greece continues under its third rescue package
Mar.	UK Government delivers Article 50 letter to European Council president, triggering the formal process of leaving the EU
	Commission publishes white paper on the future of the EU
May	Emmanuel Macron elected president of France
Jul.	Commission launches infringement proceedings against Hungary because of its laws on foreign-funded non-governmental organizations (NGOs)
Sep.	French President Macron delivers major speech on the future of the EU
Oct.	Political crisis breaks out in Spain as Catalan Parliament votes to declare independence following a referendum, which was ruled illegal by Spain's Constitutional Court
Dec.	Commission announces it will take Poland, Hungary, and Czech Republic to the European Court of Justice (ECJ) over failure of the three member states to accept the number of asylum-seekers allocated under the terms of the EU's September 2015 plan
	25 EU member states agree to Permanent Structured Cooperation (PESCO) in defence policy
	European Council agrees that Brexit talks can proceed past their first stage, announcing satisfactory progress has been made on several key issues

This chronology was compiled by Desmond Dinan, Andrew Byrne, and Daniel Kenealy.

GLOSSARY

Several of the terms below are defined and elaborated in more detail in the concept boxes of each of the chapters. Where this is the case, the box number is provided.

The EU also has its own official EU glossary, which can be found at: https://europa.eu/european-union/documents-publications/language-and-terminology_en

Absorption capacity (see Box 8.1) refers to the EU's ability to integrate new members into its system.

Accession (see Box 8.1) The process whereby a country joins the EU and becomes a member state.

Acquis communautaire (see Box 4.1) denotes the rights and obligations derived from the EU treaties, laws, and Court rulings. In principle, new member states joining the EU must accept the entire *acquis*.

Assent procedure: see **consent procedure**.

Asylum Protection provided by a government to a foreigner who is unable to stay in their country of citizenship/residence for fear of persecution.

Battle groups combine national military resources at the 'hard end' of European capabilities in specialized areas. The EU decided in 2004 to create 20 battle groups, which would be deployable at short notice for limited deployments.

Benchmarking (see Box 5.1) The use of comparison with other states or organizations with the aim of improving performance by learning from the experience of others.

Bicameralism From Latin *bi* (two) + *camera* (chamber). The principle that a legislature should comprise two chambers, usually chosen by different methods or electoral systems.

Cabinet The group of staff and advisers that make up the private offices of senior EU figures, such as commissioners.

Candidate country (see Box 8.1) refers to a country whose application is confirmed by the EU but is not yet a member.

Charter of Fundamental Rights of the European Union Adopted by the Council at the Nice Summit in 2000 but not legally binding, the Charter seeks to strengthen and promote the fundamental **human rights** of EU citizens.

Civil society (see Box 6.1) The collection of groups and associations (such as private firms and non-governmental organizations) that operate between the individual and the state.

Co-decision procedure Under this decision-making procedure the European Parliament formally shares legal responsibility for legislation jointly with the **Council of ministers**.

Cohesion policy Introduced after the first enlargement in 1973, its aim has been to reduce inequality among regions and compensate for the costs of economic integration.

Common Foreign and Security Policy (CFSP) (see Box 9.1) Created by the 1992 Maastricht Treaty as a successor to the European Political Cooperation mechanism. It has been embellished by successive new treaties and given (by the Treaty of Nice) a Brussels-based political and security committee to prepare foreign ministers' meetings and (by Lisbon) a 'new-look' **High Representative** and the EEAs.

Common market More than a free trade area, the EU common market (also called the single market) involves the free trade of goods, services, people, and capital. See also, **internal market**.

Community method Used especially in areas where common EU policies replace national policies (such as the **internal market**) the community method is a form of **supranational** policy-making in which the Union's institutions wield considerable power. Usually contrasted to the **intergovernmental** method.

Common Security and Defence Policy (CSDP) Created in 1999 to engage in the so-called 'Petersberg tasks' (named after a German castle where an earlier summit devoted to defence was held): humanitarian and rescue missions, peacekeeping, crisis management, and the vaguely specified task of 'peace-making'. It was formerly referred to as the European Security and Defence Policy (ESDP).

Conditionality (see Box 8.1) means that **accession** is conditional on fulfilling the criteria for membership.

Consent procedure (see Box 6.2) Previously known as the **assent procedure**, requires the EP's approval in a simple yes/no vote on international treaties, the **accession** of new member states, and some other decisions. The EP cannot amend proposals subject to consent. For enlargement, the approval of an absolute majority of Parliament's members is necessary.

Constructivism (-ists) (see Table 1.1) A school of thought drawing on cultural and sociological studies and emphasizing the non-rational 'social construction' of the collective rules and norms that guide political behaviour.

Consultation procedure (see Box 6.2) Decision-making procedure whereby the Council seeks the opinion of the European Parliament but need not heed that opinion.

Coreper (Committee of Permanent Representatives) The most important preparatory committee of the Council, Coreper is composed of heads of the Permanent Representation (EU ambassadors) and their supporting delegations maintained by each member state in Brussels. (See also 'Perm Reps'.)

Cotonou Agreement Agreed in the African state of Bénin in 2000 and then revised repeatedly (last in 2010). It is the successor to the Lomé Convention and is claimed to be a 'comprehensive partnership' between former European colonies and the EU.

Council of Europe (CoE) The leading human rights organization in Europe, the Council includes 47 member states each of which has signed up to the European Convention on Human Rights, a treaty designed to protect human rights, democracy, and the rule of law. The Convention is overseen by the **European Court of Human Rights**.

Council of ministers The EU institution representing the interests of the member states. National ministers from each EU member state meet in the Council to adopt laws and coordinate policies. For most EU law the Council co-decides with the European Parliament.

Court of Justice of the European Union (CJEU) The judicial authority of the EU, ensuring that EU law is applied and interpreted uniformly throughout the Union.

Customs Union (see Box 2.4) An agreement among states to abolish all customs duties and restrictions between them, and construct a common external tariff and common commercial (trade) policy.

Demandeur (see Box 4.1) French term often used to refer to those demanding something (say regional or agricultural funds) from the EU.

Democratic deficit (see Box 7.1) refers broadly to the belief that the EU lacks sufficient democratic control. Neither the Commission, which proposes legislation, nor the Council, which enacts it, is directly accountable to the public or national parliaments.

Demos From the ancient Greek, refers to 'the people', 'populace', or 'citizen body'.

Direct effect Established in the 1963 *van Gend en Loos* case, the doctrine has become a distinguishing principle of Community law. Under direct effect Community law applies directly to individuals (not just states) and national courts must enforce it.

Directive (see Box 5.1) The most common form of EU legislation. It stipulates the ends to be achieved but allows each member state to choose the form and method for achieving that end.

Directorates General (DGs) The primary administrative units within the Commission, comparable to national ministries or departments. There are about 20 DGs, each focusing on a specific area of policy such as competition or trade.

Economic and Monetary Union (EMU) A package of measures designed to harmonize the economic and monetary policies of participating member states. It includes the free movement of capital and convergence of monetary policies. Its most visible element is a single currency—the euro—adopted in 1999, with notes and coins circulating in 2002. By 2008, 15 member states were members of EMU.

Elysèe Treaty (1963) A treaty of friendship and cooperation signed between Germany and France in 1963.

Empty Chair Crisis (see Box 2.2) Protesting the Commission's plans to subject more decisions to **qualified majority voting**, French president De Gaulle pulled France out of all Council meetings in 1965, thereby leaving one chair empty.

Enhanced cooperation: see **flexible integration**.

Europe Agreements Signed in the early 1990s, these cooperation agreements between the EU and several East European countries were viewed as a first step towards **accession**.

European Central Bank (ECB) Established in 1998 and based in Frankfurt, the ECB is the institution of the EU that manages the euro. It is charged with keeping prices stable and it conducts EU economic and monetary policy. The ECB sets interest rates for the Eurozone.

European Citizens' Initiative A request addressed to the European Commission from at least one million EU citizens drawn from at least seven of the 28 member states to propose a specific piece of legislation in a policy area where the EU has competence to legislate.

European Commission The EU's executive body, representing the interests of the EU as a whole. The Commission proposes legislation, enforces European law, manages and implements EU policies and the budget, and represents the EU outside of Europe.

European Convention on Human Rights (ECHR) (see Box 7.1) formally the *Convention for the Protection of Human Rights and Fundamental Freedoms* is an international treaty drafted in 1950 by the then newly formed **Council of Europe**. All (the now 47) Council of Europe member states are party to the Convention. Any person who feels his or her rights, as defined in the Charter, have been violated by a state can appeal to the **European Court of Human Rights**. Judgements finding violations are binding on the states concerned.

European Council Made up on the heads of state or government of the EU member states, the European Council is the political apex of the EU. It defines the general political direction and priorities of the EU.

European Court of Auditors (ECA) The ECA is the independent external auditor of the EU. It audits the revenue and expenditure of the EU, checking that funds are correctly raised and spent. It is responsible for reporting fraud and corruption to the European Anti-Fraud Office. Established in 1977, the ECA is based in Luxembourg

European Court of Human Rights An international court set up in 1959, the Court hears cases that may involve the violation of the rights—civil and political—set out in the European Convention on Human Rights. The decisions of the Court are binding. The Court is based in Strasbourg and its jurisdiction covers citizens in the 47 member states of the **Council of Europe** that have ratified the European Convention on Human Rights. The Court is not part of the EU's institutional architecture and should not be confused with the European Court of Justice.

European Court of Justice (ECJ): see **Court of Justice of the European Union**.

European Defence Agency (EDA) was created in 2004 'to support the member states and the Council in their effort to improve European defense capabilities [particularly] in the field of crisis management and to sustain' the ESDP. It aims to move the EU towards more cooperation in arms production and procurement.

European Defence Community (EDC) A French-inspired, American-backed proposal for a European army. Tabled in 1950, the plan collapsed following its rejection by the French National Assembly in 1954.

European Economic Area (EEA) (see Box 8.1) is an arrangement which extends the EU's **single market** to Norway, Iceland, and Liechtenstein.

European Economic and Social Committee (EESC) The EESC is an advisory body that represents the interests of workers' and employers' organizations across and within the EU. It was established in 1957 and is based in Brussels. It often writes opinions to the European Commission, Council, and Parliament about proposed EU legislation.

European External Action Service (EEAS) (see Box 9.1) Created by the **Lisbon Treaty** and became active in 2010. It works under the authority of the **High Representative** and brings under one roof EU (Commission and Council) and national diplomats. One intended effect of the EEAS is to make the Union's missions in foreign capitals more like real embassies, with clout and resources.

European integration (see Box 1.5) The process whereby sovereign European states relinquish (surrender or pool) national **sovereignty** to maximize their collective power and interests.

European Investment Bank (EIB) Jointly owned by the EU's member states, the EIB borrows money in the capital markets and lends it to projects that support the objectives and aims of the EU. Each EU member state provides an EIB director, with a further director representing the European Commission. Established in 1958 and based in Luxembourg, the EIB approved projects worth more than 74 billion euros in 2016.

Europeanization (see Box 4.1) The process whereby national systems (institutions, policies, governments) adapt to EU policies and integration more generally, while also themselves shaping the EU.

European Parliament (EP) The only directly elected body of the EU. Its 751 members (MEP's) represent the EU's citizens. Elections are held every five years. The Parliament has gained power over the decades and is now a co-legislator (along with the Council) for nearly all EU law.

European Political Cooperation (EPC) The precursor to the **Common Foreign and Security Policy (CFSP)**, the EPC was launched in 1970 as a way for member states to coordinate their foreign policies and speak (and sometimes act) together when national policies overlapped.

European Security and Defence Policy (ESDP): see **Common Security and Defence Policy**.

Europol The European police office designed to improve the effectiveness with which police forces across the EU could cooperate across national borders.

Eurozone (see Box 5.1) The countries that are part of the **Economic and Monetary Union**

(EMU). By 2008, 15 member states belonged to the Eurozone.

Federalism (see Box 5.1) Principle of sharing power and **sovereignty** between levels of **governance**, usually between central or federal level, and substate (state, provincial, Länder) level.

Flexible integration Also called 'reinforced' or 'enhanced cooperation', flexible integration denotes the possibility for some member states to pursue deeper integration without the participation of others. Examples include EMU and the Schengen Agreement.

Fonctionnaires EU officials are international civil servants, who have successfully passed an entrance exam known as the 'concours' and are involved in policy-making in the EU's institutions.

Free trade area (FTA) (see Box 2.4) An area in which restrictive trading measures are removed and goods can travel freely among its signatory states. These states retain authority to establish their own tariff levels and quotas for third countries.

Frontex is the EU's agency for the management of its external border. It was created in 2005 to coordinate member states' operational cooperation in external border controls, provide training to national border guards, carry out risk analyses, organize joint control operations, and assist member states in migrant return operations.

Globalization (see Box 1.5) The process by which the world becomes increasingly interconnected and interdependent because of increasing flows of trade, ideas, people, and capital.

Governance (see Box 1.5) Established patterns of rules, principles, and practices that enable a community to be governed even without a government or ruler. The term is usefully applied to the EU because of its lack of identifiable government.

Gross domestic product (GDP) An index of the total value of all goods and services

produced by a country, not counting overseas operations.

Gross national product (GNP) An index of the total value of all goods and services produced by a country, including overseas trade. Most common measure of a country's material wealth.

High Representative for foreign affairs and security policy This post was established in the Treaty of Amsterdam. Javier Solana, who had previously served as Spanish foreign minister and secretary general of NATO, was the first High Representative. The High Representative manages the EU's **Common Foreign and Security Policy**, including the **Common Security and Defence Policy**, and chairs the Foreign Affairs Council of the Council of the European Union. The High Representative is appointed by the **European Council**, acting by **QMV**, and serves a five-year term.

Intergovernmental conferences (IGCs) Conferences bringing together representatives of member states to hammer out deals and consider amendments to the treaties, or other history-making decisions such as enlargement.

Intergovernmentalism (see Box 1.5) Process or condition whereby decisions are reached by specifically defined cooperation between or among governments. **Sovereignty** is not directly undermined.

Internal market More than a free trade area, an internal market signifies the free trade of goods, services, people, and capital. Also known as the **single market**.

Legal basis The basis of an EU law is the treaty article or articles (cited in the legislation) which give(s) the EU authority to act in that area and lay(s) down the decision-making rules that apply.

Legitimacy The right to rule and make political decisions. More generally, the idea that 'the existing political institutions are the most appropriate ones for society' (Lipset 1963: 64).

Liberal intergovernmentalism (-ists) (see Table 1.1) A theory of **European integration** which argues that the most important decisions taken concerning the EU reflect the preferences of national governments rather than **supranational** institutions.

Lisbon Treaty At the time of writing, the most recent revision to the EU's treaties. The Lisbon Treaty, among other things, abolished the pillar system, increased the power of the European Parliament, extended Qualified Majority Voting, and created the role of president of the **European Council**.

Lobbying (see Box 6.1) An attempt to influence policy-makers to adopt a course of action advantageous (or not detrimental) to a particular group or interest.

Luxembourg Compromise (see Box 2.2) Agreed in 1966 to resolve the 'Empty Chair Crisis', this informal agreement established that when a decision was subject to **qualified majority voting**, the Council would postpone a decision if any member states felt 'very important' interests were under threat.

Market (Box 5.1) A system of exchange bringing together buyers and sellers of goods and services.

Marshall Plan (1947) (see Box 2.2) A US aid package of $13 billion to help rebuild West European economies after the war.

Multi-level governance (see Box 1.5) A term denoting a system of overlapping and shared powers between actors on the regional, national, and **supranational** levels.

Negative integration Integration through **market**-building and the removal of obstacles to trade. Less ambitious than positive integration.

Neofunctionalism (-ists) (see Table 1.1) A theory of **European integration** which suggests

that economic integration in certain sectors will provoke further integration in other sectors, and can lead to the formation of integrated **supranational** institutions.

New institutionalism (-ists) (see Table 1.1) As applied to the EU, a theoretical approach that suggests that institutions, including rules and informal practices, can mould the behaviour of policy-makers (including national officials) in ways that governments neither plan nor control.

Non-tariff barriers (see Box 5.1) Regulations, such as national standards, that increase the cost of imports and thus have the equivalent effect of tariffs.

Ordinary Legislative Procedure (OLP): see **Co-decision procedure**.

Organization for Security and Co-operation in Europe (OSCE) (see Box 9.1) The organization brings together 57 (as of 2018) states from Europe and beyond in what is the world's largest regional security organization. It claims to take a 'comprehensive approach to security', extending especially to human rights. The OSCE works on the basis of unanimity and its decisions are politically, not legally, binding. It thus is criticized as toothless, even though its predecessor—the Conference on SCE—was important in putting into motion the changes that led to the end of the Cold War.

Path dependency The idea (developed especially by new institutionalists) that once a particular policy path or course of action is taken, it is extremely difficult to turn back because of the 'sunk costs' (time and resources already invested). Used to explain why even those policies that have outlived their usefulness remained unreformed.

'Perm Reps' Eurospeak for the permanent representatives (EU ambassador) and the permanent representations (similar to embassies) of each member state. Together the 'Perm Reps' from each of the member states make up **Coreper**.

Petersberg tasks A series of security tasks designed to strengthen European defence capability and the EU's role as a civilian power. These tasks include humanitarian, rescue, and peacekeeping operations as well as tasks involving combat forces in crisis management.

Pillars (see Box 1.2) A shorthand term for describing the 'Greek temple' architecture created by the Maastricht Treaty, with the first pillar (the pre-existing European Community) and the second (foreign and security policy) and third (justice and home affairs) pillars together constituting the 'European Union'. If ratified, the Reform Treaty would collapse the EU's pillars into one institutional structure.

Policy networks (see Table 1.1) Clusters of actors, each of whom has an interest or stake in a given policy sector and the capacity to help determine policy success or failure. Scholars applying this notion argue that analysing such networks can reveal a great deal about day-to-day decision-making in the EU.

Positive integration Integration through the active promotion of common policies which effectively replace national ones.

Public policy (see Box 5.1) A course of action (decisions, actions, rules, laws, and so on) or inaction taken by government in regard to some public problem or issue.

Qualified majority voting (QMV) (see Box 2.2) refers to the most commonly used voting method in the **Council of ministers**. Under this system each member state is granted a number of votes roughly proportional to its population.

Rapporteur (see Box 6.1) The member of the European Parliament responsible for preparing a report in one of the Parliament's committees.

Schengen Agreement (see Box 2.2) An agreement stipulating the gradual abolition of controls at borders. By 2008, 15 EU member states were signatories, as were Norway and Iceland. The UK and Ireland have not signed, and Denmark has opted out of certain aspects.

Schuman Plan (see Box 2.3) A plan proposed by the French foreign minister, Robert Schuman, in 1950 to combine the coal and steel industries of Germany and France, thus making war between them impossible. It eventually became the basis for the European Coal and Steel Community, launched by the 1950 Treaty of Paris.

Screening occurs at the start of negotiations when the applicant to the EU and the Commission examine the **acquis** to see if there are particular problems to be resolved.

Single market: see **internal market**.

Soft security is a post-Cold War concept that refers to security that is obtained through non-military policy instruments (except in cases of peacekeeping) and does not involve territorial defence of the state. It is related to the ideas of 'human security'—defence of the citizen, as opposed to the state—and 'homeland security', obtained via policies designed to eliminate internal security threats.

Sovereignty (see Box 1.5) refers to the ultimate authority over people and territory.

Subsidiarity (see Box 2.2) The idea that action should be taken at the most efficient level of **governance**, but as close to the citizens as possible.

Supranationalism (see Box 1.5) Above states or nations. Supranationalism means decisions are made by a process or institution which is largely independent of national governments. The term supranationalism is usually contrasted with intergovernmentalism.

Tour(s) de table (see Box 4.1) In the **Council of ministers** a 'tour around the table' allows each delegation to make an intervention on a given subject.

Transparency (see Box 6.1) this refers to the process of making (EU) documents and decision-making processes more open and accessible to the public.

Trilogues (Box 6.3) (*Trialogues* in French) These are three-way meetings between key representatives of the Commission, the Council, and the European Parliament designed to advance negotiations and speed-up budgetary and legislative decision-making.

Variable geometry In 'EU speak', variable geometry refers to the idea that certain groups of EU member states may wish to pursue integration in certain policy areas. Member states who were opposed to integration in a certain area would be free not to. The result of various developments of this kind would be an EU of variable geometry, in other words not all member states would be involved in all policy initiatives at all times.

The Glossary was compiled with the assistance of Louise Maythorne and Andrew Byrne.

REFERENCES

Acosta, D. and Geddes, A. (2013), 'The Development, Application and Implications of an EU Rule of Law in the Area of Migration Policy', *Journal of Common Market Studies*, 51/2: 179–93.

Adriaensen, J. (2016), *National Trade Administrations in EU Trade Policy: Maintaining the Capacity to Control* (Basingstoke: Palgrave).

Aggestam, L. and Johansson, M. (2017), 'The Leadership Paradox in EU Foreign Policy', *Journal of Common Market Studies*, 55/6: 1203–20.

Armstrong, K. and Bulmer, S. (1998), *The Governance of the Single European Market* (Manchester and New York: Manchester University Press).

Aspinwall, M. and Schneider, G. (2000), 'Same Menu, Separate Tables: The Institutionalist Turn in Political Science and the Study of European Integration', *European Journal of Political Research* 38/1: 1–36.

Authers, J. (2012), *Europe's Financial Crisis: A Short Guide to How the Euro Fell into Crisis and the Consequences for the World* (London: Prentice Hall).

Avery, G. (2004), 'The Enlargement Negotiations', in F. Cameron (ed.), *The Future of Europe, Integration and Enlargement* (London: Routledge): 35–62.

Avery, G. (2014a), *Independentism and the European Union* (Brussels: European Policy Centre).

Avery, G. (2014b), *Could an Independent Scotland Join the European Union?* (Brussels: European Policy Centre).

Avery G., Bailes J. K., and Thorhallsson B. (2011), 'Iceland's Application for European Union Membership', *Studia Diplomatica, Royal Institute for International Relations, Brussels*, 64/1: 93–119.

Aydin, U. and Thomas, K. P. (2012), 'The Challenges and Trajectories of EU Competition Policy in the Twenty-First Century', *Journal of European Integration*, 34/6: 531–47.

Bache, I. (2008), *Europeanization and Multi-Level Governance: Cohesion Policy in the European Union and Britain* (Lanham, MD: Rowman & Littlefield).

Bachtler, J., Mendez, C., and Wishlade, F. (2013), *EU Cohesion Policy and European Integration* (Farnham: Ashgate).

Bale, T., Hanley, S., and Szczerbiak, A. (2010), '"May Contain Nuts"? The Reality behind the Rhetoric Surrounding the British Conservatives' New Group in the European Parliament', *The Political Quarterly*, 81/1: 85–98.

Balfour, R. and Raik, K. (eds) (2012), 'The European External Action Service and National Diplomacies', *EPC Issue Paper*, 73, March. http://www.fiia.fi/assets/news/The%20EEAS%20and%20National%20Diplomacies.pdf

Barber, T. (2010), 'The Appointments of Herman van Rompuy and Catherine Ashton', *Journal of Common Market Studies*, 48/1: 55–67.

Barker, A. (2017), 'Brussels Hoists Gross Brexit Bill to €100', *Financial Times*, 3 May. https://www.ft.com/content/cc7eed42-2f49-11e7-9555-23ef563ecf9a

Bartolini S. (2005), *Restructuring Europe Centre Formation, System Building and Political Restructuring between the Nation State and the European Union* (Oxford: Oxford University Press).

Barysch, K., Everts, S., and Grabbe, H. (2005), *Why Europe Should Embrace Turkey* (London: Centre for European Reform).

Batora, J. (2013), 'The "Mitrailleuse Effect": The EEAS as an Interstitial Organization and the Dynamics of Innovation in Diplomacy', *Journal of Common Market Studies*, 51/4, 598–613.

Baun, M., Dürr, J., Marek, D., and Šaradín, P. (2006), 'The Europeanization of Czech Politics', *Journal of Common Market Studies*, 44/2: 249–80.

BBC (2016a), *Brexit: A Very British Coup?* Documentary. https://www.youtube.com/watch?v=IT-ScoHqMxU

BBC (2016b), 'Brexit: Sturgeon says second Scottish independence vote "highly likely"', 24 June. http://www.bbc.co.uk/news/uk-scotland-scotland-politics-36621030

BBC (2017), 'Sir Ivan Rogers' letter to staff in full', 4 January. http://www.bbc.co.uk/news/uk-politics-38503504

Beck, U. (2013), *German Europe* (Cambridge: Polity).

Beech, M. and Lee, S. (eds) (2015), *The Conservative–Liberal Coalition: Examining the Cameron–Clegg Coalition* (Basingstoke: Palgrave Macmillan).

Behr, R. (2016), 'How remain failed: the inside story of a doomed campaign', *The Guardian*, 5 July. https://www.theguardian.com/politics/2016/jul/05/how-remain-failed-inside-story-doomed-campaign

Bendiek, A. (2016) 'The Global Strategy for the EU's Foreign and Security Policy', SWP Comments, 38/August: https://www.swp-berlin.org/fileadmin/contents/products/comments/2016C38_bdk.pdf

Bennett, O. (2016), *The Brexit Club: The Inside Story of the Leave Campaign's Shock Victory* (London: Biteback Publishing).

Bergman, A. and Peterson, J. (2006), 'Security Strategy, ESDP and the Non-Aligned States', in R. Dannreuther and J. Peterson (eds), *Security Strategy and Transatlantic Relations* (London: Routledge): 147–64.

Best, E., Christiansen, T., and Settembri P. (eds) (2008), *The Institutions of the Enlarged European Union: Continuity and Change* (Cheltenham and Northampton, MA: Edward Elgar).

Bickerton, C., Hodson, D., and Puetter, U. (2015), 'The New Intergovernmentalism: European Integration in the Post-Maastrict Era', *Journal of Common Market Studies*, 53/4: 703–22.

Biermann F., Guerin, N., Jagdhuber, S., Rittberger, B., and Weiss, M. (2017), 'Political (Non-)Reform in the Euro Crisis and the Refugee Crisis: A Liberal Intergovernmentalist Explanation', *Journal of European Public Policy*. https://doi.org/10.1080/13501763.2017.1408670

Bindi, F. with Cisci, M. (2005), 'Italy and Spain: A Tale of Contrasting Effectiveness in the EU', in S. Bulmer, and C. Lequesne (eds), *The Member States of the European Union* (Oxford and New York: Oxford University Press): 142–63.

Biscop, J. (2016) 'The EU Global Strategy: Realpolitik with European Characteristics', Egmont Security Policy Brief, 75/June. http://www.egmontinstitute.be/
contentuploads/2016/06/SPB75.pdf?type=pdf

Bogdanor, V. (2007), *Democracy, Accountability and Legitimacy in the European Union*
(London: Federal Trust for Education and Research).

Börzel, T. (ed.) (2005), 'The Disparity of European Integration: Revisiting Neofunctionalism in Honour of Ernst Haas', *Journal of European Public Policy*, Special Issue, 12/2.

Börzel, T. A. and Risse, T. (2018), 'From the Euro to the Schengen Crises: European Integration Theories, Politicization and Identity Politics', *Journal of European Public Policy*,
25/1: 83–108.

Börzel, T. and Schimmelfennig, F. (2017), 'Coming Together or Drifting Apart? The EU's
Political Integration Capacity in Eastern Europe', *Journal of European Public Policy*,
24(2): 278–96.

Börzel, T. and Sedelmeier, U. (2017), 'Larger and More Law Abiding? The Impact of
Enlargement on Compliance in the European Union', *Journal of European Public Policy*,
24/2: 197–215.

Börzel, T., Dimitrova, A., and Schimmelfennig, F. (eds) (2017), 'European Union Enlargement and Integration Capacity', *Journal of European Public Policy*, Special Issue, 24/2.

Bossong, R. and Rhinard, M. (eds) (2016), *Theorizing Internal Security in the European
Union* (Oxford and New York: Oxford University Press).

Bostock, D. (2002), 'Coreper Revisited', *Journal of Common Market Studies*, 40/2: 215–34.

Bouchard, C., Peterson, J., and Tocci, N. (eds) (2013), *Multilateralism in the Twenty-First
Century: Europe's Quest for Effectiveness* (London and New York: Routledge).

Brandsma, G. J. (2015), 'Co-Decision after Lisbon: The Politics of Informal Trilogues in
European Union Lawmaking', *European Union Politics*, 16/2: 300–19.

Bretherton, C. and Vogler, J. (2006), *The European Union as a Global Actor*, 2nd edn (London and New York: Routledge).

Brown, M. L. (2017), *Regional Economic Organizations and Security Challenges* (London
and New York: Routledge).

Bulmer, S. (2009), 'Politics in Time Meets the Politics of Time: Historical Institutionalism
and the EU Timescape', *Journal of European Public Policy*, 16/2: 307–24.

Bulmer, S. (2014), 'Germany and the Eurozone Crisis: Between Hegemony and Domestic
Politics', *West European Politics*, 37/6: 1244–63.

Bulmer, S. and Burch, M. (2009), *The Europeanisation of Whitehall: UK Central Government and the European Union* (Manchester: Manchester University Press).

Bulmer, S. and Lequesne, C. (eds) (2005), *The Member States of the European Union*
(Oxford and New York: Oxford University Press).

Bulmer, S. and Lequesne, C. (2012), *The Member States of the European Union*, 2nd edn
(Oxford and New York: Oxford University Press).

Bulmer, S. and Paterson, W. (2013), 'Germany as the EU's Reluctant Hegemon? Of Economic
Strength and Political Constraints', *Journal of European Public Policy*, 20/10: 1387–405.

Bulmer, S., Burch, M., Hogwood, P., and Scott, A. (2006), 'UK Devolution and the
European Union: A Tale of Cooperative Asymmetry?', *Publius: The Journal of Federalism*,
36/1: 75–93.

Bulmer, S., Jeffery, C., and Padgett, S. (eds) (2010), *Rethinking Germany and Europe: Democracy and Diplomacy in a Semi-Sovereign State* (Basingstoke: Palgrave Macmillan).

Burchill, S., Linklates A., Devetak, R. *et al.* (2013), *Theories of International Relations*, 5th edn (Basingstoke and New York: Palgrave Macmillan).

Cafruny, A. and Ryner, M. (eds) (2003), *A Ruined Fortress? Neoliberal Hegemony and Transformation in Europe* (Oxford and Lanham, MD: Rowman & Littlefield).

Cairney, P. (2016), 'The Scottish Parliament Election 2016: Another Momentous Event but Dull Campaign', *Scottish Affairs*, 25/3: 277–93.

Caporaso, J. (2001), 'The Europeanization of Gender Equality Policy and Domestic Structural Change', in M. Green Cowles, J. Caporaso, and T. Risse (eds), *Transforming Europe: Europeanization and Domestic Change* (Ithaca, NY: Cornell University Press): 21–43.

Caporaso, J., Kim, M., Durrett, W., and Wesley, R. (2015), 'Still a Regulatory State? The European Union and the Financial Crisis', *Journal of European Public Policy*, 22/7: 889–907.

Carlsnaes, W. (2006), 'European Foreign Policy', in K. E. Jørgensen, M. A. Pollack, and B. Rosamond (eds), *Handbook of European Union Politics* (London and Thousand Oaks, CA: Sage): 545–60.

Chatterjee, P. (2004), *The Politics of the Governed: Reflections on Popular Politics in Most of the World* (New York: Columbia University Press).

Checkel, J. (1999), 'Social Construction and Integration', *Journal of European Public Policy*, 6/4: 545–60.

Checkel, J. (2001), 'Why Comply? Social Learning and European Identity Change', *International Organization*, 55/3: 553–88.

Checkel, J. (2004), 'Social Constructivisms in Global and European Politics: A Review Essay', *Review of International Studies*, 30/2: 229–44.

Checkel, J. (2006), 'Constructivism and EU Politics', in K. E. Jørgensen, M. Pollack, and B. Rosamond (eds), *Handbook of European Union Politics* (London: Sage): 57–76.

Cheneval, F. and Nicolaidis, K. (2017), 'The Social Construction of Demoicracy in the European Union', *European Journal of Political Theory*, 16/2: 235–60.

Chevenal, F. and Schimmelfennig, F. (2013), 'The Case for Democracy in the European Union', *Journal of Common Market Studies*, 51/2: 334–50.

Christiansen, T. (2016), 'After the *Spitzenkandidaten*: Fundamental Change in the EU's Political System', *West European Politics*, 39/5: 992–1010.

Cini, M. and Borragàn, N. P.-S. (eds) (2016), *European Union Politics* (Oxford and New York: Oxford University Press).

Clarke, H. D., Goodwin, M., and Cowley, P. (2017), *Brexit: Why Britain Voted to Leave the European Union* (Cambridge: Cambridge University Press).

Closa, C. and Heywood, P. S. (2004), *Spain and the European Union* (Basingstoke and New York: Palgrave).

Coen, D. and Richardson, J. (2009), *Lobbying in the European Union: Institutions, Actors and Issues* (Oxford and New York: Oxford University Press).

Commission (2013), *EU Budget 2012—Financial Report* (Brussels: Commission).

Commission (2016) Budget—Documents 2016. http://ec.europa.eu/budget/biblio/documents/2016/2016_en.cfm

Commission (2017), 'The EU Single Market: Single Market Scoreboard', July. http://ec.europa.eu/internal_market/scoreboard/

Conceição-Heldt, E. (2011), 'Variation in EU Member States' Preferences and the Commission's Discretion in the Doha Round', *Journal of European Public Policy*, 18/3: 403–19.

Cooper, R. (2004), 'Hard Power, Soft Power and the Goals of Diplomacy', in D. Held and M. Koenig-Archibugi (eds), *American Power in the 21st Century* (Oxford and Malden, MA: Polity): 168–80.

Cooper, C. (2016), 'Brexit: UK cannot have "single market a la carte", say EU leaders', *The Independent*, 29 June. http://www.independent.co.uk/news/uk/politics/brexit-uk-cannot-have-single-market-a-la-carte-say-eu-leaders-a7109141.html

Corbett, R. (2002), *The European Parliament's Role in Closer EU Integration* (Basingstoke: Macmillan).

Corbett, R. (2014), 'European Elections are Second-Order Elections: Is Received Wisdom Changing?', *Journal of Common Market Studies*, 52/6: 1194–8.

Corbett, R. (2016/17), *Brexit Briefings*. http://www.richardcorbett.org.uk/category/brexit-briefings/

Corbett, R., Jacobs, F., and Neville, D. (2016), *The European Parliament*, 9th edn (London: John Harper).

Cowles, M. G. and Curtis, S. (2004), 'Developments in European Integration Theory: The EU as "Other"', in M. G. Cowles and D. Dinan (eds), *Developments in the European Union II* (Basingstoke and New York: Palgrave): 296–309.

Culpepper, P. (2011), *Quiet Politics and Business Power: Corporate Control in Europe and Japan* (Cambridge: Cambridge University Press).

Cummings, D. (2017), 'How the Brexit Referendum was Won', *The Spectator*, 9 January. https://blogs.spectator.co.uk/2017/01/dominic-cummings-brexit-referendum-won/#

Curtice, J. (2017), 'Why Leave Won the UK's EU Referendum', *Journal of Common Market Studies*, 55/1: 19–37.

Curtin, D. (2014), 'Overseeing Secrets in the EU: A Democratic Perspective', *Journal of Common Market Studies*, 52/3: 684–700.

Damro, C. (2010), 'Market Power Europe'. MERCURY e-paper. http://www.europa.ed.ac.uk/_data/assets/pdf_file/0004/206887/Mercury-Paper-5.pdf

Damro, C. (2014), 'Market Power Europe: Externalization and Multilateralism', in C. Bouchard, J. Peterson, and N. Tocci (eds), *Multilateralism in the Twenty-First Century: Europe's Quest for Effectiveness* (London and New York: Routledge).

Damro, C. and Guay, T. (2016), *European Competition Policy and Globalization* (Basingstoke: Palgrave).

Daugbjerg, C. (2012), 'Globalisation and Internal Policy Dynamics in the Reform of the Common Agricultural Policy', in Richardson, J. (ed.), *Constructing a Policy-Making State?* (Oxford: Oxford University Press): 88–103.

De Grauwe, P. (2012), *Economics of Monetary Union*, 9th edn (Oxford: Oxford University Press).

De Ville, F. and Siles-Brügge, G. (2016), *TTIP: The Truth about the Transatlantic Trade and Investment Partnership* (Cambridge and Malden, MA: Polity).

Delreux, T. and Laloux, T. (2018), 'Concluding Early Agreements in the EU: A Double Principal-Agent Analysis of Trilogue Negotiations', *Journal of Common Market Studies*, 56/2: 300–17.

Devetak, R., Burke, A., and George, J. (eds) (2012), *An Introduction to International Relations* (Cambridge and New York: Cambridge University Press).

Dhingra, S. and Sampson, T. (2016), 'Life after Brexit: What are the UK's Options Outside the European Union?', LSE Centre for Economic Performance, Paper 01. http://cep.lse.ac.uk/pubs/download/brexit01.pdf

Diamond, L. (2015), 'Facing Up to the Democratic Recession', *Journal of Democracy*, 26/1: 141–55.

Dinan, D. (2014a), *Europe Recast: A History of European Union*, 2nd edn (Boulder, CO: Lynne Rienner Publishers and Basingstoke: Palgrave).

Dinan, D. (ed.) (2014b), *Origins and Evolution of the European Union*, 2nd edn (Oxford: Oxford University Press).

Dinan, D. (2015), 'Governance and Institutions: The Year of the *Spitzenkandidaten*', *Journal of Common Market Studies*, Special issue 53/1: 93–107.

Dinan, D., Nugent, N., and Paterson, W. (eds) (2017), *The European Union in Crisis* (Basingstoke and New York: Palgrave Macmillan).

Doherty, B., Temple Lang, J., McCrudden, C. *et al.* (2017), 'Northern Ireland and Brexit: The European Economic Area Option', European Policy Centre, Discussion Paper, 7 April. http://epc.eu/documents/uploads/pub_7576_northernirelandandbrexit.pdf

Donnelly, B. and Bigatto, M. (2008), 'The European Parliament and Enlargement', in E. Best, T. Christiansen, and P. Settembri (eds), *The Institutions of the Enlarged European Union: Continuity and Change* (Cheltenham and Northampton, MA: Edward Elgar): 82–99.

Duchêne, F. (1994), *Jean Monnet: The First Statesman of Interdependence* (New York: Norton).

Duina, F. and Lenz, T. (2017), 'Democratic Legitimacy in Regional Economic Organizations: The European Union in Comparative Perspective', *Economy & Society*. doi: 10.1080/03085147.2017.1377946.

Dur, A. and Mateo, G. (2014), 'Public Opinion and Interest Group Influence: How Citizen Groups Derailed the Anti-Counterfeiting Trade Agreement', *Journal of European Public Policy*, 21/8: 1199–217.

Dyrhauge, H. (2014), 'The Road to Environmental Policy Integration is Paved with Obstacles: Intra- and Inter-organizational Conflicts in EU Transport Decision-Making', *Journal of Common Market Studies*, 52/5: 985–1001.

Eilstrup-Sangiovanni, M. (2006), 'The Constructivist Turn in European Integration Studies', in M. Eilstrup-Sangiovanni (ed.), *Debates on European Integration: A Reader* (Basingstoke and New York: Palgrave): 393–405.

Elgström, O. (2007), 'Outsiders' Perceptions of the European Union in International Trade Negotiations', *Journal of Common Market Studies*, 45/4: 949–67.

Epstein, R. and Jacoby, W. (eds) (2014), *Journal of Common Market Studies*, Special issue on 'Eastern Enlargement Ten Years On: Transcending the East–West Divide?', 52/1.

Epstein, R. and Sedelmeier, U. (eds) (2009), *International Influence beyond Conditionality: Postcommunist Europe after EU Enlargement* (London: Routledge).

Eurobarometer (2007), *Standard Barometer 67, First Results Spring 2007* (Brussels: European Commission). http://ec.europa.eu/commfrontoffice/publicopinion/archives/eb/eb67/eb67_en.pdf

Eurobarometer (2016), *Special Eurobarometer of the European Parliament*, September/October. http://www.europarl.europa.eu/pdf/eurobarometre/2016/parlemetre/eb86_1_parlemeter_synthesis_en.pdf

European Commission (1992), 'Europe and the Challenge of Enlargement', *Bulletin of the European Communities*, Supplement 3/92, 12 June. http://aei.pitt.edu/1573/1/challenge_of_enlargement_June_92.pdf

European Commission (2016), *Annual Activity Report –2016*. Translation. https://ec.europa.eu/info/publications/annual-activity-report-2016-translation_en

European Commission (2017a), 'Annex to the Recommendation for a Council Decision'. https://ec.europa.eu/info/sites/info/files/annex-recommendation-uk-eu-negotiations_3-may-2017_en.pdf

European Commission (2017b), 'White Paper on the Future of Europe'. https://ec.europa.eu/commission/sites/beta-political/files/white_paper_on_the_future_of_europe_en.pdf

European Commission (2018), 'Internal EU27 Peparatory Discussions on the Framework for the Future Relationship: "Regulatory Issues"', 21 February. https://ec.europa.eu/commission/sites/beta-political/files/slides_regulatory_issues.pdf

European Council (2016a), 'European Council Meeting (18 and 19 February 2016)—Conclusions'. http://www.consilium.europa.eu/media/21787/0216-euco-conclusions.pdf

European Council (2016b), 'The Bratislava Declaration', 16 September. https://www.consilium.europa.eu/media/21250/160916-bratislava-declaration-and-roadmapen16.pdf

European Council (2017), 'European Council (Art. 50) Guidelines for Brexit Negotiations'. http://www.consilium.europa.eu/en/press/press-releases/2017/04/29-euco-brexit-guidelines/

European Parliament (2015), '*Spitzenkandidaten*: The Underlying Story', *EuroParlTV*. https://www.europarltv.europa.eu/en/programme/others/spitzenkandidaten-the-underlying-story

European Parliament (2017), 'Resolution on Negotiations with the United Kingdom'. http://www.europarl.europa.eu/sides/getDoc.do?pubRef=-//EP//TEXT+TA+P8-TA-2017-0102+0+DOC+XML+V0//EN&language=EN

Everts, S. (2002), *Shaping a Credible EU Foreign Policy* (London: Centre for European Reform).

Faber, G. and Orbie, J. (2009), 'Everything but Arms: Much More than Appears at First Sight', *Journal of Common Market Studies*, 47/4: 767–87.

Falkner, G., Treib, O., and Holzleithner, E. (2008), *Compliance in the Enlarged European Union* (Aldershot: Ashgate).

Farrell, M. (2007), 'From EU Model to External Policy? Promoting Regional Integration in the Rest of the World', in S. Meunier, and K. McNamara (eds), *Making History: European Integration and Institutional Change at Fifty* (Oxford and New York: Oxford University Press): 299–316.

Ford, R. and Goodwin, M. (2014) *Revolt on the Right: Explaining Support for the Radical Right in Britain* (London: Routledge).

Forsberg, T. (2011), 'Normative Power Europe, Once Again: A Conceptual Analysis of an Ideal Type', *Journal of Common Market Studies*, 49/6: 1184–204.

Fox, B. (2014), 'Secret EU Lawmaking: The Triumph of the Trilogues', *EU Observer*, 4 April. https://euobserver.com/investigations/123555

Freedland, J. (2017), 'Dover and Out', *New York Review of Books*, 12 April. http://www.nybooks.com/articles/2017/05/11/dover-and-out/

Galtung, J. (1973), *The European Community: A Superpower in the Making* (London: George Allen & Unwin).

Geddes, A. (2016), 'Britain Beyond the European Union?', in R. Heffernan, C. Hay, M. Russell, and P. Cowley (eds), *Developments in British Politics*, 10th edn (Basingstoke: Palgrave Macmillan): 264–86.

George, S. (1998), *An Awkward Partner: Britain in the European Community*, 3rd edn (Oxford: Oxford University Press).

Gillingham, J. (1991), *Coal, Steel and the Rebirth of Europe, 1945–1955* (Cambridge: Cambridge University Press).

Gillingham, J. (2003), *European Integration, 1950–2003* (Cambridge: Cambridge University Press).

Ginsberg, R. (2001), *The European Union in International Politics: Baptism by Fire* (Boulder, CO, and Oxford: Rowman & Littlefield).

Glencross, A. (2011), 'A Post-National EU? The Problem of Legitimising the EU without the Nation and National Representation', *Political Studies*, 59/2: 348–67.

Goetz, K. H. (2005), 'The New Member States and the EU: Responding to Europe', in S. Bulmer and C. Lequesne (eds), *The Member States of the European Union* (Oxford and New York: Oxford University Press): 254–84.

Goodwin, M. (2016), 'Inequality, not Personalities Drove Britain to Brexit', *Politico*, 28 June. http://www.politico.eu/article/inequality-not-personalities-drove-britain-to-brexit/

Goodwin, M. and Heath, O. (2016), 'The 2016 Referendum, Brexit and the Left Behind: An Aggregate-Level Analysis of the Result', *The Political Quarterly*, 87/3: 323–32.

Goodwin, M., Hix, S., and Pickup, M. (2015), 'What is the Likely Effect of Different Arguments on Britain's EU Referendum?', *The UK in a Changing Europe* blog, 27 November. http://ukandeu.ac.uk/what-is-the-likely-effect-of-different-arguments-on-britains-eu-referendum/

Gormley-Heenan, C. and Aughey, A. (2017), '"Waking Up in a Different Country": Brexit and Northern Ireland', *British Journal of Politics and International Relations*, 19/3: 497–511.

Grabbe, H. (2006), *The EU's Transformative Power: Europeanization through Conditionality in Central and Eastern Europe* (Basingstoke and New York: Palgrave Macmillan).

Grabbe, H. (2014), 'Six Lessons of Enlargement Ten Years On: The EU's Transformative Power in Retrospect and Prospect', *Journal of Common Market Studies*, 52/s1: 40–56.

Grant, W. (2010), 'Policy Instruments in the Common Agricultural Policy', *West European Politics*, 33/1: 22–38.

Greenwood, J. (2017), *Interest Representation in the European Union*, 4th edn (Basingstoke and New York: Palgrave).

Grimaud, M. (2018), *Small States and EU Governance: Malta in EU Decision-Making Processes* (Basingstoke: Palgrave Macmillan).

Grob-Fitzgibbon, B. (2016), *Continental Drift: Britain and Europe from the End of Empire to the Rise of Euroscepticism* (Cambridge: Cambridge University Press).

Gross, E. (2009), *The Europeanization of National Foreign Policy: Continuity and Change in European Crisis Management* (Basingstoke and New York: Palgrave Macmillan).

Guardian/ICM survey (2018), 'How Britain's Views Have Changed—Full Brexit Poll Results', 26th January. https://www.theguardian.com/politics/ng-interactive/2018/jan/26/guardian-icm-brexit-poll-full-results

Haas, E. (1958), *The Uniting of Europe: Political, Social, and Economic Forces* (Stanford, CA: Stanford University Press).

Haas, E. (1961), 'International Integration: The European and the Universal Process', *International Organization*, 15/3: 366–92.

Haas, E. (1964), *Beyond the Nation-State: Functionalism and International Organization* (Stanford, CA: Stanford University Press).

Haas, E. (2001), 'Does Constructivism Subsume Neo-functionalism?' in T. Christiansen, K. E. Jørgensen, and A. Weiner (eds), *The Social Construction of Europe* (London and Thousand Oaks, CA: Sage): 22–31.

Haas, P. (2004), 'When Does Power Listen to Truth? A Constructivist Approach to the Policy Process', *Journal of European Public Policy*, 11/4: 569–92.

Habermas, J. (2008), *Europe: The Faltering Project* (Cambridge and Malden, MA: Polity).

Häge, F. (2017), 'The Scheduling Power of the EU Council Presidency', *Journal of European Public Policy*, 24/5: 695–713.

Hagemann, S. and De Clerck-Sachsse, J. (2007), 'Decision-making in the Council of Ministers Before and After May 2004'. Special CEPS Report (Brussels: Centre for European Policy Studies).

Hall, P. (2014), 'Varieties of Capitalism and the Euro Crisis', *West European Politics*, 37/6: 1223–43.

Hall, P. and Taylor, C. (1996), 'Political Science and the Three New Institutionalisms', *Political Studies*, 44/5: 936–57.

Hancke', B. (2013), *Unions, Central Banks, and EMU: Labour Market Institutions and Monetary Integration in Europe* (Oxford: Oxford University Press).

Havighurst, A. F. (1985), *Britain in Transition: the Twentieth Century*, 4th edn (Chicago, IL: University of Chicago Press).

Hayes-Renshaw, F. (2017), 'The Council of Ministers: Conflict, Consensus and Continuity', in D. Hodson and J. Peterson (eds), *Institutions of the European Union*, 4th edn (Oxford: Oxford University Press): chapter 4.

Hayes-Renshaw, F. and Wallace, H. (2006), *The Council of Ministers*, 2nd edn (Basingstoke: Palgrave).

Heisenberg, D. (2005), 'The Institution of "Consensus" in the European Union: Formal versus Informal Decision-Making in the Council', *European Journal of Political Research*, 44/1: 65–90.

Heisenberg, D. (2007), 'Informal Decision-Making in the Council: The Secret of the EU's Success?', in S. Meunier, and K. McNamara (eds), *Making History. European Integration and Institutional Change at Fifty* (Oxford and New York: Oxford University Press): 67–88.

Helwig, N. (2013), 'EU Foreign Policy and the High Representative's Capability-expectations Gap—A Question of Political Will', *European Foreign Affairs Review*, 18/2: 235–54.

Helwig, N. (2015), 'In Search of a Role for the High Representative: The Legacy of Catherine Ashton', *The International Spectator*, 49/4: 1–17.

Helwig, N., Ivan, P., and Kostanyan, H. (2013), *The New EU Foreign Policy Architecture, Reviewing the First Two Years of the EEAS* (Brussels: Centre for European Policy Studies).

Henderson, K. (2007), *The European Union's New Democracies* (London and New York: Routledge).

Heppell, T. (2013), 'Cameron and Liberal Conservatism: Attitudes within the Parliamentary Conservative Party and Conservative Ministers', *British Journal of Politics & International Relations*, 15/3: 340–61.

Hill, C. (1993), 'The Capability–Expectations Gap, or Conceptualizing Europe's International Role', *Journal of Common Market Studies*, 31/3: 305–28.

Hill, C. (1998), 'Closing the Capabilities–expectations Gap?', in J. Peterson and H. Sjursen (eds), *A Common Foreign Policy for Europe? Competing Visions of the CFSP* (London and New York: Routledge): 91–107.

Hill, C. (2006), 'The European Powers in the Security Council: Differing Interests, Differing Arenas', in K. V. Laatikainen and K. E. Smith (eds), *The European Union at the United Nations* (Basingstoke and New York: Palgrave): 49–69.

Hill, C., Smith, M., and Vanhoonacker S. (eds) (2017), *International Relations and the European Union*, 3nd edn (Oxford and New York: Oxford University Press).

Hillebrandt, M. and Novak, S. (2016), 'Integration without Transparency? Reliance on the Space to Think in the European Council and Council', *Journal of European Integration*, 38/5: 527–40.

Hillebrandt, M. Z., Curtin, D., and Meijer, A. (2014), 'Transparency in the EU Council of Ministers: An Institutional Analysis', *European Law Journal*, 20/1: 1–20.

Hix, S. (2008), 'Towards a Partisan Theory of EU Politics', *Journal of European Public Policy*, 15/8: 1254–65.

Hix, S. (2009), *What to Expect in the 2009–14 European Parliament: Return of the Grand Coalition?* (Stockholm: Swedish Institute for European Policy Analysis).

Hix, S. and Høyland, B. (2013), 'Empowerment of the European Parliament', *Annual Review of Political Science*, 16/1: 171–89.

Hix, S., Noury, A., and Roland, G. (2007), *Democratic Politics in the European Parliament* (Cambridge: Cambridge University Press).

Hix, S., Noury, A. and Roland, G. (2009), 'Voting Patterns and Alliance Formation in the European Parliament', *Philosophical Transactions of the Royal Society B*, 364: 821–31.

Hobolt, S. (2009), *Europe in Question: Referendums on European Integration* (Oxford: Oxford University Press).

Hodson, D. (2015), 'Economic and Monetary Union', in H. Wallace, M. Pollack, and A. Young (eds), *Policymaking in the European Union*, 7th edn (Oxford: Oxford University Press): 157–80.

Hodson, D. and Peterson, J. (eds) (2017), *The Institutions of the European Union*, 4th edn (Oxford and New York: Oxford University Press).

Hoeksma, J. (2010), *A Polity called EU: The European Union as a Transnational Democracy* (Amsterdam: Europe's World).

Hoffmann, S. (1966), 'Obstinate or Obsolete: The Fate of the Nation-State and the Case of Western Europe', *Daedalus* 95/3: 862–915. Reprinted in S. Hoffmann (1995), *The European Sisyphus: Essays on Europe 1964–1994* (Boulder, CO, and Oxford: Westview Press).

Hoffmann, S. (1995), *The European Sisyphus: Essays on Europe 1964–1994* (Boulder, CO, and Oxford: Westview Press).

Holzinger, K. and Sommerer, T. (2011), '"Race to the Bottom" or "Race to Brussels"? Environmental Competition in Europe', *Journal of Common Market Studies*, 49/1: 315–39.

Hooghe, L. (2005), 'Many Roads Lead to International Norms, But Few via International Socialization: A Case Study of the European Commission', *International Organization*, 59/4: 861–98.

Hooghe, L. and Marks, G. (2001), *Multi-Level Governance and European Integration* (Lanham and Oxford: Rowman & Littlefield).

Hooghe, L. and Marks, G. (2003), 'Unraveling the Central State, but How? Types of Multi-Level Governance', *American Political Science Review*, 97/2: 233–43.

House of Lords (2006), *The Further Enlargement of the EU: Threat or Opportunity?* European Union Committee, Report with Evidence, HL Paper 273 (London: Stationery Office Ltd). http://www.publications.parliament.uk/pa/ld200506/ldselect/ldeucom/273/273.pdf

House of Lords (2009), *Codecision and National Parliamentary Scrutiny*, 17th Report of Session 2008–9 (London: HMSO).

House of Lords (2015), *Inter-Governmental Relations in the United Kingdom*, Select Committee on the Constitution, 11th Report of Session 2014–15, HL Paper 146 (London: HMSO).

Howorth, J. (2007), *Security and Defence Policy in the European Union* (Basingstoke and New York: Palgrave).

Hug, A. (2010), *Reconnecting the European Parliament and its People* (London: Foreign Policy Centre).

Hurrelmann, A. (2014), 'Democracy Beyond the State: Insights from the European Union', *Political Science Quarterly*, 129/1: 87–105.

Hyde-Price, A. (2006), 'Normative Power Europe: A Realist Critique', *Journal of European Public Policy*, 13/2: 217–34.

Independent (2017), 'Article 50 was designed for European dictators, not the UK, says man who wrote it', 29 March. http://www.independent.co.uk/news/uk/politics/article-50-design-dictators-not-uk-eu-european-lisbon-treaty-author-lord-kerr-a7655891.html

Institute for Government (2017), *The Civil Service after Article 50*. https://www.institute-forgovernment.org.uk/sites/default/files/publications/IFGJ5327_Report_Brexit_Civil_Service_080317_WEB.pdf

Jabko, N. (2006), *Playing the Market* (Ithaca, NY: Cornell University Press).

Jachtenfuchs, M. and Kasak, C. (2017), 'Balancing Sub-Unit Autonomy and Collective Problem-Solving by Varying Exit and Voice: An Analytical Perspective', *Journal of European Public Policy*, 24/4: 598–614.

Jensen, C. S. (2016), 'Neo-Functionalism', in M. Cini and N. P.-S. Borragàn (eds), *European Union Politics* (Oxford and New York: Oxford University Press): 59–70.

Jones, E. (2018), 'Towards a Theory of Disintegration', *Journal of European Public Policy*, 25/3: 440–51.

Jones, E., Menon, A., and Weatherill, S. (2012), *The Oxford Handbook of the European Union* (New York and Oxford: Oxford University Press).

Jordan, A. and Schout, A. (2006), *The Coordination of the European Union: Exploring the Capacities for Networked Governance*. Oxford: Oxford University Press.

Jørgensen K. E. (2006), 'Overview: the European Union and the World', in K. E. Jørgensen, M. A. Pollack, and B. Rosamond, *Handbook of European Union Politics* (London and Thousand Oaks CA: Sage): 507–25.

Jørgensen K. E., Pollack, M., and Rosamond, B. (eds) (2006), *Handbook of European Union Politics* (London and Thousand Oaks CA: Sage).

Journal of Common Market Studies (2014), Special issue on 'Eastern Enlargement Ten Years On: Transcending the East-West Divide?', 52/1.

Journal of European Integration (2017), Special Issue on European Boundaries, 39/5.

Journal of European Public Policy (2007), Special issue on 'Empirical and Theoretical Studies in EU Lobbying', 14/3.

Journal of European Public Policy (2013a) Special issue on 'Building Better Theoretical Frameworks of the European Union's Policy Process', 20/6.

Journal of European Public Policy (2013b) Special issue on 'Twenty Years of Legislative Codecision in the European Union', 20/7.

Journal of European Public Policy (2013c) Symposium on 'Building the European External Action Service', 20/9.

Journal of European Public Policy (2015a) Special issue on 'Legislative Lobbying in Context: The Policy and Polity Determinants of Interest Group Politics in the European Union,' 22/4.

Journal of European Public Policy (2015b), Special issue on 'Demoi-cracy in the European Union', 22/1.

Juncker, J.-C. (2017) 'State of the Union, 2017', 13 September, Brussels, at https://ec.europa.eu/commission/state-union-2017_en.

Juncos, A.E. (2016) 'Resilience as a New EU Foreign Policy Paradigm: A Pragmatist Turn?', *European Security*, 26/1: 1–18

Juncos, A. and Pomorska, K. (2014) 'Manufacturing *Esprit de Corps*: The Case of the European External Action Service', *Journal of Common Market Studies*, 52/2: 302–19.

Kaeding, M. and Stack, K. (2015) 'Legislative Scrutiny? The Political Economy and Practice of Legislative Vetoes in the European Union', *Journal of Common Market Studies*, 53:6: 1268–84.

Kassim, H., Peters, B. G., and Wright, V. (eds) (2001), *The National Co-Ordination of EU Policy: The European Level* (Oxford and New York: Oxford University Press).

Kassim, H., Peterson, J., Bauer, M., Dehousse, R., Hooghe, L., Thompson, A., and Connolly, S. (2013) *The European Commission of the Twenty-First Century: Decline or Renewal?* (Oxford: Oxford University Press).

Kastner, L. (2017) 'Business Lobbying under Salience—Financial Industry Mobilization Against the European Financial Transaction Tax', *Journal of European Public Policy*, advance online access: https://doi.org/10.1080/13501763.2017.1330357

Kelemen, R. D. (2017) 'Europe's Other Democratic Deficit: National Authoritarianism in Europe's Democratic Union', *Government and Opposition* 52(2): 211–38.

Kelemen, R. D; A. Menon, and J. Slapin (eds) (2014) *The European Union: Wider and Deeper?* Journal of European Public Policy, Special Issue, 21(5).

Kelley, J. (2006) 'New Wine in Old Wineskins: Promoting Political Reforms through the New European Neighbourhood Policy', *Journal of Common Market Studies* 44(1): 29–55.

Kenealy, D. (2014), 'How Do You Solve a Problem like Scotland? A Proposal Regarding Internal Enlargement', *Journal of European Integration*, 36/6: 585–600.

Kenealy, D. (2016) 'The Scottish Government's Brexit proposals are politically savvy and all-but-impossible', LSE Brexit blog, 22 December, at http://blogs.lse.ac.uk/brexit/2016/12/22/the-scottish-governments-brexit-proposals-are-politically-savvy-and-all-but-impossible/.

Kenealy, D. and Kostagiannis, K. (2013) 'Realist Visions of European Union: E.H. Carr and Integration', *Millennium: Journal of International Studies*, 41/2: 221–46.

Kenealy, D. and MacLennan, S. (2014), 'Sincere Cooperation, Respect for Democracy, and EU Citizenship: Sufficient to Guarantee Scotland's Future in the Union?', *European Law Journal*, 20/5: 591–612.

Keohane, R. (ed.) (1986) *Neorealism and its Critics*. New York: Columbia University Press.

Keukeleire, S. and Delreux, T. (2014), *The Foreign Policy of the European Union*, 2nd edn (Basingstoke: Palgrave Macmillan).

Kingah, S., Schmidt, V., and Yong, W. (2015) 'Setting the Scene: The European Union's Engagement with Transnational Policy Networks', *Contemporary Politics*, 21/3: 231–44.

Klüver, H. (2013) *Lobbying in the European Union: Interest Groups, Lobbying Coalitions, and Policy Change* (Oxford: Oxford University Press).

Kochenov, D. and Pech, L. (2016) 'Better Late than Never? On the European Commission's Rule of Law Framework and its First Activation', *Journal of Common Market Studies*, 54/5: 1062–74.

Korski, D. (2016) 'Why we lost the Brexit vote', *Politico*, 20 October. http://www.politico.eu/article/why-we-lost-the-brexit-vote-former-uk-prime-minister-david-cameron/.

Krasner, S. (1999) *Sovereignty: Organized Hypocrisy* (Princeton, NJ: Princeton University Press).

Krotz, U. (2009), 'Momentum and Impediments: Why Europe Won't Emerge as a Full Political Actor on the World Stage Soon', *Journal of Common Market Studies*, 47/3: 555–78.

Krotz, U. and Schild, J. (2013) *Shaping Europe: France, Germany and Embedded Bilateralism from the Elysee Treaty to Twenty-First Century Politics* (Oxford: Oxford University Press).

Kundnani, H. (2017), 'President Trump, the U.S. Security Guarantee, and the Future of European Integration', German Marshall Fund of the United States Policy Brief. http://brussels.gmfus.org/publications/president-trump-us-security-guarantee-and-future-european-integration

Laffan, B. (2017) 'Financial Control: The Court of Auditors and OLAF', in Hodson, D. and Peterson, J. (eds), *The Institutions of the European Union* (Oxford and New York: Oxford University Press): 58–79.

Laffan, B. and O'Mahony, J. (2008), *Ireland in the European Union* (Palgrave: London).

Laffan, B., O'Donnell, R., and Smith, M. (2000), *Europe's Experimental Union: Rethinking Integration* (London and New York: Routledge).

Laïdi, Z. (2008) *La Norme san la Force: l'Enigme de la Puissance Européene*, 2nd edn (Paris: Presses de Science Po).

Lavenex, S. (2004) 'EU External Governance in "Wider Europe"', *Journal of European Public Policy*, 11(4): 680–700.

Le Gloannec, A. M. (2018), *Continent by Default* (Ithaca, NY: Cornell University Press).

Leonard, M. (2005), *Why Europe Will Run the Twenty-First Century* (London and New York: Harper Collins).

Levy, D., Aslan, B., and Bironzo, D. (2016) *UK Press Coverage of the EU Referendum*, Reuters Institute for the Study of Journalism, University of Oxford. http://reutersinstitute.politics.ox.ac.uk/our-research/uk-press-coverage-eu-referendum

Lewis, J. (2005) 'The Janus Face of Brussels: Socialization and Everyday Decision-Making and Administrative Rivalry in the European Union', *International Organization*, 59/4: 937–71.

Lindberg, B., Rasmussen, A., and Warntjen, A. (eds) (2008) Special issue of *Journal of European Public Policy*, 'The Role of Political Parties in the European Union', 15/8.

Lindberg, L. (1963), *The Political Dynamics of European Economic Integration* (Stanford, CA: Stanford University Press).

Lindberg, L. and Scheingold, S. A. (1970), *Europe's Would-Be Polity: Patterns of Change in the European Community* (Englewood Cliffs, NJ: Prentice-Hall).

Ludlow, P. (2010) *Eurocomment 7* (7/8).

Lynch, P. and Whitaker, R. (2008) 'A Loveless Marriage: The Conservatives and the European People's Party', *Parliamentary Affairs*, 61:1: 31–51.

Macron, E. (2017) 'Sorbonne Speech: Initiative for Europe', 26 September, full text available. http://international.blogs.ouest-france.fr/archive/2017/09/29/macron-sorbonne-verbatim-europe-18583.html.

Majone, G. (1999), 'The Regulatory State and its Legitimacy Problems', *West European Politics* 22/1: 1–13.

Manners, I. (2002), 'Normative Power Europe: A Contradiction in Terms?', *Journal of Common Market Studies* 40/2: 235–58.

Manners, I. (2006), 'Normative Power Europe Reconsidered', *Journal of European Public Policy* 13/2: 182–99.

Mariniello, M., Sapir, A., and Terzi, A. (2015) 'The Long Road Towards the European Single Market', *Bruegel Working Paper* 2015/01.

Marsh, D. (2011), *The Euro: The Battle for the New Global Currency* (New Haven, CT: Yale University Press).

Marsh, D. (2013), *Europe's Deadlock: How the Euro Crisis Could be Solved—And Why it Won't Happen* (New Haven, CT: Yale University Press).

Martin, P. (2010), 'The US Supreme Court', in G. Peele, C. Bailey, B. Cain, and B. Guy Peters (eds), *Developments in American Politics 6* (Basingstoke and New York: Palgrave Macmillan): 132–49.

Matthijs, M. (2016) 'Powerful Rules Governing the Euro: The Perverse Logic of German Ideas', *Journal of European Public Policy*, 23/3, 375–91.

May, T. (2016) 'Britain after Brexit: A Vision of a Global Britain. https://www.gov.uk/government/speeches/we-have-voted-to-leave-the-eu-but-not-europe-article-by-theresa-may

May, T. (2017) 'We Have Voted to Leave the EU but not Europe' (published in *Le Figaro*). https://www.gov.uk/government/speeches/we-have-voted-to-leave-the-eu-but-not-europe-article-by-theresa-may

Mearsheimer, J. J. (2001), *The Tragedy of Great Power Politics* (New York and London: Norton).

Menon, A. (2011), 'Power, Institutions and the CSDP: The Promise of Institutional Theory', *Journal of Common Market Studies*, 49/1: 83–100.

Merand, F. and Saurugger, S. (2010), Special issue of *Comparative European Politics*, 8/1.

Merand F., Foucault, M., and Irondelle, B. (eds) (2011), *European Security since the Fall of the Berlin Wall* (Toronto: University of Toronto Press).

Messerlin, P. (2001), *Measuring the Costs of Economic Protection in Europe* (Washington DC: Institute for International Economics).

Meunier, S. (2017) 'Integration By Stealth: How the European Union Gained Competence over Foreign Direct Investment', *Journal of Common Market Studies*, 55/3: 593–610.

Meunier, S. and McNamara, K. (eds) (2007), *Making History: European Integration and Institutional Change at Fifty* (Oxford: Oxford University Press).

Meyer, C. O. and Strickmann, E. (2011), 'Solidifying Constructivism: How Material and Ideational Factors Interact in European Defence', *Journal of Common Market Studies*, 49/1: 61–81.

Miller, V. (2013), 'Voting Behaviour in the EU Council', House of Commons Library Standard Note S N06646.

Milward, A. (1984), *The Reconstruction of Western Europe, 1945–51* (Berkeley, CA: University of California Press).

Milward, A. (2000), *The European Rescue of the Nation-State*, 2nd edn (London: Routledge).

Milward, A. (2002) *The United Kingdom and the European Community, Volume I: The Rise and Fall of a National Strategy, 1945–1963*. London: Routledge.

Mitchell, J. (2015) 'Sea Change in Scotland', *Parliamentary Affairs*, 68 (supplement 1): 88–100.

Mitchell, J. and McHarg, A. (2017) 'Brexit and Scotland: What Does Brexit Tell Us About the UK's Territorial Constitution?', *British Journal of Politics and International Relations*, 19/3: 512–26.

Mogherini, F. (2016), 'A Global Strategy for the European Union's Foreign and Security Policy: "Shared Vision, Common Action: A Stronger Europe"'. Paper prepared for the European Union Global Strategy, June. *European Foregn Affairs Journal* 3. https://eeas.europa.eu/archives/docs/top_stories/pdf/eugs_review_web.pdf

Moore, P. (2016) 'How Britain voted', *YouGov* blog, 27 June. https://yougov.co.uk/news/2016/06/27/how-britain-voted/.

Moravcsik, A. (1993), 'Preferences and Power in the European Community: A Liberal Intergovernmentalist Approach', *Journal of Common Market Studies*, 31/4: 473–524.

Moravcsik, A. (1998), *The Choice for Europe: Social Purpose and State Power from Messina to Maastricht* (Ithaca, NY, and London: Cornell University Press and UCL Press).

Moravcsik, A. (2002), 'In Defence of the Democratic Deficit: Reassessing Legitimacy in the European Union', *Journal of Common Market Studies*, 40/4: 603–24.

Moravcsik, A. (2013) 'Did Power Politics Cause European Integration? Realist Theory meets Qualitative Methods', *Security Studies*, 22/4: 773–90.

Moravcsik, A. and Schimmelfennig, F. (2009), 'Liberal Intergovernmentalism', in A. Wiener and T. Diez (eds), *European Integration Theory*, 2nd edn (Oxford and New York: Oxford University Press): 67–89.

Morgan, G. (2005), *The Idea of a European Superstate* (Princeton, NJ: Princeton University Press).

Mosbacher, M. and Wiseman, O. (2016) *Brexit Revolt: How the UK Voted to Leave the EU* (London: Social Affairs Union).

Neheider, S. and Santos, I. (2011), 'Reframing the EU Budget Decision-Making Process', *Journal of Common Market Studies*, 49/3: 631–51.

Neustadt, R. E. (1991), *Presidential Power and the Modern Presidents: The Politics of Leadership from Roosevelt to Reagan*, rev. edn (New York and London: Free Press).

Nicolaidis, K. (2013) 'European Demoicracy and Its Crisis', *Journal of Common Market Studies*, 51/2: 351–69.

Norris, P. and Inglehart, R. (2016), 'Trump, Brexit and the Rise of Populism: Economic Have-Nots and Cultural Backlash', *Harvard Kennedy School of Government* Faculty Research Working Paper Series. https://research.hks.harvard.edu/publications/getFile.aspx?Id=1401

Novak, S. (2013), 'The Silence of Ministers: Consensus and Blame Avoidance in the Council of the European Union', *Journal of Common Market Studies*, 51/6: 1091–107.

Nugent, N. (2004), *European Union Enlargement* (Basingstoke and New York: Palgrave).

Nugent, N. (2017), *The Government and Politics of the European Union*, 8th edn (Basingstoke and New York: Palgrave Macmillan).

Nuttall, S. (2000), *European Foreign Policy* (Oxford and New York: Oxford University Press).

Nye, J. S. (2004), *Soft Power: The Means to Success in World Politics* (New York: Public Affairs).

Oliver, C. (2016) *Unleashing Demons: The Inside Story of Brexit* (London: Hodden & Stoughton).

Open Britain (2017) 'Full Text of Lord Kerr's Speech "Article 50—the Facts"', 10 November. http://www.open-britain.co.uk/full_text_of_lord_kerr_s_speech_article_50_the_facts

Orbie, J. (2009), *Europe's Global Role: External Policies of the European Union* (Farnham: Ashgate).

Owen, J. and Munro, R. (2016), *Whitehall's Preparation from the UK's Exit from the EU*. https://www.instituteforgovernment.org.uk/sites/default/files/publications/IFGJ5003_Whitehalls_preparation_131216_V10.pdf

Oxford Economics (2016), *Assessing the Economic Implications of Brexit* (Oxford: Oxford Economics).

Panke, D. (2010), *Small States in the European Union. Coping with Structural Disadvantages* (London: Ashgate).

Panke, D. (2012) 'Lobbying Institutional Key Players: How States Seek to Influence the European Commission, the Council Presidency and the European Parliament', *Journal of Common Market Studies*, 50/1: 129–50.

Papadimitriou, D. and Phinnemore, D. (2007), *Romania and the European Union* (London and New York: Routledge).

Patten, C. (2001), 'In Defence of Europe's Foreign Policy', *Financial Times*, 17 October. www.ft.com

Patten, C. (2005), *Not Quite the Diplomat: Home Truths about World Affairs* (London and New York: Allen Lane/Penguin).

Paun, A. and Munro, R. (2015), *Governing in an Ever Looser Union: How the Four Governments of the UK Cooperate, Negotiate and Compete*. https://www.instituteforgovernment.org.uk/sites/default/files/publications/Governing%20in%20an%20ever%20looser%20union%20-%20final.pdf

Pech, L. and Scheppele, K. L. (2017), 'Illiberalism Within: Rule of Law Backsliding in the EU', *Cambridge Yearbook of European Legal Studies*, 19: 3–47.

Peeters, S., Costa, H., Stuckler, D., McKee, M., and Gilmore, A. (2016), 'The Revision of the 2014 European Tobacco Products Directive: An Analysis of the Tobacco Industry's Attempts to "Break the Health Silo"', *Tobacco Control*, 25: 108–17.

Peterson, J. (1995), 'Decision-Making in the EU: Towards a Framework for Analysis', *Journal of European Public Policy*, 2/1: 69–73.

Peterson, J. (2001) 'The Choice for EU Theorists: Establishing a Common Framework for Analysis', *European Journal of Political Research*, 39/3: 289–318.

Peterson, J. (2003/4), 'Europe, America, Iraq: Worst Ever, Ever Worsening?', *Journal of Common Market Studies*, Annual Review, 42: 9–26.

Peterson, J. (2008), 'Enlargement, Reform and the European Commission: Weathering a Perfect Storm?', *Journal of European Public Policy*, 15/5: 761–80.

Peterson, J. (2009) 'Policy Networks', in A. Wiener and T. Diez (eds), *European Integration Theory*, 2nd edn (Oxford: Oxford University Press): 105–24.

Peterson, J. (2017a), 'The College of Commissioners', in D. Hodson and J. Peterson (eds), *The Institutions of the European Union*, 4th edn (Oxford: Oxford University Press): 108–37.

Peterson, J. (2017b) 'Juncker's Political Commission and an EU in Crisis', *Journal of Common Market Studies*, 55/2, March: 349–67.

Peterson, J. (2018) 'Present at the Destruction? The Liberal Order in the Trump Era', *The International Spectator*, 53/1: 28–44. https://www.tandfonline.com/eprint/YgyEEA-Qhq2SMBSAW63YY/full

Peterson, J. (2018) 'structure, Agency and Transatlantic Relations in the Trump Era', *Journal of European Integration*, 41/2 (forthcoming).

Peterson, J. and Bomberg, E. (1999), *Decision-Making in the European Union* (Basingstoke and New York: Palgrave).

Peterson, J. and Geddes, A. (2015) 'The EU as a Security Actor', in D. Kenealy, J. Peterson, and R. Corbett (eds), *The European Union: How Does it Work?*, 4th edn (Oxford and New York: Oxford University Press): 187–207.

Peterson, J. and Helwig, N. (2017), 'Common Foreign and Security Policy: Institutionalizing Europe's Global Role', in D. Hodson and J. Peterson (eds), *The Institutions of the European Union*, 4th edn (Oxford and New York: Oxford University Press): 307–33.

Pierson, P. (1996), 'The Path to European Integration', *Comparative Political Studies* 29/2: 123–63.

Pierson, P. (2000), 'Increasing Returns, Path Dependence, and the Study of Politics', *American Political Science Review*, 94/2: 251–67.

Pierson, P. (2004), *Politics in Time: History, Institutions and Social Analysis* (Princeton, NJ and Woodstock: Princeton University Press).

Piris, J.-C. (2010), *The Lisbon Treaty: A Legal and Political Analysis* (Cambridge and New York: Cambridge University Press).

Piris, J.-C. (2016) 'Article 50 is not forever and the UK could change its mind', *Financial Times*, 1 September. https://www.ft.com/content/b9fc30c8-6edb-11e6-a0c9-1365ce54b926

Pisani-Ferry, J. (2014), *The Euro Crisis and its Aftermath* (Oxford: Oxford University Press).

Pollack, M. (2005), 'Theorizing the European Union: International Organization, Domestic Polity, or Experiment in New Governance?', *Annual Review of Political Science*, 8: 357–98.

Pollack, M.A. (2009), 'New Institutionalism', in A. Wiener and T. Diez (eds), *European Integration Theory*, 2nd edn (Oxford: Oxford University Press): 125–43.

Pollack, M. A. (2015), 'Theorizing EU Policy-Making', in H. Wallace, M. Pollack, and A. Young (eds), *Policy-Making in the European Union*, 7th edn (Oxford and New York: Oxford University Press): 12–45.

Preston, C. (1997), *Enlargement and Integration in the European Union* (London: Routledge).

Puchala, D. J. (1971), 'Of Blind Men, Elephants and International Integration', *Journal of Common Market Studios*, 10/3: 267–84.

Quaglia, L. (2007), *Central Banking Governance in the European Union: A Comparative Analysis* (London and New York: Routledge).

Quaglia, L. (2010), *Governing Financial Services in the European Union* (London and New York: Routledge).

Rasmussen, A. (2012), 'Twenty Years of Co-Decision since Maastricht: Inter- and Intra-institutional Implications', *Journal of European Integration*, 34/7: 735–51.

Rasmussen, A. (2015), 'The Battle for Influence: The Politics of Business Lobbying in the European Parliament', *Journal of Common Market Studies*, 53/2: 365–82.

Redmond, J. (2007), 'Turkey and the EU: Troubled European or European Trouble?', *International Affairs* 83/2: 305–17.

Rieger, E. (2005), 'Agricultural Policy: Constrained Reforms', in H. Wallace, W. Wallace, and M. Pollack (eds), *Policy-Making in the European Union*, 5th edn (Oxford: Oxford University Press): 161–90.

Rifkin, J. (2004), *The European Dream* (Cambridge: Polity).

Risse, T. (2009), 'Social Constructivism', in A. Wiener and T. Diez (eds), *European Integration Theory*, 2nd edn (Oxford: Oxford University Press): 144–61.

Risse, T. (2010), *A Community of Europeans: Transnational Identities and Public Spheres* (Ithaca, NY: Cornell University Press).

Roche, M. (2010), *Exploring the Sociology of Europe: An Analysis of the European Social Complex* (London: SAGE).

Rodrick, D. (2011), *The Globalization Paradox* (New York: W.W. Norton and Company).

Roederer-Rynning, C. (2015), 'The Common Agricultural Policy—The Fortress Challenged', in W. Wallace, M. Pollack, and A. Young (eds), *Policy-Making in the European Union*, 7th edn (Oxford and New York: Oxford University Press): 196–219.

Roederer-Rynning, C. and Greenwood, J. (2016), 'The European Parliament as a Developing Legislature: Coming of Age in Trilogues', *Journal of European Public Policy*, 24/5: 735–54.

Rogers, J. (2009), 'From "Civilian Power" to "Global Power": Explicating the European Union's "Grand Strategy" through the Articulation of Discourse Theory', *Journal of Common Market Studies*, 47/4: 831–62.

Rosamond, B. (2013), 'Theorizing the EU after Integration Theory', in M. Cini and N. Pérez-Solórzano Borragán (eds), *European Union Politics*, 4th edn (Oxford and New York: Oxford University Press): 85–102.

Rosamond, B. (2016), 'Theorizing the EU after Integration Theory', in M. Cini and N. Pérez-Solórzano Borragán (eds), *European Union Politics*, 5th edn (Oxford and New York: Oxford University Press): 79–96.

Rosato, S. (2011), *Europe United: Power, Politics and the Making of the European Community* (Ithaca NY and London: Cornell University Press).

Rosato, S. (2012), 'Europe Troubles: Power Politics and the State of the European Project', *International Security*, 35/4: 45–86.

Rowe, C. (2012), 'Social and Regional Interests: The Economic and Social Committee and Committee of the Regions', in D. Hodson and J. Peterson (eds), *The Institutions of the European Union*, 4th edn (Oxford: Oxford University Press).

Rynning, S. (2005), 'Return of the Jedi: Realism and the Study of the European Union', *Politique Europeenne* Research Paper. https://www.cairn.info/revue-politique-europeenne-2005-3-page-10.htm

Sandholtz, W. and Stone Sweet, A. (1998), *European Integration and Supranational Governance* (Oxford: Oxford University Press).

Saurugger, S. (2014) 'Europeanisation in Times of Crisis', *Political Studies*, 12/2: 181–92.

Sbragia, A. (2001), 'Italy Pays for Europe: Political Leadership, Political Choice, and Institutional Adaptation', in M. Green Cowles, J. Caporaso, and T. Risse (eds), *Transforming Europe: Europeanization and Domestic Change* (Ithaca, NY: Cornell University Press): 79–96.

Schimmelfennig, F. (2003), *The EU, NATO and the Integration of Europe* (Cambridge: Cambridge University Press).

Schimmelfennig, F. (2015), 'What's the News in the "New Intergovernmentalism"? A Critique of Bickerton, Hodson and Puetter', *Journal of Common Market Studies*, 53:4: 723–30.

Schimmelfennig, F. and Sedelmeier, U. (2002), 'Theorizing EU Enlargement: Research Focus, Hypotheses, and the State of Research', *Journal of European Public Policy* 9(4): 500–28.

Schimmelfennig, F. and Sedelmeier, U. (2004). 'Governance by Conditionality: EU Rule Transfer to the Candidate Countries of Central and Eastern Europe', *Journal of European Public Policy*, 11(4): 661–79.

Schimmelfennig, F. and Sedelmeier, U. (2005a), *The Europeanization of Central and Eastern Europe* (Ithaca, NY: Cornell University Press).

Schimmelfennig, F. and Sedelmeier, U. (2005b), *The Politics of European Union Enlargement: Theoretical Approaches* (London: Routledge).

Schimmelfennig, F. and Winzen, T. (2017), 'Eastern Enlargement and Differentiated Integration: Towards Normalization', *Journal of European Public Policy*, 24(2): 239–58.

Schmidt, V. (2013), 'Democracy and Legitimacy in the European Union Revisited: Input, Output *and* "Throughput"2', *Political Studies*, 61: 2–22.

Schneider C. J. (2008), *Conflict, Negotiation and European Union Enlargement* (Cambridge: Cambridge University Press).

Schoeller, M. (2018), 'The Rise and Fall of Merkozy: Franco-German Bilateralism as a Negotiation Strategy in Eurozone Crisis Management', *Journal of Common Market Studies*, advanced online access. doi: 10.1111/jcms.12704

Schultz, M. (2013), 'Europe's budget deal is flawed', *Financial Times*, 17 February.

Scicluna, N. (2017), 'Integration through the Disintegration of Law? The ECB and EU Constitutionalism in the Crisis', *Journal of European Public Policy*, advance online access: https://doi.org/10.1080/13501763.2017.1362026

Sedelmeier, U. (2005), *Constructing the Path to Eastern Enlargement: The Uneven Policy Impact of EU Identity* (Manchester: Manchester University Press).

Sedelmeier, U. (2008) 'After Conditionality: Post-Accession Compliance with EU Law in East Central Europe', *Journal of European Public Policy* 15/6: 806–25.

Sedelmeier, U. (2014), 'Anchoring Democracy from Above? The European Union and Democratic Backsliding in Hungary and Romania after Accession', *Journal of Common Market Studies* 52/1:105–21.

Sedelmeier, U. (2015), 'Enlargement: Constituent Policy and Tool for External Governance', in Helen Wallace, Mark Pollack, and Alasdair Young (eds), *Policy-Making in the European Union*, 7th edn (Oxford: Oxford University Press, 2015): 407–35.

Sedelmeier, U. (2016), 'Protecting Democracy inside the European Union? The Party Politics of Sanctioning Democratic Backsliding in the European Parliament', MAXCAP Working Paper No. 27, July 2016. http://userpage.fu-berlin.de/kfgeu/maxcap/system/files/maxcap_wp_27.pdf

Settembri, P. (2007), 'The Surgery Succeeded. Has the Patient Died? The Impact of Enlargement on the European Union', paper presented at the Global Fellows Forum, NYU Law School, New York: 5 April 2007. http://www.nyulawglobal.org/fellowsscholars/documents/gffsettembripaper.pdf

Shipman, T. (2016), *All Out War: The Full Story of How Brexit Sank Britain's Political Class* (Glasgow: Harper Collins).

Short, C. (2000), 'Aid that doesn't help', *Financial Times*. 23 June. http://www.ft.com

Siedentop, L. (2000), *Democracy in Europe* (Harmondsworth: Allen Lane/Penguin Press).

Sjursen, H. (ed.) (2006a), *Questioning EU Enlargement: Europe in Search of Identity* (London: Routledge).

Sjursen, H. (ed.) (2006b), 'What Kind of Europe? European Foreign Policy in Perspective', special issue of *Journal of European Public Policy* 13/2.

Slapin, J. B. (2008), 'Bargaining Power at Europe's Intergovernmental Conferences: Testing Institutionalism and Intergovernmental Theories', *International Organization* 62/1: 131–62.

Smeets, S. and Vennix, J. (2014), '"How to Make the Most of Your Time in the Chair": EU Presidencies and the Management of Council Debates', *Journal of European Public Policy*, 21/10: 1435–51.

Smith, M. E. (2003), *Europe's Foreign and Security Policy* (Cambridge and New York: Cambridge University Press).

Smith, K. E. (2014), *European Union Foreign Policy in a Changing World*, 3rd edn (Oxford and Malden, MA: Polity).

Smith, K. E. (2017), 'EU Member States at the UN: A Case of Europeanization Arrested?', *Journal of Common Market Studies*, 55/3: 628–44.

Smith, M. E. (2015), 'The New Intergovernmentalism and Experential Learning in the Common Security and Defence Policy', in C. Bickerton, D. Hodson, and U. Puetter (eds),

The New Intergovernmentalism: States and Supranational Actors in the Post-Maastricht Era (Oxford and New York: Oxford University Press).

Söderbaum, F. and Sbragia, A. (2010), 'EU Studies and the 'New Regionalism': What Can be Gained from Dialogue?', *Journal of European Integration*, 32/6: 563–82.

Stiglitz, J. (2016), *The Euro and its Threat to the Future of Europe* (London: Allen Lane).

Stolfi, F. (2013), 'The Monti Government and the European Union', in C. Radaelli and A. di Virgilio (eds), *Italian Politics 2012* (New York: Berghahn Books): 173–87.

Swales, K. (2016), 'Understanding the Leave Vote', NatCen Social Research Briefing Paper. https://whatukthinks.org/eu/wp-content/uploads/2016/12/NatCen_Brexplanations-report-FINAL-WEB2.pdf

Tallberg, J. (2004), 'The Power of the Presidency: Brokerage, Efficiency and Distribution in EU Negotiations', *Journal of Common Market Studies*, 42/5: 999–1022.

Tatham, M. (2013), 'Paradiplomats against the State: Explaining Conflict in State and Substate Interest Representation in Brussels', *Comparative Political Studies*, 46/1: 63–94.

Tatham M. and Thau, M. (2014), 'Territorial Interest Representation in the European Union: Actors, Objectives and Strategies', *European Union Politics*, 15/2: 256–77.

Thierse, S. (2017), 'Policy Entrepreneurship in the European Parliament: Reconsidering the Influence of Rapporteurs', *Journal of European Public Policy*, advance online access. https://doi.org/10.1080/13501763.2017.1409794

Thomson, R. (2008), 'The Council Presidency in the European Union: Responsibility with Power', *Journal of Common Market Studies*, 46/3: 593–617.

Tocci, N. (2011), *Turkey's European Future: Behind the Scenes of America's Influence on EU–Turkey Relations* (New York and London: New York University Press).

Toje, A. (2010), *The European Union as a Small Power: After the Post-Cold War* (Basingstoke and New York: Palgrave).

Toje, A. (2011), 'The European Union as a Small Power', *Journal of Common Market Studies*, 49/1: 43–60.

Tonra, B. (2001), *The Europeanisation of National Foreign Policy: Dutch, Danish and Irish Foreign Policy in the European Union* (Aldershot and Brookfield VT: Ashgate).

Tonra, B. and Christiansen, T. (eds) (2004), *Rethinking European Union Foreign Policy* (Manchester and New York: Manchester University Press).

Toshkov, D. (2017) 'The Impact of the Eastern Enlargement on the Decision-Making Capacity of the European Union', *Journal of European Public Policy*, 24:2, 177–96.

Toshkov, D., Kortenska, E., Dimitrova, A., and Fagan, A. (2014), 'The "Old" and the "New" Europeans: Analyses of Public Opinion on EU Enlargement in Review' (MAXCAP Working Paper 2). http://userpage.fu-berlin.de/kfgeu/maxcap/system/files/maxcap_wp_02.pdf

UK Government (2013), 'EU Speech at Bloomberg', 23 January. https://www.gov.uk/government/speeches/eu-speech-at-bloomberg.

UK Government (2016), *Scotland's Place in Europe* (Edinburgh: Scottish Government).

UK Government (2017a), 'The government's negotiating objectives for exiting the EU:

PM speech', 17 January. https://www.gov.uk/government/speeches/the-governments-negotiating-objectives-for-exiting-the-eu-pm-speech

UK Government (2017b), 'PM's Florence Speech: A New Era of Cooperation and Partnership between the UK and the EU', 22 September. https://www.gov.uk/government/speeches/pms-florence-speech-a-new-era-of-cooperation-and-partnership-between-the-uk-and-the-eu

Vachudova, M. (2005), *Europe Undivided: Democracy, Leverage, and Integration after Communism* (Oxford: Oxford University Press).

Vachudova, M, (2009), 'Corruption and Compliance in the EU's Post-Communist Members and Candidates', *JCMS Annual Review of the European Union in 2008*, 47/s1: 43–62.

Van Esch, F. and de Jong, E. (2017), 'National Culture Triumps EU Socialization: European Central Bankers' Views of the Euro Crisis', *Journal of European Public Policy*, advance online access. https://doi.org/10.1080/13501763.2017.1391862

Van Middelaar, L. (2013), *The Passage to Europe: How a Continent Became a Union* (New Haven, CT and London: Yale University Press).

Van Rompuy, H. (2012), Speech at the Humboldt University, Walter Hallstein Institute for European Constitutional Law, 'The discovery of co-responsibility: Europe in the debt crisis', 6 February. http://www.consilium.europa.eu/uedocs/cms_data/docs/pressdata/en/ec/127849.pdf

Van Schendelen, M. (2013), *The Art of Lobbying the EU: More Machiavelli in Brussels*, rev. edn (Chicago, IL: University of Chicago Press).

Vanhoonacker, S. and Pomorska, K. (2013), 'The European External Action Service and Agenda-setting in European Foreign Policy', *Journal of European Public Policy*, 20/9: 1316–31.

Vanke, J. (2010), *Europeanism and European Union: Interests, Emotions, and Systemic Integration in the Early European Economic Community* (Palo Alto, CA: Academica Press).

Varoufakis, Y. (2016), *Adults in the Room: My Battle with Europe's Deep Establishment* (Oxford: Bodley Head).

Verhofstadt, G. (2017), 'We can deliver a Brexit deal that works for all', *Financial Times*, 7 May. https://www.ft.com/content/2494db66-31ae-11e7-9555-23ef563ecf9a

Vicere, M. (2016), 'The Roles of the President of the European Council and the High Representative in Leading EU Foreign Policy on Kosovo', *Journal of European Integration*, 38/5: 557–70.

Wall, S. (2012), *The Official History of Britain and the European Community, Volume II: From Rejection to Referendum, 1963-1975* (London: Routledge).

Wallace, H. (1989), 'Widening and Deepening: The European Community and the New European Agenda', *RIIA Discussion Paper*, No. 23 (London: Royal Institute of International Affairs).

Wallace, H. (2000), 'The Policy Process', in H. Wallace and W. Wallace (eds), *Policy-Making in the European Union* 4th edn (Oxford and New York: Oxford University Press): 39–64.

Wallace, H. (2005), 'Exercising Power and Influence in the European Union: The Roles of Member States', in S. Bulmer and C. Lesquene (eds), *The Member States of the European Union* (Oxford and New York: Oxford University Press): 25–44.

Wallace, H. and Reh, C. (2015), 'An Institutional Anatomy and Five Policy Modes', in H. Wallace, M. Pollack, and A. Young (eds), *Policy-Making in the European Union*, 7th edn Oxford: Oxford University Press: 72–112

Wallace, H., Pollack, M., and Young, A. (eds) (2015), *Policy-Making in the European Union*, 7th edn (Oxford: Oxford University Press).

Waltz, K. N. (2002), 'Structural Realism after the Cold War', in G. J. Ikenberry (ed.), *America Unrivaled: The Future of the Balance of Power* (Ithaca, NY and London: Cornell University Press): 29–67.

Webber, D. (2014) 'How Likely is it that the European Union will Disintegrate? A Critical Analysis of Competing Theoretical Perspectives', *European Journal of International Relations*, 20/2: 341–65.

Weber, K., Smith, M. E., and Baun, M. (eds) (2007), *Governing Europe's Neighborhood: Partners or Periphery?* (Manchester and New York: Manchester University Press).

Weiler, J. H. H. (1998), 'Ideas and Idolatry in the European Construct', in B. McSweeney (ed.), *Moral Issues in International Affairs* (Basingstoke and New York: Macmillan.

Wendt, A. (1992), 'Anarchy is What States Make of It: The Social Construction of Power Politics', *International Organization,* 46/3: 391–426.

Wendt, A. (1999), *Social Theory of International Politics* (Cambridge: Cambridge University Press).

West European Politics (2011), Special issue, 'Linking Inter- and Intra-institutional Change in the European Union', 34/1.

White, B. (2001), *Understanding European Foreign Policy* (Basingstoke and New York: Palgrave).

Whitman, R. (2017), 'Devolved External Affairs: The Impact of Brexit', *Chatham House*. https://www.chathamhouse.org/publication/devolved-external-affairs-impact-brexit

Whitman, R. and Wolf, S. (eds) (2010), *The European Neighbourhood Policy in Perspective: Context, Implementation and Impact* (Basingstoke: Palgrave Macmillan).

Wiener, A., and Diez, T. (eds) (2009), *European Integration Theory* (London: Oxford University Press).

Wincott, D. (ed.) (2017), 'Studying Brexit's Causes and Consequences', special issue of *British Journal of Politics & International Relations*, articles in issues 19/3 and 19/4.

Wolf, M. (2004), *Why Globalization Works* (New Haven, CT: Yale University Press).

Wolff, G. (2017), 'Beyond the Juncker and Schauble Visions of Euro-area Governance', *Bruegel Policy Brief*, November 2017, Issue 6.

Woll, C. (2013), 'Lobbying under Pressure: The Effect of Salience on EU Hedge Fund Regulation', *Journal of Common Market Studies*, 51/3: 555–72.

Wurzel, R., Zito, A., and Jordan, A. (2013), *Environmental Governance in Europe: A Comparative Analysis of New Environmental Policy Instruments* (Cheltenham, UK: Edward Elgar Publishing).

Young, A. and Peterson, J. (2014), *Parochial Global Europe: Twenty-First Century Trade Politics* (Oxford and New York: Oxford University Press).

Young, A. R. (2017), *The New Politics of Trade: Lessons from TTIP* (Newcastle: Agenda).

Young, H. (1998), *This Blessed Plot: Britain and Europe from Churchill to Blair* (Basingstoke: Palgrave Macmillan).

Zeff, E. and Pirro, E. (2015), *The European Union and the Member States*, 3rd edn (Boulder, CO: Lynne Rienner).

INDEX

bicameralism
  definition 148
Black Sea region
  Turkey's proximity to 182
Blair, Tony 212, 218–19,
border controls 27, 250
  abolition of 27
  between Republic of Ireland and Northern
      Ireland 227, 231, 233–4
Bosnia-Herzegovina 174, 180
  as potential member 186
Bosnian crisis 206
Brazil
  economic competition from 202
  member of Mercosur 32
Brexit 9, 19, 161, 189–90, 197, 216–36, 239
  hard vs soft 228–31
  how to leave the EU 223–6
  'Irish question' 227, 231, 233–4
  negotiations 42, 126, 224–6
  reasons for the referendum 218–20
  referendum (2016) 218–23
  referendum campaign 220–2
  revoking Article 50 226
  understanding the referendum result 222–3
  UK constitutional politics 232–5
budget 71, 82-3, 104
  bargaining 105
  breakdown of spending 114
  controlling increases in 83
  disputes 40
  EU and national compared 104
  procedure 149
budget deficit requirements
      111–12
Bulgaria 27, 78, 81, 82, 179
  accession 19, 40
  governance problems 179
  non-participation in Schengen Agreement 27
Bundesbank 38, 71
Bundesrat
  compared to European Council 152
Bunia
  military intervention in 208
Buttiglione, Rocco 63

C

Cameron, David 42, 52, 86, 151, 217–21, 236
Canada 108, 147, 212, 229, 230, 231
  EU–Canada trade deal as example of foreign
      policy community system
      199, 204
  free trade deal with 202
  member of NAFTA 32

capital
  free movement of 108
capitalism 85
carbon emissions
  trading 108
Caribbean 36, 194
Cartels 110
Cassis de Dijon case (1979) 66
Central Europe 40, 42, 169–70, 176, 177, 179, 183,
      189, 222
  challenges of competition policy 110
  excluded from Schuman Plan 29
  political and economic change 178, 196
  role during 2015–16 migration 'crisis' 42
central planning
  transitional to market economy 176
Charter of Fundamental Rights 8, 41, 149
'Chicken War' 34
China 194
  APEC membership 32
  Belt and Road Initiative 13
  bilateral economic agreement with 204
  competition from 202, 213
Christian Democrats 62, 158, 160, 162
Churchill, Winston 26
Citizens' Initiative 54, 125, 138
civil society
  definition 124
climate change 8, 54, 60, 72, 108, 203, 248
co-decision 39, 63, 117, 129, 133, 140
coal and steel 5, 12, 18, 30
  pooling via European Coal and Steel
      Community 28–9, 33, 68, 218
Cockfield, Lord Arthur 53
Cohesion Fund 71, 82, 105, 115
cohesion policy 37, 82, 113, 115, 120, 169, 179,
      182
  effect of enlargement on 40
Cohn-Bendit, Daniel 157
Cold War 13, 26–9, 38–9, 179, 198
  end of 40, 172, 175–6
College of Commissioners *see* European
      Commission
collegiality
  principle of 52, 158
Cologne summit (1999) 206
commercial policy *see* trade policy
Commissioner for External Relations 56
Commissioners *see* European Commission
Committee of Independent Experts 204
Committee of Permanent Representatives
      (Coreper) 35, 56, 59, 130, 224
Committee of the Regions (CoR) *see* European
      Committee of the Regions
Common Agricultural Policy (CAP) 14, 32, 35, 105,
      113–14, 115, 230